The English Legal System

CONTENTS

PREFACE

The book is intended for any first time student of the English Legal System. In particular, the coverage of topics is suitable for the new AS specifications in Law, but the book is also suitable for those starting degree or similar courses. The book does not assume any prior knowledge and starts with an introduction to types of law, in particular the critical distinction between civil and criminal law. The first chapter also introduces jurisprudential concepts and discusses law and morality and law and justice using recent cases. This section has been deliberately kept fairly brief as I have always felt that an 'in depth' study of jurisprudence at an early stage of a legal course is not desirable.

The order of topics is then fairly traditional, starting with the sources of law and going on to look at the criminal justice system, the civil justice system, and legal personnel. The chapters on criminal justice take the student through the entire process starting with the commission of crimes and police powers, covering prosecution, both pre-trial and the process in the courts and finishing with sentencing. The civil justice chapters also endeavour to give comprehensive coverage including pre-litigation matters, the courts, tribunals, arbitration and ADR, remedies and enforcement of judgments. The chapters on legal personnel cover both the professionals

and lay participation and the problem of financing litigation. The final chapter covers three loosely connected areas on protection of rights: judicial review, Ombudsmen and the European Convention on Human Rights.

I have tried to keep to the principles of explaining legal points simply and clearly, but at the same time providing sufficient depth for the more able students. Articles, cases and other 'live' material are used to illustrate points and to provide examples of the legal system at work today. Many of these items have also been used to give students the opportunity to do activities and exercises to help their understanding of topics. Key fact charts on many topics are included.

In this third edition I have tried to update the text thoroughly. At the same time I have shortened some topics, especially custom and equity. I have added extra activities. A number of these are based on using the Internet; this is in an attempt to encourage students to do research. Finally, at the request of a number of students I have included a small number of cartoons to cheer them up during their study of the English Legal System.

The law is stated as I believe it to be on 1 February 2002.

TABLE OF ACTS OF PARLIAMENT

TABLE OF CASES

INDEX OF KEY FACT CHARTS AND SIMILAR REVISION AIDS

ACKNOWLEDGEMENTS

The author and publishers would like to thank the following for permission to reproduce material: ABTA for the extract on page 115; Claire Dyer for the article on page 41; Derek Edmunds for the article on pages 233–4; *The Guardian* for the articles on pages 123, 209; Crown copyright is reproduced with the permission of Her Majesty's Stationery Office: Recorded Crime Figure 81, Claim Form page 94; Law Reform page 46; Arrests for Notifiable Offences and the Operation of Certain Police Powers under PACE Figure 82; Offenders sentenced at Magistrates' Court and Crown Court by types of sentence page 174; Jury Service pages 242, 243; *The Independent* for the articles on pages 4, 126; Sir Frederick Lawton for the article on page 180; *The New Law Journal* for the articles on page 161; *The Daily Telegraph* for the article on pages 5, 197; *The Times* for the articles on pages 4, 5, 6, 7, 57, 86, 154, 180, 215, 225, 234, 252; Pat Murray for the cartoons on pages 60, 112, 187, 288; PA Photos for the photograph on page 212.

Every effort has been made to obtain permission with reference to copyright material. The publishers apologise if inadvertently any sources remain unacknowledged and will be glad to make the necessary arrangements at the earliest opportunity.

Chapter 1

THE RULE OF LAW

1.1 What is law?

Law can affect many aspects of our lives, yet most people living in England and Wales have little understanding of the legal system that operates in these countries. For many their main awareness comes from newspaper articles with headlines such as 'Murderer jailed for life'; 'Young offender goes free'; 'Burglar caught'. This type of headline appears so frequently that it is not surprising that, when law is mentioned, many people only think of the criminal law and the courts that deal with this type of case. In reality the law covers an enormous range of situations and the legal system in England and Wales has a variety of courts and methods for dealing with different types of cases.

1.1.1 Different types of law

Since the law does cover such a wide variety of matters it can be helpful to divide it into different categories. The first distinction is that between international and national (municipal) law; national law can then be classified into public and private law; finally these classifications can be sub-divided into a number of different categories. These divisions are explained below.

International and national law

International law is concerned with disputes between nations; much of this law comes from treaties which have been agreed by the governments of the countries. National law is the law which applies within a country: each country will have its own national law and there are often wide differences between the law of individual countries. This can be shown by the fact that Scotland has its own law and legal system which are quite separate from the law and legal system which operate in England and Wales. For example, while serious criminal cases are tried by jury in both systems, the Scottish jury has 15 members and the decision can be made by a simple majority of eight to seven. In contrast the jury in England and Wales has 12 members, at least 10 of whom must agree on the decision.

Public and private law

Within national law there is usually a clear distinction between public and private law. Public law involves the State or government in some way, while private law is concerned with disputes between private individuals or businesses. Both public and private law can be sub-divided into different categories.

Public law

There are three main types of law in this category. These are:

1. **Constitutional law**
   This controls the method of government and any disputes which arise over such matters as who is entitled to vote in an election, or who is allowed to become a Member of Parliament, or whether an election was carried out by the correct procedure.
2. **Administrative law**
   This controls how Ministers of State or other public bodies such as local councils should operate. An important part of this is the right to judicial review of certain decisions (this is dealt with more fully in Chapter 16).

3. **Criminal law**

This sets out the types of behaviour which are forbidden at risk of punishment. A person who commits a crime is said to have offended against the State, and so the State has the right to prosecute them. This is so even though there is often an individual victim of a crime as well. For example, if a defendant commits the crime of burglary by breaking into a house and stealing, the State prosecutes the defendant for that burglary, although it is also possible for the victim to bring a private prosecution if the State does not take proceedings. However, if there is a private prosecution, the State still has the right to intervene and take over the matter. At the end of the case, if the defendant is found guilty, the court will punish the defendant for the offence, because he or she has broken the criminal law set down by the State. The victim will not necessarily be given any compensation, since the case is not viewed as a dispute between the burglar and the householder. However, the criminal courts have the power to order that the offender pays the victim compensation and can make such an order, as well as punishing the offender.

Private law

This is usually called civil law and has many different branches. The main ones are contract, tort, family law, law of succession, company law and employment law. This book does not deal with the actual legal rules of any of these areas, only with the system for dealing with disputes. However, it is sensible to have some idea of what types of dispute may be involved in these areas of law, so look at the following situations.

- A family complain that their package holiday did not match what was promised by the tour operator and that they were put into a lower grade hotel than the one they had paid for

- A woman has bought a new car and discovers the engine is faulty
- A man who bought a new car on hire-purchase has failed to pay the instalments due to the hire-purchase company

All these situations come under the law of contract. There are, of course, many other situations in which contracts can be involved.

Now look at the next list of situations; they are also civil matters, but of a different type.

- A child passenger in a car is injured in a collision (the tort of negligence)
- A family complain that their health is being affected by the noise and dust from a factory which has just been built near their house (the tort of nuisance)
- A woman is injured by faulty machinery at work (the tort of negligence, but may also involve occupiers' liability and/or employer's duty under health and safety regulations)
- A man complains that a newspaper has written an untrue article about him, which has affected his reputation (the tort of defamation)

All these cases come under the law of tort. A tort occurs where the civil law holds that, even though there is no contract between them, one person owes a legal responsibility of some kind to another person, and there has been a breach of that responsibility. There are many different types of tort, and the above examples demonstrate only some of them. Many cases arise from road traffic crashes, since drivers owe a duty of care to anyone who might be injured by their negligent driving.

Other divisions of private (civil) law concentrate on particular topics. Family law covers such matters as whether a marriage is valid, what the rules are for divorce and who should have the day-to-day care of any children of the family. The law of succession is concerned both with regulating who inherits property when a person dies without making a will, and also what the rules are for

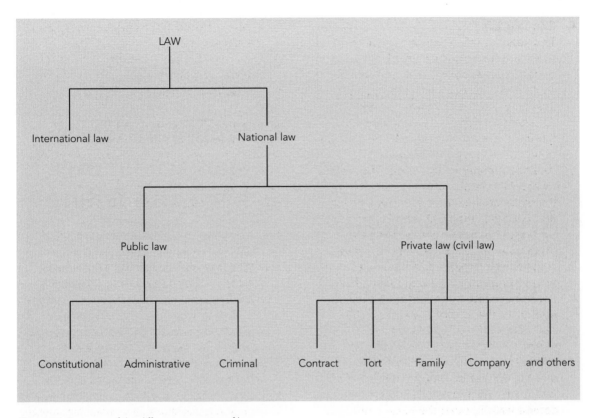

```
                              LAW
                               |
          _____
         |                                        |
   International law                         National law
                                                  |
                        _____
                       |                                                  |
                  Public law                                    Private law (civil law)
                       |                                                  |
          _____|_____                    _____
         |             |            |                  |       |        |         |          |
  Constitutional  Administrative  Criminal          Contract  Tort   Family   Company   and others
```

Figure 1.1 Summary of the different categories of law

making a valid will. Company law is very important in the business world: it regulates how a company should be formed, sets out formal rules for running companies, and deals with the rights and duties of shareholders and directors. Employment law covers all aspects of employment, from the original formation of a contract of employment to situations of redundancy or unfair dismissal. As well as these areas of private law, there are also laws relating to land, to copyright and patents, to marine law and many other topics, so it can be seen that civil law covers a wide variety of situations.

It is important to realise that civil law is very different from criminal law. The first point is shown in Figure 1.1 above. Criminal law is part of public law while civil law is the

separate category of private law. The reason that criminal law is part of public law is that crime is regarded as an action against the state and society as a whole. Civil law is called private law because the issues it deals with are between two individuals. The two types of law have different aims and are dealt with in different courts.

On the next three pages there are five newspaper articles. Some are about civil law and some are about criminal law. Do the activity based on these and then read section 1.1.2 to get a clearer understanding of the differences between the two.

Activity

Read the following newspaper articles and answer the questions on page 6.

SOURCE A

Negligent officials ordered to pay disabled boxer

The boxer Michael Watson, who suffered brain damage during a world championship bout with Chris Eubank, won a historic High Court case yesterday, raising questions about the future of the professional sport in this country.

In what was described as a landmark decision, the British Boxing Board of Control was found to have been negligent and liable for compensation for the injuries that left Mr Watson with only half his brain functioning, partially paralysed and confined to a wheelchair . . .

Eight years of litigation have followed Mr Watson's injury on 21 September 1991. The legal costs alone are said to amount to £500,000. In addition there will be financial compensation for Mr Watson . . . The actual amount will be decided by a High Court judge.

Taken from an article by Kim Sengupta in *The Independent*, 24 September 1999

SOURCE B

Would-be lawyer sues school over her Latin failure

A leading independent school is being sued by its former deputy head girl for £150,000 after she failed to achieve a top grade in her Latin A-level. Katherine Norfolk claims that Hurstpierpoint College in West Sussex is responsible for poor teaching that led to her being given an E grade, which she says will damage her career and salary prospects . . . Miss Norfolk had been a star pupil and had been predicted to gain an A grade in her Latin exam. She had won the school prize for Latin every year, according to papers lodged in the High Court. But when her A-level results came through last autumn she received an A in History, a B in French but a fail in Latin. After being re-marked twice she was awarded an E . . . Miss Norfolk is suing mainly for the loss of potential earnings, but also for the loss of esteem among her peers and for the distress caused by failing to achieve a higher grade.

Adapted from an article by David Brown and John Shaw in *The Times*, 1st October 2001.

SOURCE C

Bungling burglar in box gets a year inside

A father who persuaded his son to mail him in a cramped wooden box was jailed for a year yesterday. John Whalley, 53, tried to use the 'Trojan Horse' scheme to get into a parcel depot, which he intended to burgle.

Instead he found himself stuck overnight at the wrong warehouse and was caught by a guard after leaving the 2 metre by 1/2 metre box for a walk. A jury refused to accept his defence that he allowed himself to be posted for a bet.

At Birmingham Crown Court, Assistant Recorder Alan Mainds said: 'There is a danger of people applauding those who cheat others out of property by this sort of cunning means. I'm not going to fall into this trap.'

Whalley's son, Steven, 22, was put on probation for 18 months. Both had been found guilty of conspiracy to burgle the City Link warehouse in Saltley, Birmingham.

The Times, 20 July 1996

SOURCE D

£14,000 for girl whose ear-piercing went wrong

A vicar's step-daughter has been awarded almost £14,000 compensation after an ear-piercing left her disfigured. Katrina Healey, now 15, lost part of her ear after a piercing gun was used instead of a specialist needle to insert a gold stud near the top of her ear.

. . . Katrina defied her parents to have her ear pierced when she was 12, getting a friend over the age of 18 to sign the consent form in H Warner and Sons jewellers' shop in Barnsley, South Yorks. Afterwards she underwent three hospital operations after her ear swelled and she developed an abscess. A judge at Barnsley County Court has awarded her £13,900 in damages after her parents sued the jewellers.

Adapted from an article by Paul Stokes in *The Daily Telegraph*, 6 October 2001

SOURCE E

Man who destroyed river gets £1,500 fine

A demolition contractor who dumped deadly chemicals, 'destroying a river' and costing £500,000 in clean up costs, was ordered to do 200 hours' community service and fined £1,500 yesterday.

Ed Gallagher, chief executive of the Environment Agency, which brought the prosecution, said last night that it was disappointed by the sentence. 'We are concerned that some people might think that the laws on the environment are not tough enough,' he said.

Raymond Hake, of Taunton, Somerset, was found guilty at Yeovil Magistrates' Court under the Water Resources Act 1991 after disposing of an estimated 250 gallons of lindane, a pesticide, and mercury into Mill Stream at Somerton, Somerset. The maximum sentence for the offence was a fine of up to £20,000 and six months in jail.

Taken from an article by Nick Nuttall in *The Times*, 27 July 1996

— QUESTIONS —

❶ Identify which of these articles is referring to civil cases and which to criminal cases. (If you wish to check that you are right before continuing with the rest of the questions, turn to the start of Appendix 1 page 290.)

❷ Look at the articles which you have identified as criminal cases and state in which courts the defendants were tried.

❸ Look at the articles which you have identified as civil cases and state which courts are mentioned.

❹ In the criminal cases the defendants all received some form of punishment. List the different punishments used in the cases.

❺ Two of the civil cases have been decided. Identify these and, for each, state how long the time delay is between the incident which caused the claim and the actual decision.

❻ What do the people in the civil cases hope to receive as a result of their claim?

1.1.2 Distinctions between criminal cases and civil cases

There are many differences between criminal cases and civil cases (you should already have noticed some from the articles):

- **The cases take place in different courts.** In general, criminal cases will be tried in either the Magistrates' Court or the Crown Court, while civil cases are heard in the High Court or the County Court. (Note that some civil matters, especially family cases, can be dealt with in the Magistrates' Court – see Sections 10.1.1 and 14.1.5 for further details.)

- **The person starting the case is given a different name:** in criminal cases they are referred to as the prosecutor, while in civil cases they are called the claimant (pre-1999, the plaintiff). As already stated, the criminal case is taken on behalf of the State and there is a Crown Prosecution Service responsible for conducting cases, though there are other State agencies who may prosecute certain types of crime, as for example the Environment Agency in source E above. Civil cases are started by the person (or business) who is making the claim.

- **The terminology used is different.** A defendant in a criminal case is found guilty or not guilty (an alternative way of putting it is to say the defendant is convicted or acquitted), whereas a defendant in a civil case is found liable or not liable. At the end of a criminal case those who are found guilty of breaking the law may be punished, while at the end of a civil case anyone found liable will be ordered to put right the matter as far as possible. This is usually done by an award of money in compensation, known as damages, though the court can make other orders such as an injunction to prevent similar actions in the future, or an order for specific performance where the defendant who broke a contract is ordered to complete that contract.

- **The standard of proof is different.** Criminal cases must be proved 'beyond reasonable doubt'. This is a very high standard of proof, and is necessary since a conviction could result in a defendant serving a long prison sentence. Civil cases have only to be proved 'on the balance of probabilities', a lower standard in which the judge decides who is most likely to be right. This difference in the standard to which a case has to be proved means that even though a defendant in a criminal case has been acquitted, a civil case based on the same facts against that defendant can still be successful. Such situations are not common, but one is illustrated in the article on the right.

It is more common for a civil action to follow a successful criminal case, especially in road accident cases. A defendant may be found guilty of a driving offence, such as going through a red traffic light or driving without due care and attention; this is a criminal case. Anyone who was injured or had property damaged as a result of the incident could bring a civil action to claim compensation. The fact that the defendant had already been convicted of a driving offence will make it easier to prove the civil case.

In the English legal system an understanding of these basic distinctions between civil and criminal cases is important. To help you, a chart of the main differences is provided in Figure 1.2.

Judgment overtakes Brink's-Mat accused 11 years later

Eleven years after a man was acquitted of the £26 million Brink's-Mat bullion robbery, a High Court judge ruled that he was involved and must repay the value of the gold.

Anthony White, acquitted at the Old Bailey in 1984 of taking part in Britain's biggest gold robbery, was ordered to repay the £26,369,778 value and £2,188,600 in compensation. His wife Margaret was ordered to pay £1,084,344. Insurers for Brink's-Mat had sued the couple for the value of the proceeds.

Mr Justice Rimmer told Mr White that his acquittal did not mean that the Old Bailey jury had been satisfied he was innocent; only that he was not guilty according to the standard of proof required in criminal cases . . .

The case against the Whites is the latest and almost the last in a series of actions since the 1983 robbery brought by insurers for Brink's-Mat against people either convicted or suspected of taking part in the robbery and of handling the proceeds.

Using the lower standards of proof in civil courts and in actions for seizure of assets, lawyers believe that they will recoup at least £20 million.

Taken from an article by Stewart Tendler in *The Times*, 2 August 1995

	CIVIL CASES	CRIMINAL CASES
Purpose of the law	To uphold the rights of individuals	To maintain law and order; to protect society
Person starting the case	The individual whose rights have been affected	Usually the State through the police and Crown Prosecution Service
Legal name for that person	Claimant	Prosecutor
Courts hearing cases	County Court or High Court Some cases dealt with in tribunals	Magistrates' Court or Crown Court
Standard of proof	The balance of probability	Beyond reasonable doubt
Person/s making the decision	Judge (or panel of judges) Very rarely a jury	Magistrates OR jury
Decision	Liable or not liable	Guilty or not guilty
Powers of the court	Usually an award of damages, also possible: injunction, specific performance of a contract, rescission or rectification	Prison, fine, probation, discharge, community service order, curfew order etc (see Chapter 11)

Figure 1.2 *Distinctions between civil and criminal cases*

1.1.3 Definition of 'law'

So far we have only considered some divisions of law, and briefly introduced the system which applies in England and Wales. It is now necessary to look more widely at, and to discuss what is meant by, law in general terms and to compare it with concepts of morality and justice.

It is not easy to give a simple one sentence definition of law – however, legal theorists have tried to provide such a definition. John Austin, writing in the early nineteenth century, defined law as being a command issued from a superior (the State) to an inferior (the individual) and enforced by sanctions. This definition, however, does not truly apply to regulatory law such as that setting out how a will should be made; nor does it cover the concept of judicial review, where individuals may challenge the 'command' made by a Minister of State.

Austin was writing at a time when the law was much less developed than it is today, so it is not surprising that his definition does not cover all types of law today.

Sir John Salmond defined law as being 'the body of principles recognised and applied by the state in the administration of justice'. This is a much broader definition than Austin's and is probably the nearest that one can get to a workable 'one sentence' definition. Law could also be described as a formal mechanism of social control. It is formal because the rules set down in the law can be enforced through the courts and legal system, while in a broad sense all law could be said to be involved in some area of social control.

Law and rules

Law applies throughout a country to the people generally. There are other rules that apply only to certain groups or in limited situations: for example all sports have a set of rules to be followed, and the sanction applied for breaking the rules may be that a free kick is given to the other side, or that a player is sent off, or in serious cases a player is banned from competing for a certain number of weeks or months.

There are also unwritten 'rules' within communities. These come from local custom or practice, or they may be connected to religious beliefs. They enforce what is regarded by the community as the norm for behaviour. If you break such rules, others in the community may disapprove of your behaviour, but there is no legal sanction to force you to comply or to punish you if you refuse to do so. Such normative values are often connected with sexual behaviour and the concept of morality. The relationship of law and morality is explored in the next section of this chapter.

Codes of law

In some civilisations or countries, an effort has been made to produce a complete set of rules designed to deal with every possible situation that might arise. Some of the early major civilisations attempted this, notably the code of Justinian in Roman times. In the eighteenth century, Frederick the Great of Prussia compiled a code of 17,000 'rules' which he saw as a complete and ideal set of laws. In France, Napoleon also codified the law, and this Napoleonic Code is still the basis of French law today. In theory this idea of a complete code is attractive. It makes the law more accessible so that everyone knows exactly what their rights and duties are; however, law needs to be able to change and develop with the needs of society, and a fully codified system would prevent any such change.

Definition of a legal system

One of the best known definitions comes from Professor Hart. He listed five factors which had to co-exist to create a legal system. These were:

1. Rules which either forbade certain conduct or compelled certain conduct on pain of sanctions
2. Rules requiring people to compensate those whom they injured
3. Rules stating what needs to be done in certain 'mechanical' areas of law such as making a contract or making a will
4. A system of courts to determine what the rules are, whether they have been broken and what the appropriate sanction is
5. A body whose responsibility it is to make rules, and amend or repeal them as necessary

These would appear to be the minimum requirements for a legal system. Considering these in the context of the English legal system, the first three types of rule all exist – the first one being our criminal law, and the second two being part of the civil law; there are courts to deal with the points in factor 4; and Parliament is the legislative (law-making) body (5).

1.2 Law and morality

The moral values of communities lay down a framework for how people should behave. Concepts of morality differ from culture to culture, although most will outlaw extreme behaviour such as murder. Often morality is based on religious ideas: the Bible teachings provide a moral code for Christian communities, and the teachings in the Koran for Muslims. The law of a country will usually reflect the moral values accepted by the majority of the country, but the law is unlikely to be exactly the same as the common religious moral code. One example is adultery: this is against the moral code for both Christians and Muslims but is not considered a crime in Christian countries; however, in some Muslim countries (though not all) it is against the criminal law.

The moral standards of a community are recognised as having a profound influence on the development of law, but in complex societies, morality and law are never likely to be co-extensive. Major breaches of a moral code (such as murder and robbery) will also be against the law, but in other matters there may not be consensus.

In England and Wales there has been a move away from religious belief and the way that the law has developed reflects this. Abortion was legalised in 1967, yet many people still believe it is morally wrong. A limited form of euthanasia has been accepted as legal with the ruling in *Airedale NHS Trust* v *Bland* (1993), where it was ruled that medical staff could withdraw life support systems from a patient who could breathe unaided, but who was in a persistent vegetative state. This ruling meant that they could withdraw the feeding tubes of the patient, despite the fact that this would inevitably cause him to die. Again, many groups believe that this is immoral as it denies the sanctity of human life.

There are also differences between law and morality in the way the two develop and the sanctions imposed. The following is a suggested list of such differences.

1. Morality cannot be deliberately changed; it evolves slowly and changes according to the will of the people. Law can be altered deliberately by legislation: this means that behaviour which was against the law can be 'de-criminalised' overnight. Equally, behaviour which was lawful can be declared unlawful.
2. Morality is voluntary with consequences, but generally carrying no official sanction (though some religions may 'excommunicate'); morality relies for its effectiveness on the individual's sense of shame or guilt. Law makes certain behaviour obligatory with legal sanctions to enforce it.
3. Breaches of morality are not usually subject to formal adjudication; breaches of law will be ruled on by a formal legal system.

Activity

In *Re A (Conjoined twins)* (2000) the Court of Appeal had to decide whether doctors should operate to separate Siamese twins when it was certain that the operation would kill one twin as she could not exist without being linked to her twin.

A Search back copies of newspapers on the Internet (or on CD Rom) for fuller reports of this case.

B Discuss:

1. Whether this sort of decision should be made by judges.
2. Whether you think that, knowing one child would die, it was right for the operation to go ahead.

1.2.1 Natural law and positivism

A major debate is whether law and morality should reflect each other exactly. The idea of natural law is that the two should coincide and that there is a divine source for the law. Taken to the extreme, the supporters of natural law would say that legal rules which did not conform with moral laws should be ignored. In other words, if the legal rules of a country are in contrast to the moral laws, the legal rules should be disobeyed. Positivists, on the other hand, hold that if legal rules have been enacted by the correct procedures, then those legal rules must be obeyed, even if they are not liked and are in conflict with morality.

1.2.2 The Hart Devlin debate

Professor Hart has argued strongly that there should be a clear separation of law and morality. For him morality is a matter of private judgment, while a legal system should be based on logical ideas producing 'correct' decisions from rules. However, he does concede that society could not exist without a form of morality which mirrors and supplements the legal rules.

Lord Devlin felt that society required the observance of certain moral principles and, even if public opinion was changing, the law should still support those moral principles.

English law still takes this line in some cases. A strong example was the case of *R* v *Brown* (1993), where a group of men took part in sadomasochistic acts against each other. This was done in private, all the men involved were adult and had consented to the acts. There were some injuries caused but the court accepted that these were transient and minor. Despite all these facts the House of Lords ruled that their behaviour was a breach of the criminal law of assault and they could not claim the defence of consent to excuse their acts. The House of Lords was imposing a certain standard of what was considered as acceptable behaviour. However the judges in the House of Lords were not unanimous as two of the five judges disagreed with the decision.

Activity

The following statements are brief extracts from some of the judgments in the case of *R* v *Brown*. Look at the different approaches shown by the judges and decide which side of the Hart Devlin debate they each support.

Lord Templeman: 'The question whether the defence of consent should be extended to the consequences of sadomasochistic encounters can only be decided by consideration of policy and public interest.' At the end of this judgment he also said 'Society is entitled and bound to protect itself against a cult of violence. Pleasure derived from the infliction of pain is an evil thing. Cruelty is uncivilised.'

Lord Slynn: 'Adults can consent to acts in private which do not result in serious bodily harm, so that such acts do not constitute criminal assaults for the purposes of the 1861 [Offences against the Person] Act. In the end it is a matter of policy in an area where social and moral factors are extremely important and where attitudes could change. It is a matter of policy for the legislature to decide. It is not for the courts in the interests of paternalism or in order to protect people from themselves to introduce into existing statutory crimes relating to offences against the person, concepts which do not properly fit there.'

1.3 Law and justice

It is often said that the law provides justice, yet this is not always so. Justice is probably the ultimate goal towards which the law should strive, but it is unlikely that law will ever produce 'justice' in every case.

First there is the problem of what is meant by 'justice'. The difficulty of defining justice was commented on by Lord Wright, who said:

'the guiding principle of a judge in deciding cases is to do justice; that is justice according to the law, but still justice. I have not found any satisfactory definition of justice . . . what is just in a particular case is what appears just to the just man, in the same way as what is reasonable appears to be reasonable to the reasonable man.'

In some situations people's concept of what is justice may not be the same. Justice can be seen as applying the rules in the same way to all people, but even this may lead to perceived injustices – indeed rigid application of rules may actually produce injustice.

Activity

Read the facts of the following case and use the case and the questions below as the basis of a discussion on the concept of justice.

Case *Revill* v *Newbery* (1996)

Facts Mark Revill, aged 21, with another man attempted to break into a brick shed on William Newbery's allotment at about 2 o'clock in the morning. Mr Revill and his companion had already that night stolen cars and caused criminal damage elsewhere, and intended to steal items from the shed. Mr Newbery, who was aged 76, was sleeping in the shed in order to protect his property after earlier thefts and vandalism. He had with him an air rifle and a single barrelled 12-bore shotgun and ammunition for both guns. When he was awakened by the noise of the two men trying to break in, he loaded the shotgun, poked it through a small hole in the door and fired. The shot hit Mr Revill on the right upper arm and chest.

Criminal proceedings Mr Revill was prosecuted for various criminal offences he had committed that night, pleaded guilty and was sentenced. Mr Newbery was prosecuted for wounding Mr Revill, but was found not guilty by the jury at the Crown Court.

Civil proceedings Mr Revill then brought a civil case against Mr Newbery claiming damages for the injuries he had suffered from the shotgun blast. In this case the judge awarded Mr Revill damages of £12,100 but reduced the amount to £4,033 because the judge held that Mr Revill was two-thirds to blame for what had happened. This meant that Mr Newbery was ordered to pay Mr Revill £4,033.

Mr Newbery appealed against this order but the Court of Appeal dismissed his appeal saying that his conduct was 'clearly dangerous and bordered on the reckless'. One of the judges pointed out that: 'Violence may be returned with necessary violence but the force used must not exceed the limits of what is reasonable in the circumstances.'

QUESTIONS

❶ Should a criminal be able to use the legal rules to claim for injuries caused by another person? Is it justice to award damages to someone who was injured while carrying out criminal activities?

❷ Bearing in mind the fact that Mr Newbery had fired without warning, was the decision in the civil case brought by Mr Revill, that Mr Newbery should pay a reduced amount of damages to Mr Revill for the injuries, a just one?

❸ Mr Newbery was found not guilty of a criminal charge of wounding Mr Revill. Was this a 'just' decision?

Conclusion

From sections 1.2 and 1.3 it is clear that the three concepts of law, morality and justice are quite distinct. There is, however, a large overlap between law and morality, law and justice and also morality and justice. This idea of the overlapping of the three is illustrated in diagram form in Figure 1.3

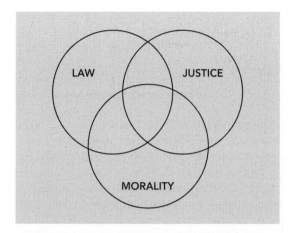

Figure 1.3 Diagram of the relationship of law, morality and justice

1.4 Rights and duties

The law gives rights to individuals and methods of enforcing those rights. Quite often the law is involved in a balancing act, trying to ensure that one person's rights do not affect another person's rights. In order to keep the balance the law also imposes duties on people.

This is more easily understood by looking at examples. In the law of contract, where one person buys a digital television from a shop each party will have rights and duties under this contract. For example, the shop has the right to be paid the agreed price for the TV, while the buyer has the right to have a set which is in working order.

The idea of rights and duties can also be seen clearly in employment law. An employer has a duty to pay wages to the employee, while the employee has the right to sue for any wages which are owed. An employee has a duty to obey reasonable lawful orders while an employer has a right to expect this and may be able to dismiss the employee if there is a serious breach. An employer has a duty to provide a safe system of work for all employees, while an employee has the right to claim compensation if he is injured because the employer has broken this duty. These are just a few of the rights and duties of employers and employees and this balancing of their rights and duties is also shown in Figure 1.4.

Even where there is no contract or agreement between the parties, the law can impose rights and duties on people. An example of this is the right to use one's own land (this includes a house or a flat) as one wants to. The law recognises that people have the right to enjoy the use of their own property, but this right is balanced by the right of other land users to enjoy the use of their properties. So the tort of nuisance allows a claim to be made if one's enjoyment of land is affected by too much noise, smoke, smells or other nuisances coming from another person's land.

Even in the criminal law this idea of rights and duties can be seen. The criminal law imposes a duty on all citizens to obey the law or face possible punishment. This duty is imposed to protect other citizens or society as a whole. In this way the law upholds the rights of people not to be assaulted or to have their possessions stolen or whatever else the particular crime involves.

Employer	Employee
Duty to pay employee -→	Right to claim for unpaid wages
Right to dismiss employee for serious misconduct ◄- - - - - - - - - - - -	Duty to obey reasonable orders
Duty to provide safe system of work -→	Right to claim if injured because of unsafe system

Figure 1.4 Balancing rights and duties in employment law

Chapter 2

THE DEVELOPMENT OF ENGLISH LAW

The law of England and Wales has been built up very gradually over the centuries. There is not just one way of creating or developing law; there have been, and still are, a number of different ways. These methods of developing law are usually referred to as sources of law. Historically, the most important ways were custom and decisions of judges. Then, as Parliament became more powerful in the eighteenth and early nineteenth centuries, Acts of Parliament were the main source of new laws, although judicial decisions were still important as they interpreted the Parliamentary law and filled in gaps where there was no statute law (statute law is explained in Chapter 3). During the twentieth century, statute law and judicial decisions continued to be the major sources of law but, in addition, two new sources of law became increasingly important: these were delegated legislation and European law. All these sources of law have combined to make our present day law as indicated by Figure 2.1

All these sources of law are examined in turn in this chapter and Chapters 3 and 4.

2.1 Customs

These are rules of behaviour which develop in a community without being deliberately invented. There are two main types of custom: general customs and local customs.

2.1.1 General customs

Historically these are believed to have been very important in that they were, effectively, the basis of our Common law

(see section 2.2). It is thought that following the Norman conquest (as the country was gradually brought under centralised government) the judges appointed by the kings to travel around the land making decisions in the King's name based at least some of their decisions on the common customs. This idea caused Lord Justice Coke in the seventeenth century to describe these customs as being 'one of the main triangles of the laws of England'. However, other commentators dispute this theory.

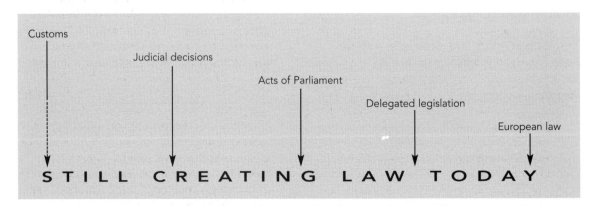

Figure 2.1 Historical development of sources of law

Today, Michael Zander writes that probably a high proportion of the so-called customs were almost certainly invented by the judges. In any event, it is accepted that general customs have long since been absorbed into legislation or case law and are no longer a creative source of law.

2.1.2 Local customs

This is the term used where a person claims that he is entitled to some local right, such as a right of way or a right to use land in a particular way, because this is what has always happened locally. Such customs are an exception to the general law of the land, and will only operate in that particular area.

Since there were (or still are) exceptions to the general common law, the judges, from the earliest times, established a series of rigorous tests or hurdles that had to be passed before they recognised any local custom. These tests still exist today and are used on the rare occasions that a claim to a right comes before the courts because of a local custom. The tests are as follows:

- The custom must have existed since 'time immemorial'
- The custom must have been exercised peaceably, openly and as of right
- The custom must be definite as to locality, nature and scope
- The custom must be reasonable

It is very unusual for a new custom to be considered by the courts today and even rarer for the courts to decide that it will be recognised as a valid custom, but there have been some such cases. For example in *Egerton* v *Harding* (1974) the court decided that there was a customary duty to fence land against cattle straying from the common. Another case was *New Windsor Corporation* v *Mellor* (1974) where a local authority was prevented from building on land because the local people proved there

was a custom that they had the right to use the land for lawful sports. Although customs may develop, they are not part of the law until recognised by the courts; it is the judges who decide which customs will be recognised as enforceable at law.

2.2 Common law

Clearly the legal system in England and Wales could not rely only on customs. Even in Anglo-Saxon times there were local courts which decided disputes, but it was not until after the Norman conquest in 1066 that a more organised system of courts emerged. This was because the Norman kings realised that control of the country would be easier if they controlled, among other things, the legal system. The first Norman king, William the Conqueror, set up the Curia Regis (the King's Court) and appointed his own judges. The nobles who had a dispute were encouraged to apply to have the King (or his judges) decide the matter.

As well as this central court, the judges were sent to major towns to decide any important cases. This meant that judges travelled from London all round the country that was under the control of the King. In the time of Henry II (1154–89) these tours became more regular and Henry divided up the country into 'circuits' or areas for the judges to visit. Initially the judges would use the local customs or the old Anglo-Saxon laws to decide cases, but over a period of time it is believed that the judges on their return to Westminster in London would discuss the laws or customs they had used, and the decisions they had made, with each other. Gradually, the judges selected the best customs and these were then used by all the judges throughout the country. This had the effect that the law became uniform or 'common' through the whole country, and it is from here that the phrase 'common law' seems to have developed.

COMMON LAW	
Different meanings	**Distinguishes it from:**
The law developed by the early judges to form a 'common' law for the country	The local laws used prior to the Norman conquest
The law which has continued to be developed by the judges through the doctrine of judicial precedent Judge-made law	Laws made by a legislative body, such as Acts of Parliament or delegated legislation
The law operated in the common law courts before the reorganisation of the courts in 1873–75	Equity – the decisions made in the Chancery courts

Figure 2.2 Different meanings of the term 'common law'

Common law is the basis of our law today: it is unwritten law that developed from customs and judicial decisions. The phrase 'common law' is still used to distinguish laws that have been developed by judicial decisions, from laws that have been created by statute or other legislation. For example, murder is a common law crime while theft is a statutory crime. This means that murder has never been defined in any Act of Parliament, but theft is now defined by the Theft Act 1968.

Common law also has another meaning, in that it is used to distinguish between rules that were developed by the common law courts (the King's courts) and the rules of Equity which were developed by the Lord Chancellor and the Chancery courts.

2.3 Equity

Historically this was an important source and it still plays a part today with many of our legal concepts having developed from equitable principles. The word 'equity' has a meaning of 'fairness', and this is the basis on which it operates, when adding to our law.

2.3.1 The development of equity

Equity developed because of problems in the common law. Only certain types of case were recognised. The law was also very technical; if there was an error in the formalities the person making the claim would lose the case.

Another major problem was the fact that the only remedy the common law courts could give was 'damages' – that is an order that the defendant pay a sum of money to the plaintiff by way of compensation. In some cases this would not be the best method of putting matters right between the parties. For example in a case of trespass to land, where perhaps the defendant had built on his neighbour's land, the building would still be there and the plaintiff would have lost the use of that part of his land. In such a situation the plaintiff would probably prefer to have the building removed, rather than be given money in compensation.

People who could not obtain justice in the common law courts appealed directly to the King. Most of these cases were referred to the King's Chancellor, who was both a lawyer and a priest, and who became known as the keeper of the King's conscience. This was because the Chancellor based his decisions on principles of natural justice and fairness, making a decision on what seemed 'right' in the particular case rather than on the strict following of previous precedents. He was also prepared to look beyond legal documents, which were considered legally binding by the common law courts, and to take account of what the parties had intended to do.

To ensure that the decisions were 'fair' the Chancellor used new procedures such as subpoenas, which ordered a witness to attend court or risk imprisonment for refusing to obey the Chancellor's order. He also developed new remedies which were able to compensate plaintiffs more fully than the common law remedy of damages. The main equitable remedies were: injunctions; specific performance; rescission; and rectification. These are all still used today and are explained more fully in Chapter 6.

Eventually a Court of Chancery under the control of the Chancellor came into being which operated these rules of fairness or equity. Equity was not a complete system of law; it merely filled the gaps in the common law and softened the strict rules of the common law.

Conflict between equity and common law

The two systems of common law and equity operated quite separately, so it was not surprising that this overlapping of the two systems led to conflict between them. One of the main problems was that the common law courts would make an order in favour of one party and the Court of Chancery an order in favour of the other party. The conflict was finally resolved in the *Earl of Oxford's case* (1615) when the King ruled that equity should prevail; in other words,

the decision made in the Chancery court was the one which must be followed by the parties. This ruling made the position of equity stronger and the same rule was subsequently included in section 25 of the Judicature Act 1873.

2.3.2 The relevance of equity today

Equitable rights, interests and remedies remain important in the law today. Concepts such as mortgages and trusts are founded on the idea that one person owns the legal interest in property but has to use that property for the benefit of another. This other person is said to have an equitable interest in the property. It is difficult to imagine life today without mortgages – the vast majority of homeowners buy their property with the aid of a mortgage. Trusts are widely used in setting up such matters as pension funds, as well as within families when property is settled on younger members of the family or between husband and wife.

Modern use of equitable remedies

Equitable remedies are still important and used in a variety of circumstances.

For example, injunctions are often ordered in cases of domestic violence as a protection for the abused partner. Such an injunction often forbids the violent partner from entering the premises where the other partner is living or even going with a certain distance of the place. Injunctions are also used to prevent trespass to land or to prevent excessive noise, or smoke or other nuisances. They are used in employment law in various situations. For example a former employee can be prevented from disclosing trade secrets to anyone, or an injunction may be granted against a trade union to prevent unlawful industrial action.

2.4 Judicial precedent

Judicial precedent refers to the source of law where past decisions of the judges create law for future judges to follow. This source of law is also known as case-law. It is a major source of law, both historically and today.

2.4.1 The doctrine of *stare decisis*

The English system of precedent is based on the Latin maxim *stare decisis et non quieta movere* (usually shortened to *stare decisis*) which loosely translated means: 'stand by what has been decided and do not unsettle the established'. This supports the idea of fairness and provides certainty in the law.

Ratio decidendi

Precedent can only operate if the legal reasons for past decisions are known, therefore at the end of a case there will be a judgment – a speech made by the judge giving the decision and, more importantly, explaining the reasons for that decision. In a judgment the judge is likely to give a summary of the facts of the case, review the arguments put to him by the advocates in the case, and then explain the principles of law he is using to come to the decision. These principles are the important part of the judgment and are known as the *ratio decidendi* which means the reason for deciding (and is pronounced 'ray-she-o des-id-end-i'). This is what creates a precedent for judges to follow in future cases. Sir Rupert Cross defined the *ratio decidendi* as 'any rule expressly or impliedly treated by the judge as a necessary step in reaching his conclusion'.

Obiter dicta

The remainder of the judgment is called *obiter dicta* ('other things said') and judges in future cases do not have to follow it. Sometimes a judge will speculate on what his decision would have been if the facts of the case had been different. This hypothetical situation is part of the *obiter dicta* and the legal reasoning put forward may be considered in future cases, although, as with all *obiter* statements, it is not binding precedent. A major problem when looking at a past judgment is to divide the *ratio decidendi* from the *obiter dicta*, as the judgment is usually in a continuous form, without any headings specifying what is meant to be part of the *ratio decidendi* and what is not.

Judgments

It is also worth realising that there can be more than one speech at the end of a case, depending on the number of judges hearing the case. In courts of first instance there will be only one judge and therefore one judgment. However, in the appeal courts (the Divisional Courts, the Court of Appeal and the House of Lords) cases are heard by at least two judges and up to a maximum of seven judges in the House of Lords, therefore there can be more than one judgment. The fact that there are two or more judges does not mean that there will always be several judgments as it is quite common for one judge to give the judgment and the other judge/judges simply to say 'I agree'! However, in cases where there is a particularly important or complicated point of law, more than one judge may want to explain his legal reasoning on the point. This can cause problems in later cases as each judge may have had a different reason for his decision, so there will be more than one *ratio decidendi*. (By the way, the plural of *ratio* is *rationes*.) As well as learning the Latin phrases *ratio decidendi*, *obiter dicta* and *stare decisis* there are some English phrases which are important for understanding the concept of judicial precedent. These are original or declaratory precedent, binding precedent and persuasive precedent.

Original precedent

If the point of law in a case has never been decided before, then whatever the judge decides will form a new precedent for future cases to follow, i.e. it is an original precedent. As there are no past cases for the judge to base his decision on, he is likely to look at cases which are the closest in principle and he may decide to use similar rules. This way of arriving at a judgment is called reasoning by analogy. Some legal commentators used to hold that the judge is only declaring what the law is (that is, the law has always been there, but it is the first time a judge has had to decide it). This view holds that judges do not create law, they merely declare what it has always been. Nowadays it is accepted that judges do have a law-making role in these situations – when a new point has to be decided, the judge is creating new law.

This idea of creating new law by analogy can be seen in *Hunter and others* v *Canary Wharf Ltd and London Docklands Development Corporation* (1995). Part of the decision involved whether the interference with television reception by a large building was capable of constituting an actionable private nuisance. The facts of the case were that in 1990 a tower known as the Canary Wharf Tower was built by the first defendant in an enterprise zone in East London. The tower was about 250 metres high and over 50 metres square. The claimant, and hundreds of others suing with her, claimed damages from the first defendant for interference over a number of years with reception of television broadcasts at their homes in East London. The interference was claimed to have been caused by the tower.

Activity

Read the following extract from the judgment in this case of *Hunter and others* v *Canary Wharf Ltd and London Docklands Development Corporation*. Then answer the question below.

When the case was heard on appeal in the Court of Appeal, Lord Justice Pill giving judgment said:

> '*Lord Irving (counsel for the defendants) submits that interference with television reception by reason of the presence of a building is properly to be regarded as analogous to loss of aspect (view). To obstruct the receipt of television signals by the erection of a building between the point of receipt and the source is not in law a nuisance. In* **Aldred's Case** *(1611) Wray CJ cited what he had said in* **Bland** *v* **Moselely**: "*for prospect, which is a matter only of delight and not of necessity, no action lies for stopping thereof, and yet it is a great recommendation of a house if it has a long and large prospect . . . But the law does not give an action for such things of delight*".*
>
> *I accept the importance of television in the lives of very many people. However, in my judgment the erection or presence of a building in the line of sight between a television transmitter and other properties is not actionable as an interference with the use and enjoyment of land. The analogy with loss of prospect is compelling. The loss of a view, which may be of the greatest importance to many householders, is not actionable and neither is the mere presence of a building in the sight line to the television transmitter.*'

QUESTIONS

❶ With what did Lord Justice Pill say that interference with television broadcasts was analogous?

❷ Do you think that the judge was correct to say that the two situations are analogous? Give reasons for your answer.

❸ By drawing this analogy does it mean that the claimant won or lost the case?

Binding precedent

This is a precedent from an earlier case which must be followed even if the judge in the later case does not agree with the legal principle. A binding precedent is only created when the facts of the second case are sufficiently similar to the original case and the decision was made by a court which is senior to (or in some cases the same level as) the court hearing the later case.

Persuasive precedent

This is a precedent that is not binding on the court, but the judge may consider it and decide that it is a correct principle so he is persuaded that he should follow it. Persuasive precedent comes from a number of sources as follows:

1. **Courts lower in the hierarchy**
   Such an example can be seen in *R v R* (1991) where the House of Lords agreed with and followed the same reasoning as the Court of Appeal in deciding that a man could be guilty of raping his wife.

2. **Decisions of the Judicial Committee of the Privy Council**
   This court is not part of the court hierarchy in England and Wales and so its decisions are not binding, but, since many of its judges are also members of the House of Lords, their judgments are treated with respect and may often be followed. An example of this can be seen in the law on remoteness of damages in the law of tort and the decision made by the Privy Council in the case of *The Wagon Mound (No 1)* (1961).

3. **Statements made obiter dicta**
   (particularly where the comment was made in a House of Lords decision)
   This is clearly seen in the law on duress as a defence to a criminal charge, where the House of Lords in *R v Howe* (1987) ruled that duress could not be a defence to a charge of murder. In the

judgment the Lords also commented, as an *obiter* statement, that duress would not be available as a defence to someone charged with attempted murder. When, later, in *R v Gotts* (1992) a defendant charged with attempted murder tried to argue that he could use the defence of duress, the *obiter* statement from *Howe* was followed as persuasive precedent by the Court of Appeal.

4. **A dissenting judgment**
   Where a case has been decided by a majority of judges (for example 2–1 in the Court of Appeal), the judge who disagreed will have explained his reasons. If that case goes on appeal to the House of Lords, or if there is a later case on the same point which goes to the House of Lords, it is possible that the House of Lords may prefer the dissenting judgment and decide the case in the same way. The dissenting judgment has persuaded them to follow it.

5. **Decisions of courts in other countries**
   This is especially so where the other country uses the same ideas of common law as in our system. This applies to Commonwealth countries such as Canada, Australia and New Zealand.

2.4.2 Precedent and the hierarchy of the courts

In England and Wales our courts operate a very rigid doctrine of judicial precedent which has the effect that:

- Every court is bound to follow any decision made by a court above it in the hierarchy
- In general, appellate courts (courts which hear appeals) are bound by their own past decisions

So the hierarchy of the courts is the next important point to get clear. Which courts

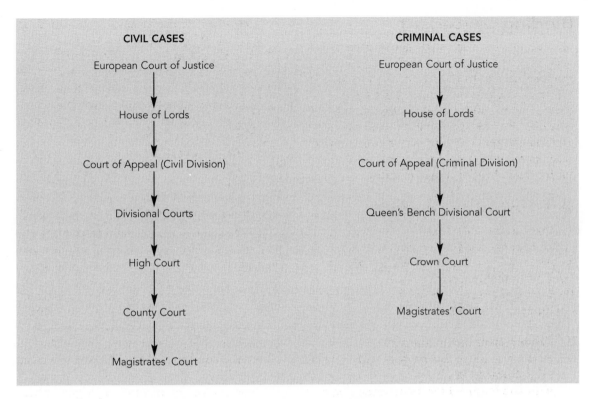

CIVIL CASES

European Court of Justice

↓

House of Lords

↓

Court of Appeal (Civil Division)

↓

Divisional Courts

↓

High Court

↓

County Court

↓

Magistrates' Court

CRIMINAL CASES

European Court of Justice

↓

House of Lords

↓

Court of Appeal (Criminal Division)

↓

Queen's Bench Divisional Court

↓

Crown Court

↓

Magistrates' Court

Figure 2.3 *Cascade model of judicial precedent operating in the hierarchy of the courts*

come where in the hierarchy? Figure 2.3 shows this in the form of a cascade model and Figure 2.4 gives each court and its position in respect of the other courts. The position of each court is also considered in this section and in sections 2.4.3 and 2.4.4.

The European Court of Justice

Since 1973 the highest court affecting our legal system is the European Court of Justice. For points of European law, a decision made by this court is binding on all other courts in England and Wales. However, there are still laws which are unaffected by European Union law and for these the House of Lords is the supreme court. An important feature of the European Court of Justice is that it is prepared to overrule its own past decisions if it feels it is necessary. This flexible approach to past precedents is seen in other legal systems in Europe, and is a

contrast to the more rigid approach of our national courts.

House of Lords

The most senior national court is the House of Lords and its decisions bind all other courts in the English legal system. The House of Lords is not bound by its own past decisions, although it will generally follow them. This point is discussed in detail in section 2.4.3.

Court of Appeal

At the next level down in the hierarchy is the Court of Appeal which has two divisions: Civil and Criminal. Both divisions of the Court of Appeal are bound to follow decisions of the European Court of Justice and the House of Lords. In addition they must usually follow past decisions of their own; although there are some limited exceptions to this rule, and the Court of

Court	Courts bound by it	Courts it must follow
European Court	All courts	None
House of Lords	All other courts in the English legal system	European Court
Court of Appeal	Itself (with some exceptions) Divisional Courts All other lower courts	European Court House of Lords
Divisional Courts	Itself (with some exceptions) High Court All other lower courts	European Court House of Lords Court of Appeal
High Court	County Court Magistrates' Court	European Court House of Lords Court of Appeal Divisional Courts
Crown Court	Possibly Magistrates' Court	All higher courts

County Court and Magistrates' Court do not create precedent and are bound by all higher courts

Figure 2.4 The courts and precedent

Appeal (Criminal Division) is more flexible where the point involves the liberty of the subject. The position of the two divisions is discussed in detail in section 2.4.4.

Divisional Courts

The three Divisional Courts (Queen's Bench, Chancery and Family) are bound by decisions of the European Court of Justice, the House of Lords and the Court of Appeal. In addition the Divisional Courts are bound by their own past decisions, although they operate similar exceptions to those operated by the Court of Appeal. This was decided in *Police Authority for Huddersfield v Watson* (1947). It is also probably correct to say that the Divisional Courts have the same flexibility as the Criminal Division of the Court of Appeal where the case involves a person's liberty. Certainly this was the attitude taken in *R v Greater Manchester Coroner, ex parte Tal* (1984). In *C v DPP* (1996) the court refused to follow earlier

decisions that, in order for a child aged 10–13 to be guilty of a criminal offence, the prosecution must prove that the child knew what they were doing was seriously wrong. However, the House of Lords overruled this decision.

The High Court

This is bound by decisions of all the courts above and in turn it binds the lower courts. High Court judges do not have to follow each others' decisions but will usually do so. In *Colchester Estates (Cardiff) v Carlton Industries plc* (1984) it was held that where there were two earlier decisions which conflicted, then, provided the first decision had been fully considered in the later case, that later decision should be followed.

Inferior courts

These are the Crown Court, the County Court and the Magistrates' Court. They are bound to follow decisions by all higher courts and it is unlikely that a decision by an inferior court can create precedent. The one exception is that a ruling on a point of law by a judge in the Crown Court technically creates precedent for the Magistrates' Court. However, since such rulings are rarely recorded in the law reports, this is of little practical effect.

2.4.3 The House of Lords and judicial precedent

The main debate about the House of Lords is the extent to which it should follow its own past decisions and the ideas on this have changed over the years. Originally the view was that the House of Lords had the right to overrule past decisions, but gradually during the nineteenth century this more flexible approach disappeared. By the end of that century, in *London Street Tramways* v *London County Council* (1898), the House of Lords held that certainty in the law was more important than the possibility of individual hardship being caused through having to follow a past decision. So from 1898 to 1966 the House of Lords regarded itself as being completely bound by its own past decisions unless the decision had been made *per incuriam*, that is 'in error'. However, this idea of error referred only to situations where a decision had been made without considering the effect of a relevant statute.

This was not felt to be satisfactory, as the law could not alter to meet changing social conditions and opinions, nor could any possible 'wrong' decisions be changed by the courts. If there was an unsatisfactory decision by the House of Lords, then the only way it could be changed was by Parliament passing a new Act of Parliament. This happened in the law about intention as an element of a criminal offence. The House of Lords in *DPP* v *Smith* (1961) had ruled that an accused could be guilty of murder if a reasonable person would have foreseen

that death or very serious injury might result from the accused's actions. This decision was criticised as it meant that the defendant could be guilty even if he had not intended to cause death or serious injury, nor even realised that his actions might have that effect. Eventually Parliament changed the law by passing the Criminal Justice Act 1967.

The Practice Statement

It was realised that the House of Lords should have more flexibility. For today's system of judicial precedent the critical date is 1966, when the Lord Chancellor issued a Practice Statement announcing a change to the rule in *London Street Tramways* v *London County Council*. The Practice Statement said:

'Their Lordships regard the use of precedent as an indispensable foundation upon which to decide what is the law and its application to individual cases. It provides at least some degree of certainty upon which individuals can rely in the conduct of their affairs, as well as a basis for orderly development of legal rules.

Their Lordships nevertheless recognise that the rigid adherence to precedent may lead to injustice in a particular case and also unduly restrict the proper development of the law. They propose, therefore, to modify their present practice and while treating former decisions of this House as normally binding, to depart from a previous decision when it appears right to do so.

In this connection they will bear in mind the danger of disturbing retrospectively the basis on which contracts, settlement of property and fiscal arrangements have been entered into and also the especial need for certainty as to the criminal law. This announcement is not intended to affect the use of precedent elsewhere than in this House.'

KEY FACTS

1898	House of Lords decides in the case of *London Street Tramways* that it is bound to follow its own previous decisions
1966	Issue of the Practice Statement House of Lords will depart from previous decisions when 'it is right to do so'
1968	First use of Practice Statement in *Conway* v *Rimmer* Only involves technical law on discovery of documents
1972	First major use of Practice Statement in *Herrington* v *British Railways Board* on the duty of care owed to child trespassers
1980s and 1990s	House of Lords shows an increasing willingness to use Practice Statement to overrule previous decisions eg *R* v *Shivpuri* (criminal attempts) *Pepper* v *Hart* (use of *Hansard* in statutory interpretation)

Figure 2.5 *Key fact chart for the operation of judicial precedent in the House of Lords*

Use of the Practice Statement

Since 1966, this Practice Statement has allowed the House of Lords to change the law if it believes that an earlier case was wrongly decided. It has the flexibility to refuse to follow an earlier case when 'it appears right to do so'. This phrase is, of course, very vague and gives little guidance as to when the House of Lords might overrule a previous decision. In fact the House of Lords has been reluctant to use this power, especially in the first few years after 1966. The first case in which the Practice Statement was used was *Conway* v *Rimmer* (1968), but this only involved a technical point on discovery of documents. The first major use did not occur until 1972 in *Herrington* v *British Railways Board* (1972), which involved the law on the duty of care owed to a child trespasser. The earlier case of *Addie* v *Dumbreck* (1929) had decided that an occupier of land would only owe a duty of care for injuries to a child trespasser, if those injuries had been caused

deliberately or recklessly. In *Herrington* the Lords held that social and physical conditions had changed since 1929, and the law should also change.

There was still great reluctance in the House of Lords to use the Practice Statement, as can be seen by the case of *Jones* v *Secretary of State for Social Services* (1972). This case involved the interpretation of the National Insurance (Industrial Injuries) Act 1946 and four out of the seven judges hearing the case regarded the earlier decision in *Re Dowling* (1967) as being wrong. Despite this the Lords refused to overrule that earlier case, preferring to keep to the idea that certainty was the most important feature of precedent. The same attitude was shown in *Knuller* v *DPP* (1973) when Lord Reid said:

> 'Our change of practice in no longer regarding previous decisions of this House as absolutely binding does not mean that whenever we think a previous precedent was wrong we should reverse it. In the

general interest of certainty in the law we must be sure that there is some very good reason before we so act.'

From the mid-1970s onwards the House of Lords showed a little more willingness to make use of the Practice Statement. For example in *Miliangos* v *George Frank (Textiles) Ltd* (1976) the House of Lords used the Practice Statement to overrule a previous judgment that damages could only be awarded in sterling. More recently in *Murphy* v *Brentwood District Council* (1990), the House of Lords overruled the decision in *Anns* v *Merton London Borough* (1977) regarding the test for negligence in the law of tort. Another major case was *Pepper* v *Hart* (1993) where the previous ban on the use of *Hansard* in statutory interpretation was overruled.

The Practice Statement in criminal law

The Practice Statement stressed that criminal law needs to be certain, so it was not surprising that the House of Lords did not rush to overrule any judgments in criminal cases. The first use in a criminal case was in *R* v *Shivpuri* (1986) which overruled the decision in *Anderton* v *Ryan* (1985) on attempts to do the impossible. The interesting point was that the decision in *Anderton* had been made less than a year before, but it had been severely criticised by academic lawyers. In *Shivpuri* Lord Bridge said:

'I am undeterred by the consideration that the decision in Anderton v Ryan was so recent. The Practice Statement is an effective abandonment of our pretention to infallibility. If a serious error embodied in a decision of this House has distorted the law, the sooner it is corrected the better.'

In other words, the House of Lords recognised that they might sometimes make errors and the most important thing then was to put the law right. Where the Practice

Statement is used to overrule a previous decision, that past case is then effectively ignored. The law is now that which is set out in the new case.

Conclusion

So is the House of Lords making enough use of the Practice Statement? Alan Patterson, in his work *The Law Lords*, points out that the Practice Statement has had a greater impact than thought. He demonstrates this by showing that between 1966 and 1980 some 29 cases involved the possibility of the House of Lords overruling an earlier precedent of its own. While they only actually used the Practice Statement in eight out of those 29 cases, at least one of the judges in the House of Lords was prepared to overrule a previous precedent in another ten cases. Since 1980 cases such as *R* v *Shivpuri* and *Pepper* v *Hart* suggest that the Lords are more prepared to use the Practice Statement.

Activity

Read the following passage which comes from an extra explanatory note which was given to the press when the Practice Statement was issued and answer the questions below.

'The statement is one of great importance, although it should not be supposed that there will frequently be cases in which the House thinks it right not to follow their own precedent. An example of a case in which the House might think it right to depart from a precedent is where they consider that the earlier decision was influenced by the existence of conditions which no longer prevail, and that in modern conditions the law ought to be different.

One consequence of this change is of major importance. The relaxation of the rule of judicial precedent will enable the House of Lords to pay greater attention to judicial decisions reached in the superior courts of the Commonwealth, where they differ from earlier decisions of the House of Lords. That could be of great help in the development of our own law. The superior courts of many other countries are not rigidly bound by their own decisions and the change in the practice of the House of Lords will bring us more into line with them.'

QUESTIONS

❶ Why is the Practice Statement of great importance?

❷ Does the note suggest that the Practice Statement is likely to be used often?

❸ Do you agree that 'in modern conditions the law ought to be different'? Give reasons and examples to support your answer.

❹ Why should the House of Lords want to consider decisions from Commonwealth countries? What authority do such decisions have in the English legal system?

2.4.4 The position of the Court of Appeal

As already stated there are two divisions of this court, the Civil Division and the Criminal Division, and the rules for precedent are not quite the same in these two divisions. However, both divisions of the Court of Appeal are bound by decisions of the European Court of Justice and the House of Lords. This is true even though there have been attempts in the past, mainly by Lord Denning, to argue that the Court of Appeal should not be bound by the House of Lords. In *Broome v Cassell & Co Ltd* (1971) Lord Denning refused to follow the earlier decision of the House of Lords in *Rookes v Barnard* (1964) on the circumstances in which exemplary damages could be awarded.

Again in the cases of *Schorsch Meier GmbH v Henning* (1975) and *Miliangos v George Frank (Textiles) Ltd* (1976) the Court of Appeal under Lord Denning's leadership refused to follow a decision of the House of Lords in *Havana Railways* (1961) which said that damages could only be awarded in

sterling (English money). Lord Denning's argument for refusing to follow the House of Lords' decision was that the economic climate of the world had changed, and sterling was no longer a stable currency; there were some situations in which justice could only be done by awarding damages in another currency. The case of *Schorsch Meier GmbH v Henning* was not appealed to the House of Lords, but *Miliangos v George Frank (Textiles) Ltd* did go on appeal to the Lords, where it was pointed out that the Court of Appeal had no right to ignore or overrule decisions of the House of Lords. The more unusual feature of *Miliangos* was that the House of Lords then used the Practice Statement to overrule its own decision in *Havana Railways*.

 Comment

Should the Court of Appeal have to follow House of Lords' decisions?

The main argument in favour of the Court of Appeal being able to ignore House of Lords' decisions is that very few cases reach the House of Lords, so that if there is an error in the law it may take years before a suitable case is appealed all the way to the House of Lords. The cases of *Schorsch Meier* and *Miliangos* illustrate the potential for injustice if there is no appeal to the House of Lords. What would have happened if the Court of Appeal in *Schorsch Meier* had decided that it had to follow the House of Lords' decision in *Havana Railways*? It is quite possible that the later case of *Miliangos* would not have even been appealed to the Court of Appeal. After all, why waste money on an appeal when there have been previous cases in both the Court of Appeal and the House of Lords ruling on that point of law? The law would have been regarded as fixed and it might never have been changed.

On the other hand, if the Court of Appeal could overrule the House of Lords, the system of precedent would break down and the law would become uncertain. There would be two conflicting precedents for lower courts to choose from. This would make it difficult for the judge in the lower court. It would also make the law so uncertain that it would be difficult for lawyers to advise clients on the law. However, since the case of *Miliangos*, there has been no further challenge by the Court of Appeal to this basic idea (in our system of judicial precedent) that lower courts must follow decisions of courts above them in the hierarchy.

Effect of the Human Rights Act 1998

Section 2(1)(a) of the Human Rights Act 1998 states that courts must take into account any judgment or decision of the European Court of Human Rights. In the case of *Re Medicaments (No 2), Director General of Fair Trading* v *Proprietary Association of Great Britain* (2001) the Court of Appeal refused to follow the decision of the House of Lords in *R* v *Gough* (1996) because it was slightly different to decisions of the European Court of Human Rights.

The *Director General* case was about whether a decision should be set aside because of the risk of bias on the part of one of the panel. In *Gough* the test for bias included the appeal court deciding whether there was a real danger that the tribunal was biased. The Court of Appeal said that in the European Court of Human Rights cases the emphasis was on the impression which the facts would give on an objective basis. This they claimed was a 'modest adjustment' of the test in *Gough*. However, this appears to be one situation in which the Court of Appeal need not follow a House of Lords decision.

This Court of Appeal decision, rather than the House of Lords view, was followed by the High Court in *M* v *Islington London*

Borough Council (2001). It was held that a District Judge should not have heard care proceedings involving a particular child. This was because he had been involved with a local planning group at one meeting of which mention of problems of this child in the community had been discussed. There was no suggestion that the judge was biased but, applying the *Re Medicaments* test, the circumstances were such as to lead a fair-minded and informed observer to conclude that there was a real possibility of bias.

The Court of Appeal and its own decisions

The first rule is that decisions by one division of the Court of Appeal will not bind the other division. However, within each division, decisions are normally binding, especially for the Civil Division. This rule comes from the case of *Young* v *Bristol Aeroplane Co Ltd* (1944) and the only exceptions allowed by that case are:

- Where there are conflicting decisions in past Court of Appeal cases, the court can choose which one it will follow and which it will reject
- Where there is a decision of the House of Lords which effectively overrules a Court of Appeal decision the Court of Appeal must follow the the decision of the House of Lords
- Where the decision was made *per incuriam*, that is carelessly or by mistake because a relevant Act of Parliament or other regulation has not been considered by the court

The Civil Division of the Court of Appeal under Lord Denning tried to challenge the rule in *Young's* case, claiming that as it had made the earlier decision it could change it. As Lord Denning said in *Gallie* v *Lee* (1969): 'It was a self-imposed limitation and we who imposed it can also remove it.' This view was not shared by the other judges in the Court of Appeal, as is shown by the statement of Russell LJ in the same case of *Gallie* v *Lee* where he said: 'The availability of the House of Lords to correct errors in the Court of Appeal makes it, in my view, unnecessary for the court to depart from its existing discipline.'

However, in *Davis* v *Johnson* (1979) the Court of Appeal, unusually sitting as a full court of five judges, refused to follow a decision made only days earlier regarding the interpretation of the Domestic Violence and Matriminial Proceedings Act 1976. The case went to the House of Lords on appeal where the Law Lords, despite agreeing with the actual interpretation of the law, ruled that the Court of Appeal had to follow its own previous decisions and said that they 'expressly, unequivocally and unanimously reaffirmed the rule in *Young* v *Bristol Aeroplane*'.

Since this case and, perhaps more especially since the retirement of Lord Denning, the Court of Appeal has not challenged the rule in *Young's* case, though it has made some use of the *per incuriam* exception allowed by *Young's* case. For example in *Williams* v *Fawcett* (1986) the Court refused to follow previous decisions because these had been based on a misunderstanding of the County Court rules dealing with procedure for committing to prison those who break court undertakings. In *Rickards* v *Rickards* (1989) the court refused to follow a case it had decided in 1981. This was because of the fact that, in the previous case, it had misunderstood the effect of a House of Lords' decision. Even though the court did not follow its own previous decision Lord Donaldson said that it would only be in 'rare and exceptional cases' that the Court of Appeal would be justified in refusing to follow a previous decision. *Rickards* v *Rickards* was considered a 'rare and exceptional' case because the mistake was over the critical point of whether the court had power to hear that particular type of case. Also it was very unlikely that the case would be appealed to the House of Lords. In *Rakhit* v *Carty* (1990), the Court refused to follow decisions made in 1982 and 1988 because a relevant provision of the Rent Act 1977 had not been considered.

The Court of Appeal (Criminal Division)

The Criminal Division as well as using the exceptions from *Young's* case, can also refuse to follow a past decision of its own if the law has been 'misapplied or misunderstood'. This extra exception arises because in criminal cases people's liberty is involved. This idea was recognised in *R* v *Taylor* (1950) by the Court of Criminal Appeal, which was the court that existed before the creation of the Court of Appeal (Criminal Division). Once the Court of Appeal (Criminal Division) was set up, the same point was made in *R* v *Gould* (1968). Also in *R* v *Spencer* (1985) the judges said that there should not in general be any difference in the way that precedent was followed in the Criminal Division and in the Civil Division, 'save that we must remember that we may be dealing with the liberty of the subject and if a departure from authority is necessary in the interests of justice to an appellant, then this court should not shrink from so acting'.

Activity

Read the following comments by Lord Scarman in his judgment in *Tiverton Estates Ltd* v *Wearwell Ltd* (1975) and answer the questions below.

'The Court of Appeal occupies a central, but intermediate position in our legal system. To a large extent, the consistency and certainty of the law depend upon it . . . If, therefore, one division of the court should refuse to follow another because it believed the other's decision to be wrong, there would be a risk of confusion and doubt arising where there should be consistency and certainty.

The appropriate forum for the correction of the Court of Appeal's errors is the House of Lords, where the decision will at least have the merit of being final and binding, subject only to the House's power to review its own decisions. The House of Lords as the court of last resort needs this power of review; it does not follow that an intermediate court needs it.'

QUESTIONS

❶ Why did Lord Scarman describe the Court of Appeal as occupying 'a central but intermediate position'?

❷ Do you agree with his view that there would be a 'risk of confusion and doubt' if the Court of Appeal was not obliged to follow its own past decisions?

❸ Describe the situations in which the Court of Appeal may refuse to follow its own past decisions.

❹ Why does the House of Lords need the power of review?

2.4.5 Distinguishing, overruling and reversing

Distinguishing

This is a method which can be used by a judge to avoid following a past decision which he would otherwise have to follow. It means that the judge finds that the material facts of the case he is deciding are sufficiently different for him to draw a distinction between the present case and the previous precedent. He is not then bound by the previous case.

KEY FACTS

General rules	Comment
Bound by European Court of Justice	Since 1972 all courts in England and Wales are bound by the European Court of Justice.
Bound by House of Lords	This is because the House of Lords is above the Court of Appeal in the court hierarchy. Also necessary for certainty in the law. Court of Appeal tried to challenge this rule in *Broome* v *Cassell* (1971) and also in *Miliangos* (1976). The House of Lords rejected this challenge. The Court of Appeal must follow decisions of the House of Lords.
Bound by its own past decisions	Decided by the Court of Appeal in *Young's case* (1944), though there are minor exceptions (see below). In *Davis* v *Johnson* (1979) the Court of Appeal tried to challenge this rule but the House of Lords confirmed that the Court of Appeal had to follow its own previous decisions.

Exceptions	Comment
Exceptions in *Young's case*	Court of Appeal need not follow its own previous decisions where: • there are conflicting past decisions • there is a House of Lords' decision which effectively overrules the Court of Appeal decision • the decision was made *per incuriam* (in error).
Limitation of *per incuriam*	Only used in 'rare and exceptional cases' (*Rickards* v *Rickards* (1989)).
Special exception for the Criminal Division	If the law has been 'misapplied or misunderstood' (*R* v *Gould* (1968)).

Figure 2.6 Key fact chart for the Court of Appeal and the doctrine of precedent

KEY FACTS

Concept	Definition	Comment
stare decisis	Stand by what has been decided	Follow the law decided in previous cases for certainty and fairness
ratio decidendi	Reason for deciding	The part of the judgment which creates the law
obiter dicta	Others things said	The other parts of the judgment – these do not create law
binding precedent	A previous decision which has to be followed	Decisions of higher courts bind lower courts
persuasive precedent	A previous decision which does not have to be followed	The court may be 'persuaded' that the same legal decision should be made
original precedent	A decision in a case where there is no previous legal decision or law for the judge to use	This leads to judges 'making' law
distinguishing	A method of avoiding a previous decision because facts in the present case are different	e.g. *Balfour* v *Balfour* not followed In *Merritt* v *Merritt*
overruling	A decision which states that a legal rule in an earlier case is wrong	e.g. in *Pepper* v *Hart* the House of Lords overruled *Davis* v *Johnson* on the use of *Hansard*
reversing	Where a higher court in the same case overturns the decision of the lower court	This can only happen if there is an appeal in the case

Figure 2.7 Key fact chart for the basic concepts of judicial precedent

Two cases demonstrating this process are *Balfour* v *Balfour* (1919) and *Merritt* v *Merritt* (1971). Both cases involved a wife making a claim against her husband for breach of contract. In *Balfour* it was decided that the claim could not succeed because there was no intention to create legal relations; there was merely a domestic arrangement between a husband and wife and so there was no legally binding contract. The second case was successful because the court held that the facts of the two cases were sufficiently different in that, although the parties were husband and wife, the

agreement was made after they had separated. Furthermore the agreement was made in writing. This distinguished the case from *Balfour*; the agreement in *Merritt* was not just a domestic arrangement but meant as a legally enforceable contract.

Overruling

This is where a court in a later case states that the legal rule decided in an earlier case is wrong. Overruling may occur when a higher court overrules a decision made in an earlier case by a lower court, for example the House of Lords overruling a decision of the Court of Appeal. It can also occur where the European Court of Justice overrules a past decision it has made; or when the House of Lords uses its power under the Practice Statement to overrule a past decision of its own.

An example of this was seen in *Pepper* v *Hart* (1993) when the House of Lords ruled that *Hansard* (the record of what is said in Parliament) could be consulted when trying to decide what certain words in an Act of Parliament meant. This decision overruled the earlier decision in *Davis* v *Johnson* (1979) when the House of Lords had held that it could not consult *Hansard*.

Reversing

This is where a court higher up in the hierarchy overturns the decision of a lower court on appeal in the same case. For example, the Court of Appeal may disagree with the legal ruling of the High Court and come to a different view of the law; in this situation they reverse the decision made by the High Court.

2.4.6 Judicial law-making

Although there used to be a school of thought that judges did not actually 'make' new law but merely declared what the law had always been, today it is well recognised that judges do use precedent to create new law and to extend old principles. There are many areas of law which owe their existence to decisions by the judges.

Law of contract

Nearly all the main rules which govern the formation of contracts come from decided cases. Many of the decisions were made in the nineteenth century, but they still affect the law today.

Tort of negligence

The law of negligence in the law of tort is another major area which has been developed and refined by judicial decisions. An important starting point in this area of law was the case of *Donoghue* v *Stevenson* (1932) in which the House of Lords, when recognising that a manufacturer owed a duty of care to the 'ultimate consumer', created what is known as the 'neighbour test'. Lord Atkin in his judgment in the case said: 'You must take reasonable care to avoid acts or omissions which you can reasonably foresee would be likely to injure your neighbour'. This concept has been applied by judges in several different situations, so that the tort of negligence has developed into a major tort. An interesting extension was in the case of *Ogwo* v *Taylor* (1987) where it was held that a man, who negligently started a fire in his roof when trying to burn off paint with a blow torch, owed a duty of care to a fireman who was injured trying to put out the fire.

There have also been major developments in case-law on liability for nervous shock where there has been negligence. The House of Lords laid down the guidelines for this area of law in the case of *Alcock* v *Chief Constable of South Yorkshire* (1991) which involved claims made by people who had lost relatives in the Hillsborough tragedy. The law of negligence has also been extended in cases on liability for economic loss.

Criminal law

In the criminal law the judges have played a major role in developing the law on intention. For example, it is only because of judicial decisions that the intention for murder covers not only the intention to kill but also the intention to cause grievous bodily harm. Judicial decisions have also effectively created new crimes, as in *Shaw* v *DPP* (1962) which created the offence of conspiracy to corrupt public morals and *R* v *R* (1991) when it was decided that rape within marriage could be a crime.

However, there have been cases in which the House of Lords has refused to change the law, saying that such a change should only be made by Parliament. This happened in *C v DPP* (1995) when it refused to abolish the presumption that children between ten and 14 were incapable of having the necessary intention to commit a crime. (This presumption meant that there always had to be evidence that the child knew he or she was doing something which was seriously wrong.) In fact the Government did change the law later in the Crime and Disorder Act 1998.

◄ Comment

Should judges make law?

It is argued that it is wrong for judges to make law. Their job is to apply the law. It is for Parliament to make the law. Parliament is elected to do this but judges are not. This means that law-making by judges is undemocratic.

But, in reality judges have to make law in some situations. The first is where a case involves a legal point which has never been decided before. As there is no law on it, the judge in the case has to make a decision. After all, the parties in the case would not want the judge to refuse to deal with the case; they want the matter decided.

The second area is more controversial. This is where judges overrule old cases and in doing so create new law. It is important for the law to be updated in this way. Law for the twenty first century needs to be based on today's society and values. Law decided a hundred years or more ago may no longer be suitable. Ideally, Parliament should reform the law, but Parliament is sometimes slow to do this. If judges never overruled old cases, then the law might be 'out of date'.

An example of this is the case of *R v R* (1991). In this case a man was charged with raping his wife. The point the court had to decide was whether, by being married, a woman automatically consented to sex with her husband and could never say 'no'. The old law dated back to 1736 when it was said that 'by their mutual matrimonial consent the wife hath given up her herself in this kind to her husband, which she cannot retract'. In other words, once married, a woman was always assumed to consent and could not go back on this. This was still held to be the law in *R v Miller* (1954), even though the wife had already started divorce proceedings. Parliament had not done anything to reform this law.

So, when the case of *R v R* came before the courts, the judges had to decide whether to follow the old law, or whether they should change the law to match the ideas of the late twentieth century. In the House of Lords, the judges pointed out that 'the status of women and the status of a married woman in our law have changed quite dramatically. A husband and wife are now for all practical purposes equal partners in marriage'. As a result it was decided that if a wife did not consent to sex then her husband could be guilty of rape. The House of Lords stated that the common law (judge-made law) 'is capable of evolving in the light of changing social, economic and cultural developments'. This clearly recognises that judges in the House of Lords can, and will, change the law if they think it necessary.

Effect of new Act of Parliament

However precedent is subordinate to statute law, delegated legislation and European regulations. This means that if (for example) an Act of Parliament is passed and that Act contains a provision which contradicts a previously decided case, that case decision will cease to have effect; the Act of Parliament is now the law on that point. This happened when Parliament passed the Law Reform (Year and a Day Rule) Act in 1996.

Up to then judicial decisions meant that a person could only be charged with murder or manslaughter if the victim died within a year and a day of receiving his injuries. The Act enacted that there was no time limit, and a person could be guilty even if the victim died several years later, so cases after 1996 follow the Act and not the old judicial decisions.

2.4.7 Comparison with other legal systems

Codes of law

Most countries have some system of considering past case decisions, but these are rarely as rigid as the system of judicial precedent followed in England and Wales. In countries which have a code of law, precedent plays a much less important part. This civil system is operated in many continental countries; the judges are less likely to make law, the code should provide for all situations and so the judge's task is to interpret the code. Since the code is the fountain of the law, judicial decisions are not followed so closely. Even judges in lower courts can refuse to follow a decision by another court if they feel that the code was not correctly interpreted.

Less rigid precedent

Even in other countries which have a common law system similar to England's where case decisions form a major part of the law, the doctrine of precedent is not applied so strictly. For example, in the United States of America a previous precedent is likely to be ignored if it fails to meet with academic approval: if there is considerable criticism of the decision by leading academic lawyers, judges in later cases are likely to take note of that criticism and rule differently. This has happened in England in the case of *R v Shivpuri* (1986), but this is a rare happening, while in America it occurs more frequently.

Also in America, cases where the panel of judges disagreed (so that the decision may have been by three judges to two) are likely to be overruled in the future. In England, the fact that the majority was so slender does not make the precedent less valuable.

Prospective overruling

The other difference is that in America the concept of prospective overruling is used. This means that the law is not changed in the case before the court, but it is changed for the future. In England, the judges cannot do this; if their decision changes the law then it is changed in the actual case. This has been described as 'dog's law'; that is you do not know you have done wrong until the court changes the law in your case, in just the way that a dog does not know it has done wrong until you punish him. This is what happened in the case of *R v R* (1991) when it was decided that rape within marriage could be a crime. Until that case, previous decisions had held that this was not a crime. This can be viewed as unfair to the parties in a case. The American use of prospective overruling is preferable in such cases.

Retrospective overruling can also lead to other possibly unfair situations. In *R v Governor of Brockhill Prison (ex parte Evans)* (1997), a prison governor had worked out when a prisoner should be released according to rules set out in three decisions of the Queen's Bench Divisional Court. However, the Divisional Court later ruled that those three cases were wrong and gave a new approach to calculating release dates. This new approach meant that the prisoner should have been released 59 days earlier. Since the law changes retrospectively it meant that the prisoner had been unlawfully detained and was entitled to claim compensation for this. This was so even though when the calculations were made the governor was applying the law correctly as it then was.

Activity

Discuss whether you think the prisoner in *R v Governor of Brockhill Prison (ex parte Evans)* (1997) should have received compensation.

2.4.8 Advantages and disadvantages of precedent

As can be seen from the previous sections there are both advantages and disadvantages to the way in which judicial precedent operates in England and Wales. In fact it could be said that every advantage has a corresponding disadvantage. The main advantages are:

1. **Certainty**
   Because the courts follow past decisions, people know what the law is and how it is likely to be applied in their case; it allows lawyers to advise clients on the likely outcome of cases; it also allows people to operate their businesses knowing that financial and other arrangements they make are recognised by law. The House of Lords' Practice Statement points out how important certainty is.

2. **Consistency and fairness in the law**
   It is seen as just and fair that similar cases should be decided in a similar way, just as in any sport it is seen as fair that the rules of the game apply equally to each side. The law must be consistent if it is to be credible.

3. **Precision**
   As the principles of law are set out in actual cases the law becomes very precise; it is well illustrated and gradually builds up through the different variations of facts in the cases that come before the courts.

4. **Flexibility**
   There is room for the law to change as the House of Lords can use the Practice Statement to overrule cases. The ability to distinguish cases also gives all courts some freedom to avoid past decisions and develop the law.

5. **Time-saving**
   Precedent can be considered a useful time saving device. Where a principle has been established, cases with similar facts are unlikely to go through the lengthy process of litigation.

The main advantages have been summed up very neatly as follows:

'The main advantages of the precedent system are said to be certainty, precision and flexibility. Legal certainty is achieved in theory at least, in that if the legal problem raised has been solved before, the judge is bound to adopt that solution. Precision is achieved by the sheer volume of reported cases containing solutions to innumerable factual situations. No code or statute could ever contain as much.

Flexibility is achieved by the possibility of decisions being overruled and by the possibility of distinguishing and confining the operation of decisions which appear unsound.'

However, there are disadvantages as follows:

1. **Rigidity**
   The fact that lower courts have to follow decisions of higher courts, together with the fact that the Court of Appeal has to follow its own past decisions, can make the law too inflexible so that bad decisions made in the past may be perpetuated. There is the added problem that so few cases go to the House of Lords. Change in the law will only take place if parties have the courage, the persistence and the money to appeal their case.

a   # Re S (adult: refusal of medical treatment)

FAMILY DIVISION
SIR STEPHEN BROWN P
12 OCTOBER 1992

b   *Medical treatment – Adult patient – Consent to treatment – Right to refuse consent – Refusal on religious grounds – Discretion of court to authorise emergency operation – Health authority seeking authority to carry out emergency Caesarian section operation on pregnant woman – Operation in vital interests of patient and unborn child – Patient objecting to operation on religious grounds – Whether court should exercise inherent jurisdiction to authorise operation.*

c
A health authority applied for a declaration to authorise the surgeons and staff of a hospital under the authority's control to carry out an emergency Caesarian section operation upon a 30-year-old woman patient who had been admitted to hospital with ruptured membranes and in spontaneous labour with her third pregnancy and who had continued in labour since then. She was six days overdue
d   beyond the expected date of birth and had refused, on religious grounds, to submit herself to such an operation. The surgeon in charge of the patient was emphatic in his evidence that the operation was the only means of saving the patient's life and that her baby could not be born alive if the operation was not carried out.

e
Held – The court would exercise its inherent jurisdiction to authorise the surgeons and staff of a hospital to carry out an emergency Caesarian section operation upon a patient contrary to her beliefs if the operation was vital to protect the life of the unborn child. Accordingly, a declaration would be granted that such an operation and any necessary consequential treatment which the
f   hospital and its staff proposed to perform on the patient was in the vital interests of the patient and her unborn child and could be lawfully performed despite the patient's refusal to give her consent to the operation (see p 672 *c d and g*, post).

Notes
For consent to medical treatment, see 30 *Halsbury's Laws* (4th edn reissue) para 39,
g   and for cases on the subject, see 33 *Digest* (Reissue) 273, 2242–2246.

Cases referred to in judgment
AC, Re (1990) 573 A 2d 1235, DC Ct of Apps (en banc).
T (adult: refusal of medical treatment), Re [1992] 4 All ER 649, CA.

h   **Application**
A health authority applied for a declaration to authorise the surgeons and staff of a hospital under the health authority's control to carry out an emergency Caesarian operation on a patient, Mrs S. The facts are set out in the judgment.

j   *Huw Lloyd* (instructed by *Beachcroft Stanleys*) for the health authority.
James Munby QC (instructed by the *Official Solicitor*) as amicus curiae.

SIR STEPHEN BROWN P. This is an application by a health authority for a declaration to authorise the surgeons and staff of a hospital to carry out an emergency Caesarian operation upon a patient, who I shall refer to as 'Mrs S'.

Figure 2.8 Law Report in the case of Re S

Mrs S is 30 years of age. She is in labour with her third pregnancy. She was admitted to a hospital last Saturday with ruptured membranes and in spontaneous labour. She had continued in labour since. She is already six days overdue beyond the expected date of birth, which was 6 October, and she has now refused, on religious grounds, to submit herself to a Caesarian section operation. She is supported in this by her husband. They are described as 'born-again Christians' and are clearly quite sincere in their beliefs.

I have heard the evidence of P, a Fellow of the Royal College of Surgeons who is in charge of this patient at the hospital. He has given, succinctly and graphically, a description of the condition of this patient. Her situation is desperately serious, as is also the situation of the as yet unborn child. The child is in what is described as a position of 'transverse lie', with the elbow projecting through the cervix and the head being on the right side. There is the gravest risk of a rupture of the uterus if the section is not carried out and the natural labour process is permitted to continue. The evidence of P is that we are concerned with 'minutes rather than hours' and that it is a 'life and death' situation. He has done his best, as have other surgeons and doctors at the hospital, to persuade the mother that the only means of saving her life, and also I emphasise the life of her unborn child, is to carry out a Caesarian section operation. P is emphatic. He says it is absolutely the case that the baby cannot be born alive if a Caesarian operation is not carried out. He has described the medical condition. I am not going to go into it in detail because of the pressure of time.

I have been assisted by Mr Munby QC appearing for the Official Solicitor as amicus curiae. The Official Solicitor answered the call of the court within minutes and, although this application only came to the notice of the court officials at 1.30 pm, it has come on for hearing just before 2 o'clock and now at 2.18 pm I propose to make the declaration which is sought. I do so in the knowledge that the fundamental question appears to have been left open by Lord Donaldson MR in *Re T (adult: refusal of medical treatment)* [1992] 4 All ER 649, heard earlier this year in the Court of Appeal, and in the knowledge that there is no English authority which is directly in point. There is, however, some American authority which suggests that if this case were being heard in the American courts the answer would be likely to be in favour of granting a declaration in these circumstances: see *Re AC* (1990) 573 A 2d 1235 at 1240, 1246–1248, 1252.

I do not propose to say more at this stage, except that I wholly accept the evidence of P as to the desperate nature of this situation, and that I grant the declaration as sought.

Declaration that a Caesarian section and any necessary consequential treatment which the hospital and its staff proposed to perform on the patient was in the vital interests of the patient and her unborn child and could be lawfully performed despite the patient's refusal to give her consent. No order as to costs.

Bebe Chua   Barrister.

Figure 2.8 Law Report in the case of Re S – continued

2. Complexity

Since there are nearly half a million reported cases it is not easy to find all the relevant case law even with computerised databases. Another problem is in the judgments themselves, which are often very long with no clear distinction between comments and the reasons for the decision. This makes it difficult in some cases to extract the *ratio decidendi*; indeed in *Dodd's Case* (1973) the judges in the Court of Appeal said they were unable to find the *ratio* in a decision of the House of Lords.

3. Illogical distinctions

The use of distinguishing to avoid past decisions can lead to 'hair-splitting' so that some areas of the law have become very complex. The differences between some cases may be very small and appear illogical.

4. Slowness of growth

Judges are well aware that some areas of the law are unclear or in need of reform, however they cannot make a decision unless there is a case before the courts to be decided. This is one of the criticisms of the need for the Court of Appeal to follow its own previous decisions, as only about 50 cases go to the House of Lords each year. There may be a long wait for a suitable case to be appealed as far as the House of Lords.

2.4.9 Law reporting

In order to follow past decisions there must be an accurate record of what those decisions were. Written reports have existed in England and Wales since the thirteenth century, but many of the early reports were very brief and, it is thought, not always accurate. The earliest reports from about 1275 to 1535 were called Year Books, and contained short reports of cases, usually written in French. From 1535 to 1865 cases were reported by individuals who made a business out of selling the reports to lawyers. The detail and accuracy of these reports varied enormously. However, some are still occasionally used today.

In 1865 the Incorporated Council of Law Reporting was set up – this was controlled by the courts. Reports became accurate, with the judgment usually noted down word for word. This accuracy of reports was one of the factors in the development of the strict doctrine of precedent. These reports still exist and are published according to the court that the case took place in. For example, cases references abbreviated to 'Ch' stand for 'Chancery' and the case will have been decided in the Chancery Division; while 'QB' stands for 'Queen's Bench Division'.

There are also other well established reports today, notably the All England series (abbreviated to All ER) and the Weekly Law Reports (WLR). Newspapers and journals also publish law reports, but these are often abbreviated versions in which the law reporter has tried to pick out the essential parts of the judgment.

On pages 35 and 36 a law report in the case of *Re S* (1992) is set out in full for you to see.

If you look at that report you will see at the very top of the page it shows in which court the case took place with 'Fam D' standing for 'Family Division' of the High Court. On the second page of the report it has the reference [1992] 4 All ER, showing that the report is from the fourth volume of the All England Reports for 1992. In the report itself there are lower case letters down the side for ease of reference; this is done in all law reports. So using those look at *(a)* where the name of the case is given, and immediately below that is the court, the judge who decided the case and then the date on which it was decided. At *(b)* there is a summary of what the case is about and the key legal points it involved; this is a quick method of checking whether the case is relevant to the point you are researching. Then at *(c)* and *(d)* you will see what is called the headnote which has a résumé of the facts of the case followed at *(e)* and *(f)* by a statement of what the court decided. All this is written by the barrister who reported the case and it is not part of the judgment. The name of the barrister who reported the case is given at the end of the report.

Further down is a list of previous cases which were referred to in the judgment. In this instance there are only two, but in some cases there may be quite a long list. Right at the bottom of the first page of the report, the judgment starts. One interesting point in this judgment is that the judge, Sir Stephen Brown P, states that there is no English authority on the matter. This is at *(f)* on the second page. He then goes on to say that there is some American authority. A decision by the American courts would, of course, only be persuasive precedent. This is an unusually short law report, but the same pattern is followed in reports generally and it is a useful illustration of law reporting.

Internet law reports

All High Court, Court of Appeal and House of Lords cases are now reported on the Internet. Some websites give the full report free, others give summaries or an index of cases. There are also subscription sites which give a very comprehensive service of law reports.

Activity

Search at least one website address and find a recent law report. Some suggestions for websites are given below.

www.lawreports.co.uk gives summaries of important cases
www.publications.parliament.uk gives reports of House of Lords cases
www.courtservice.gov.uk gives recent cases under What's New

Chapter 3

LEGISLATION

In today's world there is often a need for new law to meet new situations. Clearly the method of judicial law-making through precedents is not suitable for major changes to the law, nor is it a sufficiently quick, efficient law-making method for a modern society. The other point to be made is that judges are not elected by the people and in a democracy the view is that laws should only be made by the elected representatives of society. So, today, the main legislative body in the United Kingdom is Parliament.

Laws passed by Parliament are known as Acts of Parliament or statutes, and this source of law is usually referred to as statute law. About 60 to 70 Acts are passed each year. In addition to Parliament as a whole enacting law, power is delegated to government ministers and their departments to make detailed rules and regulations, which supplement Acts of Parliament. These regulations are known as delegated legislation.

3.1 Acts of Parliament

3.1.1 Parliament

Members of Parliament

Parliament consists of the House of Commons and the House of Lords. The members of the House of Commons are elected by the public, with the country being divided into constituencies and each of these returning one Member of Parliament (MP). There must be a general election at least once every five years, though such an election can be called sooner by the Prime Minister. In addition, there may be individual by-elections in constituencies where the MP has died or retired during the current session of Parliament. The Government of the day is formed by the political party which has a majority in the House of Commons.

The House of Lords

Originally the members of the House of Lords were mainly those who had inherited a title. These were the hereditary peers. In addition, the judges who sat as Law Lords and also the most senior bishops in the country were members of the House of Lords. During the twentieth century the awarding of a title for life (a life peerage) became more common. The Prime Minister nominated people who should receive a title for their lifetime, but this title would not pass on to their children. The title was then awarded by the Monarch. In this way people who had served the country and were thought to be suitable members of the House of Lords were able to bring their expertise to the House. Most life peerages were given to former politicians who had retired from the House of Commons. For example, Margaret Thatcher, who had been Prime Minister in the 1980s, was made a life peer.

Reform of the House of Lords

By 1999, there were over 1,100 members of the House of Lords, of whom 750 were hereditary peers. The Labour Government decided that in a modern society an inherited title should not automatically allow someone to participate in making law. They felt that some of the members should be elected and some should be nominated. To help decide exactly what reforms should be made, a Royal

Commission was set up to consider how members of the House of Lords should be selected. In the meantime the right of most of the hereditary peers to sit in the House of Lords was abolished in November 1999. Only 92 hereditary peers were allowed to continue to be members of the House of Lords.

The Wakeham Commission reported in 2000 and recommended that one third of the House should be elected. Also, that there should be a limit on the system of political patronage whereby the Prime Minister nominates people to the House of Lords. The Commission recommended that an independent Appointments Commission could reject poorly qualified nominees and also be able to appoint 'people's peers'.

In 2001 some so-called people's peers were appointed to the House of Lords by the Prime Minister. These were supposed to be ordinary people who had been recommended by other ordinary people. However, the list was mainly of already famous people, rather than 'Mr Joe Public'.

In December 2001 the Government issued a White Paper setting out the changes they wished to see to the House of Lords. This allows for only 20 per cent of the House to be elected and another 20 per cent selected by the Appointments Commission. The remainder would be nominated by the political parties in proportion to their share of the vote in the previous general election. This would make the House of Lords more party political than it used to be.

3.1.2 Influences on Parliamentary law-making

When a Government is formed, it will have a programme of reforms it wishes to carry out. These will have been set out in its party manifesto on which it asked people to vote for it in the General Election. Also, at the start of each Parliamentary session, the Government announces (in the Queen's Speech) what particular laws it intends introducing during that session. So most new legislation is likely to arise from Government policy.

However, there are other influences on what law is enacted: European law can lead to new Acts of Parliament which are passed in order to bring our law in line with the European law. This may be to implement a specific European Regulation or Directive, as in the case of the Consumer Protection Act 1987, or because a decision of the European Court of Justice has shown that our law does not conform with the Treaty of Rome, as with the Sex Discrimination Act 1986. The effect of European law is considered in more detail in Chapter 4.

Other outside influences include proposals for law reform put forward by law reform agencies, commissions or inquiries into the effectiveness of existing law. These law reform agencies are dealt with in detail in Chapter 5. In addition specific events may also play a role in formulating the law. A particularly tragic example was the massacre in March 1996 of 16 young children and their teacher in Dunblane by a lone gunman. After this there was an inquiry into the laws on gun-ownership. By March 1997 Parliament passed the Firearms (Amendment) Act 1997 banning private ownership of most handguns.

Pressure groups may also cause the Government to reconsider the law on certain areas. This was seen in 1994 when the Government agreed to reduce the age of consent for homosexual acts in private from 21 to 18. Then in 2000 the age of consent was further reduced to 16. Another clear example of the Government bowing to public opinion and the efforts of pressure groups was the introduction of the Disability Discrimination Act 1995. The progress of this Act through the various Parliamentary stages illustrates many of the points made in this chapter and is considered in section 3.1.6.

3.1.3 The pre-legislative procedure

On major matters a Green Paper may be issued by the Minister with responsibility for that matter. The use of Green Papers was introduced in 1967 by the then Labour Government. A Green Paper is a consultative document on a topic in which the Government's view is put forward with proposals for law reform. Interested parties are then invited to send comments to the relevant Government Department, so that a full consideration of all sides can be made and necessary changes made to the Government's proposals. Following this the Government will publish a White Paper with its firm proposals for new law.

Consultation before any new law is framed is valuable as it allows time for mature consideration. Governments have been criticised for sometimes responding in a 'knee-jerk' fashion to incidents and, as a result, rushing law through that has subsequently proved to be unworkable. This occurred with the Dangerous Dogs Act 1991.

Activity

Read the following article and answer the questions below

Judge reprieves Dempsey, the harmless pit bull

A High Court judge, who reprieved a pit bull terrier from death row yesterday, savaged the Dangerous Dogs Act (1991) which he said would have sent a 'perfectly inoffensive animal to the gas chamber'.

Dempsey, dubbed Britain's most expensive dog after a long legal battle to save her, will be returned to her overjoyed owner after Lord Justice Staughton and Mr Justice Rougier quashed a destruction order by Ealing Magistrates' Court in 1992.

Dempsey's only crime was being the wrong kind of dog, Judge Rougier said. Magistrates sentenced her to be destroyed after the nephew of her owner, Dianne Fanneran, took her muzzle off in public when she became ill, and she was spotted by a policeman.

Mr Justice Rougier said: 'It seems to me that, while acknowledging the need to protect the public . . . the Dangerous Dogs Act bears all the hallmarks of an ill-thought-out piece of legislation, no doubt drafted in response to another pressure group . . .'

The Act was rushed through in 1991 by the then Home Secretary, Kenneth Baker, after pit bull terriers attacked a man in Lincoln and a 6-year-old girl in Bradford. It requires them to be put down unless they are neutered, tattooed, microchipped, registered, muzzled and kept on a lead in public.

Taken from an article by Clare Dyer in *The Guardian*, 23 November 1995

QUESTIONS

❶ Why was the Dangerous Dogs Act 1991 passed?
❷ Why was Dempsey in breach of the Act?
❸ What did Mr Justice Rougier say about the Act?
❹ How might this problem with the Act have been avoided by the Government when formulating the legislation?

3.1.4 Introducing an Act of Parliament

The great majority of Acts of Parliament are introduced by the Government – these are initially drafted by lawyers in the civil service who are known as Parliamentary Counsel to the Treasury. Instructions as to what is to be included and the effect the proposed law is intended to have, are given by the government department responsible for it.

Bills

When the proposed Act has been drafted it is published, and at this stage is called a Bill. It will only become an Act of Parliament if it successfully completes all the necessary stages in Parliament. Even at this early stage there are difficulties, as the draftsmen face problems in trying to frame the Bill. It has to be drawn up so that it represents the Government's wishes, while at the same time using correct legal wording so that there will not be any difficulties in the courts applying it. It must be unambiguous, precise and comprehensive. Achieving all of these is not easy, and there may be unforeseen problems with the language used, as discussed in the section on statutory interpretation. On top of this there is usually pressure on time, as the Government will have a timetable of when they wish to introduce the draft Bill into Parliament.

Private Members' Bills
Ballot

Bills can also be sponsored by individual MPs. The Parliamentary process allows for a ballot each Parliamentary session in which 20 private members are selected who can then take their turn in presenting a Bill to Parliament. The time for debate of private members' Bills is limited, usually only being debated on Fridays, so that only the first six or seven members in the ballot have a realistic chance of introducing a Bill on their chosen topic. Relatively few private members' Bills become law, but there have been some important laws passed as the result of such Bills. A major example was the Abortion Act 1967 which legalised abortion in this country. More recent examples are the Computer Misuse Act 1990, the Timeshare Act 1992 and the Marriage Act 1994, which was introduced by Giles Brandreth, the MP for Chester, allowing people to marry in any registered place, not only in Register Offices or religious buildings.

10 minute rule

Backbenchers can also try to introduce a Bill through the '10-minute' rule, under which any MP can make a speech of up to 10 minutes supporting the introduction of new legislation. This method is rarely successful unless there is no opposition to the Bill, but some Acts of Parliament have been introduced in this way, for example the Bail (Amendment) Act 1993 which gave the prosecution the right to appeal against the granting of bail to a defendant. Members of the House of Lords can also introduce private members' Bills.

Public and Private Bills

A public Bill involves matters of public policy which will affect either the whole country or a large section of it. Most of the Government Bills are in this category, for example the Disability Discrimination Act 1995, the Crime and Disorder Act 1998, the Access to Justice Act 1999 and the Powers of Criminal Courts (Sentencing) Act 2000. However, not all Bills are aimed at changing the law for the entire country; some are designed to pass a law which will affect only individual people or corporations. A recent example of this was the University College London Act 1996 which was passed in order to combine the Royal Free Hospital School of Medicine, the Institute of Neurology and the Institute of Child Health with University College.

3.1.5 The process in Parliament

In order to become an Act of Parliament, the Bill will usually have to be passed by both Houses of Parliament, and in each House there is a long and complex process. A Bill may start in either the House of Commons or the House of Lords, with the exception of finance Bills which must start in the House of Commons. All Bills must go through the following stages:

1. **First Reading**

   This is a formal procedure where the name and main aims of the Bill are read out. Usually no discussion takes place, but there will be a vote on whether the House wishes to consider the Bill further. The vote may be verbal: this is when the Speaker of the House asks the members as a whole how they vote and the members shout out 'Aye' or 'No'. If it is clear that nearly all members are in agreement, either for or against, there is no need for a more formal vote. If it is not possible to judge whether more people are shouting 'Aye' or 'No' there will be a formal vote in which the members of the House vote by leaving the Chamber and then walking back in through one of two special doors on one side or the other of the Chamber. There will be two 'tellers' positioned at each of these two voting doors to make a list of the Members voting on each side. These tellers count up the number of MPs who voted for and against and declare these numbers to the Speaker in front of the members of the House.

2. **Second Reading**

   This is the main debate on the whole Bill in which MPs debate the principles behind the Bill. The debate usually focuses on the main principles rather than the smaller details. Those MPs who wish to speak in the debate must catch the Speaker's eye, since the Speaker controls all debates and no-one may speak without being called on by the Speaker. At the end of this a vote is taken in the same way as for the First Reading; obviously there must be a majority in favour for the Bill to progress any further.

3. **Committee Stage**

   At this stage a detailed examination of each clause of the Bill is undertaken by a committee of between 16 and 50 MPs. This is usually done by what is called a Standing Committee, which, contrary to its name, is a committee chosen specifically for that Bill. The membership of such a committee is decided 'having regard to the qualifications of those members nominated and to the composition of the House'. So, although the Government will have a majority, the opposition and minority parties are represented proportionately to the number of seats they have in the House of Commons. The members of Parliament nominated for each Standing Committee will usually be those with a special interest in, or knowledge of, the subject of the Bill which is being considered. For finance Bills the whole House will sit in committee.

4. **Report Stage**

   At the Committee stage amendments to various clauses in the Bill may have been voted on and passed, so this report stage is where the committee report back to the House on those amendments. (If there were no amendments at the Committee stage, there will not be a 'Report' stage – instead the Bill will go straight on to the Third Reading.) The amendments will be debated in the House and accepted or rejected. Further amendments may also be added. The Report stage has been described as 'a useful safeguard against a small Committee amending a Bill against the wishes of the House, and a necessary opportunity for second thoughts'.

5. **Third Reading**

This is the final vote on the Bill. It is almost a formality since a Bill which has passed through all the stages above is unlikely to fail at this late stage. In fact in the House of Commons there will only be an actual further debate on the Bill as a whole if at least six MPs request it. However, in the House of Lords there may sometimes be amendments made at this stage.

6. **The House of Lords**

If the Bill started life in the House of Commons it is now passed to the House of Lords where it goes through the same five stages outlined above and, if the House of Lords makes amendments to the Bill, then it will go back to the House of Commons for it to consider those amendments. If the Bill started in the House of Lords then it passes to the House of Commons.

Parliament Acts

The power of the House of Lords is limited by the Parliament Acts 1911 and 1949. These allow a Bill to become law even if the House of Lords rejects it, provided that the Bill is re-introduced into the House of Commons in the next session of Parliament and passes all the stages again there. The principle behind the Parliament Acts is that the House of Lords is not an elected body, and its function is to refine and add to the law rather than oppose the will of the democratically elected House of Commons. In fact there have only been four occasions when this procedure has been used to by-pass the House of Lords after it had voted against a Bill. The last occasion was the War Crimes Act in 1991.

Sometimes the threat of using the Parliament Acts is enough to persuade the House of Lords to vote for the Bill on the second occasion. This happened with the reducing of the age of consent for homosexual acts from 18 to 16. The House of Lords initially rejected this when it was part of the Crime and Disorder Bill in 1998. In order to make sure the rest of that Bill was passed, the Government withdrew the section on the age of consent. However, in 2000 a new Bill (the Sexual Offences (Amendment) Bill) was put before Parliament to make the change in the law. The Government said that if necessary it would use the Parliament Acts to pass the law. After this the House of Lords eventually passed the Bill and the age of consent was reduced to 16.

7. **Royal Assent**

The final stage is where the monarch formally gives approval to the Bill and it then becomes an Act of Parliament. This is now a formality and, under the Royal Assent Act 1961, the monarch will not even have the text of the Bills to which she is assenting; she will only have the short title. The last time that a monarch refused assent was in 1707, when Queen Anne refused to assent to the Scottish Militia Bill.

Commencement of an Act

Following the Royal Assent the Act of Parliament will come in force on midnight of that day, unless another date has been set. However, there has been a growing trend for Acts of Parliament not to be implemented immediately. Instead the Act itself states the date when it will commence or passes responsibility on to the appropriate minister to fix the commencement date. In the latter case the minister will bring the Act into force by issuing a commencement order. This can cause problems of uncertainty as it is difficult to discover which sections of an Act have been brought into force. The Disability Discrimination Act 1995 is a good example of an Act where the sections are being brought in bit by bit. The part of the Act

KEY FACTS

Green Paper	Consultation document on possible new law
White Paper	Government's firm proposals for new law
First Reading	Formal introduction of Bill into the House of Commons
Second Reading	Main debate on Bill's principles
Committee Stage	Clause by clause consideration of the Bill by a select committee
Report Stage	Committee reports suggested amendments back to the House of Commons
Third Reading	Final debate on the Bill
Repeat of process in the House of Lords	All stages are repeated BUT if the House of Lords votes against the Bill, it can go back to the House of Commons and, under the Parliament Acts 1911 and 1949, become law if the House of Commons passes it for the second time (rare occurrence)
Royal Assent	A formality – normally Acts of Parliament come into force at midnight after receiving the Royal Assent

Figure 3.1 Key fact chart for the legislative process

giving employment rights was mostly brought into force in 1996. However, some parts of the Act which give disabled people rights to access to goods and services are not going to be law until the year 2004. Some parts which relate to access to transport may not be law until 2010.

It may be that some sections or even a whole Act will never become law. An example of this is the Easter Act 1928, which was intended to fix the date of Easter Day. Although this Act passed all the necessary Parliamentary stages, and was given the Royal Assent, it has never come into force.

It can be seen that with all these stages it usually takes several months for a Bill to be passed. However, there have been occasions where all parties have thought a new law is needed urgently and an Act has been passed in less than 24 hours. This happened with the Northern Ireland Bill in 1972.

Activity

Look up a recent Act on the Internet. If you do not know of any try the website *www.hmso.gov.uk*

Choose an Act and now search for the debates in Parliament on that Act (try *www.parliament.uk*). Don't forget it would be called a Bill before it is passed.

Example of an Act

On page 46 is a reproduction of the Law Reform (Year and a Day Rule) Act 1996 (Figure 3.2). This shows what an Act of Parliament looks like. The name of the Act is given immediately under the Royal coat of arms and underneath the name '1996 CHAPTER 19' means that it was the nineteenth Act to be passed in 1996. Next follows a short statement or preamble about the purpose of

ELIZABETH II   c. 19

Law Reform (Year and a Day Rule) Act 1996

1996 CHAPTER 19

An Act to abolish the "year and a day rule" and, in consequence of its abolition, to impose a restriction on the institution in certain circumstances of proceedings for a fatal offence. [17th June 1996]

B E IT ENACTED by the Queen's most Excellent Majesty, by and with the advice and consent of the Lords Spiritual and Temporal, and Commons, in this present Parliament assembled, and by the authority of the same, as follows:—

1. The rule known as the "year and a day rule" (that is, the rule that, for the purposes of offences involving death and of suicide, an act or omission is conclusively presumed not to have caused a person's death if more than a year and a day elapsed before he died) is abolished for all purposes. *Abolition of "year and a day rule".*

2.—(1) Proceedings to which this section applies may only be instituted by or with the consent of the Attorney General. *Restriction on institution of proceedings for a fatal offence.*

(2) This section applies to proceedings against a person for a fatal offence if—

    (a) the injury alleged to have caused the death was sustained more than three years before the death occurred, or

    (b) the person has previously been convicted of an offence committed in circumstances alleged to be connected with the death.

(3) In subsection (2) "fatal offence" means—

    (a) murder, manslaughter, infanticide or any other offence of which one of the elements is causing a person's death, or

    (b) the offence of aiding, abetting, counselling or procuring a person's suicide.

Figure 3.2 The Law Reform (Year and a Day Rule) Act 1996

the Act. Then there is a formal statement showing that the Act has been passed by both Houses of Parliament and received the Royal Assent; this is included in all Acts. After this comes the body of the Act, which is set out in sections; this is an unusually short Act as it has only three sections.

Section 1 abolishes the 'year and a day rule'. Note that the Act actually refers to it in those terms; this is because the rule was a part of the common law and was never written down in any statute. Section 2 sets out when the consent of the Attorney-General is needed before a prosecution can be started. The last section gives the name by which the Act may be cited and it also sets out that the Act does not apply to cases in which the incident which led to death occurred before the Act was passed. Section 3 is concerned with the commencement of the Act; this sets the commencement date for section 2 at two months after the Act is passed. As section 1 is not specifically mentioned, the normal rule that an Act comes into effect on midnight of the date on which it receives the Royal Assent applies to that section.

3.1.6 Following the Disability Discrimination Act 1995 through the legislative stages

This section looks at how the Disability Discrimination Act 1995 eventually became law. For many years backbenchers had tried to steer private members' Bills aimed at preventing discrimination against disabled people through Parliament. Until 1993–94 all such Bills had been voted against in the early stages. This demonstrates that, even where the Bill involves what many people would accept as sensible measures, it is difficult for a private member's Bill to succeed unless it has the backing of the Government. However in the 1993–94 session of Parliament the Civil Rights (Disabled Persons) Bill was introduced as a

private member's Bill, and was successful up to, and including, the Committee Stage, but was then defeated by procedural means at the Report stage. This defeat caused public outcry as can be seen from the article following.

Scott filibuster kills disabled bill

The Government was accused last night of cynically exploiting the funeral of John Smith to kill a Bill on disabled people's rights.

Nicholas Scott, Minister for Social Security, faced a fresh storm of protest and angry demands from his own daughter, Victoria, for his resignation after he helped to block the Civil Rights (Disabled Persons) Bill, which would have banned discrimation against the disabled at work.

'It was a terrible experience. I feel very angry and terribly upset,' said Ms Scott, a parliamentary liaison officer for the Royal Association for Disability and Rehabilitation, who watched her father filibuster for more than an hour at the despatch box and talk out the Bill.

The coup de grâce was delivered when a Tory MP, Liam Fox, the parliamentary aide to Michael Howard, the Home Secretary, forced a vote and halted discussion at 2 pm. The Bill was shelved because – with many Labour MPs attending Mr Smith's funeral in Edinburgh – there were too few MPs in the House to take the vote.

Adapted from an article by Colin Brown, Chief Political Correspondent in *The Independent*, 21 May 1994

Government Green Paper

The backlash from this defeat of the Civil Rights (Disabled Persons) Bill was probably a main factor in the Government's decision to issue a Green Paper in July 1994, entitled *A Consultation on Government Measures to Tackle Discrimination Against Disabled People*. This set out proposals for limited reform of the law so that discrimination against disabled people is prevented both in the labour market and in access to goods and services. One of the points for consideration was the definition of 'disability' and who should and should not be included. A brief extract of the Green Paper on this point is set out in Figure 3.3 showing how views are sought on such points.

Government White Paper

Following the consultation on the Green Paper, the Government then published its firm proposals for a new discrimination law in a White Paper *Ending Discrimination Against Disabled People*. This committed the Government to legislating against discrimination.

The Disability Discrimination Bill was published at the same time, but did not cover all the proposals contained in the White Paper.

The Bill's progress through Parliament

The progress of the Bill was unusual in that at the same time a revised version of the Civil Rights (Disabled Persons) Bill had again been introduced into the House of Commons as a private member's Bill, so that initially two Bills on the same subject, though with striking differences in their approach, were being considered by Parliament. The Civil Rights (Disabled Persons) Bill was eventually abandoned. Figure 3.4 gives the timetable of the Disability Discrimination Bill's progress through Parliament, and demonstrates the length of time that a major

Bill can take, especially when there are disputes about its contents and several amendments are made to it at various stages.

The Bill also shows how the House of Lords can refine and add to Bills. For instance the definition of disabled was extended to cover those who had had a disability, even though they may not be disabled at the time of the discrimination. This was an important change since it provides a potential remedy for those who are discriminated against because they have suffered from a disability in the past.

Despite the time taken on this Act, some parts are still not in force. Also, the Government decided it was necessary to amend some parts of the Act. For example, the Disability Rights Commission was established in April 2000 by another Act of Parliament. This was because the original Disability Council was not given enough powers in the 1995 Act.

A White paper *Valuing People* was published in March 2001, so it is likely that there will be further legislation on rights for disabled people.

3.1.7 Criticism of the legislative process

There are many criticisms which can be made about the legislative process. In fact the Renton Committee on the Preparation of Legislation which reported in 1975 pointed out that there had been criticism for centuries, quoting Edward VI as saying more than four hundred years ago: 'I would wish that . . . the superfluous and tedious statutes were brought into one sum together, and made more plain and short, to the intent that men might better understand them'.

The Renton Committee said there were four main categories of complaint:

Definition of disabled people who would benefit from the right

2.18 Disabilities are sometimes obvious, sometimes hidden. A disability can affect a person's ability to do some types of work but not others. Someone with a broken leg has a temporary mobility problem but is not considered to be a disabled person. People who have periodic attacks of hay fever are also not considered disabled but someone with a periodic condition that has a more severe effect, such as arthritis, may well be.

2.19 Some definitions which have recently been proposed are wide in scope and, moreover, contain elements which could lead to considerable uncertainty. These include allowing a wide range of non-disabled people (for example, people who are reputed to be disabled) to complain that they have been discriminated against on grounds of disability.

2.20 The Government considered that a workable employment right should be based on a definition that:

– is confined to people who have a substantial and long-term disability or a disability which has substantial or long-term effects;
– in principle covers physical, sensory and mental impairments;
– is as straightforward and easy to interpret as possible.

2.21 One approach would be to define disability broadly in primary legislation (in line with the first two criteria above) while providing a means of clarifying this in Regulations, specifying the inclusion or exclusion of conditions about which there may be doubt. Any clear-cut definition will create difficult borderline cases but the availability of a Regulation making power would allow changes to be made in the light of experience. The Code of Practice could give practical guidance on the meaning of the definition.

2.22 An alternative approach would be to list in Regulations every condition or limitation which would allow a person to be within the scope of the right. Such a list could be changed in the light of experience.

2.23 *Views are sought on what types or degrees of disability the definition should cover and what conditions might be excluded or included.*

Figure 3.3 Extract from 'A Consultation on Government Measures to Tackle Discriminiation Against Disabled People'

1. The language used in many Acts was obscure and complex.
2. Acts were 'over-elaborate' because draftsmen tried to provide for every contingency.
3. The internal structure of many Acts was illogical with sections appearing to be out of sequence, making it difficult for people to find relevant sections.
4. There was a lack of clear connection between Acts, so that it was not easy to trace all the Acts on a given topic. In addition, the frequent practice of amending small parts of one Act by passing another increased the difficulty of finding out what the law was.

The Committee made 81 recommendations, but only about half of these have been fully implemented.

Accessibility

Ideally the laws of the land should be easily accessible to citizens but there are some major problems which create difficulties not only for ordinary citizens, but also for lawyers and even in some cases for the Lord Chancellor! As already mentioned it is difficult to discover which Acts and/or which sections have been brought into force. For example the Criminal Justice and Public. Order Act 1994 was divided into 12 parts containing 172 sections, many of which have several subsections, and it also had 11 schedules. The commencement provisions are contained in section 172 and this is what it says about which parts will come into force immediately:

'172 (4) "The following provisions and their related amendments, repeals and revocations shall come into force on the

12 January 1995	First Reading in House of Commons
24 January 1995	Second Reading in House of Commons
31 January to 28 February 1995	Bill considered by Standing Committee E in 13 sittings Some small Government amendments made
27/28 March 1995	Report Stage in House of Commons
28 March 1995	Third Reading in House of Commons
29 March 1995	First Reading in House of Lords
22 May 1995	Second Reading in House of Lords
13/15/27 June 1995	Bill considered by a Committee of the Whole House A number of major amendments were made
18/20 July 1995	Report Stage in the House of Lords More amendments made
24 October 1995	Third Reading in House of Lords
31 October 1995	Bill returned to House of Commons for it to consider the amendments made by the House of Lords House of Commons rejected one the Lords' amendments and, unusually, made further amendments of its own
6 November 1995	House of Lords considered House of Commons' amendments and accepted them
8 November 1995	Royal Assent

Figure 3.4 *Timetable of the Disability Discrimination Bill through Parliament*

passing of this Act, namely sections 5 to 15 (and Schedules 1 and 2), 60, 63, 65, 68 to 71, 77 to 80, 83, 90, Chapters I and IV of Part VIII, sections 142 to 148, 150, 158(1), (3) and (4), 166, 167, 171, paragraph 46 of Schedule 9 and this section." '

All the other sections were to be brought into force on days to be appointed by the Secretary of State or the Lord Chancellor. In this sort of situation it is no wonder that it is difficult to discover which sections are in operation. In fact section 44 relating to the abolition of committal proceedings in Magistrates' Courts was superseded by the Criminal Investigation and Procedure Act 1996, without even having been brought into effect.

Another example of how complex an Act can become with different dates for commencement is the Consumer Credit Act 1984. The final commencement order was made in 1989 and a table containing an outline guide to the commencement dates runs to 11 pages. Even the Lord Chancellor when asked which provisions in Acts passed between 1989 and 1992 remained to be brought into force, said that it was not possible, 'other than at disproportionate cost', to identify those provisions but he believed the percentage was around one per cent.

Activity

Find the commencement section or Schedule in a recent Act of Parliament.

This can be done by looking at a printed copy of an Act in a library or on the Internet. There is usually a list of contents at the start of an Act.

Other problems

Many statutes are amended by later statutes so that it is necessary to read two or sometimes more Acts together to make sense of provisions. The law may also be added to by delegated legislation in the form of statutory instruments. All this increases the difficulty of discovering the law that is actually in force.

The language used in Acts is not always easily understood and apart from the obvious difficulties this causes it also results in many cases going to court. In fact about 75 per cent of cases heard by the House of Lords in its judicial capacity each year involve disputes over the interpretation of Acts.

In 1992 the report of a Hansard Society Commission under Lord Rippon underlined five principles for democratic law-making. These were that:

- Laws are made for the benefit of the citizens and all citizens should therefore be involved as fully and openly as possible in the legislative process
- Statute law has to be rooted in the authority of Parliament and thoroughly exposed to democratic scrutiny
- Statute law should be as certain and intelligible as possible
- Statute law has to be as accessible as possible
- Getting the law right is as important as getting it passed quickly

If these guidelines were to be followed there would be an improvement to the quality of the statute book. In addition, codification and/or consolidation could be used to make the law more accessible. Under this, all the law on one topic could be brought together into one Act of Parliament, making it both more accessible and, hopefully, more comprehensible.

3.1.8 Parliamentary sovereignty

Parliamentary law is sovereign over other forms of law in England and Wales. This means that an Act of Parliament can completely supersede any custom, judicial precedent, delegated legislation or previous Act of Parliament. However European law has undermined the sovereignty of Parliament in some areas of law and this is explored more fully in Chapter 4.

The concept of the sovereignty of Parliamentary law is based on the idea of democratic law-making. A member of Parliament is elected by the voters in the constituency, so that in theory that MP is participating in the legislative process on the behalf of those voters. However, this is a very simplistic view since:

- MPs usually vote on party lines rather than how their particular constituents wish
- Many MPs are elected by only a very small majority and if there were several candidates in the election, it may well be that the MP was only actually voted for by about 30 per cent or even fewer of the voters.
- Parliamentary elections only have to take place once every five years, so that an MP who votes against the wishes of his constituents is not immediately replaced

In addition the ideal concept of democracy is lost because much of the drafting of Parliamentary law is done by civil servants who are not elected. Finally there is the point that the House of Lords is not an elected body.

3.2 Delegated legislation

This is law made by some person or body other than Parliament, but with the authority of Parliament. That authority is usually laid down in a 'parent' Act of Parliament known as an enabling Act which creates the framework of the law and then delegates power to others to make more detailed law in the area. Examples of enabling Acts include the Access to Justice Act 1999 which gives the Lord Chancellor wide powers to alter various aspects of the legal funding schemes; and the Disability Discrimination Act 1995 which gave the Secretary of State powers to make regulations on several points, both in relation to discrimination in employment and in the provision of services. For example section 46 of that Act gives power to make 'rail vehicle accessibility' regulations, which are aimed at making it possible for disabled persons to get on and off trains and to travel in them, safely and easily.

3.2.1 Types of delegated legislation

Orders in Council

The Queen and the Privy Council have the authority to make Orders in Council under the Emergency Powers Act 1920, but this authority will usually only be exercised in times of emergency when Parliament is not sitting.

Statutory instruments

Ministers and Government departments are given authority to make regulations for areas under their particular responsibility. Thus the Lord Chancellor was given power regarding the legal aid schemes, while the Minister for Transport will be able to deal with necessary road traffic regulations. The use of statutory instruments is a major method of law-making as there are about 3,000 statutory instruments brought into force each year.

Bylaws

These can be made by local authorities to cover matters within their own area, for example Norfolk County Council can pass laws affecting the whole county, while a District or Town council can only make bylaws for its district or town. Many local bylaws will involve traffic control, such as parking restrictions.

Bylaws can also be made by public corporations and certain companies for matters within their jurisdiction which involve the public. This means that bodies such as the British Airports Authority and the railways can enforce rules about public behaviour on their premises. An example of such a bylaw is the smoking ban on the London Underground system.

3.2.2 The need for delegated legislation

1. Parliament does not have time to consider and debate every small detail of complex regulations.
2. In addition Parliament may not have the necessary technical expertise or knowledge required; for example health and safety regulations in different industries need expert knowledge, while local parking regulations need local knowledge. Modern society has become very complicated and technical, so that it is impossible for members of Parliament to have all the knowledge needed to draw up laws on controlling technology, ensuring environmental safety, dealing with a vast array of different industrial problems or operating complex taxation schemes. It is thought that it is better for Parliament to debate the main principles thoroughly, but leave the detail to be filled in by those who have expert knowledge of it.
3. Ministers can have the benefit of further consultation before regulations are drawn up. We have already considered

the consultation process, which took place before the Disability Discrimination Act 1995 was passed, but there was also consultation afterwards over the regulations which amplify the definition of disability.

4. As already seen the process of passing an Act of Parliament can take a considerable time and in an emergency, Parliament may not be able pass law quickly enough. This is another reason why delegated legislation is sometimes preferred. It can also be amended or revoked easily when necessary, so that the law can be kept up to date, and Ministers can respond to new or unforeseen situations by amending or amplifying statutory instruments.

3.2.3 Control of delegated legislation

As delegated legislation in many instances is made by non-elected bodies and, since there are so many people with the power to make delegated legislation, it is important that there should be some control over this. Control is exercised by Parliament and by the courts. In addition there may sometimes be a Public Inquiry before a law is passed on an especially sensitive matter, such as planning laws which may affect the environment.

Control by Parliament

This is fairly limited, though obviously Parliament has the initial control with the enabling Act which sets the parameters within which the delegated legislation is to be made. In addition, a Delegated Powers Scrutiny Committee was established in 1993 in the House of Lords to consider whether the provisions of any Bills delegated legislative power inappropriately. It reports its findings to the House of Lords before the Committee stage of the Bill, but has no power to amend Bills. The main problem is that there is no general provision that the

regulations made under the enabling Act have to be laid before Parliament for the MPs to consider them. However a few enabling Acts will say that this has to happen.

Affirmative resolutions

A small number of statutory instruments will be subject to an affirmative resolution. This means that the statutory instrument will not become law unless specifically approved by Parliament. The need for an affirmative resolution will be included in the enabling Act. For example section 166(6) of the Criminal Justice and Public Order Act 1994 allows the Secretary of State to make regulations extending the situations in which sale of tickets for sporting events by unauthorised persons (i.e. ticket touts) is a criminal offence. However, section 172(5) specifically says that this can only be done if 'a draft of the order has been laid before, and approved by a resolution of, each House'. One of the disadvantages of this procedure is that Parliament cannot amend the statutory instrument; it can only be approved, annulled or withdrawn.

Negative resolutions

Most other statutory instruments will be subject to a negative resolution, which means that the relevant statutory instrument will be law unless rejected by Parliament within 40 days. Individual Ministers may also be questioned by MPs in Parliament on the work of their departments, and this can include questions about proposed regulations.

Scrutiny Committee

A more effective check is the existence of a Joint Select Committee on Statutory Instruments (formed in 1973), usually called the Scrutiny Committee. This committee reviews all statutory instruments and, where necessary, will draw the attention of both Houses of Parliament to points that need further consideration. However, the review is a technical one and not based on policy. The main grounds for referring a statutory instrument back to the Houses of Parliament are that:

- It imposes a tax or charge – this is because only an elected body has such a right
- It appears to have retrospective effect which was not provided for by the enabling Act
- It appears to have gone beyond the powers given under the enabling legislation or it makes some unusual or unexpected use of those powers
- It is unclear or defective in some way

The Scrutiny Committee can only report back its findings; it has no power to alter any statutory instrument. The Hansard Society in their 1992 report found that some of the critical findings of the Committee were ignored by Ministers.

Control by the courts

Delegated legislation can be challenged in the courts on the ground that it is *ultra vires*, i.e. it goes beyond the powers that Parliament granted in the enabling Act. This questioning of the validity of delegated legislation may be made through the judicial review procedure (see Chapter 16), or it may arise in a civil claim between two parties, or on appeal (especially case-stated appeals).

Any delegated legislation which is ruled to be *ultra vires* is void and not effective. This was illustrated by *R v Home Secretary, ex parte Fire Brigades Union* (1995) where changes made by the Home Secretary to the Criminal Injuries Compensation scheme were held to have gone beyond the power given to him in the Criminal Justice Act 1988.

The courts will presume that unless an enabling act expressly allows it, there is no power to do any of the following:

- Make unreasonable regulations – in *Strictland v*

Hayes Borough Council (1896) a bylaw prohibiting the singing or reciting of any obscene song or ballad and the use of obscene language generally, was held to be unreasonable and so *ultra vires*, because it was too widely drawn in that it covered acts done in private as well as those in public
- Levy taxes
- Allow sub-delegation

It is also possible for the courts to hold that delegated legislation is *ultra vires* because the correct procedure has not been followed. For example in the *Aylesbury Mushroom* case (1972) the Minister of Labour had to consult 'any organisation . . . appearing to him to be representative of substantial numbers of employers engaging in the activity concerned'. His failure to consult the Mushroom Growers' Association, which represented about 85 per cent of all mushroom growers meant that his order establishing a training board was invalid as against mushroom growers, though it was valid in relation to others affected by the order, such as farmers, as the minister had consulted with the National Farmers' Union.

In *R v Secretary of State for Education and Employment, ex parte National Union of Teachers* (2000) a High Court judge ruled that a statutory instrument setting conditions for appraisal and access to higher rates of pay for teachers was beyond the powers given under the Education Act 1996. In addition, the procedure used was unfair as only four days had been allowed for consultation.

Statutory instruments can also be declared void if they conflict with European Union legislation.

3.2.4 Criticisms of the use of delegated legislation

1. The main criticism is that it takes law-making away from the democratically

elected House of Commons and allows non-elected people to make law. This is acceptable provided there is sufficient control, but, as already seen, Parliament's control is fairly limited. This criticism cannot be made of bylaws made by local authorities since these are elected bodies and accountable to the local citizens.

2. Another problem is that of sub-delegation, which means that the law-making authority is handed down another level. This causes comments that much of our law is made by civil servants and merely 'rubber-stamped' by the Minister of that department.

3. The large volume of delegated legislation also gives rise to criticism since it makes it difficult to discover what the present law is. This problem is aggravated by a lack of publicity, as much delegated legislation is made in private in contrast to the public debates of Parliament.

4. Finally, delegated legislation shares with Acts of Parliament the same problem of obscure wording that can lead to difficulty in understanding the law. This difficulty of how to understand or interpret the law is dealt with in section 3.3.

KEY FACTS

Definition
- Law made by bodies other than Parliament, but with the authority of Parliament

Types of delegated legislation
- Orders in Council
  - Made by Crown and Privy Council
- Statutory instruments
  - Made by Government Ministers
- Bylaws
  - Made by local authorities and public corporations

Reasons for delegated legislation
- Knowledge and expertise
- Saving of Parliamentary time
- More flexible than Acts of Parliament

Control over delegated legislation
- By Parliament
  - Affirmative/negative resolutions
  - Scrutiny Committee
- By the courts
  - Judicial review
  - Doctrine of *ultra vires*

Disadvantages of delegated legislation
- Undemocratic
- Risk of sub-delegation
- Large volume
- Lack of publicity

Figure 3.5 Key fact chart for delegated legislation

3.3 Statutory interpretation

As seen at the beginning of this chapter, many statutes are passed by Parliament each year. The meaning of the law in these statutes should be clear and explicit but this is not always achieved. In order to help with the understanding of a statute Parliament sometimes includes sections defining certain words used in that statute: such sections are called interpretation sections. In the Theft Act 1968, for example, the definition of 'theft' is given in section one, and then sections two to six define the key words in that definition. To help the judges with general words, Parliament has also passed the Interpretation Act 1978 which makes it clear that, unless the contrary appears, 'he' includes 'she', and singular includes plural.

Despite these aids, many cases come before the courts because there is a dispute over the meaning of an Act of Parliament. In such cases the court's task is to decide the exact meaning of a particular word or phrase. There are many reasons why the meaning may be unclear:

- **A broad term**
  There may be words designed to cover several possibilities; this can lead to problems as to how wide this should go. In the Dangerous Dogs Act 1991 there is a phrase: 'any dog of the type known as the pit bull terrier' which seems simple but has led to problems. What is meant by 'type'? Does it mean the same as 'breed'? In *Brock* v *DPP* (1993) this was the key point in dispute and the Queen's Bench Divisional Court decided that 'type' had a wider meaning than 'breed'. It could cover dogs who were not pedigree pit bull terriers, but had a substantial number of the characteristics of such a dog.

- **Ambiguity**
  This is where a word has two or more meanings; it may not be clear which meaning should be used.

- **A drafting error**
  The Parliamentary Counsel who drafted the original Bill may have made an error which has not been noticed by Parliament; this is particularly likely to occur where the Bill is amended several times while going through Parliament.

- **New developments**
  New technology may mean that an old Act of Parliament does not apparently cover present day situations. This is seen in the case of *Royal College of Nursing* v *DHSS* (1981) where medical science and methods had changed since the passing of the Abortion Act in 1967. This case is discussed more fully in section 3.3.4.

- **Changes in the use of language**
  The meaning of words can change over the years. This was one of the problems in the case of *Cheeseman* v *DPP* (1990). *The Times* law report of this case is set out below in the activity section.

Activity

Read the following law report and answer the questions below.

Lurking policemen not 'passengers'

Cheeseman* v *Director of Public Prosecutions

Before Lord Justice Bingham and Mr Justice Waterhouse

[Judgment October 19]

Police officers who witnessed a man masturbating in a public lavatory were not 'passengers' within the meaning of section 28 of the Town Police Clauses Act 1847 when they had been stationed in the lavatory following complaints.

The Queen's Bench Divisional Court so held in allowing an appeal by way of case stated by Ashley Frederick Cheeseman against his conviction by Leicester City Justices of an offence of wilfully and indecently exposing his person in a street to the annoyance of passengers.

Section 81 of the Public Health Amendment Act 1902 extended the meaning of the word 'street' in section 28 to include, *inter alia*, any place of public resort under the control of the local authority.

Mr Stuart Rafferty for the appellant: Mr David Bartlett for the prosecution.

LORD JUSTICE BINGHAM, concurring with Mr Justice Waterhouse, said that *The Oxford English Dictionary* showed that in 1847 when the Act was passed 'passenger' had a meaning, now unusual except in the expression 'foot-passenger' of 'a passer by or through: a traveller (usually on foot); a wayfarer'.

Before the meaning of 'street' was enlarged in 1907 that dictionary definition of passenger was not hard to apply: it clearly covered anyone using the street for ordinary purposes of passage or travel.

The dictionary definition could not be so aptly applied to a place of public resort such as a public lavatory, but on a commonsense reading when applied in context 'passenger' had to mean anyone resorting in the ordinary way to a place for one of the purposes for which people would normally resort to it.

If that was the correct approach, the two police officers were not 'passengers'. They were stationed in the public lavatory in order to apprehend persons committing acts which had given rise to earlier complaints. They were not resorting to that place of public resort in the ordinary way but for a special purpose and thus were not passengers.

Solicitors: Bray & Bray, Leicester: CPS Leicester.

The Times Law Report, 2 November 1990

QUESTIONS

❶ In this case the meaning of the word 'street' was important. How did the court discover the meaning of the word in this case?

❷ The meaning of the word 'passenger' was also important. How did the court discover what this word meant in 1847?

❸ The court decided that 'passenger' meant 'a passer by or through; a traveller (usually on foot); a wayfarer'. Why did that definition **not** apply to the police officers who arrested the defendant?

❹ The defendant was found not guilty because of the way the court interpreted 'passenger'. Do you think this was a correct decision? Give reasons for your answer.

3.3.1 Literal approach versus purposive approach

The case of *Cheeseman* illustrates several of the problems of statutory interpretation. It is an example of the courts taking the words literally. However, it can be argued that the defendant was 'wilfully and indecently exposing his person in a street' and that he was caught doing that. Is it important whether the police officers were 'passengers'? After all, they were there because of previous complaints about this type of behaviour and presumably the defendant thought they were ordinary members of the public. Some people would argue that the whole purpose of the Act was to prevent this type of behaviour; this is the purposive approach to statutory interpretation – instead of looking at the precise meaning of each word, a broader approach is taken.

This conflict between the literal approach and the purposive approach is one of the major issues in statutory interpretation. Should judges examine each word and take the words literally or should it be accepted that an Act of Parliament cannot cover every situation and that the meanings of words cannot always be exact? In European law the purposive approach is taken. The Treaty of Rome sets out general principles but without explicit details. As Lord Denning said of the Treaty in *Bulmer Ltd v Bollinger S.A. (1974)*:

> 'It lays down general principles. It expresses its aims and purposes. All in sentences of moderate length and commendable style. But it lacks precision. It uses words and phrases without defining what they mean. An English lawyer would look for an interpretation clause, but he would look in vain. There is none. All the way through the Treaty there are gaps and lacunas. These have to be filled in by the judges.'

In fact, since European treaties, regulations and directives are issued in several languages it would be difficult, if not impossible, to take the meanings of words literally. It is not always possible to have an exact translation from one language to another.

In English law the judges have not been able to agree on which approach should be used, but instead, over the years they have developed three different rules of interpretation. These are:

- The literal rule
- The golden rule
- The mischief rule

These rules take different approaches to interpretation and some judges prefer to use one rule, while other judges prefer another rule. This means that in English law the interpretation of a statute may differ according to which judge is hearing the case. However, once an interpretation has been laid down, it may then form a precedent for future cases under the normal rules of judicial precedent. Since the three rules can result in very different decisions, it is important to understand them.

3.3.2 The literal rule

Under this rule courts will give words their plain, ordinary or literal meaning, even if the result is not very sensible. This idea was expressed by Lord Esher in *R v Judge of the City of London Court (1892)* when he said:

> 'If the words of an act are clear then you must follow them even though they lead to a manifest absurdity. The court has nothing to do with the question whether the legislature has committed an absurdity.'

The rule developed in the early nineteenth century and has been the main rule applied ever since then. It has been used in many cases, even though the result has made a nonsense of the law. This is illustrated in *Whiteley v Chappell (1868)* where the defendant was charged under a section which made it an offence to impersonate 'any person entitled to vote'. The defendant had pretended to be a person whose name was on the voters' list, but who had died. The court held that the defendant was not guilty since a dead person is not, in the literal meaning of the words, 'entitled to vote'.

The rule is also criticised because it can lead to what are considered harsh decisions, as in *London & North Eastern Railway Co v Berriman (1946)* case where a railway worker was killed while doing maintenance work, oiling points along a railway line. His widow tried to claim compensation because there had not been a look-out man provided by the railway company in accordance with a regulation under the Fatal Accidents Act which stated that a look-out should be provided for men working on or near the railway line 'for the purposes of relaying or repairing' it. The court took the words 'relaying' and 'repairing' in their literal meaning and said that oiling points was maintaining the line and not relaying or repairing so that Mrs Berriman's claim failed.

With decisions such as the two above it is not surprising that Professor Michael Zander has denounced the literal rule as being mechanical and divorced from the realities of the use of language.

3.3.3 The golden rule

This rule is a modification of the literal rule. The golden rule starts by looking at the literal meaning but the court is then allowed to avoid an interpretation which would lead to an absurd result. There are two views on how far the golden rule should be used. The first is very narrow and is shown by Lord Reid's comments in *Jones v DPP* (1962) when he said:

> 'It is a cardinal principle applicable to all kinds of statutes that you may not for any reason attach to a statutory provision a meaning which the words of that provision cannot reasonably bear. If they are capable of more than one meaning, then you can choose between those meanings, but beyond this you cannot go.'

So under the narrow application of the golden rule the court may only choose between the possible meanings of a word or phrase. If there is only one meaning then that must be taken. This narrow view can be seen in practice in *R v Allen* (1872) where section 57 of the Offences against the Person Act 1861 made it an offence to 'marry' whilst one's original spouse was still alive (and there had been no divorce). The word 'marry' can mean to become legally married to the other person or in a more general way it can mean that the person takes part or 'goes through' a ceremony of marriage. The court decided that in the Offences against the Person Act 1861 the word had this second meaning of go through a ceremony of marriage. This was because a person who is still married to another person cannot legally marry anyone else, so if the first meaning of being legally married was applied then there would be the absurd situation that no-one could ever be guilty of bigamy.

The second and wider application of the golden rule is where the words have only one clear meaning, but that meaning would lead to a repugnant situation. In such a case the court will invoke the golden rule to modify the words of the statute in order to avoid this problem. A very clear example of this was the case of *Re Sigsworth* (1935), where a son had murdered his mother. The mother had not made a will, so normally her estate would have been inherited by her next of kin according to the rules set out in the Administration of Estates Act 1925. This meant that the murderer son would have inherited as her 'issue'. There was no ambiguity in the words of the Act, but the court was not prepared to let a murderer benefit from his crime, so it was held that the literal rule should not apply, the golden rule would be used to prevent the repugnant situation of the son inheriting. Effectively the court was writing into the Act that the 'issue' would not be entitled to inherit where they had killed the deceased.

3.3.4 The mischief rule

This rule gives a judge more discretion than the other two rules. The definition of the rule comes from *Heydon's case* (1584), where it was said that there were four points the court should consider. These, in the original language of that old case, were:

1. 'What was the common law before the making of the Act?
2. What was the mischief and defect for which the common law did not provide?
3. What was the remedy the Parliament hath resolved and appointed to cure the disease of the commonwealth?
4. The true reason of the remedy.
   Then the office of all the judges is always to make such construction as shall suppress the mischief and advance the remedy.'

Under this rule therefore, the court should look to see what the law was before the Act

No, Romeo, I am not a prostitute!

was passed in order to discover what gap or 'mischief' the Act was intended to cover. The court should then interpret the Act in such a way that the gap is covered. This is clearly a quite different approach to the literal rule.

The mischief rule was used in *Smith v Hughes* (1960) to interpret section 1(1) of the Street Offences Act 1959 which said 'it shall be an offence for a common prostitute to loiter or solicit in a street or public place for the purpose of prostitution'. The court considered appeals against conviction under this section by six different women. In each case the women had not been 'in a street'; one had been on a balcony and the others had been at the windows of ground floor rooms, with the window either half open or closed. In each case the women were attracting the attention of men by calling to them or tapping on the window, but they argued that they were not guilty under this section since they were not literally 'in a street or public place'. The court decided that they were guilty, with Lord Parker saying:

'For my part I approach the matter by considering what is the mischief aimed at

by this Act. Everybody knows that this was an Act to clean up the streets, to enable people to walk along the streets without being molested or solicited by common prostitutes. Viewed in this way it can matter little whether the prostitute is soliciting while in the street or is standing in the doorway or on a balcony, or at a window, or whether the window is shut or open or half open.'

A similar point arose in *Eastbourne Borough Council v Stirling* (2000) where a taxi driver was charged with 'plying for hire in any street' without a licence to do so. His vehicle was parked on a taxi rank on the station forecourt. He was found guilty as, although he was on private land, he was likely to get customers from the street. The court referred to *Smith v Hughes* and said that it was the same point. A driver would be plying for hire in the street when his vehicle was positioned so that the offer of services was aimed at people in the street.

Another case in which the House of Lords used the mischief rule was *Royal College of Nursing v DHSS* (1981). In this case the wording of the Abortion Act 1967 which provided that a pregnancy should be 'terminated by a registered medical practitioner', was in issue. When the Act was passed in 1967 the procedure to carry out an abortion was such that only a doctor (a registered medical practitioner) could do it. From 1972 onwards improvements in medical technique meant that the normal method of terminating a pregnancy was to induce premature labour with drugs. The first part of the procedure was carried out by a doctor, but the second part was performed by nurses without a doctor present. The court had to decide if this procedure was lawful under the Abortion Act. The case went to the House of Lords where the majority (three) of the judges held that it was lawful, whilst the other two said that it was not lawful.

The three judges in the majority based their decision on the mischief rule, pointing out that the mischief Parliament was trying to remedy was the unsatisfactory state of the law before 1967 and the number of illegal abortions. They also said that the policy of the Act was to broaden the grounds for abortion and ensure that they were carried out with proper skill in hospital. The other two judges took the literal view and said that the words of the Act were clear and that terminations could only be carried out by a registered medical practitioner. They said that the other judges were not interpreting the Act but 'redrafting it with a vengeance'.

It is clear that these three rules can lead to different decisions on the meanings of words and phrases. Below is an activity based on a real case in which the different rules could result in different decisions.

Activity

Read the facts of the case set out below then apply the different rules of interpretation.

CASE: *Fisher* v *Bell* (1960) 1 QB 394
The Restriction of Offensive Weapons Act 1959 s1(1)
      'Any person who manufactures, sells or hires or offers for sale or hire or lends or gives to any other person – (a) any knife which has a blade which opens automatically by hand pressure applied to a button, spring or other device in or attached to the handle of the knife, sometimes known as a "flick knife" . . . shall be guilty of an offence.'

FACTS: The defendant was a shop keeper, who had displayed a flick knife marked with a price in his shop window; he had not actually sold any. He was charged under *s*1 (1) and the court had to decide whether he was guilty of offering the knife for sale. There is a technical legal meaning of 'offers for sale', under which putting an article in a shop window is not an offer to sell. (Students of contract law should know this rule!)

QUESTIONS

Consider the phrase 'offers for sale' and explain how you think the case would have been decided using:

(a) The literal rule

(b) The golden rule

(c) The mischief rule

Note: the court's decision on the case is given on Page 290.

3.3.5 Rules of language

Even the literal rule does not take words in complete isolation. It is common sense that the other words in the Act must be looked at to see if they affect the word or phrase which is in dispute. In looking at the other words in the Act the courts have developed a number of minor rules which can help to make the meaning of words and phrases clear where a particular sentence construction has been used. These rules, which have Latin names, are:

1. **The *ejusdem generis* rule**
   This states that where there is a list of words followed by general words, then the general words are limited to the same kind of items as the specific words. This is easier to understand by looking at cases. In *Powell* v *Kempton Park Racecourse* (1899) the defendant was charged with keeping a 'house, office, room or other place for betting'. He had been operating betting at what is known as Tattersall's Ring, which is outdoors. The court decided that the general words 'other place' had to refer to indoor places since all the words in the list were indoor places and so the defendant was not guilty.
   There must be at least two specific words in a list before the general word or phrase for this rule to operate. In *Allen* v *Emmerson* (1944) the court had

to interpret the phrase 'theatres and other places of amusement' and decide if it applied to a funfair. As there was only one specific word 'theatres', it was decided that a funfair did come under the general term 'other places of amusement' even though it was not of the same kind as theatres.

2. ***Expressio unius exclusio alterius* (the mention of one thing excludes others)**
Where there is a list of words which is not followed by general words, then the Act applies only to the items in the list. In *Tempest v Kilner* (1846) the court had to considered whether the Statute of Frauds 1677 (which required a contract for the sale of 'goods, wares and merchandise' of more than £10 to be evidenced in writing) applied to a contract for the sale of stocks and shares. The list 'goods, wares and merchandise' was not followed by any general words, so the court held that only contracts for those three types of things were affected by the statute; because stocks and shares were not mentioned they were not caught by the statute.

3. ***Noscitur a sociis* (a word is known by the company it keeps)**
This means that the words must be looked at in context and interpreted accordingly; it involves looking at other words in the same section or at other sections in the Act. Words in the same section were important in *Inland Revenue Commissioners v Frere* (1965), where the section set out rules for 'interest, annuities or other annual interest'. The first use of the word 'interest' on its own could have meant any interest paid, whether daily, monthly or annually. Because of the words 'other annual interest' in the section, the court decided that 'interest' only meant annual interest.

Other sections of the Act were considered by the House of Lords in *Bromley London Borough Council v Greater London Council* (1982). The issue in this case was whether the GLC could operate a cheap fare scheme on their transport systems, where the amounts being charged meant that the transport system would run at a loss. The decision in the case revolved around the meaning of the word 'economic'. The House of Lords looked at the whole Act and, in particular, at another section which imposed a duty to make up any deficit as far as possible. As a result they decided that 'economic' meant being run on business lines and ruled that the cheap fares policy was not legal since it involved deliberately running the transport system at a loss and this was not running it on business lines.

3.3.6 Presumptions

The courts will also make certain presumptions or assumptions about the law, but these are only a starting point. If the statute clearly states the opposite, then the presumption will not apply and it is said that the presumption is rebutted. The most important presumptions are:

1. **A presumption against a change in the common law**
In other words it is assumed that the common law will apply unless Parliament has made it plain in the Act that the common law has been altered. An example of this occurred in *Leach v R* (1912), where the question was whether a wife could be made to give evidence against her husband under the Criminal Evidence Act 1898. Since the Act did not expressly say that this should happen, it was held that the common law rule that a wife could not be compelled to give evidence still applied. If there had been explicit words saying that a wife was compellable then the old common law would not apply. This is now the position

under section 80 of the Police and Criminal Evidence Act 1984, which expressly states that in a crime of violence one spouse can be made to give evidence against the other spouse.

2. **A presumption that *mens rea* is required in criminal cases**
The basic common law rule is that no-one can be convicted of a crime unless it is shown that they had the required intention to commit it. In *Sweet* v *Parsley* (1970) the defendant was charged with being concerned with the management of premises which were used for the purposes of smoking cannabis. The facts were that the defendant was the owner of premises which she had leased out and the tenants had smoked cannabis there without her knowledge. She was clearly 'concerned in the management' of the premises and cannabis had been smoked there, but because she had no knowledge of the events she had no *mens rea*. The key issue was whether *mens rea* was required; the Act did not say there was any need for knowledge of the events. The House of Lords held that she was not guilty as the presumption that *mens rea* was required had not been rebutted.

3. **A presumption that the Crown is not bound** by any statute unless the statute expressly says so.

4. **A presumption that legislation does not apply retrospectively**
This means that no Act of Parliament will apply to past happenings; each Act will normally only apply from the date it comes into effect.

3.3.7 Unified approach

So how do all these rules fit together? Sir Rupert Cross wrote that there was a unified approach to interpretation, so that:

1. A judge should start by using the grammatical and ordinary or, where appropriate, technical meaning of the words in the general context of the statute.
2. If the judge considers that this would produce an absurd result, then he may apply any secondary meaning which the words are capable of bearing.
3. The judge may read in words which he considers to be necessarily implied by the words which are in the statute, and he has a limited power to add to, alter or ignore words in order to prevent a provision from being unintelligible, unworkable or absurd.
4. In applying these rules the judge may resort to the various aids and presumptions (see sections 3.3.6 and 3.3.9).

However, this unified approach is based on the literal approach and does not allow for the purposive approach. Today there is a move towards the purposive approach, although not all judges agree that it should be used.

Comment

Should there be one preferred rule?
It would be helpful if there was one specific method of statutory interpretation which was always used in cases. At the moment it is entirely up to the individual judge who is hearing the case to use whichever rule or approach he wants. Some judges may use the literal rule; other judges may use the mischief rule or the modern purposive approach. This makes it difficult for lawyers to advise on what meaning a court may put on a disputed phrase in an Act of Parliament.

In some instances, a judge may decide to use the literal rule in one case and the mischief rule in another case. This happened with Lord Parker, who used the mischief rule in *Smith* v *Hughes* (see section 3.3.4) but in the case of *Fisher* v *Bell* he used the literal rule. It could be said that this means that a judge decides what result he wants in the case and then finds the rule which brings about that result.

In 1969 the Law Commission proposed that Parliament should pass an Act of Parliament which would mean that the mischief rule was to be used in order 'to promote the general legislative purpose'. However, this proposal has been ignored, although Lord Scarman in both 1980 and 1981 introduced a Bill on the matter into the House of Lords. The first time he was forced to drop the proposal; the second time the House of Lords voted for it, but the matter was never taken to the House of Commons.

There is an argument that, even if there were an Act of Parliament, there would still be variations in which rule judges would use. This has been shown in New Zealand, which has a law that encourages interpretation 'as will best ensure the attainment of the object of the Act'. Even though this should mean that this is done in every case, one writer points out that it is sometimes difficult to discover which approach has been used and 'the most that can be said is that some judges at some periods have been fairly consistent in using the approach that they prefer'.

3.3.8 The purposive approach

This goes beyond the mischief rule in that the court is not just looking to see what the gap was in the old law; the judges are deciding what they believe Parliament meant to achieve. The champion of this approach in English law was Lord Denning. His attitude towards statutory interpretation is shown when he said in the case of *Magor and St Mellons* v *Newport Corporation* (1950):

'We sit here to find out the intention of Parliament and carry it out, and we do this better by filling in the gaps and making sense of the enactment than by opening it up to destructive analysis.'

However his attitude was criticised by judges in the House of Lords when they heard the appeal in the case. Lord Simonds called Lord Denning's approach 'a naked usurpation of the legislative function under the thin disguise of interpretation' and pointed out that 'if a gap is disclosed the remedy lies in an amending Act'.

Another judge, Lord Scarman said:

'If Parliament says one thing but means another, it is not, under the historic principles of the common law, for the courts to correct it. The general principle must surely be acceptable in our society. We are to be governed not by Parliament's intentions but by Parliament's enactments.'

This speech shows the problem with the purposive approach. Should the judges refuse to follow the clear words of Parliament? How do they know what Parliament's intentions were? Opponents of the purposive approach say that it is impossible to discover Parliament's intentions; only the words of the statute can show what Parliament wanted.

European influence

The purposive approach is the one preferred by most European countries when interpreting their own legislation. It is also the approach which has been adopted by the European Court of Justice (see Chapter 4) in interpreting European law. Since the United Kingdom became a member of the European Union in 1973 the influence of the European preference for the purposive approach has affected the English courts in two ways. Firstly they have had to accept that at least for law which has been passed as a result of having to conform with a European law, the purposive approach is the correct one to use. Secondly, the fact that judges are having to use the purposive approach for European law is making them more accustomed to it, and therefore more likely to apply it to English law.

3.3.9 Finding Parliament's intention

There are certain ways in which the courts can try to discover the intention of Parliament and certain matters which they can look at in order to help with the interpretation of a statute.

Intrinsic aids

These are matters within the statute itself that may help to make its meaning clearer. The court can consider the long title, the short title and the preamble (if any). Older statutes usually have a preamble which sets out Parliament's purpose in enacting that statute. Modern statutes either do not have a preamble or contain a very brief one, for example the Theft Act 1968 states that it is an Act to modernise the law of theft. The long title may also explain briefly Parliament's intentions. An unusual approach was taken in the Arbitration Act 1996 where a statement of the principles of the Act is set out in section 2. This is a new development in statutory drafting and one that could both encourage and help the use of the purposive approach.

The other useful internal aids are any headings before a group of sections, and any schedules attached to the Act. There are often also marginal notes explaining different sections, but these are not generally regarded as giving Parliament's intention as they will have been inserted after the Parliamentary debates and are only helpful comments put in by the printer.

Extrinsic aids

These are matters which are outside the Act – it has always been accepted that some external sources can help explain the meaning of an Act. These undisputed sources are:

- Previous Acts of Parliament on the same topic
- The historical setting
- Earlier case law
- Dictionaries of the time

So far as other extrinsic aids are concerned, attitudes have changed. Originally the courts had very strict rules that other extrinsic aids should not be considered, however, for the following three aids the courts' attitude has changed. These three main extrinsic aids are:

- *Hansard*: the official report of what was said in Parliament when the Act was debated
- Reports of law reform bodies, such as the Law Commission, which led to the passing of the Act
- International conventions, regulations or directives which have been implemented by English legislation

The use of Hansard

Until 1992 there was a firm rule that the courts could not look at what was said in the debates in Parliament. Some years earlier Lord Denning had tried to attack this ban on *Hansard* in *Davis v Johnson* (1979), which involved the interpretation of the Domestic Violence and Matrimonial Proceedings Act 1976. He admitted that he had indeed read *Hansard* before making his decision, saying:

'Some may say . . . that judges should not pay any attention to what is said in Parliament. They should grope about in the dark for the meaning of an Act without switching on the light. I do not accede to this view'

In the same case the House of Lords disapproved of this and Lord Scarman explained their reasons by saying:

'Such material is an unreliable guide to the meaning of what is enacted. It promotes confusion, not clarity. The cut and thrust of debate and the pressures of executive responsibility . . . are not always conducive to a clear and unbiased explanation of the meaning of statutory language.'

However, in *Pepper v Hart* (1993) the House of Lords relaxed the rule and accepted that *Hansard* could be used in a limited way. This case was unusual in that seven judges heard the appeal, rather than the normal panel of five. These seven judges included the Lord Chancellor, who was the only judge to disagree with the use of *Hansard*. The majority ruled that *Hansard* could be consulted. Lord Browne-Wilkinson said in his judgment that:

'the exclusionary rule should be relaxed so as to permit reference to parliamentary materials where: (a) legislation is ambiguous or obscure, or leads to an absurdity; (b) the material relied on consists of one or more statements by a minister or other promoter of the Bill together if necessary with such other parliamentary material as is necessary to understand such statements and their effect; (c) the statements relied on are clear. Further than this I would not at present go.'

So *Hansard* may be considered but only where the words of the Act are ambiguous or obscure or lead to an absurdity. Even then *Hansard* should only be used if there was a clear statement by the Minister introducing the legislation, which would resolve the ambiguity or absurdity. The Lord Chancellor opposed the use of *Hansard* on practical grounds, pointing out the time and cost it would take to research *Hansard* in every case.

The only time that a wider use of *Hansard* is permitted is where the court is considering

an Act that introduced an international convention or European Directive into English law. This was pointed out by the Queen's Bench Divisional Court in *Three Rivers District Council and others v Bank of England (No 2)* (1996). In such a situation it is important to interpret the statute purposively and consistently with any European materials and the court can look at Ministerial statements, even if the statute does not appear to be ambiguous or obscure.

Since 1992 *Hansard* has been referred to in a number of cases, even sometimes when there did not appear to be any ambiguity or absurdity. The Lord Chancellor's predictions on cost have been confirmed by some solicitors, with one estimating that it had added 25 per cent to the bill. On other occasions it is clear that *Hansard* has not been helpful or that the court would have reached the same conclusion in any event. This has tended to bear out the findings of a study of 34 cases by Vera Sachs in 1982 which concluded that 'in every case studied the disputed clause was either undebated or received obscure and confusing replies from the Minister'.

Law Reform Reports

As with *Hansard*, the courts used to hold that reports by law reform agencies should not be considered by the courts. However this rule was relaxed in the *Black Clawson* case in 1975, when it was accepted that such a report should be looked at to discover the mischief or gap in the law which the legislation based on the report was designed to deal with (see Chapter 5 for more detail on law reform agencies).

International conventions

In *Fothergill v Monarch Airlines Ltd* (1980) the House of Lords decided that the original convention should be considered as it was possible that in translating and adapting the convention to our legislative process, the

KEY FACTS

	BRIEF DEFINITION	CASE EXAMPLES
Literal approach	• Approaching problems of statutory interpretation by taking the words at their face value	*Fisher* v *Bell*
Purposive approach	• Looking at the reasons why a law was passed and interpreting the words accordingly	*R* v *Registrar-General, ex parte Smith*
The 'three rules'		
Literal rule	• Words given ordinary, plain, grammatical meaning	*Whiteley* v *Chappell*
Golden rule	• Avoids absurd or repugnant situations	*R* v *Allen*
Mischief rule	• Looks at the gap in the previous law and interprets the words 'to advance the remedy'	*Smith* v *Hughes*
Rules of language		
Ejusdem generis	• General words which follow a list are limited to the same kind	*Powell* v *Kempton Park*
Expressio unius	• The express mention of one thing excludes others	*Tempest* v *Kilner*
Noscitur a sociis	• A word is known by the company it keeps	*IRC* v *Frere*
Presumptions	• No change to common law • Crown not bound • *Mens rea* required • No retrospective effect	*Leach* v *R* *Sweet* v *Parsley*
Aids to finding Parliament's intention	• Intrinsic – within the Act e.g. interpretation section • Extrinsic – outside the Act e.g. *Hansard*, Law Commission Reports	*Pepper* v *Hart* *Black Clawson case*

Figure 3.6 *Key fact chart for statutory interpretation*

true meaning of the original might have been lost. The House of Lords in that same case also held that an English court could consider any preparatory materials or explanatory notes published with an international convention. The reasoning behind this was that other countries allowed the use of such material, known as *travaux préparatoires*, and it should therefore be allowed in this country in order to get uniformity in the interpretation of international rules.

Explanatory notes

Since 1998 explanatory notes have been produced alongside new Bills. (Remember that before a law becomes an Act of Parliament, it is referred to as a Bill.) These notes are much fuller than any previous explanatory memorandum. They are produced by the Government department responsible for the Bill. The notes usually explain the background to any proposed law, summarise its main provisions and, where a point is complicated, give worked examples. These notes are updated as the Bill progresses through Parliament and, when the Bill becomes an Act of Parliament, a final version of the notes is published.

These notes are a potential new extrinsic aid to statutory interpretation. They could be helpful to courts when they have to interpret a law. However, the notes are not part of the law. This is likely to cause conflict on whether they should be used for statutory interpretation. Judges who use the purposive approach are likely to support their use, but judges who use the literal approach will not use them. This is because explanatory notes are not intended to have legal effect; they are not part of the Act itself and using them introduces the risk of changing the meaning of what is stated in the Act. As the use of these notes only started in 1998 there have not yet been any cases on whether or not they can be used in statutory interpretation.

3.3.10 Interpretation of European law

European Union Law

Where the law to be interpreted is based on European law, the courts must interpret it in the light of the wording and purpose of the European law. This is because the Treaty of Rome, which sets out the duties of European Member States, says that all Member States are required to 'take all appropriate measures . . . to ensure fulfilment of the obligations'. The European Court of Justice in the *Marleasing* case (1992) ruled that this includes interpreting national law in every way possible in the light of the text and aim of the European law.

An example of the English courts interpreting law by looking at the purpose of the relevant European Union law is *Diocese of Hallam Trustee* v *Connaughton* (1996). This case is discussed in full in the chapter on European law at 4.2.1.

3.3.11 The Human Rights Act 1998

Section 3 of the Human Rights Act says that, so far as it is possible to do so, legislation must be read and given effect in a way which is compatible with the rights in the European Convention on Human Rights. This applies to any case where one of the rights is concerned, but it does not apply where there is no involvement of human rights.

A good example of the difference the Human Rights Act has made to interpretation is *R* v *Offen* (2001). This case considered the meaning of the word 'exceptional' in the Crime (Sentences) Act 1997 where any offender committing a second serious offence must be given a life sentence unless there are 'exceptional circumstances'. Before the Human Rights Act came into force the courts in *R* v *Kelly* (2000) had said that 'exceptional' was an ordinary English adjective, saying:

> 'To be exceptional a circumstance need not be unique or unprecedented or very rare; but it cannot be one that is regularly or routinely or normally encountered.'

This led to a strict approach where offenders were given life sentences even when the earlier crime had been committed a long time ago and the second offence was not that serious of its type.

In *Offen* the Court of Appeal said that this restricted approach could lead to the sentence being arbitrary and disproportionate and a breach of Articles 3 and 5 of the European Convention on Human Rights. In order to interpret the Crime (Sentences) Act in a way which was compatible with the Convention, it was necessary to consider whether the offender was a danger to the public. If he was not then he was an exception to the normal rule in the Act and this could be considered exceptional circumstances so that a life sentence need not be given.

3.3.12 Conclusion

The attitude of English courts to interpretation has changed over recent years with a move towards the purposive approach and the increasing use of extrinsic aids. However the method used in interpreting a statute is still left to the individual judge and it quite possible that one judge will prefer the literal view, while another judge could form the opposite conclusion by applying the mischief rule or the purposive approach.

A final case illustrates this dilemma. In *R v Registrar-General, ex parte Smith* (1990), the court had to consider section 51 of the Adoption Act 1976 which stated:

> '(1) Subject to subsections (4) and (6), the Registrar-General shall on an application made in the prescribed manner by an adopted person a record of whose birth is kept by the Registrar-General and who has attained the age of 18 years supply to that person . . . such information as is necessary to enable that person to obtain a certified copy of the record of his birth.'

Subsection (4) said that before supplying that information the Registrar-General had to inform the applicant about counselling services available. Subsection (6) stated that if the adoption was before 1975 the Registrar-General could not give the information unless the applicant had attended an interview with a counsellor.

The case involved the application by Charles Smith for information to enable him to obtain his birth certificate. Mr Smith had made his application in the correct manner and was prepared to see a counsellor. On a literal view of the Act the Registrar-General had to supply him with the information, since the Act uses the phrase 'shall . . . supply'. The problem was that Mr Smith had been convicted of two murders and was detained in Broadmoor as he suffered from recurring bouts of psychotic illness. A psychiatrist thought that it was possible he might be hostile towards his natural mother. This posed a difficulty for the court: should they apply the clear meaning of the words in this situation? The judges in the Court of Appeal decided that the case called for the purposive approach, saying that, despite the plain language of the Act, Parliament could not have intended to promote serious crime. So, in view of the risk to the applicant's natural mother if he discovered her identity, they ruled that the Registrar-General did not have to supply any information.

Chapter 4

EUROPEAN LAW

On the first of January 1973 the United Kingdom joined what was then the European Economic Community, and another source of law came into being: European law. Since then it has had an increasing significance as a source of law. The European Economic Community was originally set up by Germany, France, Italy, Belgium, The Netherlands and Luxembourg in 1957 by the Treaty of Rome. The name 'European Union' was introduced by the Treaty of European Union in 1993. The Union currently has 15 Member States but the Treaty of Nice (2000) allows for an increase of up to 27 Member States from the year 2005.

Article 2 of the Treaty of Rome, as amended by the Single European Act 1986 and the Treaty of European Union, sets out the aims of the Union. This Article says:

> 'The Community shall have as its task, by establishing a common market and an economic and monetary union and by implementing the common policies or activities referred to in Article 3 and 3a, to promote throughout the Community a harmonious and balanced development of economic activities, sustainable and non-inflationary growth respecting the environment, a high degree of convergence of economic performance, a high level of employment and of social protection, the raising of the standard of living and quality of life, and economic and social cohesion and solidarity among Member States.'

Although the stress is on trade, economic and related matters, there has been a great influence on law in the United Kingdom in a number of 'spin-off' areas, especially laws on employment and sex equality. The aim of the Union is that in these common matters, the laws of all Member States should be harmonised.

Treaty of Amsterdam

This came into effect in 1999. It added a new Article to the Treaty of Rome which allows the Council to 'take appropriate action to combat discrimination based on sex, racial or ethnic origin, religion or belief, disability, age or sexual orientation'. The Treaty also re-numbered all the Articles in the Treaty of Rome. The new numbers are used throughout this chapter.

4.1 The institutions of the European Union

In order to implement the aims of the Treaty of Rome, the European Union has a vast and complex organisation with institutions established by the Treaty of Rome. The main institutions which exercise the functions of the Union are:

- The Council of the European Union
- The Commission
- The European Parliament
- The European Court of Justice

In addition there are a number of ancillary bodies, the most important of which is the Economic and Social Committee.

4.1.1 The Council of the European Union

The government of each nation in the Union sends a representative to the Council. The

Foreign Minister is usually a country's main representative, but a government is free to send any of its ministers to Council meetings. This means that usually the minister responsible for the topic under consideration will attend the meetings of the Council, so that the precise membership will vary with the subject being discussed. For example the Minister for Agriculture will attend when the issue to be discussed involves agriculture. Twice a year government heads meet in the European Council or 'Summit' to discuss broad matters of policy. The Member States take it in turn to provide the President of the Council, each for a six month period. To assist with the day-to-day work of the Council there is a committee of permanent representatives known as Coreper.

The Council is the principal decision-making body of the Union. Voting in the Council is on a weighted basis with each country having a number of votes roughly in proportion to the size of its population. There are a total of 87 votes, and the majority required to pass a measure varies. Key matters can only be agreed if there is a unanimous vote, but for most issues a qualified majority is required, in which at least 62 of the votes must be in favour. Individual Member States also have a right to veto in certain circumstances where they consider the proposal being discussed to be a 'very important interest' of their country.

4.1.2 The Commission

This consists of 20 Commissioners who are supposed to act independently of their national origin. The Commissioners are appointed for a five year term and can only be removed during this term of office by a vote of censure by the European Parliament. Each Commissioner heads a department with special responsibility for one area of Union policy, such as economic affairs, agriculture and the environment.

The Commission as a whole has several functions as follows:

- It is the motive power behind Union policy as it proposes policies and presents drafts of legislation to the Council for the Council's consideration. In its own booklet on Union law, the European Union says the relationship between the Commission and the Council can be briefly summarised by saying 'the Commission proposes and the Council disposes'.
- The Commission is also the 'guardian' of the treaties. It ensures that treaty provisions and other measures adopted by the Union are properly implemented. If a Member State has failed to implement Union law within its own country, or has infringed a Provision in some way, the Commission has a duty to intervene and, if necessary, refer the matter to the European Court of Justice. The Commission has performed this duty very effectively, and as a result there have been judgments given by the Court against Britain and other Member States.
- It is responsible for the administration of the Union and has executive powers to implement the Union's budget.

Activity

1. Use the Internet to find out more about the European Commission. Find out who are the Commissioners for the United Kingdom
2. In 1999 the Commission was forced to resign and a new Commission appointed. Using CD ROMS, find newspaper reports about this.

4.1.3 The Assembly (otherwise known as the European Parliament)

Parliament's main function is to discuss proposals put forward by the Commission, but it has no direct law-making authority.

The 626 members of the European Parliament are directly elected by the people of the Member States in elections which take place once every five years. Within the Parliament the Members do not operate in national groups, but form political groups with those of the same political allegiance. The Assembly meets on average about once a month for sessions that can last up to a week. It has standing committees which discuss proposals made by the Commission and then report to the full Parliament for debate. Decisions made by the Parliament are not binding, though they will influence the Council of Ministers.

The main criticism is that the Parliament has no real power, even though the Single European Act 1986 did enhance its position. In particular the assent of Parliament is required to any international agreements the Union wishes to enter into. This allows it an important role in deciding whether new members should be admitted to the Union. It also has some power over the Union budget, especially in non-obligatory expenditure, where it has the final decision on whether to approve the budget or not.

4.1.4 The Economic and Social Committee

This advises the Council and the Commission on economic matters. It is made up of representatives of influential interest groups such as manufacturers, farmers, employees and businesses. It must be consulted on proposed Union measures and although its role is purely consultative, it does exert strong influence on the Union's decision-making process.

4.1.5 The European Court of Justice

Its function is set out in Article 220 of the Treaty of Rome. This states that the court must 'ensure that in the interpretation and application of the Treaty the law is observed'. The court sits in Luxembourg and has 15 judges, one from each Member State. For a full court all the judges will sit, but it also sits in chambers of five judges or three judges. Judges are appointed under Article 222 of the Treaty of Rome from those who are eligible for appointment to the highest judicial posts in their own country or who are leading academic lawyers. Each judge is appointed for a term of six years, and can be re-appointed for a further term of six years. The judges select one of themselves to be President of the Court.

The Court is assisted by nine Advocates General who also hold office for six years. Each case is assigned to an Advocate General whose task under Article 223 is to research all the legal points involved and 'to present publicly, with complete impartiality and independence, reasoned conclusions on cases submitted to the Court of Justice with a view to assisting the latter in the performance of its duties'.

Key functions

The court's task is to ensure that the law is applied uniformly in all Member States and it does this by performing two key functions.

The first is that it hears cases to decide whether Member States have failed to fulfil obligations under the Treaties. Such actions are usually initiated by the European Commission, although they can also be started by another Member State. An early example of such a case was *Re Tachographs: The Commission v United Kingdom* (1979) in which the court held that the United Kingdom had to implement a Council Regulation on the use of mechanical recording equipment (tachographs) in road vehicles used for the carriage of goods. (see section 4.2.2 for further information on the effect of Regulations).

Preliminary rulings

The second key function is that it hears references from national courts for preliminary rulings to clarify the scope and meaning of European law. This function is a very important one since rulings made by the European Court of Justice are then binding on courts in all Member States. This ensures that the law is indeed uniform throughout the European Union. A request for a preliminary ruling is made under Article 234 of the Treaty of Rome. This says that:

'the Court of Justice shall have jurisdiction to give preliminary rulings concerning:

(a) the interpretation of treaties;

(b) the validity and interpretation of acts of the institutions of the Union;

(c) the interpretation of the statutes of bodies established by an act of the Council, where those statutes so provide.

Where such a question is raised before any court or tribunal of a Member State, that court or tribunal may, if it considers that a decision on the question is necessary to enable it to give judgment, request the Court of Justice to a ruling thereon.

Where any such a question is raised in a case pending before a court or tribunal of a Member State against whose decisions there is no judicial remedy under national law, that court or tribunal shall bring the matter before the Court of Justice.'

This Article, therefore, creates both a discretionary referral for any court or tribunal in Member States, and a mandatory referral (i.e. referrals which have to be made because there is no further appeal possible within the Member State's judicial system). Applied to the court structure in England and Wales, this means that the House of Lords must refer questions of European law, since it is the highest appeal court in our system. However, the Court of Appeal does not have to refer

questions. It has a choice, it may refer if it wishes or it may decide the case without any referral. The same is true of all the lower courts in the English court hierarchy.

However, even courts at the bottom of the hierarchy can refer questions of law under Article 234, if they feel that a preliminary ruling is necessary to enable a judgment to be given. An example of this was in *Torfaen Borough Council* v *B & Q* (1990) when Cwmbran Magistrates' Court made a reference on whether the restrictions which then existed on Sunday were in breach of the Treaty of Rome.

Discretionary referrals

In *Bulmer* v *Bollinger* (1974) the Court of Appeal set out the approach to be used when deciding whether a discretionary referral should be made to the European Court of Justice. The guidelines given by this case start by underlining Article 234 where it is pointed out that a reference should be made only if a ruling by the European Court is necessary to enable the English court to give judgment in the case. In this sense necessary means that the ruling would be conclusive in the case; if other matters remain to be decided then the ruling would not be considered necessary. The other guidelines are as follows:

- There is no need to refer a question which has already been decided by the European Court of Justice in a previous case
- There is no need to refer a point which is reasonably clear and free from doubt; this is known as the '*acte clair*' doctrine
- The court must consider all the circumstances of the case, especially:
  1. The length of time which may elapse before a ruling is made; the delay may cause injustice in an urgent case, and it takes about 18 months to get a ruling
  2. The possible overloading of the European Court of Justice, which is turn will cause more delay

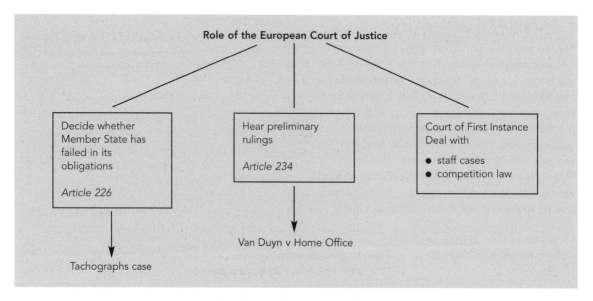

Role of the European Court of Justice

Decide whether Member State has failed in its obligations	Hear preliminary rulings	Court of First Instance Deal with
Article 226	*Article 234*	• staff cases • competition law

Tachographs case

Van Duyn v Home Office

Figure 4.1 Role of the European Court of Justice

3. The difficulty and importance of the case
4. The expense which will be involved
5. The wishes of the parties; on this point it must be noted that the situation is different to an appeal in that the parties cannot make a reference themselves; it is the court which makes the reference
• That the English court retains the discretion on whether to refer or not

The first case to be referred to the European Court of Justice by an English court was *Van Duyn* v *Home Office* (1974) and since then, there have been many referrals from various courts, though there have been signs that English courts are more prepared to hold that the Treaty is clear and can be applied directly by the English court. For instance in *Pickstone* v *Freemans plc* (1988) the Court of Appeal held that Article 141 of the Treaty of Rome on equality of treatment of men and women was clear and could be applied directly (see also *Diocese of Hallam Trustee* v *Connaughton* in section 4.2.1).

The European Court of Justice accepts that even mandatory referrals under Article 234 need not be made if the point is clear. This

was seen in *CILFIT Srl* v *Ministro della Sanita* (1982), which involved a reference from the Italian Court of Cassation. The European Court of Justice said that 'the correct application of Community law may be so obvious as to leave no scope for any reasonable doubt as to the manner in which the question is to be resolved'. The *CILFIT* case also indicated that in order for there to be an obligation to refer the case, the point of European law must be relevant to enable the court to give judgment. Finally there is no obligation to refer if the question raised is 'materially identical with a question which has already been the subject of a preliminary ruling in a similar case'.

Whenever a reference is made the European Court of Justice only makes a preliminary ruling on the point of law; it does not actually decide the case. The case then returns to the original court for it to apply the ruling to the facts in the case.

Court of First Instance

Since 1988 there has also existed a Court of First Instance which was created to relieve the European Court of Justice of some of its

KEY FACTS

Council of Ministers	• Consists of ministers from each Member State • Responsible for broad policy decisions • Under Article 249 can issue regulations, directives and decisions
Commission	• 20 Commissioners whose duty it is to act in Union's interest • Proposes legislation • Tries to ensure the implementation of the Treaties and can bring court action against Member States who do not comply with EU law
Economic and Social Committee	• Non-elected consultative body to represent such groups as employers, employees, consumer associations etc
Assembly or European Parliament	• Members voted for by electorate in each of the Member States • Consultative body, has limited powers
European Court of Justice	• Judges from each Member State, assisted by Advocates-General • Rules on European law when cases are referred under Article 234

Figure 4.2 Key fact chart on the institutions of the European Union

heavy workload. This court hears staff cases, i.e. disputes between the European Institutions and their employees. It also hears complex economic cases in the field of competition law, 'anti-dumping' law and under the European Coal and Steel Community Treaty. The Court of First Instance has 12 judges and operates in chambers of six, four or three judges.

Differences in the operation of the European Court of Justice and the English courts

When compared to English courts there are several major differences in the way the European Court of Justice operates. First the emphasis is on presenting cases 'on paper'. Lawyers are required to present their arguments in a written form and there is far less reliance on oral presentation of a case. This requirement is, of course, partly because of the wide range of languages involved, though French is the traditional language of the Court. It also represents the traditional method of case presentation in other European countries. An interesting point to note is that the English system in some areas is now beginning to use this 'paper' submission.

A second major difference is the use of the Advocate General. This independent lawyer is not used in the English system. However in the European Court of Justice the Advocate General who was assigned to the case will present his findings on the law after the parties have made their submissions. The court, therefore, has the advantage of having all aspects of the law presented to them.

The deliberations of the judges are secret and where necessary the decision will be made by a majority vote. However, when the judgment is delivered, again in a written form, it is signed by all the judges who formed part of the panel, so that it is not known if any judges disagreed with the majority. This contrasts strongly with the

English system, whereby a dissenting judge not only makes it known that he disagrees with the majority, but also usually delivers a judgment explaining his reasoning.

The other points to be noted are that the European Court of Justice is not bound by its own previous decisions and that it prefers the purposive approach to interpretation.

The court has wide rights to study extrinsic material when deciding the meaning of provisions and may study preparatory documents. The European Court of Justice is important, not only because its decisions are binding on English courts, but also because its attitude to interpretation is increasingly being followed by English courts. Indeed for any decision on a national law passed to implement some point of Union law the European Court of Justice said in *von Colson v Land Nordrhein-Westfalen* (1984):

> *'national courts are required to interpret their national law in the light of the wording and the purpose of the directive.'*

4.2 European sources of law

These are classed as primary and secondary sources of law. Primary sources are mainly the Treaties, the most important of which is the Treaty of Rome itself. Secondary sources are legislation passed by the Institutions of the Union under Article 249 of the Treaty of Rome. This secondary legislation is of three types: regulations, directives and decisions, all of which are considered below.

4.2.1 Treaties

So far as our law is concerned all treaties signed by our head of government become part of English law automatically. This is as a result of the European Communities Act 1972, section 2(1) which states that:

> *'All such rights, powers, liabilities, obligations and restrictions from time to time created or arising by or under the Treaties and all such remedies and procedures from time to time provided for by or under the Treaties, as in accordance with the Treaties are without further enactment to be given legal effect or used in the United Kingdom, shall be recognised and available in law and be enforced, allowed and followed accordingly.'*

This not only makes Community law part of our law but also allows individuals to rely on it. In the case of *Van Duyn* v *Home Office* (1974) the European Court of Justice held that an individual was entitled to rely on Article 39 giving the right of freedom of movement. The Article had direct effect and conferred rights on individuals which could be enforced not only in the European Court of Justice, but also in national courts.

As a result of this citizens of the United Kingdom are entitled to rely on the rights in the Treaty of Rome and other treaties, even though those rights may not have been specifically enacted in English law. This is clearly illustrated by the case of *Macarthys Ltd* v *Smith* (1980). In this case Wendy Smith's employers paid her less than her male predecessor for exactly the same job. As the two people were not employed at the same time by the employer there was no breach of English domestic law. However, Wendy Smith was able to claim that the company which employed her was in breach of Article 141 of the Treaty of Rome over equal pay for men and women and this claim was confirmed by the European Court of Justice.

The growing influence of European law is shown in that British courts are now prepared to apply European Treaty law directly rather than wait for the European Court of Justice to make a ruling on the point. This is illustrated in *Diocese of Hallam*

Trustee v *Connaughton* (1996). In this case the Employment Appeal Tribunal had to consider facts which had some similarity to the Wendy Smith case, Josephine Connaughton was employed as director of music by the Diocese of Hallam from 1990 to September 1994, at which time her salary was £11,138. When she left the position, the post was advertised at a salary of £13,434, but the successful applicant, a man, was actually appointed at a salary of £20,000. In other words, where in Wendy Smith's case she had discovered that her male predecessor was paid more than she was, in the *Connaughton* case it was the immediate successor who was receiving considerably higher pay.

The Employment Appeal Tribunal considered Article 141 of the Treaty of Rome and decided as a preliminary point that its provisions were wide enough to allow Miss Connaughton to make a claim, saying 'We are sufficiently satisfied as to the scope of Article 141 so as to decide this appeal without further reference to the European Court of Justice'. Similarly the House of Lords in *R* v *Secretary of State ex parte EOC* (1994) decided, without referring the case to the European Court of Justice, that the longer period of qualification for redundancy for those working less than 16 hours a week discriminated against women and was contrary to Article 141.

4.2.2 Regulations

Under Article 249 of the Treaty of Rome the European Union has the power to issue regulations which are 'binding in every respect and directly applicable in each Member State'. Such regulations do not have to be adopted in any way by the individual states as Article 249 makes it clear that they automatically become law in each member country.

This 'direct applicability' point was tested in *Re Tachographs: Commission* v *United Kingdom* (1979), where a regulation

KEY FACTS

Type of law	Effect	Source
Treaties	Directly applicable	Section 2(1) of the European Communities Act 1972
	Have direct effect (both vertically and horizontally) if give individual rights and are clear	*Macarthys* v *Smith* (1979)
Regulations	Directly applicable Have direct effect (both vertically and horizontally) if give individual rights and are clear	Article 249 of the Treaty of Rome
Directives	NOT directly applicable Have vertical direct effect if give individual rights and are clear NO horizontal direct effect But individual can claim against state for loss caused by failure to implement	Article 249 of the Treaty of Rome *Marshall* case *Duke* v *GEC Reliance* *Francovich* v *Italian Republic*

Figure 4.3 Key fact chart showing effect of EU laws

requiring mechanical recording equipment to be installed in lorries was issued. The United Kingdom government of the day decided not to implement the regulation, but to leave it to lorry owners to decide whether or not to put in such equipment. When the matter was referred to the European Court of Justice it was held that Member States had no discretion in the case of regulations. The wording of Article 249 was explicit and meant that regulations were automatically law in all Member States. States could not pick and choose which ones they would implement. In this way regulations make sure that laws are uniform across all the Member States.

4.2.3 Directives

Directives are the main way in which harmonisation of laws within Member States is reached. There have been directives covering many topics including company laws, banking, insurance, health and safety of workers, equal rights, consumer law and social security. As with regulations, it is Article 249 of the Treaty of Rome that gives the power to the Union to issue directives. There is, however, a difference from regulations in that Article 249 says such directives 'bind any Member state to which they are addressed as to the result to be achieved, while leaving to domestic agencies a competence as to form and means'. This means that Member States will pass their own laws to bring directives into effect (or implement them) and such laws have to be brought in within a time limit set by the European Commission.

The usual method of implementing directives in the United Kingdom is by Statutory Instrument. An example is the Unfair Terms in Consumer Contracts Regulations 1994, which implemented a directive aimed at giving consumers protection from unfair terms in contracts. Directives can, however, be implemented by other law-making methods. An example is the Consumer Protection Act 1987. A directive on liability for defective products was issued in July 1985. (By the way this was some nine years after the proposal had first been put forward by the Commission!) The directive had to be implemented by 30 July 1988. This was done in this country by Parliament passing the Consumer Protection Act 1987, which came into force on 1 March 1988.

Working Time Directive

Another example of a directive is the Working Time Directive which was issued in 1993. This directive gave detailed instructions of the maximum number of hours that should be worked, the rest periods and the amount of paid holiday to which workers were entitled. It should have been implemented by November 1996 but the United Kingdom Government did not implement it until October 1998 with the Working Time Regulations 1998.

Direct effect

Where Member States have not implemented a directive within the time laid down the European Court of Justice has developed the concept of 'direct effect'.

If the purpose of a directive is to grant rights to individuals and that directive is sufficiently clear, it may be directly enforceable by an individual against the Member State. This will be so even though that state has not implemented the directive, or has implemented it in a defective way. The important point is that an individual who is adversely affected by the failure to implement only has rights against the state. This is because of the concepts of vertical effect and horizontal effect explained below.

Vertical direct effect

In *Marshall v Southampton and South West Hampshire Area Health Authority* (1986) the

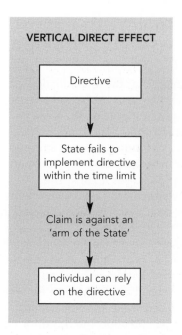

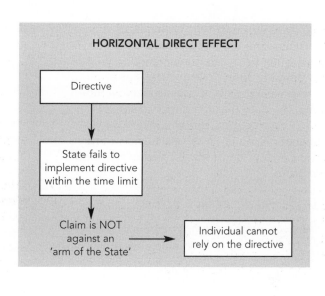

Figure 4.4 Diagram illustrating vertical and horizontal direct effect

facts were that Miss Marshall was required to retire at the age of 62 when men doing the same work did not have to retire until age 65. Under the Sex Discrimination Act 1975 in English law this was not discriminatory. However, she was able to succeed in an action for unfair dismissal by relying on the Equal Treatment Directive 76/207. This directive had not been fully implemented in the United Kingdom but the European Court of Justice held that it was sufficiently clear and imposed obligations on the Member State. This ruling allowed Miss Marshall to succeed in her claim against her employers because her employers were 'an arm of the state'; i.e. they were considered as being part of the State. The directive had vertical effect allowing her to rely on it take action against them. This idea of vertical effect is shown in a diagram form in Figure 4.4.

The concept of the state for these purposes is quite wide, as it was ruled by the European Court of Justice in *Foster* v *British Gas plc* (1990) that the state was:

'a body, whatever its legal form, which has been made responsible, pursuant to a measure adopted by the State, for providing a public service under the control of the State and has for that purpose special powers beyond those which result from the normal rules applicable in relations between individuals.'

In view of this wide definition the House of Lords decided that British Gas, which at the time was a nationalised industry, was part of the State, and Foster could rely on the Equal Treatment Directive.

The concept of vertical effect means that a Member State cannot take advantage of its own failure to comply with European law and implement a directive. Individuals can rely on the directive when bringing a claim against the state.

This concept of vertical effect was used in the case of *Gibson* v *East Riding of Yorkshire Council* (1999). In this case Mrs Gibson was employed as a part-time swimming instructor. She did not get paid holidays. The Employment Appeal Tribunal held that under the Working Time Directive she was entitled to four weeks' paid holiday from November 1996, the date that the directive should have been implemented. Her employers were an 'emanation of the State' and could not rely on the lack of domestic legislation to defeat her claim.

Horizontal direct effect

Directives which have not been implemented do not, however, give an individual any rights against other people. So in *Duke v GEC Reliance Ltd* (1988), Mrs Duke was unable to rely on the Equal Treatment Directive as her employer was a private company. This illustrates that directives do not have horizontal effect and this has been confirmed by an Italian case, *Paola Faccini Dori v Recreb Srl* (1994), in which the Italian Government failed to implement directive 85/447 in respect of consumer rights to cancel certain contracts. Dori could not rely on the directive in order to claim a right of cancellation against a private trader.

Duty to interpret national law in the light of directives

Even where a directive has not been implemented, national courts have a duty to interpret their national law in the light of the wording and purpose of any relevant directive. This was pointed out by the European Court of Justice in the case of *Marleasing SA v LA Comercial Internacional de Alimentacion SA* (1992).

It had also been said by the European Court of Justice in the earlier case of *von Colson v Land Nordrhein-Westfalen* (1984) that 'national courts are required to interpret their national law in the light of the wording and the purpose of the directive'.

Actions against the State for failure to implement a directive

Clearly it is unfair that these conflicting doctrines of vertical and horizontal effect should give rights to individuals in some cases and not in others. The European Court of Justice has developed another strategy under which it may be possible to take an action to claim damages against the Member State which has failed to implement the European directive. This was decided in *Francovich v Italian Republic* (1991) where the Italian Government failed to implement a directive aimed at protecting wages of employees whose employer became insolvent. As a result when the firm for which Francovich worked went into liquidation owing him wages, he sued the State for his financial loss. The European Court of Justice held that he was entitled to compensation. The court repeated this view of the law in *Paola Faccini Dori v Recreb Srl*, when it said that:

> 'Community law required the member states to make good damage caused by a failure to transpose a directive, provided three conditions were fulfilled;
> First, the purpose of the directive had to be to grant rights to individuals.
> Second, it had to be possible to identify the content of those rights on the basis of the provisions of the directive.
> Finally, there had to be a causal link between the breach of the state's obligations and the damage suffered.'

In *R v HM Treasury, ex parte British Telecommunications plc* (1996) the European Court of Justice held that although a directive on telecommunications had been incorrectly implemented in English law, compensation was not payable as the breach of Community law was not sufficiently serious.

The principle of Member States being liable

to pay compensation has been extended to other breaches by Member States of Community law. This was seen in the joined cases of *Brasserie du Pêcheur SA* v *Federation of Republic of Germany* and *R* v *Secretary of State for Transport, ex parte Factortame Ltd (No 4) (1996)* which are considered at 4.3.

![Comment icon] **Comment**

The importance of rulings of the European Court of Justice

The development of the concept of direct effect has been a very important one for the effectiveness of EU law. If the European Court of Justice had not developed this concept citizens of Member States would not have been able to enforce the rights given to them.

In particular where the Government has not implemented a directive, the rights of individuals in many important areas, especially employment law and discrimination, would have been lost. The rulings of the European Court of Justice have allowed individuals to rely on EU law in claims against the State or an arm of the State, and also forced the Government to implement EU law more fully.

The development of the *Francovich* principle has provided citizens with a remedy against the State, when otherwise they would not have had one. However, this brings its own problems as the European Court of Justice has no mechanism for enforcing its judgments.

4.2.4 Decisions

This does not refer to decisions made by the European Court of Justice, but to decisions issued under the power of Article 249. Such decisions may be addressed either to a Member State or an individual (person or company). Article 249 says that they are 'binding in every respect for the addressees named therein'. They are generally administrative in nature.

Article 249 also allows for recommendations and opinions to be issued, but these have no binding force.

Activity

Below in Source A are set out extracts from Articles 1 and 2 of the Equal Treatment Directive 76/207. Read these and then apply them, giving reasons for your decision, to the facts set out in Source B.

SOURCE A
Council Directive No. 76/207

Article 1

1. The purpose of this Directive is to put into effect in the Member States the principle of equal treatment as regards access to employment, including promotion, and to vocational training and as regards working conditions . . . This principle is hereinafter referred to as the 'principle of equal treatment'.

Article 2

1. For the purposes of the following provisions, the principle of equal treatment shall mean that there shall be no discrimination whatsoever on the grounds of sex either directly or indirectly by reference in particular to marital or family status.

2. This Directive shall be without prejudice to the right of Member States to exclude from its field of application those occupational activities and, where appropriate, the training leading thereto, for which, by reason of their nature or the context in which they are carried out, the sex of the worker constitutes a determining factor.

3. This Directive shall be without prejudice to provisions concerning the protection of women, particularly as regards pregnancy and maternity.

4. This Directive shall be without prejudice to measures to promote equal opportunity for men and women, in particular by removing existing inequalities which affect women's opportunities in the areas referred to in Article 1(1).

SOURCE B

Case facts: Amy Austin and Ben Bowen are employed by Green Gardens Ltd. There is a vacancy for a promotion to section manager, and both have applied for the post. Green Gardens have interviewed Amy and Ben and decided that both are equally qualified for the position. In this situation, if there are fewer women employed at the relevant level, Green Gardens have a policy of appointing the female applicant.

Ben complains that this is discriminatory and contrary to the Equal Treatment Directive.

4.3 Conflict between European law and national law

European law takes precedence over national law. This was first established in *Van Gend en Loos* (1963) which involved a conflict of Dutch law and European law on customs duty. The Dutch government argued that the European Court of Justice had no jurisdiction to decide whether European law should prevail over Dutch law; that was a matter for the Dutch courts to decide. However the European Court rejected this argument. In *Costa* v *ENEL* (1964) the European Court of Justice held that even if there was a later national law it did not take precedence over the European law. In this case the European Court of Justice said:

KEY FACTS

1963	*Van Gend en Loos*	European Court of Justice has right to decide whether Community law or national law prevails
1964	*Costa* v *ENEL*	European law takes precedence over national law
1974	*Van Duyn* v *Home Office*	Principle of direct applicability Citizens can rely directly on an article of the Treaty of Rome which confers rights on individuals
1986	*Marshall* v *Southampton etc Health Authority*	Vertical direct effect of directives In an action against the state individuals can rely on a directive which has not been implemented
1991	*Francovich* v *Italy*	Individual can claim compensation from state for its failure to implement directive
1996	*Brasserie du Pêcheur Factortame No 4*	State liable to compensate for breaches of Community law

Figure 4.5 Key fact chart of some important decisions of the European Court of Justice

'the Member States have limited their sovereign rights, albeit within limited fields, and have thus created a body of law which binds both their nationals and themselves.'

This conflict was seen clearly in the *Factortame* case (1990) when the European Court of Justice decided that Britain could not enforce the Merchant Shipping Act 1988. This Act had been passed to protect British fishermen by allowing vessels to register only if 75 per cent of directors and shareholders were British nationals. It was held that this contravened the Treaty of Rome.

This breach of Community law has had another effect in that the European Court of Justice held in a later action in the joined cases of *Brasserie du Pêcheur SA* v *Federation of Republic of Germany* and *R* v *Secretary of State for Transport, ex parte Factortame Ltd (No 4)* (1996) that governments were liable for financial loss suffered as a result of their breach of European law. In *Brasserie du Pêcheur* a French company claimed that it was forced to discontinue exports of beer to Germany, because the German authorities considered that the beer did not comply with the purity requirements laid down in German law. In *Factortame* European fishermen claimed that they had been deprived of the right to fish as result of the Merchant Shipping Act 1988. In both cases there was a claim for compensation from the state concerned.

The European Court of Justice held that Community law did give the right to compensation provided that three conditions were met. These were:

- The rule of Community law infringed must be intended to confer rights on individuals
- The breach must be sufficiently serious
- There must be a direct causal link between the breach of the obligation resting on the state and the damage sustained by the injured parties

4.3.1 The effect of European law on the sovereignty of Parliament

From the cases given above it can be seen that Member States, including Britain, have definitely transferred sovereign rights to a Community created by them. None of the states can reverse this process by means of unilateral measures which are inconsistent with the Community concept.

It is also a principle of the Treaty of Rome that no Member State may call into question the status of Community law as a system of uniformly and generally applicable law throughout the Community. It therefore follows from this, that Community law which is enacted in accordance with the power laid down in the Treaties, has priority over any conflicting law of Member States. This is true both of national laws which were enacted before the Community law and also of national laws which were enacted after the relevant Community law.

While Britain is member of the European Union it is therefore true to say that the sovereignty of Parliament has been affected and that, in the areas it operates, European law has supremacy over national law.

Chapter 5

LAW REFORM

5.1 Law reform and the need for an independent law reform body

In Chapters 2, 3 and 4 we examined the different sources of law, and saw that the law of England and Wales comes from a variety of sources. This fact makes it important to keep the law under review, to ensure that it is reformed when necessary, and to try to keep it in an accessible and manageable state. There are many influences on the way our law is formed and the impetus for reform can come from a number of sources. Some of these will have more effect than others, while in some situations there may be competing interests in the way that the law should be reformed.

The Government of the day effectively has the major say in what laws will be enacted, and the Government will set out its agenda for law reform in each session of Parliament. However, much of this will be concerned with more politically motivated areas, rather than 'pure law' reform. In addition, we have already seen with the Dangerous Dogs Act 1991 in Chapter 3 that Acts of Parliament can actually lead to more confusion and complication of the law. This is especially true where one Act is used to amend another so that the law is contained in a series of Acts, all of which must be consulted before the law can be discovered.

Pressure groups can provide the impetus for law reform. Where a subject has a particularly high profile, Parliament may bow to public opinion and alter the law (we saw this in the Disability Discrimination Act 1995). The Law Commission (see section 5.4) in its consultation process will also receive the views of pressure groups with a special interest in the area of law under review.

As seen in Chapter 2, judges play a role in law reform by means of judicial precedent. In some instances they may actually create new law, as occurred in *R* v *R* (1991), when the courts ruled that a man could be guilty of raping his wife. In some cases the courts may feel unhappy with the decision they have to come to because of the clear wording of an existing Act of Parliament or because they are bound by a previous precedent. In this situation the judges may when giving judgment draw attention to the need for reform. This happened in *R* v *Preddy* (1996) where it was clear that there was a gap in the criminal law which meant that people who had committed mortgage frauds were not guilty of any offence.

The Law Commission recommended that two new offences should be created. These were obtaining a money transfer by deception and retaining credits from dishonest sources. Parliament passed the Theft (Amendment) Act 1996 to do this. So the judges highlighted the problem with the law; the Law Commission reported on it and this led to Parliament creating new law.

However, these influences do not lead to our law developing in an organised and controlled way. The law needs to be reformed so that it adapts to the changing needs of society. This may require new laws to be passed or, in some cases, old laws to be cancelled. Confused law also creates expense. Simpler law would save legal fees.

5.1.1 History of law reform bodies

The need to have a body supervising systematic reform has been recognised for centuries, with various Lord Chancellors (as far back as 1616) calling for the appointment of 'law commissioners' to revise the laws and keep them up to date. Prior to the nineteenth century, there were no organised efforts at law reform. In the nineteenth century there were piecemeal reforms, with some statutes which codified parts of the criminal law and others codifying the common law on specialised areas of contract law. Much of this reform was carried out by individuals, such as Judge Chalmers, whose work led to the Bills of Exchange Act 1882 and the Sale of Goods Act 1893.

In the twentieth century; calls for an institution to be set up with responsibility for law reform led to the creation in 1934 of the Law Revision Committee. This has been described as the 'source of the modern machinery of law reform', but it only operated until the outbreak of World War II in 1939. After the war, from 1945 to 1952, there was no permanent law reform body, but the Government set up various *ad hoc* committees (a committee created just for that occasion) to deal with specific problems. From 1952 onwards there have been various more permanent, though part-time, committees set up, but it was not until 1965 that a full-time body with wide responsibility came into existence in the shape of the Law Commission (see section 5.4).

5.2 Law Reform Committee

This was created in 1952 and was in effect a revival of the pre-war Law Revision Committee. It is part-time and considers only small areas of the civil law, often rather narrow and technical points, which are referred to it by the Government. Its proposals have led to Parliament passing such Acts as the Occupiers' Liability Act 1957, the Civil Evidence Act 1968 and the Latent Damage Act 1986. The Law Commission has consulted this committee on areas of civil law such as trust law.

5.3 Criminal Law Revision Committee

This was set up in 1957 and was another part-time body which recommended changes to the criminal law. This Committee sat monthly until 1986 and produced 18 reports. Many of its smaller, specific recommendations became law, though its recommendations for broad changes to the law were often not taken up due to lack of parliamentary time. One of its main achievements was the virtual codification of theft and related offences in the Theft Act 1968, although another Theft Act had to be passed in 1978 to overcome problems under section 16 of the original Act.

Lord Scarman pointed out in a letter to *The Times* in 1996 that the members of the Committee included both academics and those with long practical experience of working in the criminal justice system. He felt that this gave the Committee the expertise to deal with reform of the criminal law which is needed, and that some of the poor drafting of recent law could have been avoided if the Committee had been consulted.

5.4 The Law Commission

This is the main law reform body. It was set up in 1965 by the Law Commissions Act. It is a full-time body and consists of a chairman, who is a High Court judge, and four other

Law Commissioners. There are also support staff to assist with research and four Parliamentary Draftsmen who help with the drafting of proposed Bills. The Commission considers areas of law which are believed to be in need of reform. The role of the Law Commission is set out in section three of the Law Commissions Act which states:

> 'It shall be the duty of each of the Commissions to take and keep under review all the law with which they are respectively concerned with a view to its systematic development and reform, including in particular the codification of such law, the elimination of anomalies, the repeal of obsolete and unnecessary enactments, the reduction of the number of separate enactments and generally the simplification and modernisation of the law.'

5.4.1 The way in which the Law Commission works

Topics may be referred to it by the Lord Chancellor on behalf of the Government, or it may itself select areas in need of reform and seek Governmental approval to draft a report on them. The following article shows the start of the procedure which eventually led to the Law Reform (Year and a Day Rule) Act 1996.

The Law Commission works by researching the area of law that is thought to be in need of reform. It then publishes a consultation paper seeking views on possible reform. The consultation paper will describe the current law, set out the problems and look at options for reform (often including explanations of the law in other countries).

Following the response to the consultation paper, the Commission will then draw up positive proposals for reform. These will be presented in a report which will also set out

Medical advances force review of murder

The technology of the life support machine has led the Government to re-examine the definition of murder. The Home Secretary has asked the Law Commission to consider scrapping urgently a 300-year-old law preventing prosecution for murder if the victim dies more than a year and a day after the crime.

Michael Howard is bowing to medical technology which can keep comatose assault victims alive for years on life support machines. However, he has refused to support a clause tabled by the Labour MP Alan Milburn to change the law as part of the criminal justice bill.

Speaking yesterday at the Commons committee considering the bill, David MacLean, junior Home Office minister, said that he accepted the case for Labour's new clause 5, but it was not practical because it did not include manslaughter and the matter was being referred instead to the Law Commission. The Home Office said that it was a complex area needing careful consideration and should be properly addressed.

Taken from an article by Alice Thomson in *The Times*, 4 March 1994

the research that led to the conclusions. There will often be a draft Bill attached to the report with the intention that this is the exact way in which the new law should be formed. Such a draft Bill must, of course, go before Parliament and go though the necessary Parliamentary stages if it is to become law.

Activity

Look at the Law Commission's website (www.lawcom.gov.uk) and find an area of law which it is currently researching for reform.

5.4.2 Repeal and consolidation

Repeal

There are many very old and sometimes ridiculous statutes which are still on the statute book, but which have long since ceased to have any relevance. In order to get rid of this problem, the Law Commission prepares a Statute Law (Repeals) Bill for Parliament to pass. For example, the Statute Law Repeals Act 1995 repealed 223 whole Acts or orders and the redundant parts of 259 others. In the previous 26 years similar Repeal Acts had repealed almost 1,600 complete Acts, as well as parts of many more. This 'tidying-up' of the statute book helps to make the law more accessible.

Consolidation

This is needed because in some areas of law there are a number of statutes, each of which sets out a small parts of the total law. For example the law on sentencing offenders under the age of 17 was amended more than 10 times and it was necessary to consult each of the relevant Acts to get a full picture of the law. The aim of consolidation is to draw all the existing provisions together in one Act. This is another way in which the law is being made more accessible. The Law Commission produces about five Consolidation Bills each

year, though it is perhaps true to say that as fast as one area is consolidated, another area is being fragmented by further Acts of Parliament!

This happened with the law on sentencing. The law was consolidated in the Powers of Criminal Courts (Sentencing) Act 2000. However, within a few months the law was changed again by the Criminal Justice and Courts Services Act 2000, which renamed some of the community penalties and also created new powers of sentencing.

5.4.3 Codification

Codification involves bringing together all the law on one topic into one source of law. It was specially referred to by section three of the Law Commissions Act 1965 as part of the Law Commission's role. Indeed when the Law Commission was first formed in 1965 an ambitious programme of codification was announced, aimed at codifying family law, contract law, landlord and tenant laws and the law of evidence. However, the Law Commission has gradually abandoned these massive schemes of codification in favour of what might be termed the 'building-block' approach. Under this it has concentrated on codifying small sections of the law that can be added to later.

In fact the whole concept of codification is the subject of debate. Those in favour of it say that it makes the law both accessible and understandable. In addition it gives consistency and certainty: the law is contained in one place and both lawyers and the people can easily discover what the law is. The opposite viewpoint is that a very detailed code makes the law too rigid; while if a code is drafted in broad terms without detail, it will need to be interpreted by the courts and in this way would be just as uncertain as the existing common law.

5.4.4 Success of the Law Commission

Although the Law Commission has not achieved its original ideas of codification, it has been successful in dealing with smaller areas of law. The success rate of the Law Commission's proposals was initially high, and its first 20 law reform programmes were enacted within an average of two years. These included the Unfair Contract Terms Act 1977, the Criminal Attempts Act 1981, the Supply of Goods and Services Act 1982 and the Occupiers' Liability Act 1984.

In fact, in the first 10 years of its existence it had a high success rate with 85 per cent of its proposals being enacted by Parliament. During the next 10 years, however, only 50 per cent of its suggested reforms became law. This lack of success was due to lack of Parliamentary time, and an apparent disinterest by Parliament in technical law reform. The rate hit an all-time low in 1990 when not one of its reforms was enacted by Parliament and, by 1992, there was a backlog of 36 Bills which Parliament had failed to consider.

Jellicoe procedure

This problem was tackled by the introduction in 1994 of a special procedure, known as the Jellicoe procedure, which uses the Special Public Bills Committee of the House of Lords to debate non-controversial Bills. This has helped to speed up the introduction of reforms suggested by the Law Commission to such an extent that in the 13 months from December 1994 to December 1995 13 reports became law. Unfortunately this procedure has not been used recently.

Criminal code

The reform of the criminal law is the biggest unresolved problem. The Law Commission worked with three leading academics to produce a draft criminal code which was published in 1985. Part one covered general principles of criminal liability, while part two dealt with specific offences which were grouped into five chapters containing linked offences (for example offences against, the person). The offences covered by the code were said to cover between 90 and 95 per cent of the work of the criminal courts.

This Code was laid before Parliament but not considered. In view of the amount of law covered in it, the Law Commission decided to split it into manageable sections and produce draft Bills on each of these. The first such draft Bill was on offences against the person and was published in 1993. This aimed at simplifying some of the areas of law which have become very complex and which create difficulties for the courts and defendants. For example in 1994 the House of Lords spent two days considering what the words 'inflict' and 'cause' meant in the Offences Against the Person Act 1861. This sort of dispute would be avoided by the implementation of the draft Bill.

However, Parliament has failed to find the necessary time to debate the proposal and by the end of 2001 (16 years after the original code was formulated) this area of law was still awaiting reform. This perhaps re-inforces the words of Lord Scarman, the first Chairman of the Law Commission when he said:

> *'Parliament, in matters of law reform, is an extremely amateur and indolent body. It requires advice and it requires spurring on and to be stimulated into action.'*

◀ Comment

The Law Commission was set up by Parliament; many of its law reform projects have been referred to it by the Government. Yet, despite this, Parliament is slow to implement the reforms recommended by the Law Commission and make them into law.

It is true that the Law Commission has had a major impact, with more than two-thirds of its reports becoming law, but a number of reports still await Government action. This is partly due to limited Parliamentary time, but also partly due to lack of commitment to reform of 'lawyers' law'. Perhaps delegated legislation could be used in some areas of technical law. But this raises the problem that law should only be made by our democratically elected Parliament. Using delegated legislation is undesirable in politically sensitive areas of law-making.

Another way in which more might be achieved is if a separate Ministry of Justice were to be created as new Government department. This would then provide more support for law reform and create more pressure on Governments to act on proposals of the Law Commission.

While the present system exists it is likely that the words on the Internet home page of the Law Commission in 1999 will remain true. 'Much has already been done, but there is still much more to be done.'

5.5 Royal Commissions

Apart from the full-time bodies there are also temporary committees or Royal Commissions set up to investigate and report on one specific area of law. These are dissolved after they have completed their task. Such Royal Commissions were used frequently from 1945 to 1979, but from 1979 to 1990 when Margaret Thatcher was Prime Minister, none were set up. In the 1990s there was a return to the use of such commissions.

Some Royal Commissions have led to important changes in the law; the Royal Commission on Police Procedure (the Phillips Commission) reported in 1981 and many of its recommendations were given effect by the Police and Criminal Evidence Act 1984. However the Government does not always act on recommendations as was seen with the Pearson Commission on Personal Injury cases which reported in 1978.

With the Runciman Commission (the Royal

KEY FACTS

Originated	By the Law Commissions Act 1965
Personnel	Chairman and four other Commissioners
	Support staff including Parliamentary draftsmen
Function	Under s3 Law Commissions Act 1965 to 'keep the law under review'
Success rate	First 10 years – 85 per cent of proposals enacted
	Second 10 years – 50 per cent of proposals enacted
	1990 – no enactments
	1994 onwards – use of Jellicoe procedure leads to greater action
Recent reforms	Law Reform (Year and a Day Rule) Act 1996 allows prosecutions for murder where victim dies more than a year and a day after the attack
	Contract (Rights of Third Parties) Act 1999 which allows third parties to claim under a contract made for their benefit

Figure 5.1 Key fact chart on the Law Commission

Commission on Criminal Justice) which reported in 1993, the Government implemented many of the proposals but not all.

In 1999 a Royal Commission (the Wakeham Commission) considered how the House of Lords could be reformed. In December 2001, the Government issued a White Paper showing that they were only partly accepting the proposals of the Commission.

5.5.1 Reviews by judges

Apart from actual Royal Commissions, judges may be asked to lead an investigation into technical areas of law. Recent examples of this have been the Woolf Committee on civil justice which led to major reforms of the civil court system in 1999 (see chapter 6) and the review of the criminal justice system carried out by Sir Robin Auld in 2001 (see Chapters 9 and 10).

CIVIL CASES

As already stressed in Chapter 1, it is important to understand the differences between civil cases and criminal cases. Civil cases cover a wide range of matters, so there cannot be a very specific definition which will cover all of them. However, a basic definition for civil claims is to say that these arise when an individual or a business believes that their rights have been infringed in some way. Some of the main areas of civil law are contract law, the law of tort, family law, employment law and company law.

As well as dealing with different areas of law, the types of dispute that can arise within the field of civil law are equally varied. A company may be claiming that money is owed to it (contract law); this type of claim may be for a few pounds or for several million. An individual may be claiming compensation for injuries suffered in an accident (the tort of negligence), while in another tort case the claim might not be for money but for another remedy: such as an injunction to prevent someone from building on disputed land. Other types of court orders include the winding up of a company which cannot pay its debts or a decree of divorce for a marriage that has failed. The list is almost endless.

6.1 Negotiation

In most civil matters people regard a court case as a last resort and will try to resolve the problem without going to court, so that when a dispute arises it is likely that some form of negotiation will take place. The most usual situation is that the person making the complaint will either go to see the other side and explain the problem (this is common where shoppers take back sub-standard goods) or they will write to the other side, setting out the complaint. Many cases will be resolved at this stage by the other party agreeing to refund money, change goods, pay the debt or take some other desired action.

The need to try to settle any dispute is stressed in the leaflets issued by the Court Service on taking action in court. Look at Figure 6.1.

If the other party will not settle the claim, then the aggrieved person must decide whether they are prepared to take the matter further. The most common next stage is to get legal advice and perhaps get a solicitor to write to the other person. This may lead to a 'bargaining' situation where a series of letters is written between the parties and eventually a compromise is reached. However, if, after all this, the other side refuses to pay the debt or compensation or whatever else is claimed, then the aggrieved person must decide if the matter is worth pursuing any further. This may involve starting a court case or an alternative form of dispute resolution may be used (these alternatives to going to court are considered in the next chapter).

Taking a case to court can be an expensive exercise, even if you decide to 'do-it-yourself' and not use a lawyer. There will be a court fee based on the type and size of the claim, which can be claimed back from the other party if you win the case, but there is always the risk that you will lose the case and have to pay the other side's costs. Even if you win, your problems may not be over as

Making a claim?
Some questions to ask yourself.

Can I settle this without going to court?

Issuing a claim at court should be your last resort. You should first consider other ways to settle the matter. For example, if you are owed money, you could write a letter to the person who owes it. Say how much they owe and what it is for, and what steps you have already taken to recover the money. Include a warning that you will issue a county court claim if they do not pay by the date you give. Sometimes this warning will encourage them to pay and you will not have to go to court. Keep a copy of your letter and any reply.

This is an example of the sort of letter you might send.

> 2 Spring Gardens
> Anytown
> AO6 3BX
>
> 10 March 1999
>
> Dear Mr Green
>
> You came to repair my central heating boiler on 6 January. I rang you on 7 January and again on 10 January to tell you it was still not working properly.
>
> You promised to call and put it right but did not. I had to get someone else to come and repair it on 26 January which cost £157 + VAT.
>
> I asked you on 2 February to pay this money because it was work you should have done.
>
> You have not paid it.
>
> If you do not pay me the money by 19 March 1999, I will issue a county court claim against you.
>
> Yours sincerely
>
> Mrs V Cross

Will I get my money?

It is important to consider whether the person, firm or company you are claiming from is likely to be able to pay. If they are:

- unemployed;
- bankrupt;

or have

- no money of their own;
- no personal property and
- nothing else of value belonging to them (such as a car) which is not hired or subject to a hire purchase or lease agreement;
- ceased to trade; or
- have other debts to pay,

the court may not be able to help you get your money. However, you may be able to get your money if you are prepared to accept small instalments over a period of time.

If the person or company is bankrupt, you will probably not get your money. You can contact the Insolvency Service at 21 Bloomsbury Street, London WC1B 3SS (telephone: 0171 637 1110). You need to tell them the full name of the person or company and their last address. They will tell you if the person is bankrupt, or if the company is in 'compulsory liquidation', which means that the company has stopped trading and probably has neither money nor other assets.

n ought to
d 'issuing a
to the
o court is

nnot settle
o issue a

, including:

of claim.
ut the
mean is the
claims in a

is designed
it will
or less (or
al injury or
m or
in Scotland

2

3

4

Figure 6.1 'Making a claim? Some questions to ask yourself.'

the other person may not have enough money to pay the claim and refund your costs. If the case is complicated it could take years to complete and may cost hundreds or thousands of pounds.

Given these problems, it is not surprising that many people who believe they have a good claim decide not to take court action.

However, starting a court case does not mean that it will actually go to court. The vast majority of cases are settled out of court so that fewer than 5 per cent of all cases started in the civil courts get as far as a court hearing. This is because the dispute is a private one between the parties involved and they can settle their own dispute at any time, even after court proceedings have been started.

6.2 Starting a court case

The civil justice system was reformed in 1999 following the Woolf Report (see 6.6).

Parties are encouraged to give information to each other, in an attempt to prevent the need for so many court cases to be started. So before a claim is issued, especially in personal injury cases, a pre-action 'protocol' should be followed. This is a list of things to be done and if the parties do not follow the procedure and give the required information to the other party, they may be liable for certain costs if they then make a court claim.

The information is usually in a letter explaining brief details of how the claim arises; why it is claimed that the other party is at fault; details of injury or other damage; and any other relevant matters. The defendant is then given three months to investigate the claim and must then reply, setting out if liability is admitted or if it is denied, with the reasons for the denial. If expert evidence is

going to be needed, then the parties should try to agree to use one expert. This should lead to many claims being settled, but there will still be some which need to go to court.

6.2.1 Which court to use

Where the decision is made to go to court, then the first problem is which court to use. The two courts which hear civil cases are:

- The County Court and
- The High Court.

For cases where the claim is for £15,000 or less, the case must be started in the County Court. For larger claims you can usually choose to start a case in either the County Court or the High Court. This is still the position after the Woolf Reforms. However, there are some restrictions laid down in the High Court and County Courts Jurisdiction Order 1991. These are that:

- Personal injury cases for less than £50,000 must be started in the County Court
- Defamation actions must be started in the High Court.

So for most cases over £15,000 a claimant will be able to choose the most convenient court for starting the case. The main points to consider in making the decision are the amount that is being claimed and whether the case is likely to raise a complex issue of law. The fact that a case is started in one court does not necessarily mean that the trial will be there; cases may be transferred from one court to the other for the actual trial, if this is thought necessary. Once a case is defended the case is then allocated to the appropriate track and at the same time it is possible for it to be transferred to another court.

6.2.2 Issuing a claim

If you are using the County Court, then you can choose to issue the claim in any of the

Claim Form	In the
	Claim No.

Claimant

SEAL

Defendant(s)

Brief details of claim

Value

Defendant's name and address		£
	Amount claimed	
	Court fee	
	Solicitor's costs	
	Total amount	
	Issue date	

The court office at

is open between 10 am and 4 pm Monday to Friday. When corresponding with the court, please address forms or letters to the Court Manager and quote the claim number.

N1 Claim form (CPR Part 7) (4.99)   *Printed on behalf of The Court Service*

Figure 6.2 Form N1

230 or so County Courts in the country. If you are using the High Court, then you can go to one of the 20 District Registries or the main court in London. You need a claim form called 'N1' (see Figure 6.2). The court office will give you notes explaining how to fill in the form.

Court staff can help to make sure that you have filled in the claim form properly, or you may get help from advice centres or a Citizens' Advice Bureau. Once the form is filled in you should photocopy it so that you have a copy for the court, a copy for yourself and a copy for each defendant. Then take the form to the court office. A court fee for issuing the claim has to be paid. This fee varies according to how much the claim is for. In 2002, the fee for a claim of up to £200 was £27, with the maximum fee for a small claim (under £5,000) being £115. Claims of £5,000 to £15,000 had a fee of £230, while at the top end of the scale claims of over £50,000 had a fee of £500.

6.2.3 Defending a case

When the defendant receives the claim form there are several routes which can be taken. They may admit the claim and pay the full amount. Where this happens the case ends. The claimant has achieved what was wanted. In other cases the defendant may dispute the claim. If the defendant wishes to defend the claim, he or she must send either an acknowledgement of service (Form N9) or a defence to the court within 14 days of receiving the claim. If only an acknowledgement of service is sent, then the defendant has an extra 14 days in which to serve the defence.

If the defendant does not do either of these things, then the claimant can ask the court to make an order that the defendant pays the money and costs claimed. This is called an order in default. Once a claim is defended the court will allocate the case to the most suitable 'track' or way of dealing with the case.

6.2.4 Allocation of cases

The decision on which track should be used is made by the District Judge in the County Court or the Master (a procedural judge) in the High Court. The tracks are:

1. **The small claims track** This is normally used for disputes under £5,000, except for personal injury cases and housing cases where the limit is usually £1,000.
2. **The fast track** This is used for straightforward disputes of £5,000 to £15,000.
3. **The multi-track** This is for cases over £15,000 or for complex cases under this amount.

To help the judge consider to which track a claim should be allocated, both parties are sent an allocation questionnaire. If it is thought necessary, the judge can allocate a case to a track that normally deals with claims of a higher value. Alternatively, if the parties agree, the judge can allocate a case to a lower-value track.

For claims over £15,000 there may also be a decision to transfer the case from the County Court to the High Court or *vice versa*. Usually claims of less than £25,000 are tried in the County Court, while claims for between £25,000 and £50,000 are generally tried in the court in which the proceedings were started. Claims for over £50,000 are usually tried in the High Court. This is shown in Figure 6.3 (overleaf).

We will now go on to consider the different courts and tracks.

6.3 Small claims

Clearly, it is important to have a relatively cheap and simple way of making a claim for a small amount of money, otherwise the costs of the action will be far more than the

Value of claim	Court in which case will usually be tried
Under £5,000	County Court small claims procedure
£5,000 to £15,000	County Court fast track procedure
£15,000 to £25,000	County Court multi-track procedure
£25,000 to £50,000	Either High Court or County Court multi-track procedure
Over £50,000	High Court multi-track procedure

Figure 6.3 *Summary of where cases are likely to be tried*

amount in dispute. For that reason the small claims procedure was started in 1973, and originally only claims of up to £75 could be made there. The limit has since been raised several times, especially in 1991 when the limit was increased to £1,000; in 1996 after the Woolf Report the limit was increased to £3,000; and in 1999 it became £5,000.

6.3.1 Small claims procedure

People are encouraged to take their own case so that costs are kept low. However, under the new rules small claims cases are started in the same way as all other cases. This makes it more difficult for the ordinary person. The use of lawyers is discouraged, as, though it is possible to have a lawyer to represent you at a small claims hearing, the winner cannot claim the costs of using a lawyer from the losing party. An alternative to using a lawyer is to have a 'lay representative', that is a non-legally qualified person, to help put your case.

Small claims cases used to be heard in private, but under the Woolf reforms they are now heard in an ordinary court. The procedure still allows the District Judge to be flexible in the way he hears the case but the process is no longer as informal as under the previous system. District Judges are encouraged to be more inquisitorial and are

given training in how to handle small claims cases, so that they will take an active part in the proceedings, asking questions and making sure that both parties explain all their important points.

6.3.2 Problems with the small claims procedure

Although the small claims procedure is quicker, cheaper and simpler than using the main County Court, there are still problems. In particular there are still delays. This occurs most frequently where the opposing party asks for extra time because they are not ready, although there has been some criticism of the court service itself in some cases where papers have been lost or cases not put down on the list for a hearing.

The hearing will take place during the daytime so that the parties will probably have to take time off to attend court. If the case is finished in one hearing then this is not too big a problem, but often the claimant will need to go to court at least two or three times before the case is complete.

Another problem is that although the initial fee for starting a claim is fairly small, all cases over £1,000 which are defended have to pay an allocation fee of £80. This is more expensive than before the 1999 reforms.

There is also the problem that legal funding is not available. This means that while the intention of the court is that it should be informal and suitable for 'do-it-yourself' litigation, there are cases in which a litigant in person can find that the other side has instructed a lawyer. This is most likely to happen where the other party is a business. As a result there may be an imbalance between the parties which is not always adequately compensated for by the District Judge in his 'interventionist' role. Some District Judges conduct the case in a formal way and are not very helpful to unrepresented claimants. John Baldwin, in his research, *Monitoring the Rise of the Small Claims Limit*, describes the extremely flexible role of the District Judge as leading to 'somewhat rough-and-ready judicial methods'.

The increasing limits of small claims appear to lead to more people using lawyers. Research by John Baldwin showed that in 1993, when the limit was only £1,000, lawyers were used in less than one in five cases. However, in 1996, when the limit was £3,000, lawyers were used in nearly half the cases studied. As the limit has since been increased to £5,000 it is probable that this trend will continue.

Finally there is the problem of enforcing the judgment. Once the court has given judgment it is up to the claimant to 'chase' for the money. So it is quite possible that you may win your case but still find that you have to spend more time and money on trying to actually get the money from the losing party. In March 1996 the National Audit Office reported that 94 per cent of plaintiffs (claimants) won their case and got judgment against the defendant. However, only 54 per cent actually received any money in satisfaction of that judgment. Indeed one out of every three successful litigants did not manage to get any money from the defendant.

6.4 County Court

There are about 230 County Courts, so that most major towns will have a court. The courts can try nearly all civil cases. The main types of cases are:

- All contract and tort claims
- All cases for the recovery of land
- Disputes over partnerships, trusts and inheritance up to a value of £30,000.

In addition some County Courts have the jurisdiction to hear divorce cases, bankruptcy cases, admiralty cases (normal limit £5,000 or £15,000 for salvage cases) and matters under the Race Relations Act 1976.

The County Court can try small claims, fast track and multi-track cases and its workload is much greater than the High Court. In 2000 nearly two million cases were started in the County Courts, although this figure includes small claims. An interesting feature is that over 800,000 of these summonses were issued through the Claims Production Centre which deals with about 135 companies such as banks, credit card issuers, mail order catalogues and the utilities, which issue a large number of summonses, usually at least 1,000 a year, against different defendants.

Despite the large total of summonses issued, only a very small number of cases actually proceed to a trial. In 2000 only 14,250 cases were tried in County Courts, while there were 55,836 cases dealt with by the small claims procedure.

Cases will nearly always be heard in open court and members of the public are entitled to attend; the exceptions to this are cases involving family matters, for example maintenance hearings, and proceedings under the Children Act 1989, which are heard in private. The whole hearing is more formal and many claimants and defendants will be represented, usually by a solicitor but sometimes by a barrister. The winner of a case may claim costs, including the cost of legal representation. All this makes a case in the County Court much more expensive than in the small claims court. John Baldwin's research found that 40 per cent of those taking cases in the main County Court viewed it as 'an inappropriate and disproportionately expensive way of resolving' their dispute.

Cases are heard by Circuit Judges, though in rare cases it is possible for a jury of eight to sit with the judge. (For further information on the use of juries in civil cases see Chapter 14.)

6.4.1 Fast track cases

Claims between £5,000 and £15,000 needed a faster and cheaper method of dealing with them. In 1998, before the Woolf reforms, the statistics for the year show that the average wait for cases in the County Court was 85 weeks from the issue of the claim to the actual hearing in court. As well as delay, cases were too expensive. Indeed, the Woolf Report found that the costs of cases were often higher than the amount claimed.

As a result of this the new fast track idea was brought in. Once a case is defended, the District Judge at the County Court will send out the allocation questionnaire and then make the decision of whether the case is suitable for the fast track. Personal injury cases and housing cases over £1,000 and up to £15,000 are also dealt with as fast track cases.

Fast track means that the court will set down a very strict timetable for the pre-trial matters. This is aimed at preventing one or both sides from wasting time and running up unnecessary costs. Once a case is set down for hearing, the aim is to have the case heard within 30 weeks. The new timetables have lessened the delays a little. In 2000 the wait from issue of claim to hearing was 74

weeks. This is an 11 week improvement on the pre-Woolf era. The 30 week limit from setting down the case to hearing is being met, with an average of 26 weeks' wait. However, the total time of 74 weeks is still a long time to wait for a trial of what is meant to be a fast track case. The actual trial will usually be heard by a Circuit Judge and take place in open court with a more formal procedure than for small claims. In order to speed up the trial itself, the hearing will be limited to a maximum of one day and the number of expert witnesses restricted, with usually only one expert being allowed.

6.4.2 Multi-track cases

Claims for more than £15,000 are usually allocated to the multi-track. If the case was started in a County Court then it is likely to be tried there, though it can be sent to the High Court, especially for claims of over £50,000. The case will be heard by a Circuit Judge who will also be expected to 'manage' the case from the moment it is allocated to the multi-track route. The judge can set timetables. It is even possible to ask the parties to try an alternative method of dispute resolution in an effort to prevent waste of costs.

6.5 High Court

The High Court is based in London but also has judges sitting at 26 towns and cities throughout England and Wales. It has the power to hear any civil case and has three divisions each of which specialises in hearing certain types of case. These divisions are the Queen's Bench Division, the Chancery Division and the Family Division.

6.5.1 Queen's Bench Division

The President of the Queen's Bench Division is the Lord Chief Justice and there are nearly 70 judges sitting in the division. It deals with contract and tort cases where the amount claimed is over £50,000, though, as seen earlier in this chapter, a claimant can start an action for any amount of £15,000 and above. The intention is that only multi-track cases should be dealt with in the High Court. Also, certain types of action are thought to be more suitable for the High Court than the County Court.

Usually cases are tried by a single judge but there is a right to jury trial for fraud, libel, slander, malicious prosecution and false imprisonment cases. When a jury is used there will be 12 members.

Commercial Court

This is a special court which is part of the Queen's Bench Division. This court has specialist judges to deal with insurance, banking and other commercial matters, for example the problems of the Lloyd's 'names' for the losses caused by large insurance claims. In this court a simplified speedier procedure is used and the case may be decided on documentary evidence.

Admiralty Court

There is also an Admiralty Court dealing with shipping and deciding such matters as claims for damage caused by collision at sea. It also decides disputes over salvage rights when a ship has sunk or been stranded. The judge in the Admiralty Court sits with two lay assessors, who are chosen from Masters of Trinity House, and who are there to advise the judge on questions of seamanship and navigation.

Also, in 1998 the Technology and Construction Court was set up to take over from what had been called the Official Referee's Court. This court deals with any cases in the Chancery or the Queen's Bench Division which involve technically complex issues, such as building and engineering disputes or litigation over computers.

Judicial review

The Queen's Bench Division also has important supervisory functions over inferior courts and other bodies with decision-making powers, such as Government ministers or local councils. Judicial review is concerned with whether a decision-making process has been carried out legally, as distinct from the merits of the decision in question, and is dealt with more fully in Chapter 16.

6.5.2 Chancery Division

The Lord Chancellor is technically the head of the division, but for practical purposes the Vice-Chancellor is the head. There are about 17 High Court judges assisting in the division. The main business of this division involves disputes concerned with such matters as insolvency, for both companies and individuals, the enforcement of mortgages, disputes relating to trust property, copyright and patents, intellectual property matters and contested probate actions. There is also a special Companies Court in the division which deals mainly with winding up companies.

Juries are never used in the Chancery Division and cases are heard by a single judge. The criticisms of cost and delay which apply to the Queen's Bench Division apply equally to the Chancery Division.

6.5.3 Family Division

The head of this division is the President and 17 High Court judges are assigned to the division. It has jurisdiction to hear wardship cases and all cases relating to children under the Children Act 1989. It also deals with other matters regarding the family, such as declarations of nullity of marriage, and grants probate in non-contentious probate cases.

Cases are heard by a single judge and, although juries were once used to decide defended divorce cases, juries are not now used in this division.

Activity

Advise the people in the following situations:

1. Sarah has bought a DVD player costing £700 from a local electrical superstore. The DVD player has never worked properly, but the store has refused to replace it or to refund the purchase price to Sarah. She wishes to claim against the store. Advise her as to which court to start the case in and how she should go about this. Also explain to her the way in which the case will be dealt with if the store defends it and there is a court hearing.

2. Thomas has been badly injured at work and alleges that the injuries were the result of his employer's failure to take proper safety precautions. He has been advised that his claim is likely to be worth £200,000. Advise him as to which court or courts could hear his case.

3. Imran wishes to start an action for defamation against a national newspaper. Advise him as to which court he should use and explain to him who tries defamation cases.

6.6 The Woolf reforms

The present system of civil justice is based on the reforms recommended by Lord Woolf in his report *Access to Justice* (1996).

In 1995 Lord Woolf thought that a civil justice system should:

- Be just in the results it delivers
- Be fair in the way it treats litigants
- Offer appropriate procedures at a reasonable cost
- Deal with cases at a reasonable speed
- Be understandable to those who use it
- Provide as much certainty as the nature of particular cases allows
- Be effective, adequately resourced and organised.

The Report found that virtually none of these points was being achieved in the civil courts, and criticised the system for being unequal, expensive, slow, uncertain and complicated. The report contained 303 recommendations. The most important ones proposed:

- Extending small claims up to £3,000
- A fast track for straightforward cases up to £10,000
- A multi-track for cases over £10,000, with capping of costs
- Encouraging the use of alternative dispute resolution
- Giving judges more responsibility for managing cases
- More use of information technology
- Simplifying documents and procedures and having a single set of rules governing proceedings in both the High Court and the County Court
- Shorter timetables for cases to reach court and for lengths of trials.

The proposal to increase the small claims limit to £3,000 was implemented before the full report was issued. Before committing itself to the remainder of the reforms, the Labour Government, which came to power in 1997, commissioned the Middleton Report as a 'second opinion'. This supported most of the Woolf proposals, but suggested that the small claims limit should be raised to £5,000 and the fast track route to £15,000. As a result of the Woolf and Middleton Reports, the civil justice system was radically reformed in April 1999.

6.6.1 The Civil Procedure Rules

From 26 April 1999, new Civil Procedure Rules were brought into effect. These use much simpler language than previous rules. They also changed the vocabulary used in court cases. For example, anyone starting a civil case is now called 'the claimant'; previously the term used in most cases was 'the plaintiff'. The document used to start cases is a claim form, rather than a writ or a summons. The new terms are used in this book, but the old terms still appear in reports of cases decided before April 1999.

Overriding objective

Rule 1.1 of the Civil Procedure Rules states that the overriding objective is to enable the court to deal with cases justly. This means that courts should try to:

- Ensure that the parties in any case are on an equal footing
- Save expense
- Deal with cases in a way which is proportionate to:
  - the amount involved (that is avoid the costs of the case being more than the amount claimed)
  - the importance of the case (for example, is there a major point of law involved?)
  - the complexity of the issues in the case
- Ensure that the case is dealt with quickly and fairly
- Allocate an appropriate share of the court's resources (so smaller claims do not take up more time than they justify).

Judges have more control over proceedings than previously. They can set timetables and make sure that the parties do not drag out a case unnecessarily. Rule 1.4 of the Civil Procedure Rules explains that as well as fixing timetables, 'active case management' by judges includes:

- Identifying the issues at an early stage
- Deciding which issues need investigation and trial
- Encouraging the parties to use alternative dispute resolution if this is appropriate
- Dealing with any procedural steps without the need for the parties to attend court
- Giving directions to ensure that the trial of a case proceeds quickly and efficiently.

6.6.2 Applying the rules in court

Case management has led to the issues in cases being identified more quickly, so that more cases are settling without the need for a trial. Judges are also staying cases so that mediation can be tried. The Centre for Dispute Resolution reported that, in 2000, 27 per cent of the disputes it dealt with were cases which had been stayed by a judge. This compared with 19 percent of cases in 1999 and only 8 per cent in 1998.

The judges are also applying the timetables strictly. This is illustrated by *Vinos v Marks and Spencer plc* (2000). In this case the claimant's solicitors had issued the claim just within the time limit and had told the defendant's insurers that they had done so. However, they were then nine days late in serving that claim on the defendant. The claim was struck out by the court because of this.

◄ Comment

The Woolf reforms have clearly had an effect on the way in which lawyers conduct litigation. There has been a move away from the adversarial attitude to one of greater co-operation. This is encouraged by the pre-action protocols which the parties have to use and which encourage early disclosure of information between the parties. As a result fewer claims are being issued in court. This is shown by the dramatic drop in the number of claims issued in the High Court in 2000 (the first full year under the Woolf reforms). Less than 27,000 claims were issued compared to 72,000 in 1999 and over 100,000 in 1998.

The main complaint by lawyers is that the costs at the start of a case are heavier than before ('front-loading'). If a case settles early these costs still have to be paid.

The other problem is that some County Courts are inefficient and provide a poor service. In September 2001 the results of a survey of solicitors found much dissatisfaction at the service being offered by the County Courts. They complained that courts could not be contacted by telephone and urgent orders often took weeks to obtain. The Central London County Court was especially poor with 96% of solicitors surveyed being dissatisfied with it.

The Property Litigation Association which conducted the survey pointed out that Lord Woolf's reforms were intended to encourage solicitors to run litigation in a cost-effective and efficient way, but that this objective was being frustrated by the courts.

6.7 Appellate courts

These are courts which hear appeals from lower courts. The main appellate courts are the Divisional Courts, the Court of Appeal and the House of Lords.

6.7.1 Divisional Courts

Each division of the High Court has what is called a Divisional Court which has the power to hear appeals from inferior courts and tribunals. For most appeals two or three of the judges from the particular division will sit together to hear the case.

Queen's Bench Divisional Court

The most important of the Divisional Courts is the Queen's Bench Divisional Court. This has two main functions.

1. It hears appeals by way of case stated from criminal cases decided in the Magistrates' Court. This is dealt with more fully in Chapter 10.
2. It has supervisory powers over inferior courts and tribunals and also over the actions and decisions of public bodies and Government ministers. This process is known as 'judicial review' and for this purpose the court has the power to make what are called 'prerogative orders'. These orders are *mandamus*, which is a command to perform a duty; prohibition, which is an order to prevent an inferior court from hearing a case which it has no power to deal with; and *certiorari*, which removes the decision to the Queen's Bench Division so that its legality can be enquired into and the decision quashed if it is found to be invalid. Judicial review and the use of prerogative orders are dealt with more fully in Chapter 16.

The Queen's Bench Divisional Court also hears applications for *habeas corpus* from those who allege that they are being unlawfully detained. This is an important way of protecting the right to liberty.

Chancery Divisional Court

This deals with only a small number of appeals, mainly from decisions made by Tax Commissioners on the payment of tax and appeals from decisions of the County Court in bankruptcy cases.

Family Divisional Court

The main function of this court is to hear appeals from the decisions of the magistrates regarding family matters and orders affecting children.

KEY FACTS

Courts dealing with civil cases	• County Court • High Court
Different tracks for claims	• Small claims • Fast track • Multi-track
Problems of civil cases	• Cost • Delay • Complexity
1999 reforms	• Encourage use of ADR • Simpler forms and language • Increase small claims limit to £5,000 • Fast track for claims between £5,000 and £15,000 • Judges responsible for case management • Strict timetables
Effect of 1999 reforms	• Cases settle earlier • Initial costs are high • Delays are getting shorter • Courts strict on timetables

Figure 6.4 Key fact chart on civil justice

6.7.2 Court of Appeal (Civil Division)

The Court of Appeal was set up by the Judicature Act 1873 and was initially intended to be the final court of appeal. However the position of the House of Lords as the final appellate court was re-instated by the Appellate Jurisdiction Act 1876. Today the Court of Appeal has two divisions, civil and criminal. There are 35 Lords Justices of Appeal and each division is presided over by its own head. The Civil Division is the main appellate court for civil cases and it is headed by the Master of the Rolls.

The Court of Appeal (Civil Division) mainly hears appeals from the following courts:

• All three divisions of the High Court
• The County Court for multi-track cases
• The Immigration Appeal Tribunal
• Some tribunals, especially the Lands Tribunal bunal.

Permission to appeal

Permission to appeal is required in most cases. It can be granted by the lower court where the decision was made or by the Court of Appeal. Permission to appeal will only be granted where the court considers that an appeal would have a real prospect of success or that there was some other compelling reason why the appeal should be heard.

Permission to appeal is not required in cases where the liberty of the individual is in issue; for example in an appeal against a committal to prison for breaking an injunction.

6.7.3 House of Lords

This is the final court of appeal in the English legal system. It hears appeals from the Court of Appeal, the Divisional Courts and, on rare occasions, direct from the High Court under what are called the 'leapfrog' provisions. Appeals are heard by the Lords of Appeal in Ordinary (the Law Lords), usually by a panel of five, but on some occasions by a panel of seven. A panel of seven was used in the case of *Pepper* v *Hart* (1993) which involved the question of whether *Hansard* could be used as an aid to statutory interpretation. (see Chapter 3)

Permission to appeal

On an appeal from the Court of Appeal or the Divisional Courts it is necessary to be given permission to appeal to the House of Lords. Under the Administration of Justice (Appeals) Act 1934 this leave can be given by either the House of Lords or the lower court. It is difficult to get leave to appeal; for example the statistics for 2000 show that out of 195 cases leave to appeal to the House of Lords was given in only 45.

In leapfrog cases from the High Court under the Administration of Justice Act 1969, not only must the House of Lords give permission to appeal, but the trial judge must also grant a certificate of satisfaction. This will be done only if the case involves a point of law of general public importance which *either* involves the interpretation of a statute *or* is one where the trial judge is bound by a previous decision of the Court of Appeal or House of Lords. This would mean that an appeal to the Court of Appeal would be of no effect as it would also be bound by that previous decision. Leapfrog appeals are rare, with permission to appeal being asked for in only two or three cases each year.

However, once over the hurdle of getting leave to appeal, there is quite a high chance that the appeal will be allowed. In 2000 over half the appeals actually heard by the House of Lords were successful. The number of appeals heard by the House of Lords is small; usually about 50 cases per year involving civil law with about three-quarters of these involving a question of statutory interpretation.

6.8 Appeal routes in civil cases

Although the detail on the appellate courts is given in section 6.7, it is probably helpful to have a list of the normal appeal routes from both the County Court and the High Court.

6.8.1 Appeals from the County Court

Since May 2000, the appeal routes from the County Court are as set out in Part 52 of the Civil Procedure Rules. This means that generally:

- for fast track cases dealt with by a District judge the appeal is heard by a Circuit judge;
- for fast track cases dealt with by a Circuit judge the appeal is heard by a High Court judge;
- for final decisions in multi track cases heard in the County Court (whether by a Circuit judge or by a District judge) the right of appeal is to the Court of Appeal.

Appeals from small claims

In October 2000 appeals against decisions in small claims cases became possible. This right of appeal was introduced in order to comply with Article 6 (the right to a fair trial) of the European Convention on Human Rights. The appeal routes are the same as for fast-track cases. This means that the appeal is to the next judge up in the hierarchy, so if the case was tried by a District judge the appeal is to a Circuit judge; if the case was dealt with by a Circuit judge then the appeal is to a High Court judge.

Second appeals

Where the first appeal is heard by a Circuit judge or a High Court judge, then there is a possible further appeal to the Court of Appeal. However, this will only happen in exceptional cases as s55 of the Access to Justice Act 1999 states that:

> no appeal may be made to the Court of Appeal . . . unless the Court of Appeal considers that
>
> (a) the appeal would raise an important point of principle or practice, or
> (b) there is some other compelling reason for the Court of Appeal to hear it.

These appeal routes are shown in Figure 6.5.

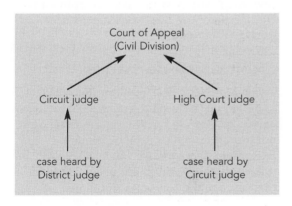

Figure 6.5 Appeal routes from the County Court

6.8.2. Appeals from the High Court

1. From a decision in the High Court the appeal usually goes to the Court of Appeal (Civil Division).

2. In rare cases there may be a 'leapfrog' appeal direct to the House of Lords under the Administration of Justice Act 1969. Such an appeal must involve a point of law of general public importance which is either concerned with the interpretation of a statute or which involves a binding precedent of the Court of Appeal or the House of Lords which the trial judge must follow. In addition the House of Lords has to give permission to appeal.

6.8.3 Further appeals

From a decision of the Court of Appeal there is a further appeal to the House of Lords but only if the House of Lords or Court of Appeal gives permission to appeal. Also note that if a point of European law is involved the case may be referred to the European Court of Justice under Article 234 of the Treaty of Rome. Such a referral can be made by any English court.

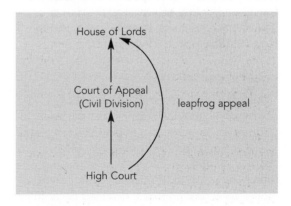

Figure 6.6 Appeal routes from the High Court

6.9 Remedies in civil cases

6.9.1 Damages

The main remedy awarded by the courts is an order that an amount of money be paid to the claimant. This is called an award of damages. The object of an award of damages in cases of breach of contract is to put the claimant in the same position, as far as money can do it, as he would have been had the contract not been broken. There is a similar aim in tort cases of awarding damages to place the claimant in the same position as if the tort had not been committed. Obviously there are many situations where monetary compensation does not really compensate for the loss caused by the breach of contract or the tort. This is particularly true of tort cases where the claimant has suffered serious personal injury and may be left with a permanent disability.

Special damages

This is the term for damages which can be calculated specifically. For example in an action for the tort of negligence following a car crash, it is possible to set out exactly the cost of repairing the car, hiring a replacement while your car is off the road and replacing damaged clothing. It will also be possible to calculate the loss of earnings that has already taken place because of the injuries, though any sick pay must be taken into account.

General damages

These are for matters which cannot be neatly itemised. In personal injury cases this will include an amount for pain and suffering and also for future loss of earnings. It will also include an amount for the cost of nursing or other necessary assistance, or for adapting a home to accommodate a disabled person. In 1994 a 37-year-old woman who was left paralysed by a car crash was awarded £3.4 million to compensate her for her injuries, loss of future earnings and the cost of care as she needed two permanent nurses. Awarding a lump sum like this is not always the most satisfactory way of dealing with monetary compensation. Professor Hazel Genn has carried out research in this area by interviewing 761 victims who received £5,000 or more by way of damages. She found that

at first most accident victims were satisfied with the amount awarded, but that 'this satisfaction drains away over time when the reality of long-term ill-effects and reduced capacity for work bite'. The other problem was the delay over receiving compensation and up to a third of the victims interviewed said they had had to borrow money or run up debts while waiting to receive compensation.

Nominal damages

Where the claimant wins the case but cannot show that there has been actual loss, it is open to the court to award a small amount of money in recognition that the claimant's rights were infringed. This usually happens in actions for torts which are 'actionable per se', that is 'of themselves' or just because they happened. An example is the tort of trespass to land, where the claimant may establish that the defendant has walked across the claimant's field without permission or lawful excuse. This is enough for the court to award nominal damages to the claimant. Of course, if in the process of crossing the field the defendant had damaged a gate then the claimant would also be entitled to specific damages to cover the cost of repairing the gate.

Exemplary damages

These are also called 'punitive damages', and this is exactly what they are – damages which are intended to punish the defendant, not merely compensate the claimant. Exemplary damages are not available for breach of contract and are only awarded in tort cases in the following situations:

- Where they are authorised by statute
- Where there has been oppressive, arbitrary or unconstitutional action by servants of the Government
- Where the defendant intended to make a profit from the tort which would be greater than any compensation due from the tort.

Exemplary damages are very rarely awarded.

6.9.2 Equitable remedies

As already seen in Chapter 2, these are remedies which have been developed by equity and the key factor of such remedies is that they are not given automatically. The court has a discretion in deciding whether or not an equitable remedy should be granted. The major equitable remedies are injunctions, specific performance, rescission and rectification.

Injunctions

Temporary injunctions called interlocutory injunctions can be granted during the course of a case. An interlocutory injunction is usually granted in order to try to preserve the *status quo* between the parties while the case is awaiting a full trial. A final injunction may be granted at the end of a case where the judge is satisfied that damages would not be an adequate remedy.

Injunctions are used in many areas of law, for example they may be used in contract law to stop a threatened breach of contract, in the law of tort to prevent the continuation of a nuisance or restrain an ongoing trespass to land, in family law to control domestic violence, or in administrative law to prevent public authorities from acting unlawfully. Breach of an injunction is a contempt of court and, in extreme cases, a person breaking an injunction can be sent to prison.

Specific performance

This is a remedy that is only used in contract law and it is an order that a contract should be carried out as agreed. It is only granted in exceptional circumstances where the court feels the common law remedy of damages could not adequately compensate the claimant, for example in a contract to purchase land. Specific performance is not ever granted to order someone to carry out personal services such as singing at a

KEY FACTS

Remedy	Effect	Comment
Damages	The defendant is ordered to pay the claimant an amount of money	There are different types of damages: • Special – for specific amounts • General – for pain and suffering • Nominal – small amount where no actual loss has been caused • Exemplary – to punish the defendant
Injunctions	Orders defendant to do or not to do something	Discretionary remedy – court may decide that damages will be sufficient
Specific performance	Orders defendant to complete contract	Discretionary remedy – only used in rare cases
Rescission	Puts parties back in their pre-contractual position	Discretionary remedy
Rectification	Alters document to show parties' real intention	Discretionary remedy

Figure 6.7 Key fact chart on remedies

concert. Nor is it granted for a breach of contract where one of the parties is a minor.

Rescission

Again this remedy is only available in contract cases. The aim of the courts in awarding rescission is to return the parties as far as possible to their pre-contractual position. The main grounds for rescission are a misrepresentation which has induced one party to enter into a contract or a mistake which has a fundamental effect on a contract.

Rectification

This is a court order that a document should be altered to reflect the parties' intention. The court will only grant such an order where it is satisfied that a mistake was made in drawing up the document so that it is not a true version of what the parties agreed.

6.10 Enforcing a judgment

When the court awards damages to the claimant, payment of those damages is due immediately unless the court has ordered payment by instalments or postponed payment for some reason, possibly pending an appeal. One of the main problems in litigation is that if the other party does not pay, it is left to the claimant to take steps to enforce the judgment; the courts will not intervene unless the claimant initiates enforcement proceedings. However the court does have various powers which can be used.

Oral examination

If the other party is an individual it is likely that the claimant will have no knowledge of his financial resources. In order to try to discover what assets the debtor has, the claimant can apply to the court for an order that the judgment debtor be orally examined before the court about his means. This allows both a court official and the applicant to cross-examine the debtor to try to discover if he is working and, if so, who his employers are and whether he owns property or has a bank account or any investments. Once this information is known it is easier to decide the most appropriate way of enforcing the judgment.

Warrant of execution

This is where the claimant applies for an order that the court bailiff seize goods belonging to the debtor and then sell them to raise money to pay the judgment. This is the most common way of trying to enforce a judgment. In 1998 about 600,000 warrants for execution were issued although the number has fallen over the large few years. This figure also illustrates the large number of cases in which the defendant fails to pay the damages awarded.

Attachment of earnings

If the debtor is working in regular employment, then it is possible to have an order made under the Attachment of Earnings Act 1971. This orders the debtor's employer to deduct money from the debtor's wages each week and send that money to the court. The court will decide a figure for the 'protected earnings' of the debtor, and the employer can only deduct from above that figure so that the debtor is left with enough money for essential living expenses.

Garnishee orders

Where the debtor has a bank account or a savings account, or where the debtor is owed money by a third party, the claimant can ask the court to order the other party to pay enough of that money to the court to satisfy the judgment.

Bankruptcy proceedings

If the judgment is for more than £750 and a warrant of execution has already been issued without success, then the claimant may apply for the debtor to be declared bankrupt. If this occurs the debtor's assets are divided among his creditors in proportion to the amount owed to them.

Despite all these methods of enforcement, some judgments will remain unpaid. Indeed the claimant may well have incurred extra court costs in trying to enforce the judgment.

6.10.1 Proposals for improving the enforcement of judgments

In 1999 the Lord Chancellor consulted on possible changes to the way in which judgments were enforced. One suggestion was to distinguish between those who 'can't pay' and those who 'won't pay', but it was accepted that in practice this would be difficult. Instead it was thought that better information about the debtor's circumstances would allow a claimant to make a more realistic decision on whether and how to enforce a judgment.

The main suggestions focus on more efficient ways of:

- Obtaining information about the debtor's circumstances; this could include allowing courts to have access to information about the debtor held by Government departments, such as tax records;
- Providing effective sanctions against debtors who will not co-operate in any way; for example using imprisonment where a debtor refuses to supply any information about his means;
- Giving the court a more active role in enforcement, especially where the claimant requests this.

Further consultations on the matter took place during 2001 but there have not been any major changes yet.

Chapter 7

ALTERNATIVE METHODS OF DISPUTE RESOLUTION

In Chapter 6 we saw that using the courts to resolve disputes can be costly, in terms of both money and time. It can also be traumatic for the individuals involved and may not lead to the most satisfactory outcome for the case. An additional problem is that court proceedings are usually open to the public and the press, so there is nothing to stop the details of the case being published in local or national newspapers. It is not surprising, therefore, that more and more people and businesses are seeking other methods of resolving their disputes. Alternative methods are referred to as 'ADR', which stands for 'Alternative Dispute Resolution', and include any method of resolving a dispute without resorting to using the courts. There are many different methods which can be used, ranging from very informal negotiations between the parties, to a comparatively formal commercial arbitration hearing.

Encouraging ADR

In the 1990s there were many moves to encourage the use of ADR, for example the Woolf Report included more use of ADR as one of its recommendations. As a result to 1999 Civil Procedure Rules allow judges to 'stay' court proceedings, that is stop the proceedings temporarily, so that the parties can try mediation or other ADR methods.

In 1996 a two year pilot scheme for court-based mediation at the Central London County Court was set up. The scheme was aimed at claims for amounts over £3,000 and parties who agreed to take part were offered a three hour mediation session at a cost of £25. If the dispute could not be resolved within the time, then it was referred to court for a court hearing in the normal way. However, the response to this scheme was disappointing. Professor Hazel Genn found that out of 4,500 cases in which mediation was offered, it was only accepted in 160 cases (about 5 per cent). Of these two out of three settled the case at the mediation session.

Divorce cases

Pilot schemes on the use of mediation in divorce cases were started in 1997. Parties were offered mediation sessions aimed at resolving any disputes about maintenance, property and especially arrangements for the care of any children. These mediation sessions were voluntary and intended to be a cheaper and more amicable way of resolving all the differences between husband and wife than fighting the issues in court. Many solicitors involved in such sessions felt that they were useful. However, the Divorce Reform Act 1996 which introduced the idea is not being brought into effect, so mediation in divorce cases will remain voluntary.

Employment cases

This is an area of law where alternative dispute resolution has long been used in the shape of ACAS (Advisory Conciliation and Arbitration Service). When any claim is filed at an employment tribunal, a copy of that claim is sent to ACAS who will then contact the two parties involved and offer to attempt to resolve the dispute without the need for the matter to go to a tribunal. ACAS has specially trained conciliation officers who have a great deal of experience of employment disputes. The success of this service can be seen from the fact that over half of all claims filed are settled in this way. However, there is criticism that the amount paid in such settlements is less than would have been awarded by a tribunal. This suggests that employees are at a disadvantage and feel under pressure to settle.

Funding of cases

Under the Access to Justice Act 1999 there are changes to the way that public funding of cases is made, including new ways of assessing whether a litigant should be funded. One of the factors which will be considered is whether another method, other than taking a court cases, is a more suitable way of dealing with the dispute. If this is so, then help with funding will be not be available. This is likely to encourage more use of alternative methods of dispute resolution.

So it can be seen that there is an increased awareness of the use of alternative dispute resolution in all sorts of disputes. However, as pointed out in the opening paragraph of this chapter, ADR includes any method of resolving a dispute, other than 'going to court' and it is important to realise that there is a wide variety of methods available. The main ones are negotiation, mediation, conciliation and arbitration and a brief summary of these is given in Figure 7.1.

Negotiation	Parties themselves
Mediation	Parties with help of neutral third party
Conciliation	Parties with help of neutral third party who plays an active role in suggesting a solution
Arbitration	Parties agree to let third party make a binding decision
Litigation	Parties go to court and a judge decides the case

Figure 7.1 Methods of dispute resolution

7.1 Negotiation

Anyone who has a dispute with another person can always try to resolve it by negotiating directly with them. This has the advantage of being completely private, and is also the quickest and cheapest method of settling a dispute. If the parties cannot come to an agreement, they may decide to take the step of instructing solicitors, and those solicitors will usually try to negotiate a settlement. In fact, even when court proceedings have been commenced, the lawyers for the parties will often continue to negotiate on behalf of their clients, and this is reflected in the high number of cases which are settled out of court. Once lawyers are involved, there will be a cost element – clearly, the longer negotiations go on, the higher the costs will be. One of the worrying aspects is the number of cases that drag on for years, only to end in an agreed settlement literally 'at the door of the court' on the morning that the trial is due to start. It is this situation that other alternative dispute resolution methods and, in particular, the new Civil Procedure Rules are aimed at avoiding.

7.2 Mediation

This where a neutral mediator helps the parties to reach a compromise solution. The role of a mediator is to consult with each party and see how much common ground there is between them. He/she will explore the position with each party, looking at their needs and carrying offers to and fro, while keeping confidentiality. A mediator will not usually tell the parties his/her own views of the merits of the dispute; it is part of the job to act as a 'facilitator', so that an agreement is reached by the parties. However, a mediator can be asked for an opinion of the merits, and in this case the mediation becomes more of an evaluation exercise, which again aims at ending the dispute.

Are you sure this is a form of Alternative Dispute Resolution?

Mediation is only suitable if there is some hope that the parties can co-operate. Companies who are used to negotiating contracts with each other are most likely to benefit from this approach. Mediation can also take different forms, and the parties will choose the exact method they want. The important point in mediation is that the parties are in control: they make the decisions.

7.2.1 Formalised settlement conference

This is a more formal method of approaching mediation. It involves a 'mini-trial' where each side presents its case to a panel composed of a decision-making executive from each party, and a neutral party. Once all the submissions have been made, the executives, with the help of the neutral advisor, will evaluate the two sides' positions and try to come to an agreement. If the executives, cannot agree, the neutral advisor, will act as a mediator between

them. Even if the whole matter is not resolved, this type of procedure may be able to narrow down the issues so that if the case does go to court, it will not take so long.

An advantage of mediation and mini-trials is that the decision need not be a strictly legal one sticking to the letter of the law. It is more likely to be based on commercial commonsense and compromise. The method will also make it easier for companies to continue to do business with each other in the future, and it may include agreements about the conduct of future business between the parties. This is something that cannot happen if the court gives judgment, as the court is only concerned with the present dispute. It avoids the adversarial conflict of the court room and the winner/loser result of court proceedings – it has been said that with mediation, everyone wins.

7.2.2 Mediation services

There are a growing number of commercial mediation services. One of the main ones is the Centre for Dispute Resolution which was set up in London in 1991. It has many important companies as members including almost all of the big London law firms. Businesses say that using the Centre to resolve disputes has saved several thousands of pounds in court costs. The typical cost of a mediator is about £1,000 to £1,500. This compares with potential litigation costs which are frequently over £100,000 and sometimes may even come to more than one million pounds, especially in major commercial cases.

The main disadvantage of using mediation services is that there is no guarantee the matter will be resolved, and it will then be necessary to go to court after the failed attempt at mediation. In such situations there is additional cost and delay through trying mediation. However the evidence is that a high number of cases will be resolved;

the Centre for Dispute Resolution claims that over 80 per cent of cases in which it is asked to act are settled. There is also the possibility that the issues may at least have been clarified, and so any court hearing will be shorter than if mediation had not been attempted.

There are also mediation services aimed at resolving smaller disputes, for example those between neighbours. An example of such a service is the West Kent Independent Mediation Service. This offers a free service that will try to help resolve disagreements between neighbours arising from such matters as noise, car-parking, dogs or boundary fence disputes. The Service is run by trained volunteers who will not take sides or make judgements on the rights and wrongs of an issue. They will usually visit the party who has made the complaint to hear their side of the matter, then, if that party agrees, ask to visit the other person and get their point of view. Finally, if both parties are willing, the mediator arranges a meeting between them in a neutral place. The parties are in control and can withdraw from the mediation process at any time.

The latest idea is Online Dispute Resolution. There are an increasing number of websites offering this, e.g. *www.theclaimroom.com* and *www.mediate.com/odr*

◀ Comment

Research into mediation has found some interesting facts showing that it has advantages and disadvantages. On the positive side Hazel Genn noted that, even if the actual mediation session did not resolve the dispute, the parties were more likely to settle the case without going to court than in non-mediated cases. However, her research also revealed disadvantages. In the Central London County Court mediation scheme, she found that the amounts paid in mediated settlements were lower than the amounts agreed in other settlements and considerably lower than amounts awarded by the courts. Given the fact that in the majority of cases the parties paid their own legal costs, mediation did not seem to offer any financial gain.

Another negative point was that Genn felt mediations were controlled by the mediators. This was despite the fact that mediators in the mediations observed all stated that the parties were in control. Successful mediation requires a skilled mediator with 'natural talent, honed skills and accumulated experience'. If these qualities are not present mediation can become a bullying exercise in which the weaker party may be forced into a settlement. This was recognised by one person who said:

'Leaning on people is the only way that you will get a settlement. If you lean on two halves of a see-saw it is usually the weaker half that will break and that is where you should apply your effort.'

However, overall Genn reached the conclusion that voluntary mediation can promote early settlement and can lead to a situation in which the sense of grievance is reduced and an acceptable settlement reached.

7.3 Conciliation

This has similarities to mediation in that a neutral third party helps to resolve the dispute, but the main difference is that the conciliator will usually play a more active role. He will be expected to suggest grounds for compromise, and the possible basis for a settlement. In industrial disputes ACAS can give an impartial opinion on the legal position. As with mediation, conciliation does not necessarily lead to a resolution and it may be necessary to continue with a court action.

7.4 Arbitration

The word 'arbitration' is used to cover two quite different processes. The first is where the courts use a more informal procedure to hear cases; this is the way proceedings in the Commercial Court of the Queen's Bench Division are described. The second meaning of the word 'arbitration' is where the parties agree to submit their claims to private arbitration; this is the type of arbitration that is relevant to alternative dispute resolution, as it is another way of resolving a dispute without the need for a court case.

Private arbitration is now governed by the Arbitration Act 1996 and section one of that Act sets out the principles behind it. This says that:

> '(a) the object of arbitration is to obtain the fair resolution of disputes by an impartial tribunal without unnecessary delay or expense;
> (b) the parties should be free to agree how their disputes are resolved, subject only to such safeguards as are necessary in the public interest.'

So arbitration is the voluntary submission by the parties, of their dispute, to the judgment of some person other than a judge. Such an agreement will usually be in writing, and indeed the Arbitration Act 1996 applies only to written arbitration agreements. The precise way in which the arbitration is carried out is left almost entirely to the parties' agreement.

7.4.1 The agreement to arbitrate

The agreement to go to arbitration can be made by the parties at any time. It can be before a dispute arises or when the dispute becomes apparent. Many commercial contracts include what is called a *Scott* v *Avery* clause, which is a clause where the parties in their original contract agree that in the event of a dispute arising between them, they will have that dispute settled by arbitration. Figure 7.2 shows a *Scott* v *Avery* clause in the author's contract for writing this book.

Where there is an arbitration agreement in a contract, the Arbitration Act 1996 states that the court will normally refuse to deal with any dispute; the matter must go to arbitration as agreed by the parties. The rules, however, are different for consumer claims where the dispute is for an amount which can be dealt with in the small claims court. In such circumstances the consumer may choose whether to abide by the agreement to go to private arbitration, or whether to insist that the case be heard in the Small Claims Court.

An agreement to go to arbitration can also be made after the dispute arises. Arbitration is becoming increasingly popular in commercial cases.

> **Arbitration**
> 24. If any difference shall arise between the PROPRIETOR and the PUBLISHERS touching the meaning of this Agreement or the rights and liabilities of the parties hereto, the same shall in the first instance be referred to the informal Disputes Settlement Scheme of the Publishers' Association, and failing agreed submission by both parties to such Scheme shall be referred to the arbitration of two persons (one to be named by each party) or their mutually agreed umpire in accordance with the provisions of the Arbitration Act 1996, or any amending or substituted statute for the time being in force.

Figure 7.2 Arbitration clause from author's contract

7.4.2 The arbitrator

Section 15 of the Arbitration Act 1996 states that the parties are free to agree on the number of arbitrators, so that a panel of two or three may be used or there may be a sole arbitrator. If the parties cannot agree on a number then the Act provides that only one arbitrator should be appointed. The Act also says that the parties are free to agree on the procedure for appointing an arbitrator. In fact most agreements to go to arbitration will either name an arbitrator or provide a method of choosing one, and in commercial contracts it is often provided that the president of the appropriate trade organisation will appoint the arbitrator. There is also the Institute of Arbitrators which provides trained arbitrators for major disputes. In many cases the arbitrator will be someone who has expertise in the particular field involved in the dispute, but if the dispute involves a point of law the parties may decide to appoint a lawyer. If there is no agreement on who or how to appoint, then, as a last resort, the court can be asked to appoint an appropriate arbitrator.

7.4.3 The arbitration hearing

The actual procedure is left to the agreement of the parties in each case, so that there are many forms of hearing. In some cases the parties may opt for a 'paper' arbitration, where the two sides put all the points they wish to raise into writing and submit this, together with any relevant documents, to the arbitrator. He will then read all the documents, and make his decision. Alternatively the parties may send all these documents to the arbitrator, but before he makes his decision both parties will attend a hearing at which they make oral submissions to the arbitrator to support their case. Where necessary witnesses can be called to give evidence. If witnesses are asked to give evidence orally then this will not normally be given on oath, i.e. the person will not have to swear to tell the truth. However, if the parties wish, then the witness can be asked to give evidence on oath and the whole procedure will be very formal. If witnesses are called to give evidence, the Arbitration Act 1996 allows for the use of court procedures to ensure the attendance of those witnesses.

The date, time and place of the arbitration hearing are all matters for the parties to decide in consultation with the arbitrator. This gives a great degree of flexibility to the proceedings; the parties can chose what is most convenient for all the people concerned.

7.4.4 The award

The decision made by the arbitrator is called an award and is binding on the parties. It can even be enforced through the courts if necessary. The decision is usually final, though it can be challenged in the courts on the grounds of serious irregularity in the proceedings or on a point of law (s 68 Arbitration Act 1996).

7.4.5 Advantages and disadvantages of arbitration

There are several advantages which largely arise from the fact that the parties have the freedom to make their own arbitration agreement, and decide exactly how formal or informal they wish it to be. The main advantages are:

- The parties may chose their own arbitrator, and can therefore decide whether the matter is best dealt with by a technical expert or by a lawyer or by a professional arbitrator
- If there is a question of quality this can be decided by an expert in the particular field, saving the expense of calling expert witnesses and the time that would be used in explaining all the technicalities to a judge.

- The hearing time and place can be arranged to suit parties
- The actual procedure used is flexible and the parties can choose that which is most suited to the situation; this will usually result in a more informal and relaxed hearing than in court
- The matter is dealt with in private and there will be no publicity
- The dispute will be resolved more quickly than through a court hearing
- Arbitration proceedings are usually much cheaper than going to court
- The award is normally final and can be enforced through the courts

However, there are some disadvantages of arbitration, especially where the parties are not on an equal footing as regards their ability to present their case. This is because legal aid is not available for arbitration and this may disadvantage an individual in a case against a business; if the case had gone to court, a person on a low income would have qualified for legal aid and so had the benefit of a lawyer to present their case. The other main disadvantages are that:

- An unexpected legal point may arise in the case which is not suitable for decision by a non-lawyer arbitrator
- If a professional arbitrator is used, his fees may be expensive
- It will also be expensive if the parties opt for a formal hearing, with witnesses giving evidence and lawyers representing both sides
- The rights of appeal are limited
- The delays for commercial and international arbitration may be nearly as great as those in the courts if a professional arbitrator and lawyers are used

This problem of delay and expense has meant that arbitration has, to some extent, lost its popularity with companies as a method of dispute resolution. More and more businesses are turning to the alternatives offered by centres such as the Centre for Dispute Resolution or, in the case of international disputes, are choosing to have the matter resolved in another country,

D Complaints
3. Disputes arising out of, or in connection with, this contract which cannot be amicably settled may (if you so wish) be referred to arbitration under a special scheme devised by arrangement with the Association of British Travel Agents (ABTA) but administered independently by the Chartered Institute of Arbitrators. The scheme provides for a simple and inexpensive method of Arbitration on documents alone, with restricted liability on you in respect of costs. The scheme does not apply to claims greater than £1,500 per person or £7,500 per booking form or to claims which are solely or mainly in respect of physical injury or illness or the consequences of such injury or illness. If you elect to use the scheme, written notice requesting arbitration must be made within 9 months after the scheduled date of return from holiday.

Figure 7.3 Optional arbitration clause in a consumer contract

One of the problems was that the law on arbitration had become complex and the Arbitration Act 1996 is an attempt to improve the process. In general it can be said that certain types of dispute are suitable for arbitration. This especially includes commercial disagreements between two businesses where the parties have little hope of finding sufficient common ground to make mediation a realistic prospect, and provided there is no major point of law involved.

Arbitration in consumer disputes

Arbitration is also offered for consumer disputes with contracts, such as those for package holidays, including the possibility of resolving a dispute by arbitration, but not as a binding agreement to go to arbitration. This optional use of arbitration in consumer disputes is a welcome move away from the previous practice of including an arbitration clause in consumer contracts so that the consumer had no choice. In other words if the consumer wanted to go ahead with the main contract, such as booking a package holiday, then they had to accept that any dispute would be dealt with by arbitration, whether they really wanted this or not. Of course, in most cases, the consumer would probably be unaware of the clause or its implications until they tried to take legal action against the company.

7.5 Tribunals

Tribunals operate alongside the court system and have become an important and integral part of the legal system. Most tribunals have been created in the second half of the twentieth century, with the development of the welfare state, in order to give people a method of enforcing their entitlement to certain social rights. However, unlike alternative dispute resolution where the parties decide not to use the courts, the parties in tribunal cases cannot go to court to resolve their dispute. The tribunal must be used instead of court proceedings.

7.5.1 Administrative tribunals

These are tribunals which have been created by statute to enforce rights which have been granted through social and welfare legislation. There are many different rights, such as: the right to a mobility allowance for those who are too disabled to walk more than a very short distance; the right to a payment if one is made redundant from work; the right not to be discriminated against because of one's sex or race and the right of immigrants to have a claim for political asylum heard. As tribunals have been set up as the welfare state has developed, new developments will often result in the creation of a new tribunal. For example following the Child Support Act 1993, the Child Support Appeals Tribunal was created. There are now 70 different types of tribunal, and many of these will have panels sitting at several places around the country so that there are over 2,000 tribunals in total.

The main types of tribunal are:

- Social security tribunals which deal with appeals against the refusal of various benefit rights
- Rent tribunals which are involved with fixing fair rents
- Immigration tribunals to hear appeals on the right of immigrants to enter and stay in this country
- The Mental Health Review Tribunal which decides if a mental patient should continue to be detained in hospital
- Employment tribunals which deal with disputes arising from employment.

7.5.2 Employment tribunals

These were originally called industrial tribunals. They were first set up in 1964 under the Industrial Training Act 1964 with only a limited role, but they have become increasingly important. The role of employment tribunals covers all aspects of work-related disputes. This includes key matters of disputed deductions from wages, unfair dismissal, redundancy and discrimination on the grounds of sex, race or disability.

7.5.3 Composition and procedure

Since the different tribunals have been set up at different times over a number of years, they do not all operate in the same way. In fact Lord Woolf in the Council on Tribunals Annual Report for 1991–92 said:

'The development of the tribunal system has been quite haphazard. It has been left very much to the inclination of particular departments of government as to whether or not a tribunal system should be created, and if so, what should be the form of that system.'

However, the majority of tribunals sit with a panel of three: a legally-qualified chairman and two lay members who have expertise in the particular field of the tribunal. For example the lay members of an industrial injuries tribunal would be medically qualified, while those on a tribunal hearing an unfair dismissal claim would be representatives of organisations for employers and employees respectively.

The procedure for each type of tribunal also tends to vary, but there are common elements in that the system is designed to encourage individuals to bring their own cases and not use lawyers. Generally there are no formal rules of evidence and procedure but the rules of natural justice apply. This means that both parties must be given an equal chance to state their side. Employment tribunals are the most formal and their procedure is similar to that of a court.

As the use of lawyers is not encouraged at tribunals, legal funding is not available for most tribunal hearings. Exceptions to this include the Mental Health Review Tribunal, the Protection of Children Tribunal, the Lands Tribunal and the Employment Appeal Tribunal, where those who come within the legal aid criteria can obtain help.

7.5.4 The Leggatt Report

In 2001 a report about the workings of tribunals was prepared under the chairmanship of Sir Andrew Leggatt. This Report on tribunals was the first since the Franks inquiry in 1957.

Some of the main recommendations included:

- The administration of tribunals should become the responsibility of the Lord Chancellor.
- There should be a single system which is divided by subject matter into Divisions; this will prevent the current problem of the isolation of individual tribunals which leads to duplication of effort and each tribunal inventing its own processes and standards.
- There should also be a single route of appeal with a right of appeal by permission on a point of law or on the basis that the decision of the tribunal was unlawful; the appeal route should be from first-tier tribunals to second-tier tribunals and from these to the Court of Appeal.

It was also recommended that there should be a Tribunals Board directing the system whose functions should include:

- advising the Lord Chancellor's Department on qualifications for chairmen
- overseeing the appointment of members
- co-ordinating their training
- investigating complaints against them and
- recommending changes to the rules of procedure governing all Divisions.

7.5.5 Control of tribunals

Since tribunals work outside the court system and are so varied in their procedures, it is important that there is some supervisory body. This was emphasised following what is called the Crichel Down Affair in which civil servants did not follow the correct procedure for offering land requisitioned during the Second World War for military purposes back to the family of the former owner. This matter was investigated by the Franks Committee which reported in 1957 and made several recommendations about decisions by civil servants and tribunals. One recommendation was that there should be an 'ombudsman' appointed to deal with complaints of maladministration, and eventually the post of Parliamentary Ombudsman was set up on 1967. The other recommendations more directly concerned with tribunals were that all tribunal chairmen should be legally qualified, and that reasons should be given for decisions. The Franks Committee also recommended that a

Council on Tribunals should be set up to oversee the whole vast array of tribunals.

Following this the Tribunals and Inquiries Act 1958 set up the Council on Tribunals to supervise and keep under review the working of tribunals. The Council has up to 15 members who visit tribunals and observe their work at first hand. It also receives complaints about tribunals and issues an annual report. The main problem is that the Council has very little power; it can only make recommendations.

The Leggatt Report recommended that the Council on Tribunals should be given an increased role with their primary duty being the championing of users' causes. The members of the Council should include some people with the experience and perspective of users.

Control by the courts

This can occur in two ways. First there is an appeal system against the decisions of some tribunals. In particular there is a right of appeal from employment tribunals to the Employment Appeals Tribunal, which is headed by a High Court judge, and from there to the Court of Appeal. Similarly, in immigration cases, there is the Immigration Appeal Tribunal which hears appeals from decisions of Immigration Adjudicators; since 1993 there has been the right to appeal from the Immigration Appeal Tribunal to the Court of Appeal on a point of law. There is also a Social Security Appeals Tribunal to hear appeals in this area, with the possibility of a further appeal to the Social Security Commissioners – again an appeal can go from here to the Court of Appeal if there is a point of law at issue.

A formal route of appeal is in itself a safeguard as well as allowing the Court of Appeal to develop the law on the basis of judicial precedent, so that the law becomes more stable and predictable.

Secondly, the Queen's Bench Divisional Court has the power to hear applications for judicial review against tribunal decisions, and can use its prerogative powers to quash a decision. This could occur, for example, where there has been a breach of natural justice.

7.5.6 Advantages and disadvantages of tribunals

Tribunals were set up to prevent the overloading of the courts with the extra cases that social and welfare rights claims generate. In 1979 the Benson Commission on legal services pointed out the importance of the role of tribunals in this respect, as they heard six times the number of cases dealt with by the courts. The amount of work can be seen by the number of appeals that are heard: in 1995 there were over 10,000 appeals to the Social Security Commissioners and just under 10,000 to the Immigration Appeal Tribunal.

For the applicant in tribunal cases, the advantages are that such cases are dealt with more cheaply, more quickly, and more informally than they would be if there was a court hearing. There is also the fact that the panel is composed of a mix of legal expertise and lay expertise in the field concerned. However, all these claims need to be evaluated.

Cost-effectiveness

As applicants are encouraged to represent themselves and not use lawyers, it is true to say that tribunal hearings do not normally involve the costs associated with court hearings. It is also rare for an order for costs to be made by a tribunal, so that an applicant need not fear a large bill if they lose the case. However, applicants who are not represented have a lower chance of winning their case than those who are represented, so the saving on cost of a lawyer may not be that

---

KEY FACTS

Types of tribunal	• Social security tribunals • Rent tribunals • Mental Health Review Tribunal • Employment tribunals
Panel hearing case	• Mostly panel of three – chairman + two lay members with knowledge of topic • Some tribunals have only one adjudicator
Method of hearing	• Informal and in private BUT employment tribunals are more formal and open to public

Legal funding availability	• ONLY for
	  – Mental Health Review Tribunal
	  – Employment Appeals Tribunal

Appeals	• Employment tribunals appeal to Employment Appeals Tribunal, then to Court of Appeal • Social security tribunals appeal to Social Security Appeals Tribunal, then to Social Security Commissioners, then to Court of Appeal
Control of tribunals	• The courts – appeal system to put right incorrect decisions – judicial review proceedings • The Council of Tribunals – reports BUT has little power

Figure 7.4 *Key fact chart on tribunals*

cost-effective. Statistics in the early 1990s showed that the success rate for those with lawyers was 49 per cent, while for those without lawyers it was 28 per cent.

Speedy hearings

This was one of the advantages of tribunal hearings, but it is no longer true to say that cases will be dealt with speedily. Reports by the Council on Tribunals have highlighted delays, due to the vast volume of work that tribunals now face, together with the fact that the lay members only sit part-time. This creates a particular problem if the case is complex and likely to last several days. An extreme example of this was seen in the case of Allison Halford who brought proceedings for sex discrimination against the Police Authorities. The case lasted 39 days, which

were spread over a period of several months, and it was more than two years from the date of her original application to the conclusion of the case. Even then the case only finished because the parties settled the matter; if the case had continued in front of the tribunal with its part-time hearings it could have taken several months more to come to a conclusion.

However, this is nothing compared with the case of *Darnell v United Kingdom* (1993) in which a doctor who was dismissed in 1984 started proceedings for unfair dismissal. The final decision in those proceedings was made in 1993 by the Employment Appeal Tribunal. In the meantime the doctor had complained to the European Court of Human Rights over the delay and this complaint was upheld.

Simple procedure

It is true that there is a more informal hearing than in court; in addition, most cases are heard in private. These comments do not apply to industrial tribunals which are open to the public and tend to be more formal. The procedure is also relatively flexible and the tribunals are not bound by strict rules of evidence. However, for individuals presenting their own cases the venue is unfamiliar and the procedure can be confusing. Where applicants are not represented, the chairman is expected to take an inquisitorial role and help to establish the points that the applicant wishes to make. This is not always achieved, as shown by research into social security cases carried out by Baldwin. Wikeley and Young in their study *Judging Social Security*, published in 1992. They found that out of the hearings they attended, the chairman's handling of the case could be described as good or excellent in 57 per cent of cases and adequate in a further quarter of cases. However, in one-sixth of cases the chairman's conduct was open to serious criticism.

This type of criticism has also been levelled at employment tribunals. In these cases an applicant in person may often find themselves opposed by a lawyer representing the employer, and so it is even more important that the proceedings should be kept simple and that the chairman should act inquisitorially to redress the balance.

The problem of the unrepresented applicant comes about because public funding is not available for most tribunals, which may put an applicant at a disadvantage if the other side (often an employer or Government department) uses a lawyer. Proposed changes to the legal aid system state that priority should be given to social welfare cases such as cases about people's basic entitlements. This includes entitlement to correct social security benefits, so it may be that public funding will eventually be available in some tribunals.

Other problems

Other problems can arise because a few tribunals still do not have to give reasons for their decisions. Nor do some tribunals follow a system of precedent, which makes it difficult to predict the outcome of cases (these criticisms do not apply to employment tribunals). In addition, there is no right of appeal from some tribunals (although an application for judicial review may be made) – this problem has lessened as a final appeal on a point of law has been brought in for both the social security cases, and immigration cases.

Impartiality

There used to be a criticism that the chairmen of tribunals were not sufficiently impartial, as they were in many cases appointed by the Minister of the Government department against whom the case was being brought. This problem was highlighted by the Franks Committee who recommended that all appointments should be impartial. Now the system is that the Independent Tribunal Service recommends potential chairmen to the Lord Chancellor. The Lord Chancellor then decides which of these people will be placed on a panel of chairmen for tribunal hearings.

7.5.7 Domestic tribunals

These are effectively 'in-house' tribunals set up by private bodies, usually for their own internal disciplinary control. They must keep to the rules of natural justice and their decisions are subject to judicial review. In addition, for many professional disciplinary tribunals there is an appeal route to the Judicial Committee of the Privy Council, in cases where the tribunal has decided to strike off a member from the professional register. For example this applies to decisions of the disciplinary committee of the General Medical Council, and also to other medical disciplinary tribunals.

Chapter 8

CRIME AND POLICE INVESTIGATIONS

Criminal cases are frequently headline news in the papers; society as a whole is concerned about the crime rate. The statistics for recorded crime show that there has been a massive increase over the last 50 years: in 1950 there were only half a million recorded crimes, but by the 1990s the figure had reached five million. For each of the years 1993 to 1998 the number of recorded crimes fell. However, in 1998–99 the number showed an increase from 4.5 million to a total of 5.4 million crimes. This increase was because of a new way of recording crime which used the number of victims whereas before this might have been classified as one incident.

Within the figures for any one year, there will be a variation in different crimes, with some showing large increases, others small increases or even a decrease. These variations can be caused by police policy in targeting certain types of crime. Full statistics for recorded crime are published by the Home Office each year, Figure 8.1 shows the change in notifiable offences between 1999–2000 and 2000–01.

Even these crime figures are not believed to give a true picture of the amount of criminal activity in England and Wales. It is thought that a large amount of crime is not recorded – this is shown by surveys such as the British Crime Survey which is conducted every two years. The newspaper article below shows the difference in the findings of the British Crime Survey with the recorded crime figures.

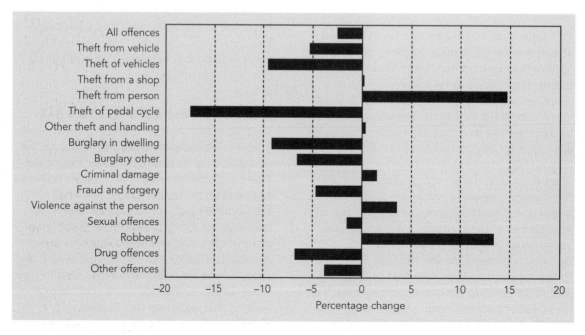

Figure 8.1 Underlying trend in notifiable offences: twelve months ending March 2001 compared to previous twelve months

Source: Notifiable Offences: Home Office Statistical Bulletin 12/01.

Detection is the deterrent

Recorded crime fell for the fifth consecutive year in yesterday's annual crime statistics. More convincingly, the authoritative British Crime Survey (BCS) showed its first ever overall drop in crime. Britain is enjoying only the second sustained drop in crime since the second world war. Recorded crime has never dropped for five successive years since criminal statistics began in 1857. This second fall coincides with the biggest increase in imprisonment ever – a 50 per cent increase in just five years. Surely, surely the two trends are connected?

Obtuse though it may seem, the answer is no. The real deterrence to criminal activity is not the severity of the penalty but the risk of being caught.

Even the experts remain puzzled by some of the trends. The drop in burglary and car crime is easy enough: increased use of security devices. A welcome reduction in fear of crime is a genuine improvement in the quality of life. But not even the Home Office research director is sure why police records show a big increase in wounding but the BCS a big drop.

It puts all statistics in perspective. Remember half of all crime is not reported to the police and only half of what is reported is recorded. Next year recorded crime will increase – they're collecting more categories of crime.

Adapted from a leading article in *The Guardian*. 14 October 1998

Activity

Look at Figure 8.1 for the changes in notifiable offences for the twelve months to March 2001

QUESTIONS

❶ What type of crime shows the biggest increase in this period?
❷ What type of crime has decreased most?
❸ What other trends are apparent from the graph?

Read the article 'Detection is the deterrent'.

QUESTIONS

❹ What difficulties are there in the accuracy of crime statistics?
❺ What is most likely to cause crime rates to drop?

Even with the variation in the rates shown by the different surveys, it is still clear that the crime rates are worryingly high. It is obviously necessary to have an authority who has sufficient power to investigate possible crimes by being able to stop suspects, search them, arrest people and interview them about suspected criminal activity. In this country the police are given this authority. However, while it is necessary that the police should have appropriate power to investigate crimes, it is also necessary to keep a balance between protecting individual liberty by preventing people from being unnecessarily harassed and/or detained, and giving the police adequate powers to prevent or detect crime.

During the 1970s and 1980s there were several serious miscarriages of justice in individual cases. Many of these miscarriages stemmed from questionable police procedures and as a result Parliament has tried to regulate this area of the law. The main police powers are set out in the Police and Criminal Evidence Act 1984 (PACE), with some additions and amendments made by the Criminal Justice and Public Order Act 1994. PACE also provides for codes of practice giving extra detail on the procedures for searching, detaining, questioning and identifying suspects, which are issued by the Home Secretary.

8.1 Legislative history

8.1.1 Royal Commission on Criminal Procedure

The Royal Commission on Criminal Procedure (the Phillips Commission) was set up in 1978 as a result of concern over police procedures. One of the main concerns was the over-use (or abuse) of what used to be called the 'sus' law under which police officers could stop people if they felt there was anything suspicious. This usually meant young men, and particularly members of ethnic minorities, were likely to be stopped, often for no real cause.

The Royal Commission found that the law on police powers that existed before 1984 was piecemeal and haphazard. There were provisions in the common law, local bylaws and over 70 different Acts of Parliament giving the right to stop, search or arrest in a variety of different circumstances. This obviously made the law confusing, both for suspects and the police. The Commission also stressed the need to find a balance between 'the interests of the community in bringing offenders to justice and the rights and liberties of persons suspected or accused of crime'. The findings of this Commission led to Parliament enacting the Police and Criminal Evidence Act 1984. This Act tried to both rationalise and modernise the law on many aspects of police

procedure. Some of the most significant changes were in the requirement that police should keep records of such matters as stops and searches, and custody records relating to those in police detention and that the police should tape-record the questioning of suspects.

8.1.2 Miscarriages of justice

When the miscarriages of justice of the 1970s and 1980s came to light, these placed doubt on police methods and interviewing techniques. However, most of the original investigations involved had been prior to the implementation of the Police and Criminal Evidence Act 1984. They also cast doubt on some of the methods used in obtaining scientific evidence. In some cases, miscarriages had arisen where the prosecution had evidence which would have helped establish the defendant's innocence, but had not disclosed that evidence to the defence.

Four of the cases involved separate allegations of terrorist activities on behalf of the IRA. These were the Guildford Four, the Birmingham Six, the Maguires and Judith Ward. The Guildford Four were convicted in 1975 of bombing a pub in Guildford and the evidence against them consisted almost entirely of confessions which were supposed to have been made to police during interviews. The original police evidence claimed that police officers had made a contemporaneous handwritten note of what was said during the interview with Armstrong, one of the four accused. Eventually a set of typed police notes with amendments, both typed and written, and rearrangement of material was discovered. This cast considerable doubt on the police version of the interview and, when the case was finally referred back to the Criminal Division of the Court of Appeal in 1989, the Court quashed the convictions.

In the Birmingham Six case, the accused claimed that they had been beaten up by the police and forced into making untrue confessions and, as with the Guildford Four case, later evidence cast doubt on police notes and the credibility of the police evidence. Later evidence also supported the men's claim that they had been beaten up by the police while in custody, being questioned about the bomb attack. There was also a problem with scientific evidence as to whether the men had handled nitroglycerine (an explosive substance). Scientific knowledge showed that such tests could be faulty and give a positive reading from quite innocent substances such as paint, or even from the washing-up liquid used to clean the dishes in which the samples were then tested. When it was first discovered that the men had tested 'positive' this had been put down to them touching adhesive tape. However, Dr Skuse, a forensic scientist, said 'categorically' in evidence that the only possible explanation of the 'positive' tests was that they had been handling explosives. Their convictions were finally quashed by the Court of Appeal.

In the case of the Tottenham Three, convictions for murder of a police officer during a riot at Broadwater Farm, Tottenham in 1985, were quashed on the grounds that police notes of an interview with one of them (Silcott) had been tampered with, prior to the evidence being given at the trial, and that another defendant (Braithwaite) had been wrongly denied access to legal advice during police interviews. Another fact was that the third defendant, Raghip, was of low intelligence. Prior to an earlier appeal the defence had obtained new evidence that the effect of this would make him abnormally suggestible under the pressure of a police interview and therefore likely to make a false confession. The defence had tried to have this evidence admitted at an earlier appeal but leave to appeal had not been given by the then Lord Chief Justice, Lord Lane.

When the case was referred back to the Court of Appeal in 1991 the judges actually apologised for the fact that the defendants had suffered as a result of the shortcomings of the criminal justice system.

The case of Stefan Kiszko was different in that scientific evidence, which supported his innocence had been available to the prosecution at the date of his trial, but this evidence had not been given at the trial nor disclosed to the defence. The details of this are given in the following article.

Evidence could have prevented prosecution: Court's quashing of murder conviction reopens questions over judicial system

The latest in the litany of miscarriages of justice is arguably the most shocking.

For even before Stefan Kiszko stood trial, there was unequivocal evidence of his innocence.

Scientists had shown that Mr Kiszko was infertile and that Lesley Molseeds's attacker was not. Mr Kiszko has a condition known as hypogonadism, making it impossible for him to secrete sperm. Spermheads were found on the dead girl's clothing.

The evidence lay buried for 16 years, until yesterday when it was used to prove his innocence.

The Lancashire police investigation into the affair will seek to discover who was involved in that suppression and whether it was deliberate, negligent or accidental.

Certainly Dr Edward Tierney, the police surgeon who ordered the tests, said he knew of the evidence's potential to clear Mr Kiszko. He said he had informed senior investigating officers in the West Yorkshire murder squad, headed by Detective Chief Supt Jack Dibb, who has since died, of its importance.

It is not known whether this information was passed to the prosecution authorities and lawyers. However, its suppression meant that Mr Kiszko served those years at first in prison and then, when his mental health deteriorated in jail, in a secure psychiatric hospital, and that the real attacker escaped justice.

An extract from an article by Heather Mills in *The Independent*, 19 February 1992.

These various cases also cast doubts on the appeal system as the defendants had appealed against conviction in all the cases, but the original appeal had not been allowed. At the same time, there was concern over the number of acquittals in criminal trials and a belief that the rules of PACE under which the police worked were too restrictive and led to many guilty people going free. It was clear that a full review of the criminal justice system was necessary, and on the same day that the convictions of the Birmingham Six were quashed by the Court of Appeal, 14 March 1991, the Home Secretary announced the setting up of a Royal Commission on Criminal Justice under the chairmanship of Lord Runciman.

8.1.3 The Runciman Commission

The terms of reference of this Royal Commission on Criminal Justice were to:

> 'examine the effectiveness of the criminal justice system in England and Wales in securing the conviction of those guilty of criminal offences and the acquittal of those who are innocent, having regard to the efficient use of resources.'

This was neatly put by Michael Zander, one of the Commission, as a remit with three distinct component elements – 'the need to convict the guilty, the need not to convict the innocent and due economy'. The Commission had 22 research studies carried out into how the criminal justice system worked in practice; it also heard evidence from over 600 organisations and its report was published in 1993, containing 352 recommendations.

These recommendations covered the spectrum of the criminal justice system and ranged from police investigations, for example, suggesting continuous videoing of police custody suites to pre-trial procedures such as the suggestion for abolishing the defendant's right to choose trial by jury. There were also recommendations about jury eligibility, and the way juries should be selected in cases where the defendant was of an ethnic minority background. These are discussed in Chapter 14. Other recommendations were concerned with the disclosure of evidence, and the setting up of an independent body to investigate possible miscarriages of justice.

The Government has been, however, somewhat selective in the implementation of these recommendations. In particular the Commission had recommended that suspects should keep the right to remain silent during a police interview, but this right was effectively eroded by subsequent legislation (as discussed in section 8.2.6.). In June 1996 the Government said it had accepted wholly or in part 204 of the 352 recommendations and was still considering 58 others; it had decided not to implement 46 and the remaining 44 were not primarily for the Government to act upon. Some of the recommendations were implemented in the Criminal Justice and Public Order Act 1994, with others being implemented by the Criminal Appeal Act 1995 and by the Criminal Procedure and Investigation Act 1996.

8.1.4 The Labour Government's policies

In May 1997 a Labour Government was elected for the first time in 18 years. In its election manifesto the party had promised to be 'tough on crime and tough on the causes of crime'. The first major piece of legislation aimed at this promise was the Crime and Disorder Act 1998. This Act added new powers to deal with persistent petty criminals and also those on the borders of committing crime. In particular it allows local authorities to seek anti-social behaviour orders against those who are sometimes called 'the neighbours from hell'. The Act also gives powers to enforce curfews against children, so that unsupervised young children are not out late, and allows police to detain school truants. These powers are given even though the children involved may not have committed any crime.

Other changes to the criminal justice system in the Crime and Disorder Act 1998 include alterations to court procedure to speed up the process; more co-operation between police and local authorities and other organisations such as the newly created Youth Offending Teams; and restrictions of the number of warnings an offender can be given before being taken to court.

8.1.5 The MacPherson Report

In 1993 a black teenager, Stephen Lawrence, was stabbed to death in a racist attack. The police handled the investigation into the murder in a very incompetent way. Some of their failings included not searching properly for evidence and suspects and not investigating tip-offs about the identify of the killers. In addition, Stephen Lawrence's parents were not treated with proper respect and sensitivity.

In 1997 the Government set up a judicial inquiry into the handling of the police investigation. This inquiry was chaired by Sir William MacPherson, a former High Court judge. A report was published in 1999. This report accused the Metropolitan Police of 'institutional racism'. It contained many recommendations about the way police and also the Crown Prosecution Service should deal with cases.

As a result of the report, the Race Relations Act 1976 was amended to make it unlawful for any public authority when carrying out their public functions, including the police, to discriminate against a person on racial grounds. This covers activities by the police such as stop and search, arrests and investigating offences.

The interests of victims and victims' families have been given a higher profile, especially in a new Code for Crown Prosecutors issued in 2000. This Code stresses that victims (or their families) should be told about decisions which make a significant difference to the case.

8.2 Police powers

The police, like everyone else, must respect the individual's civil rights. People are entitled to be allowed to move freely and to have their person and their property respected. However, as already stated, there must be sufficient powers for the police to investigate crime – Parliament has therefore given them special powers which can be used in certain circumstances. These powers include the right to stop suspects, to search them, to arrest and interview people when necessary and to take fingerprints and samples (such as blood) for scientific analysis. Without powers such as these, it would be impossible to investigate crimes. However, it is important that, at the same time, ordinary people are not unnecessarily harassed by the police and that suspects are protected from overzealous police methods. The law on police powers is mainly contained in the Police and Criminal Evidence Act 1984 and the codes of practice made under section 66 of that Act. There are five codes as follows:

1. Code A to deal with the powers to stop and search
2. Code B for the powers to search premises and seize property
3. Code C to deal with the detention, treatment and questioning of suspects
4. Code D on the rules for identification procedures
5. Code E on the tape-recording of interviews with suspects

All these codes were revised in 1999.

Serious arrestable offences

Some of the rules apply only to 'serious arrestable offences'. Those offences automatically considered as 'serious arrestable offences' under section 116 of PACE include: treason, murder, manslaughter, rape and other serious sexual offences, hijacking, kidnapping, hostagetaking, drug trafficking, some firearms offences and causing an explosion likely to endanger life or property. Other arrestable offences may only be considered as a 'serious arrestable offence' if it has had,

or is likely to have, a serious consequence such as serious harm to the State or public order, the death of any person, serious injury to any person, substantial financial gain or serious financial loss.

8.2.1 Powers to stop and search

Police powers to stop and search people and vehicles are set out in sections 1 to 7 of PACE. Section I gives the police the right to stop and search people and vehicles in a public place. 'Public place' not only means in the street, but also extends to areas such as pub car parks, and even private gardens, if the police officer has good reasons for believing that the suspect does not live at that address. To use this power under PACE a police officer must have reasonable grounds for suspecting that the person is in possession of (or the vehicle contains) stolen goods or prohibited articles. Prohibited articles includes such items as offensive weapons and articles for use in connection with burglary or theft.

As these powers are very wide there are safeguards in that the police officer must give his name and station and the reason for the search. This was shown in *Osman* v *DPP* (1999) where the officers did not give their names and station. The Queen's Bench Divisional Court held this made a search of Mr Osman unlawful and so he could not be guilty of assaulting the police in the execution of their duty. If the officer fails to give a reason for the search, then that search is unlawful. If the search is in public, the police can only request that the suspect removes outer coat, jacket and gloves (section 2(9)). The police officer must make a written report as soon as possible after the search.

Home Office statistics show that the police made increasing use of the power to stop and search. The number of stop and searches rose from just over 100,000 in 1986 to well over a million by 1998. However, after the MacPherson Report in 1999 (see 8.1.4), the number of stops and searches in 1999–2000 was well under a million at about 850,000. This was a decrease of 21 per cent on the previous twelve months. In the Metropolitan police force area, (the police force criticised in the MacPherson Report) the decrease was 41 per cent.

The code of practice A contains details and guidance on when these powers should be used. In particular it stresses that police officers must not act just because of a person's characteristics. Paragraph 1.7 of code A says:

'Reasonable suspicion can never be supported on the basis of personal factors alone. For example, a person's colour, age, hairstyle or manner of dress, or the fact that he is known to have a previous conviction for possession of an unlawful article, cannot be used alone or in combination with each other as the sole basis on which to search that person. Nor may it be found on the basis of stereotyped images of certain persons or groups as being more likely to be committing offences.'

Despite this guidance in the Code of Practice, there is still evidence that certain types of people, especially black youths, are more likely to be stopped than other groups.

A Home Office publication, *Statistics on Race and the Criminal Justice System, 2000*, shows that black people are still five times more likely than other groups to be stopped and searched. This figure is based on the resident population in each police area.

However, research by Miller, Quinton and Bland in 2000 looked at the population actually 'available' at a number of sites and compared this to stops and searches in these areas. 'Available' meant actually out in public places at times when stops and searches were most likely to happen. This research showed that there were high numbers of young men and people from ethnic minority groups in such places. This meant that when comparing statistics on stops and searches with this 'available' population, black people were not more likely to be searched.

Another point to be aware of is that these statistics do not cover situations where the search was 'voluntary'. In other words where the police officer has no right under PACE,

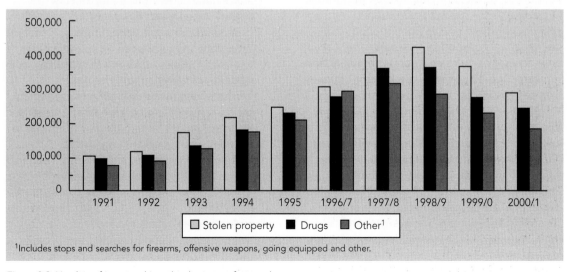

¹Includes stops and searches for firearms, offensive weapons, going equipped and other.

Figure 8.2 Number of stops and searches by reason for search

Source: *Stop and Search:* Home Office Statistical Bulletin 3/01

but by virtue of saying to someone 'let's have a look in your bag', persuades that person to co-operate and allow the search. Research in 1990 by Dixon, Coleman and Bottomley revealed that the police were aware of how few young people knew their rights and that they could be 'bamboozled' into allowing a so-called voluntary search. The codes of practice were revised in 1999 and code A tries to deal with this type of situation as it states that an officer who wishes to carry out a voluntary search 'should always make it clear that he is seeking the co-operation of the person concerned'.

Other powers to stop and search

Apart from PACE there are also other Acts of Parliament which give the police the right to stop and search in special circumstances. For example the Misuse of Drugs Act 1971 allows the police to search for controlled drugs while the Terrorism Act 2000 gives powers to stop and search where there is reasonable suspicion of involvement in terrorism.

Section 60 of the Criminal Justice and Public Order Act 1994 gives the police an additional power of the right to stop and search in anticipation of violence. This can only occur where it has been authorised by a senior police officer who reasonably believes that serious violence may take place in any locality in his area. An interesting feature of this right to stop and search is that once it has been authorised, a police officer acting under it does not have to have reasonable suspicion about the individual he stops. Section 60(5) says that: 'A constable may, in the exercise of those powers, stop any person or vehicle and make any search he thinks fit whether or not he has any grounds for suspecting that the person or vehicle is carrying weapons or (dangerous) articles'.

The extension of rights to stop and search without any reason to suspect the individual who is stopped, can be seen as an infringement of civil liberties. Such rights are, at least, of limited duration as the senior police officer authorising stop and search powers can only do so for a period of 24 hours.

Comment

Abuse of stop and search powers?

Before 1999, only 10 per cent of those stopped and searched were then arrested. This meant that of the one million or so stops and searches, 900,000 people were stopped and searched unnecessarily. In 2000 when the number of stops and searches went down, 13 per cent ended with an arrest. This shows that a more carefully targeted approach to stop and search is more likely to produce an arrest.

One main problem with stop and search procedure is that having reasonable grounds for suspecting the person is in possession of stolen goods or prohibited articles gives a wide discretion to individual police officers. The police are now keeping a database on stop/search powers which may identify officers who overuse this power.

In 1996, when the police in the Tottenham area of London were required to hand out a leaflet explaining stop and search rights, the number of stop and search incidents dropped by over 50 per cent. At the same time the proportion of arrests from stops and searches went up from 10 to 12 per cent. However, there was also an increase of 17 per cent in crimes such as burglary and street robbery in the area. So fewer stops and searches may well lead to more crimes.

Another worrying feature of stop and search powers is the large number of ethnic minority suspects who are stopped and searched.

8.2.2 Road checks

Where there is a reasonable suspicion that a person who has committed a serious arrestable offence is at large in a particular area, section 4 of PACE gives permission for road checks to be made in that area. Such a check can normally only be authorised by a high-ranking police officer, that is a superintendent or higher rank, but an officer of a lower rank can authorise a road check if it is urgent. A road check allows all vehicles in the particular locality to be stopped.

8.2.3 The power to search premises

In certain circumstances the police have the power to enter and search premises. PACE sets out most of these powers, though there are other Acts which allow the police to obtain search warrants.

Search warrants

The police can enter premises without the occupier's permission to make a search, if a warrant authorising that search has been issued by a magistrate. Such a warrant will normally be issued under section 8 of PACE. It will be granted if the magistrate is satisfied that the police have reasonable grounds for believing that a serious arrestable offence has been committed, and that there is material on the premises which is likely to be of substantial value in the investigation of the offence and relevant evidence. In addition, the magistrate should be satisfied that it is not practicable to communicate with any person entitled to grant entry or access, or that entry will be refused unless a search warrant is produced, or that the purpose of the search may be frustrated unless police arriving at the premises can gain immediate entry. Search warrants are designed to prevent evidence being removed or destroyed through the need to give warning of an intended search.

Requirements of a warrant

A warrant must specify the premises to be searched and, as far as possible, the articles or persons to be sought. The warrant only authorises one entry on one occasion and must be executed within one month from the date of issue. In addition the police are required to enter and search at a reasonable hour, unless it appears that the purpose of the search would be frustrated by an entry at a reasonable hour. They are also required to identify themselves as police officers, to show the warrant to any person at the premises and give that person a copy of the warrant.

However the courts have held that the police need not comply precisely with these requirements if the circumstances of the case make it wholly inappropriate. In particular that the identification of the searcher as a police officer and the production of the warrant need not be carried out on entry, but only before the actual search begins. This was the position in *R v Longman* (1988) where the police, who had a warrant to search premises for drugs, knew that it would be difficult to gain entry. They therefore arranged for a plain clothes policewoman to pose as a delivery girl from Interflora and get the occupants of the premises to open the door. Once the door was opened, the police burst into the premises without identifying themselves as police officers or showing the search warrant. The Court of Appeal held that force or subterfuge could be lawfully used in order to gain entry with a search warrant.

Section 16 of PACE and the code of practice B set out full guidelines for executing search warrants.

Powers to enter premises without a search warrant

Police officers may enter and search premises if it is in order to arrest a person named in an

Type of power	Law giving power	Comment
With a warrant	s 8 PACE gives power to magistrates to issue warrants	• Warrant must specify premises • *R v Longman* – need not show warrant before entry only before search
Without a warrant: (a) to arrest person (b) to search premises controlled by an arrested person	s 17 PACE s 18 PACE	*O'Loughlin* v *Chief Constable of Essex* – police must state reason for entry whenever possible
(c) to search premises which a person was in at or immediately before arrest	s32 PACE	• *R v Badham* – must make search immediately after arrest
To prevent a breach of the peace	Common law	• Applies to private homes as well as public places • *McLeod* v *Commissioner of Police for Metropolis*

Figure 8.3 Summary of police powers to enter and search premises

arrest warrant, or to arrest someone for an arrestable offence, or to recapture an escaped prisoner. This power is set out in section 17 of PACE. The police must give anybody present in the premises the reason for the entry. In *O'Loughlin* v *Chief Constable of Essex* (1998) police forced their way in without explaining that it was in order to arrest O'Loughlin's wife for criminal damage. This made the entry unlawful and O'Loughlin was able to sue the police for damages. Police can only enter without giving a reason if the circumstances make it impossible, impracticable or undesirable to give the reason.

PACE also gives the police the right to enter premises without a search warrant after making an arrest, if an officer has reasonable grounds for suspecting that there is evidence on premises relating to the offence for which the person has just been arrested, or to a possible connected or similar offence. The police can enter premises which are occupied or controlled by the person under arrest (s 18), or premises in which that person was at the time of arrest, or immediately before he was arrested (s 32). It

was held in *R v Badham* (1987) that this power under section 32 only allows a search to be made immediately after the arrest; it does not allow the police to return to the premises several hours later to make a search.

To prevent a breach of the peace

There is still a right under the common law for police to enter premises if there is need for them to deal with, or prevent, a breach of the peace. This right applies even to private homes as was shown by the case of *McLeod* v *Commission of Police of the Metropolis* (1994) in which the police had entered domestic premises when there was a violent quarrel taking place, fearing a breach of the peace.

Searching with the consent of the occupier of the premises

The police may, of course, enter and search premises without a warrant if the occupier of those premises gives them permission to do so. However, that consent must be given in writing and, if, at any time, the occupier indicates that he has withdrawn his consent, the police must stop the search and leave the premises. Figure 8.3 summarises these powers to search premises.

Unlawful entry and searches

Where the police exceed their powers, the occupier of the premises or any other person affected can make a civil claim for damages against the police under the tort of trespass. However, if the police obtain any evidence in an unlawful search, it is possible that that evidence may be used as the basis of a prosecution. The defence can try to have such evidence excluded under section 78 of PACE which says that a court may refuse to allow evidence to be given if it appears that, having regard to all the circumstances, the admission of the evidence would have such an adverse effect on the fairness of the proceedings that the court ought not to admit it. This means that it may be possible to persuade the judge at the trial to refuse to allow the prosecution to put forward any evidence obtained as a result of an unlawful search.

8.2.4 Powers of arrest

Section 24 of PACE sets out general powers of arrest, and some of these powers can be exercised by private citizens as well as by the police.

Arrestable offence

This section applies to situations which involve, or may involve, the commission of an 'arrestable offence'. So it is important to have a clear understanding of what is meant by an arrestable offence.

An arrestable offence is:

1. Any offence for which the sentence is fixed by law (for example murder which has a fixed sentence of life imprisonment).
2. Any offence for which the maximum sentence that could be given to an adult is at least five years' imprisonment. This

category covers a wide range of offences including theft (maximum sentence seven years), assault causing actual bodily harm (maximum sentence five years), rape (maximum life imprisonment) and robbery (maximum life imprisonment). Note that this does not mean the offender will actually receive the maximum sentence, merely that the maximum sentence is five years or more.
3. Any other offence which Parliament has specifically made an arrestable offence; for example taking a motor vehicle without consent has been made an arrestable offence even though the maximum sentence is only six months' imprisonment.

Section 24 PACE

Section 24 allows police and private citizens to arrest without a warrant:

1. Anyone who is in the act of committing an arrestable offence.
2. Anyone whom he has reasonable grounds for suspecting to be committing an arrestable offence.
3. Anyone who has committed an arrestable offence.
4. Where an arrestable offence has been committed, anyone whom he has reasonable grounds for suspecting to be guilty of it (even if it turns out later that he did not commit the offence).

The main point to note is that these rights of arrest are given to private citizens as well as the police, so that a private citizen may lawfully carry out an arrest.

The police also have the right to arrest:

1. Anyone who is about to commit an arrestable offence.
2. Anyone whom he has reasonable grounds for suspecting to be about to commit an arrestable offence.
3. Where there are reasonable grounds for suspecting that an arrestable offence has been committed (even if it turns out later

that no offence was committed) and there are reasonable grounds for suspecting the person arrested.

Private citizens do not have these rights, so that if there has not been an arrestable offence, no matter how suspicious the circumstances, a private citizen cannot lawfully carry out an arrest.

This was seen in the case of *R v Self* (1992) where an off-duty policeman was suspected of theft by a store detective when the officer was seen to pick up a bar of chocolate in the shop and leave without paying. The store detective, helped by another person, arrested the police officer by catching hold of him. The officer struggled to get free, kicking the two in the process. He was charged with theft of the chocolate and assault with intent to resist arrest. At his trial he was acquitted of the theft but convicted of the assaults. He appealed and the Court of Appeal held that, as the offence of theft had not been proved, there was no arrestable offence and so the arrest was not lawful. In view of this he could not be guilty of assault with intent to resist arrest, since a person is entitled to resist an unlawful attempt to arrest them.

Reasonable grounds for suspecting

Many of the police powers under section 24 require that the police have reasonable grounds for suspecting the defendant. In the case of *Castorina v Chief Constable of Surrey* (1988) the Court of Appeal held that this did not mean that there had to be sufficient grounds which would make an ordinary cautious person think that the defendant was guilty. It was enough if the facts could lead an ordinary person to *suspect* that the defendant was guilty.

Section 25 PACE

The police also have power under section 25 of PACE, which allows the police to arrest for any offence where:

1. The suspect's name and address cannot be discovered.
2. There are reasonable grounds for believing that the name and address given by the suspect are false.

This power is necessary as, if it did not exist, defendants who committed non-arrestable offences could refuse to co-operate with the police and run off, leaving the police powerless to act.

Section 25 also provides powers of arrest where there are reasonable grounds for believing that arrest is necessary to prevent that person from:

- Causing physical injury to himself or any other person
- Suffering physical injury (e.g. by trying to jump from a bridge in a suicide attempt)
- Causing loss of or damage to property
- Committing an offence against public decency
- Causing an unlawful obstruction of the highway

This section also allows the police to arrest if the arrest is reasonably believed to be necessary to protect a child, or other vulnerable person, from the person who is arrested. All these allow an arrest as a preventative measure.

Figure 8.4 gives a summary of the different powers of arrest.

Other statutory rights of arrest

The Criminal Justice and Public Order Act 1994 added an extra power of arrest to PACE. This is now in section 46A of PACE and gives the police the right to arrest without a warrant anyone who, having been released on police bail, fails to attend at the police station at the set time. The Criminal Justice and Public Order Act 1994 also gives police the right to arrest for a variety of new offences including collective and aggravated

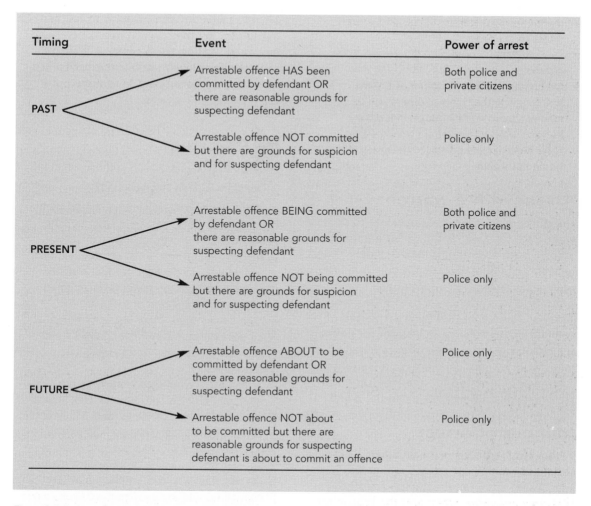

Timing	Event	Power of arrest
PAST	Arrestable offence HAS been committed by defendant OR there are reasonable grounds for suspecting defendant	Both police and private citizens
	Arrestable offence NOT committed but there are grounds for suspicion and for suspecting defendant	Police only
PRESENT	Arrestable offence BEING committed by defendant OR there are reasonable grounds for suspecting defendant	Both police and private citizens
	Arrestable offence NOT being committed but there are grounds for suspicion and for suspecting defendant	Police only
FUTURE	Arrestable offence ABOUT to be committed by defendant OR there are reasonable grounds for suspecting defendant	Police only
	Arrestable offence NOT about to be committed but there are reasonable grounds for suspecting defendant is about to commit an offence	Police only

Figure 8.4 *Powers of arrest, comparing police powers with those of private citizens*

trespass, in connection with offences committed in preparing for or attending a 'rave', or intentional harassment.

Arrest for breach of the peace

As well as rights given to them by Acts of Parliament, the police still retain a common law right to arrest where there has been, or is likely to be, a breach of the peace. This applies even if the behaviour complained of was on private premises as demonstrated by the case of *McConnell* v *Chief Constable of the Greater Manchester Police* (1990). In this case the manager of a carpet store had asked

McConnell to leave, but he had refused to do so. A police officer had then taken McConnell outside, but McConnell attempted to re-enter, so the office arrested him for conduct whereby a breach of the peace might be occasioned. McConnell later sued the police for false imprisonment arguing that the arrest was unlawful, as a breach of the peace could not occur on private premises, but the Court of Appeal held that it could do so and that the arrest was lawful.

In *Bibby* v *Chief Constable of Essex Police* (2000), the Court of Appeal summarised the conditions that must apply for this common law power of arrest to be used. These were:

- there must be a sufficiently real and present threat to the peace;
- the threat must come from the person to be arrested;
- the conduct of that person must clearly interfere with the rights of others and its natural consequence must be 'not wholly unreasonable' violence from a third party;
- the conduct of the person to be arrested must be unreasonable.

Arrest with a warrant

The police may make an application to a magistrate for a warrant to arrest a named person. Such a warrant is issued under section 1 of the Magistrates' Court Act 1980 which requires written information, supported by evidence on oath showing that a person has committed (or is suspected of committing) an offence. A warrant for arrest will only be granted if the offence involved is punishable by imprisonment, so a warrant can never be granted for offences for which are only punishable by, for example, a fine.

Manner of arrest

Whenever the police make an arrest they should at the time of, or as soon as practicable after, tell the person arrested that they are under arrest and the reason for it, even if it is perfectly obvious why they are being arrested. There is no set form of words to be used and, as is often portrayed in television dramas, it is sufficient if the arresting officer says something like 'you're nicked for theft'.

Where necessary both the police and private citizens making an arrest may use reasonable force. Section 117 of PACE covers any power of arrest under PACE, while the Criminal Justice Act 1967 s. 3 covers other arrests.

The right to search an arrested person

Where a person has been arrested the police have a right to search that person for

anything which might be used to help an escape, or anything which might be evidence relating to an offence. If such a search takes place in public the police can only require the suspect to remove outer coat, jacket and gloves.

Comment

Does arrest lead to conviction?

About two million people are arrested each year. Home Office research, *From arrest to conviction* – a survey, published in 1998, showed that far more men are arrested than women with 85 per cent of those arrested being male. Unemployment is linked to arrests as 54 per cent of those arrested were unemployed. Other key facts were that 15 per cent were under the age of 17 and just over 60 per cent had previous convictions.

Just over half of those arrested were eventually charged with a crime, with another 17 per cent being cautioned and 13 per cent dealt with in another way, such as referral to a juvenile agency. Twenty per cent of those arrested had no action taken against them. Women, juveniles, those with no previous convictions and whites were more likely to be cautioned than other groups.

The findings also showed that ethnic minority groups were more likely to have no further action taken against them, perhaps indicating that the arrest should not have taken place. Where they were charged they were more likely to have the case against them dropped by the Crown Prosecution Service. This again suggests that the police are too quick to take action against ethnic minority groups. However, the research on which the study was based took place in 1993 and 1994 and since then there have a number of initiatives which may have changed the patterns. These initiatives include ethnic monitoring of stops, searches, arrests and cautions.

Activity

State whether there has been a lawful arrest in the following situations. Give reasons for your answers.

QUESTIONS

❶ After an incident in which a man was stabbed and seriously hurt, a police officer grabs hold of Damon. When Damon protests and asks why, the police officer says 'you know what it's for'. The police officer did not see the incident but was told by someone else at the scene that Damon was responsible.

❷ Tony, a taxi driver, sees Gary climbing out of the window of a house. Tony catches hold of Gary and takes him to a nearby police station.

❸ Amanda is stopped by the police for speeding. When one of the police officers asks her her name, she replies 'Superwoman'. She is then asked for her address and refuses to give it. The police officer arrests her and takes her to the police station.

8.2.5 Powers of detention

Once a person has been arrested and taken to a police station there are rules setting out very strict time limits on how long they may be held there. These limits are longer if the offence being investigated is a serious arrestable offence. There are also rules about the treatment of people in detention; these are contained in PACE as amended by the Criminal Justice and Public Order Act 1994, together with code of practice C.

Time limits on detention

For most offences the police may only detain a person for a maximum of 24 hours and must then either charge them with an offence or release them. For serious arrestable offences the police may detain the person for an initial period of 36 hours and may then apply to the Magistrates' Court for permission to detain him for up to a maximum of 96 hours. The detainee has the right to be represented and oppose such an application. There is an exception under

Time factor	Event(s)
Start of detention	Arrested person arrives at police station and the custody officer decides there is reason to detain him/her
Six hours	First review by custody officer
15 hours and every nine hours thereafter	Second and subsequent reviews by custody officer
24 hours	Police must charge or release arrested person unless he is being held in connection with a serious arrestable offence
36 hours	Police may apply to magistrates to extend the period of detention for a serious arrestable offence
96 hours	Maximum time for detaining an arrested person (except under Prevention of Terrorism (Temporary Provisions) Act 1989). Police must charge or release suspect

Figure 8.5 Time limits on detention of a suspect

the Prevention of Terrorism (Temporary Provisions) Act 1989 which allows for detention of 48 hours and up to another five days with the Home Secretary's permission. The time limits on detention are set out in Figure 8.5. The detention must also be reviewed by the custody officer. Initially this must be not later than six hours after the detention, and then at intervals of not less than nine hours. If at any time the custody officer becomes aware that there are no grounds for continuing the detention, then he is under a duty to order an immediate release from custody. Also, while a person remains in custody under powers of detention, the custody officer must keep a record of all events that occur (such as interviews or visits to the cell by police officers).

Rights of a detained person

Detainees must be told their rights by the custody officer. These rights include:

- Having someone informed of the arrest
- Being told that independent legal advice is available free and being allowed to consult privately with a solicitor
- Being allowed to consult the code of practice

The right to have someone informed of the arrest

The right to have someone informed of the arrest is given by section 56 of PACE. The arrested person can nominate any friend, relative or any other person who they think is likely to take an interest in their welfare. The person nominated by the detainee must be told of the arrest and where the person is being held. This should normally be done as soon as practicable, but, in the case of a serious arrestable offence a senior police officer may authorise that there be a delay of up to 36 hours. This can only be done if there are reasonable grounds for believing that telling the named person will lead to: interference; harm to evidence or to other

persons; the alerting of others involved in the offence or hinder the recovery of property obtained through the offence. Code C states that, in addition to the right to have someone informed of the arrest, a detained person should be allowed to speak on the telephone 'for a reasonable time to one person'. If the suspect is under the age of 18 the police must also contact a person 'responsible for his welfare' and inform them of the arrest.

The right to legal advice

A detained person may either contact their own solicitor, or they can use the system of duty solicitors which is provided free for anyone under arrest. In fact the code of practice tries to make sure that detained people are aware of their right to legal advice. Under the code the custody officer, when authorising the detention of someone at the police station, must get the suspect to sign the custody record at that time saying whether he/she wishes to have legal advice. Police stations must have posters 'prominently displayed' advertising the right to free legal advice, and an arrested suspect must not only be told orally of this right, but also given a written notice of it.

It is possible for a senior police officer to authorise a delay to a suspect's right to see a solicitor in the case of a serious arrestable offence for up to 36 hours. However, this can only occur if there are reasonable grounds for believing that giving access to a solicitor will lead to: interference with, or harm to, evidence or to other persons; the alerting of others involved in the offence, or hinder the recovery of property obtained through the offence. The case of *R v Samuel* (1988) stressed that it would only be on rare occasions that such a delay was justified, and that it must be based on specific aspects of the case, not a general assumption that access to a solicitor might lead to the alerting of accomplices. In *Samuel*'s case, the defendant was a 24-year-old man, whose

KEY FACTS

Right	Source	Comment
To have someone informed of detention	s.56 PACE	Can be delayed for up to 36 hours if serious arrestable offence
To speak to someone on the telephone	Code of Practice C	Not compulsory – police can refuse
To be told of their right to legal advice	Code of Practice C	Notices displayed in police stations Duty of custody officer to bring this to the suspect's attention
To legal advice	s.58 PACE	Can be delayed for up to 36 hours if serious arrestable offence BUT only in exceptional circumstances: R v Samuel
To have appropriate adult present at interview	Code of Practice C	Applies to those under 17 and also to mentally ill or handicapped: R v Aspinall
Right to consult the Codes of Practice	The Codes of Practice	

Figure 8.6 *Key fact chart on rights of suspects in police detention*

mother had already been informed of her son's arrest some hours before he was refused access to a solicitor. The Court of Appeal felt that if anyone was likely to be alerted then it would already have happened, and that there was no reason to deny Samuel his 'fundamental freedom' of consulting a solicitor. As his final interview with the police had taken place after his solicitor had been refused access, the evidence of what was said at that interview was inadmissable in court and so Samuel's conviction for robbery was quashed.

8.2.6 Police interviews of suspects

Any detained person may be questioned by the police. All interviews at a police station must be tape-recorded and trials are being conducted on the feasibility of videoing rather than just audio-taping. A problem in many cases is that questioning of the suspect starts before they arrive at the police station (possibly in the police car on the way to the station) and these informal interviews are not recorded. In many cases, the defendant challenges the truth of police evidence about an alleged informal interview. In order to protect suspects from the possibility of police fabricating evidence of a confession made outside the police station, the Runciman Commission recommended that if a confession was allegedly made outside the police station, then that confession should be put to the suspect at the beginning of any tape-recorded interview that subsequently takes place. This allows a suspect a chance to make comments about it in the taped interview.

Suspects have the right to have a solicitor present at any interview, unless it is one of the rare occasions referred to in *Samuel* above. However, if the suspect does not ask for a solicitor, the police may conduct the interview without one being present. In addition, if the matter is urgent or the solicitor likely to be delayed for some time, the police have the right to start questioning a suspect before a solicitor arrives.

If the suspect is under the age of 17 or is mentally handicapped then there must be an 'appropriate adult' present during all interviews. This right is in addition to the right to legal advice. Research suggests that many mentally vulnerable individuals are not being given this protection; the Runciman Commission recommended that the police should be given clearer guidelines on identifying suspects who need an appropriate adult. The Commission also suggested there should be trials of the use of 'duty psychiatrist schemes' to see whether a permanent scheme would be appropriate in busy city centre police stations.

In *R v Aspinall* (1999) the Court of Appeal ruled that a defendant who suffered from schizophrenia should have had an appropriate adult present when interviewed by police. This was so even though the defendant appeared able to understand the police questions. The interview was, therefore, not admissible as evidence.

Treatment of suspects and exclusion of evidence

The law gives some protection to suspects as to the way they should be treated whilst being detained and questioned. Section 76 of PACE states that the court shall not allow statements which have been obtained through oppression to be used as evidence. Oppression is defined as including torture, inhuman or degrading treatment and the use or threat of violence. Code C also gives protection to suspects who are being

questioned in regard to the physical conditions of the interview. For example, the code states that interview rooms must be adequately lit, heated and ventilated and that suspects must be given adequate breaks for meals, refeshments and sleep.

In theory the treatment of a suspect is monitored by the custody officer who is supposed to keep accurate records of all happenings during the detention period. This should include the length and timing of interviews and other matters, such as visits of police officers to the defendant's cell, so that any breaches of the rules will be obvious. However, research by Sanders and Bridge suggests that a substantial minority of custody records (about 10 per cent) are falsified.

The right to silence

Until the Criminal Justice and Public Order Act 1994 was enacted, defendants could refuse to answer any questions without any adverse conclusion being drawn on their silence if the case came to trial. In fact, the previously used caution given before a police interview commenced, contained the phrase 'you do not have to say anything'. This right to remain silent was considered by the Runciman Commission, which recommended that it should be retained in essence. However, the Government decided that this rule was allowing guilty people to go free and that the right to silence should be curbed. This was done by sections 34 to 39 of the Criminal Justice and Public Order Act 1994.

These sections allow inferences to be made from the fact that a defendant has refused to answer questions. As a result the wording of the caution given to a suspect before interviewing commences now states:

'You do not have to say anything. But it may harm your defence if you do not mention when questioned something which you later rely on in court. Anything you do say may be given in evidence.'

KEY FACTS

Power	Sections in PACE or other Act	Code of practice	Comments
Stop and search	ss 1–7 of PACE also other Acts e.g. Misuse of Drugs Act 1971	A	• Must be in a public place and must have reasonable grounds for suspecting person
Enter premises	With search warrant (s 8 PACE) OR to arrest person (s 17 PACE) OR to prevent breach of the peace	B	• Magistrates issue warrant • Even applies to private homes
Arrest	With a warrant OR under sections 24 or 25 of PACE	–	• Magistrates issue warrant • Must have reasonable grounds

Detention	ss 34–46 PACE Limits 24 hours OR 36 (extendible to 96) for serious arrestable offence	C	• Detainee has rights to:
			  – have someone told
			  – to be told of availability of legal advice
			  – to see Code of Practice

Searches	ss 54, 55 PACE	C	• Intimate search must be by person of same sex
Fingerprinting	ss 61 PACE		• Intimate samples must be taken by qualified person
Samples	ss 62, 63 PACE		
Police interviews	s 53 PACE Also ss 34–39 Criminal Justice and Public Order Act 1994 re 'silence'	E	• Police must caution • Should tape-record • Appropriate adult present for those under 17

Figure 8.7 Key fact chart on police powers

This change in the law does not mean that the defendant can be forced to speak; he can still remain silent. At any trial which follows however, the judge may comment on the defendant's failure to mention a crucial matter, and this failure can form part of the evidence against him. It is argued that this alters the basic premise of criminal trials that the prosecution must prove the defendant's guilt. However a defendant's silence is not enough for a conviction on its own; there must be prosecution evidence as well. This is made clear by the Court of Appeal's ruling in *R v Cowan* (1995) in which the Lord Chief Justice, Lord Taylor said that to give a correct direction of the law to the jury:

'(1) The judge will have told the jury that the burden of proof remains upon the prosecution throughout . . .
(2) It is necessary for the judge to make clear to the jury that the defendant is entitled to remain silent. That is his right and choice. The right of silence remains.

(3) An inference from failure to give evidence cannot on its own prove guilt. That is expressly stated in s 38(3) of the Act.

(4) Therefore, the jury must be satisfied that the prosecution have established a case to answer before drawing any inferences from silence.'

Under the Criminal Justice and Public Order Act 1994 an adverse inference could only be drawn if the defendant was aged 14 or over. The Crime and Disorder Act 1998 allows an adverse inference to be drawn from the defendant's failure to answer questions or give evidence regardless of the defendant's age, so that the rule will apply to 10 to 13 year olds as well as older defendants.

One interesting point to note is that other enactments have already removed the right to silence in certain cases. In particular, under the Criminal Justice Act 1987 s 2, the Director of the Serious Fraud Office can require anyone whom he thinks has relevant information to attend to answer questions. Failure to comply with such a requirement is a criminal offence.

8.2.7 Searches, fingerprints and body samples

When a person is being held at a police station the police have no automatic right to search them. However, the custody officer has a duty to record everything a person has with them when they are brought to the police station, and if the custody officer thinks a search is necessary to carry out this duty, then a non-intimate search may be made.

Strip searches

These are defined in code C as searches 'involving the removal of more than outer clothing'. The code stresses that a strip search may only take place if it is necessary to remove an article which a person in detention should not be allowed to keep, and there is reasonable suspicion that the person might have concealed such an article.

Such searches should not take place in an area where the search can be seen by any person who does not need to be present, nor by a member of the opposite sex. Suspects should not normally be required to remove all their clothing at the same time. A man should be allowed to put his shirt back on before he removes his trousers and a woman should be given a robe or similar garment to wear once she has removed her top garment.

Intimate searches

In addition a high-ranking police officer can authorise an intimate search, if there is reason to believe that the person has with them an item which could be used to cause physical injury to themselves or others or that he/she is in possession of a Class A drug. An intimate search is defined as 'a search which consists of the physical examination of a person's body orifices other than the mouth'. If it is a drugs related search then it may only be carried out by a suitably qualified person, for example a doctor or nurse. If it is a search for other items then, if practicable, it should be carried out by a suitably qualified person, but can be by another person if a high-ranking police officer authorises it.

Fingerprints and body samples

While a person is detained the police may take fingerprints and non-intimate body samples such as hair and saliva without the person's consent. If necessary the police may use reasonable force to obtain these. There are different rules for intimate samples. Intimate samples are defined by the Criminal

Justice and Public Order Act 1994 as:

'(a) a sample of blood, semen or any other tissue fluid, urine or pubic hair;
(b) a dental impression;
(c) a swab taken from a person's body orifice other than the mouth.'

These can only be taken by a registered medical practitioner or a nurse. Although a sample will only be taken where there is reasonable ground for suspecting involvement in a particular recordable offence, the sample may then be checked against information held on other crimes. Any fingerprints or samples taken must be destroyed, if the suspect is not charged or is later found not guilty.

Activity

Advise whether or not in the following situations there have been breaches of the rules in PACE and the codes of practice.

QUESTIONS

❶ Leroy, aged 23, has been arrested on suspicion of murder. He is taken to the police station at 7 am. The custody officer tells him that he will not be allowed to see a lawyer. Leroy is interviewed for eight hours that day about the alleged murder. He continually denies any involvement and demands to see a lawyer. The police take his fingerprints and a sample of saliva for DNA testing. Leroy spends the night in the police station cells. The following morning the police finally allow him to make a telephone call to his brother at 11 am.

❷ Martin, aged 16, has been arrested for breaking into an office and stealing money. The police believe he may have been responsible for several other burglaries and that he has an accomplice. On the way to the police station they question him about this. At the police station he is taken into an

interview room and told that the police have enough evidence 'to lock him up for years' but that if he tells them who was with him, the police will only caution him. Martin asks if he can see his father but the police refuse to call his father until Martin signs an admission.

8.3 Complaints against the police

Citizens who believe that the police have exceeded their powers can complain to the police authorities. Any complaint about police behaviour must be recorded. The type of complaint then determines how it is dealt with, although in all instances, the police are under a duty to take steps to obtain and/or preserve evidence which is relevant to the complaint. Minor complaints will be dealt with informally, and if the complaint is proved, the individual will receive an apology and that will probably be an end of the matter. If disciplinary action is thought to be necessary, then the complaint should be investigated by the police force concerned; if it involves a high-ranking officer, the investigation is carried out by another police force.

8.3.1 Police Complaints Authority

Serious complaints are referred to the Police Complaints Authority (PCA) which was set up by PACE. The powers of the PCA are now governed by the Police Act 1996. Complaints alleging that the conduct complained of resulted in the death of, or serious injury to, someone must be referred to the PCA, and any investigation of the complaint will be supervised by them. This is to counter the criticism that investigation of police behaviour is carried out by the police themselves, who cannot be considered as sufficiently independent. The Police Act 1996 underlines that complaints against senior police officers must be investigated by another police force. Where an investigation discloses that a police officer may have committed a criminal offence, then the file must go to the Director of Public Prosecutions, who will decide whether criminal proceedings should be brought.

8.3.2 Court actions

Where the police have committed a crime in the unlawful execution of their duties, criminal proceedings may be brought against them. Such proceedings are usually for assault and may be commenced by a private prosecution or, as seen above, by the State.

If there is a breach of civil rights, citizens may also be able to take proceedings in the civil courts against the police. This can be done under a claim in tort for trespass to property, as would be the case if the police entered premises without a search warrant or other permission, or for trespass to the person where any arrest is unlawful. There can also be civil proceedings for false arrest or malicious prosecution.

Chapter 9

PRE-TRIAL PROCEDURE IN CRIMINAL CASES

The criminal law is set down by the State. A breach of the criminal law can lead to a penalty, such as imprisonment or a fine, being imposed on the defendant in the name of the State. Therefore, bringing a prosecution for a criminal offence is usually seen as part of the role of the State. Indeed, the majority of criminal prosecutions are conducted by the Crown Prosecution Service which is the state agency for criminal prosecutions (the role of the Crown Prosecution Service is dealt with in section 9.3).

It is also possible for a private individual or business to start a prosecution. Big shops often conduct their own prosecutions in shoplifting cases, and bodies like the RSPCA regularly bring prosecutions. However, it is unusual for an individual to bring a prosecution. This will probably only happen where the police have refused to act to investigate a complaint, or where the Crown Prosecution Service have decided to drop a case after the police had brought charges. The article on page 154 shows a successful private prosecution for rape.

In order to start a prosecution, the individual must present a written account of the alleged offence to a magistrate and, if the magistrate is persuaded that there is sufficient reason, he or she will issue a summons to be served on the defendant. The summons sets out a date on which the case will be heard at the Magistrates' Court. The Attorney-General does have the right, on behalf of the State, to take over any private criminal prosecution and to then decide whether the prosecution should continue or not.

However, regardless of whether the prosecution has been brought by the State or by a private individual, the same matters have to be dealt with and the defendant will probably have to attend court more than once before the trial takes place.

9.1 Pre-trial hearings

All criminal cases will first go to the Magistrates' Court but it is unusual for a case to be completed at this first hearing, although it is possible for minor offences to be dealt with at this point. This would only be where the defendant pleads guilty and is either already legally represented or does not want legal representation. For most driving offences there is a special procedure which allows the defendant to plead guilty by post, so that no attendance at court is necessary. Even in these cases the magistrates may need to adjourn the case to get further information about the defendant.

9.1.1 Categories of offences

The type of offence that is being dealt with affects the number and type of pre-trial hearings, and where the final trial will take place. Criminal offences are divided into three main categories. These are:

1. **Summary offences**
    These are the least serious offences and are always tried in the Magistrates' Court. They include nearly all driving offences, common assault and criminal damage which has caused less than £5,000 worth of damage.

Category of offence	Place of trial	Examples of offences
Summary	Magistrates' Court	Driving without insurance Taking a vehicle without consent Common assault
Triable either way	Magistrates' Court OR Crown Court	Theft Assault causing actual bodily harm Obtaining property by deception
Indictable	Crown Court	Murder Manslaughter Rape Robbery

Figure 9.1 The three categories of offence

2. Triable either way offences

These can be regarded as the middle range of crimes and they include a wide variety of offences, such as theft and assault causing actual bodily harm. As the name implies, these cases can be tried in either the Magistrates' Court or the Crown Court.

Plea before venue

The first stage in deciding where a triable either way case will be dealt with is called plea before venue. This means that the defendant is first asked whether he pleads guilty or not guilty. If he pleads guilty, the case is automatically heard by the magistrates, although they can still send the defendant to the Crown Court for sentence if they feel this is necessary.

Mode of trial

Where the defendant pleads not guilty a decision has to made as to where the trial takes place. This is called 'mode of trial' procedure. Even where the case is going to be tried at the Crown Court, preliminary matters are still dealt with at the Magistrates' Court before the case is committed to the Crown Court for trial.

3. Indictable offences

These are the more serious crimes and include murder, manslaughter and rape. All indictable offences must be tried at the Crown Court, but the first hearing is dealt with at the Magistrates' Court. After this the case is transferred to the Crown Court.

Note that there are recommendations for reform which may change this system. See section 10.6 The Auld Review.

9.1.2 Pre-trial procedure in cases which are to be tried in the Magistrates' Court

It is possible for cases to be dealt with on a first appearance in court but often an adjournment may be needed. This could be because the Crown Prosecution Service has not got all the information required to complete the case, or because the defendant wants to get legal advice. Another reason for adjourning a case is where the magistrates want pre-sentence reports on a defendant who pleads guilty, before they decide what sentence to impose. When a defendant wishes to plead not guilty, there will almost always have to be an adjournment, as witnesses will have to be brought to court. One of the main points to be decided on an adjournment is whether the defendant should be remanded on bail or in custody (see section 9.2).

Early administrative hearings

In order to prevent unnecessary delays, the first hearing is now an early administrative hearing (EAH). The hearing can be dealt with by a single lay magistrate, or even by the clerk of the court. The hearing is aimed at discovering if the defendant wants to apply for legal aid and, if so, enquiring into whether he is eligible for it; requesting pre-sentence or medical reports if these are appropriate; and deciding if the defendant should be remanded in custody or on bail. There is a limit on the clerk's powers in this last respect as the clerk cannot change any conditions where bail has previously been granted.

The use of early administrative hearings is one of the suggestions made in the Narey Report, *Reducing delay in the Criminal Justice System*. Pilot schemes of measures to reduce delay found that the average wait between the defendant being charged with a crime and the matter being completed in the Magistrates' Court was reduced from 85 days to 30 days.

9.1.3 Cases going for trial at the Crown Court

Triable either way offences

For these there will be further hearings at the Magistrates' Court for the plea before venue and mode of trial to be decided. If the case is to go for trial to the Crown Court, then there will be committal proceedings where the magistrates check that there is sufficient evidence to justify sending the case for trial. See section 10.1.5 for more detail.

Indictable offences

Committal proceedings for indictable offences were abolished by the Crime and Disorder Act 1998. As a result since January 2001 indictable offences are sent to the Crown Court immediately after the early administrative hearing in the Magistrates' Court. Al other pre-trial matters are dealt with by a judge at the Crown Court.

9.2 Bail

An important pre-trial matter to be decided is whether the defendant should stay in custody while awaiting the trial or whether bail should be granted. A person can be released on bail at any point after being arrested by the police. Being given bail means that the person is allowed to be at liberty until the next stage in the case.

9.2.1 Police powers to grant bail

The police may release a suspect on bail while they make further inquiries. This means that the suspect is released from police custody on the condition that they return to the police station on a specific date in the future.

The police can also give bail to a defendant who has been charged with an offence. In this case the defendant is bailed to appear at the local Magistrates' Court on a set date. The decision on whether to grant bail or not is made by the custody officer under section 38 of PACE as amended by the Criminal Justice and Public Order Act 1994. The custody officer can refuse bail if the suspect's name and address cannot be discovered, or if there is a doubt as to whether the name and address given are genuine. Apart from this, the normal principles as to when bail should be granted apply. These are set out in the Bail Act 1976 and are given in section 9.2.2. If any person granted bail by the police fails to surrender to that bail, (i.e. attend at the next stage of the case) then the police are given the right to arrest them.

Conditional bail

The Criminal Justice and Public Order Act 1994 gave the police the power to impose conditions on a grant of bail. The types of conditions include asking the suspect to surrender his passport, report at regular intervals to the police station or get another person to stand surety for him. These conditions can be only imposed in order to make sure that the suspect surrenders to bail, does not commit an offence while on bail and does not interfere with witnesses or interfere in any other way with the course of justice.

No police bail

Where, having charged a defendant with a crime, the police are not prepared to allow bail, they must bring the defendant in front of the Magistrates' Court at the first possible opportunity. If (as usually happens) the magistrates cannot deal with the whole case at that first hearing, the magistrates must then make the decision as to whether the defendant should be given bail or remanded in custody. The question as to whether bail should be given can also be considered by a court at any later stage of the criminal proceedings.

Statistics published by the Home Office show that the majority of those prosecuted are summonsed to court, rather than charged. This means that the question of bail or custody is not relevant, they are automatically at liberty. Of those who are charged, about five out of every six are released on bail by the police pending the court proceedings, so in fact only a small number of defendants are refused bail by the police. In these cases the courts must then decide whether to grant bail.

9.2.2 The Bail Act 1976

This is the key act, starting with the assumption that an accused person should be granted bail, though this right is limited for certain cases (see section 9.2.3). Section 4 of the Bail Act 1976 gives a general right to bail, but the court need not grant a defendant bail if it is satisfied that there are substantial grounds for believing that the defendant, if released on bail, would:

1. Fail to surrender to custody
2. Commit an offence while on bail
3. Interfere with witnesses or otherwise obstruct the course of justice

The court can also refuse bail if it is satisfied that the defendant should be kept in custody for his own protection.

In deciding whether to grant bail, the court will consider various factors including:

- The nature and seriousness of the offence (and the probable method of dealing with it)
- The character, antecedents (that is, past record), associations and community ties of the defendant
- The defendant's record as respects the fulfilment of his obligations under previous grants of bail in criminal proceedings; in other words has he turned up (surrendered to his bail) on previous occasions
- The strength of the evidence against him

If a defendant is charged with an offence which is not punishable by imprisonment, bail can only be refused if the defendant has previously failed to surrender to bail and there are grounds for believing that he will not surrender on this occasion.

A court can make conditions for the granting of bail. These are similar to conditions which can be set by the police and may include the surrender of passport and/or reporting to a police station. The court can also make a condition as to where the accused must reside while on bail; this could be at a home address or at a bail hostel.

Sureties

The court (and the police) can require a surety for bail. A surety is another person who is prepared to promise to pay the court a certain sum of money if the defendant fails to attend court. This promise is called a recognisance and no money is paid unless the defendant fails to answer to his bail. This system is different from that of other countries, especially America, where the surety must pay the money into court before the defendant is released on bail, but gets the money back when the defendant attends court as required.

Renewed applications and appeals

Normally only one further application can be made to the magistrates, unless there is a change of circumstance. The defendant can appeal against a refusal to grant bail. Such an appeal is made to a judge in chambers in the Queen's Bench Division of the High Court. A defendant who has been sent for trial to the Crown Court can also apply there for bail.

9.2.3 Amendments to the Bail Act 1976

During the 1980s and early 1990s there was concern that the Bail Act 1976 allowed bail to be given too freely and, that, as a result, dangerous defendants were being released on bail and in some cases defendants were committing further offences while on bail. This first led to the passing of section 153 of the Criminal Justice Act 1988 which amended the Bail Act, so that a court is required to give reasons for granting bail where the offence charged is murder, manslaughter or rape. However, there were still cases in which an offender released on bail by magistrates, committed further serious offences while on bail.

The following year the Bail (Amendment) Act 1993 gave the prosecution the right to

appeal to a judge at the Crown Court against the granting of bail provided:

- The offence charged carries a maximum sentence of at least five years' imprisonment, or is the offence of taking a conveyance without consent
- The prosecution objected to bail
- The prosecution give immediate verbal notice of the intention to appeal followed by a written notice to the magistrates within two hours

Section 26 of the Criminal Justice and Public Order Act 1994 amended the Bail Act so that the presumption in favour of bail is removed where it appears that the defendant has committed a triable either way offence or an indictable offence, while already on bail for another offence. However the court can still decide to grant bail.

Section 25 of the Criminal Justice and Public Order Act 1994 also barred the courts from granting bail in cases of murder, attempted murder, manslaughter, rape or attempted rape where the defendant had already served a custodial sentence for such an offence on a previous occasion. This total bar on bail was challenged as being in breach of the Convention on Human Rights and so, in 1998, the Government abolished this provision. Instead, the rule introduced by section 56 of the Crime and Disorder Act 1998 is that a defendant can only be granted bail in such cases if the court is satisfied that there are exceptional circumstances.

Activity

Look up the Law Commission's website and find out what it has recommended in relation to the need for bail rules to comply with the European Convention on Human Rights.

Then check to see whether these recommendations are being implemented by the Government.

KEY FACTS

Bail can be granted by	• police • magistrates • Crown Court
Bail Act 1976	There is a presumption in favour of bail BUT • bail need not be given where defendant has committed offence while already on bail • must be exceptional circumstances for bail to be granted for murder, attempted murder, manslaughter, rape or attempted rape where the defendant has already served a custodial sentence for such an offence
In all cases bail can be refused if there are reasonable grounds for believing the defendant:	• would fail to surrender • would commit further offences • would interfere with witnesses
Conditions can be imposed	• sureties • residence in bail hostel • curfew • hand in passport etc.
Comment	Many of those in prison are awaiting trial and could have been given bail Problem of balancing this against need to protect public

Figure 9.2 Key fact chart on bail

9.2.4 Balancing conflicting interests

It is argued that too many people are refused bail as about 20 per cent of those in our prisons are defendants who have not yet been tried, but who are remanded in custody. Some of these will be found not guilty, but will not be entitled to any compensation for the time they spent in custody. Even where the defendant is later found guilty, statistics show that 60 per cent are given non-custodial sentences.

The problem is that the criminal justice system has to balance the conflicting interests of the defendant (who is presumed innocent at this stage and entitled to his liberty) against the needs of the public to be protected from potentially dangerous criminals. The case of Andrew Hagans was an extreme example of what can happen where bail is granted too readily, but it is also important that the public are protected from other criminal behaviour. A Home Office survey suggested that about 10 per cent of those on bail commit further offences during the bail period, while a survey by Morgan in 1992 found that up 16 per cent of burglaries are committed by an offender who is already on bail for another offence.

The changes made by the Bail (Amendment) Act 1993 and the Criminal Justice and Public Order Act 1994 are attempts to keep the right balance between the defendant's civil rights and the protection of the public.

There is also the provision of bail hostels run by the probation service which are available in some areas. These provide a fixed address for homeless defendants who might otherwise be refused bail because of their homeless state. They also provide some degree of supervision for those on bail. However, there is a shortage of places in bail hostels and other alternatives need to be considered. One of these is the possibility of 'electronic tagging' of defendants on bail. The first such schemes were not very successful, with defendants having a high rate of offending while on bail. However, curfew orders are being used more often as a condition of bail.

Activity

Consider each of the following situations and explain with reasons whether you think bail would be granted or not.

1. Alex, aged 19 is charged with a robbery in which he threatened a shopkeeper with a gun and stole £2000. He has no previous convictions and lives at home with his mother.

2. Homer, aged 43, is charged with three offences of burglary. He has been convicted of burglary on two occasions in the past.

3. Melanie, aged 21, is charged with theft of items from a sportswear shop. She is currently unemployed and living rough. She has no previous convictions.

9.3 Crown Prosecution Service (CPS)

Before 1986 prosecutions brought by the state were normally conducted by the police. This led to criticism as it was thought

that the investigation of crime should be separate from the prosecution of cases. The Royal Commission on Criminal Procedure (the Phillips Commission), whose report led to the enactment of PACE, had also pointed out that there was no uniform system of prosecution in England and Wales. The Commission thought it was desirable to have an independent agency to review and conduct prosecutions. Eventually the Crown Prosecution Service (CPS) was established by the Prosecution of Offences Act 1985 and began operating in 1986.

9.3.1 Organisation of the CPS

The head of the CPS is the Director of Public Prosecutions (DPP), who must have been qualified as a lawyer for at least 10 years. The DPP is appointed by, and is subject to supervision by, the Attorney-General. Below the DPP are Chief Crown Prosecutors who each head one of the 42 areas into which the country is divided up. Each area is sub-divided into branches, each of which is headed by a Branch Crown Prosecutor. Within the branches there are several lawyers and support staff, who are organised into teams and given responsibility for cases.

At the beginning there were serious problems due to staff shortages and lack of co-ordination between police and local crown prosecutors. Both these problems have now been largely overcome, although there is still tension between the police and the CPS over the number of cases the CPS discontinues after the police have started proceedings against a defendant. This point is explored further in section 9.3.3.

9.3.2 The functions of the CPS

These involve all aspects of prosecution and can be summarised as:

- Giving advice to police on the admissibility of evidence at the stage before a charge is brought; this should avoid charges being brought unnecessarily
- Reviewing all cases passed to them by the police to see if there is sufficient evidence for a case to proceed, and whether it is in the public interest to do so; this is to avoid weak cases being brought to court
- Being responsible for the case after it has been passed to them by the police
- Conducting the prosecution of cases in the Magistrates' Court; this is usually done by lawyers working in the Crown Prosecution Service as Crown Prosecutors or lay presenters.
- Conducting cases in the Crown Court. This can either be by instructing an independent lawyer to act as prosecuting counsel at court or, from April 2000 under the Access to Justice Act 1999, Crown Prosecutors with the appropriate advocacy qualifications can conduct the case themselves.

On a practical level, once a defendant has been charged or summonsed with an offence the police role is at an end. They must send the papers for each case to the CPS – each case is then assigned to a team in the local branch of the CPS, and that team will be responsible for the case throughout the prosecution process. This is aimed at ensuring continuity and better communication in each case.

9.3.3 Discontinuance of cases

Once papers are received, the CPS is under a duty to review the case to see if the prosecution should continue. There have been criticisms over the number of cases in which the CPS decide that the prosecution should be discontinued. In order to overcome some of this criticism the DPP, in 1994, issued a revised code of practice for the CPS and the code was amended again in 2000. This code shows the factors taken into account when deciding whether to go ahead with a prosecution.

Evidential test

The two main factors are the 'evidential test' and the 'public interest test'. The first is concerned with whether there is sufficient evidence to provide a 'realistic prospect of conviction' in the case. Under this the CPS has to consider what the strength of the evidence is, and whether magistrates or a jury are more likely than not to convict. It will ask itself whether the evidence is admissible or whether it has been obtained by breaching the rules of PACE; whether a witness's background may weaken the case (for example the witness has a dubious motive so that the evidence is unreliable) and how strong the evidence of identification of the defendant is.

Public interest test

The second test, whether it is in the public interest to continue with the case, is more controversial as it involves very wide-ranging considerations. The code of practice gives lists of some 'common public interest factors' both for and against prosecution. It stresses that the lists are not exhaustive and that the factors that will apply depend on the facts in each case. These factors are reproduced in the activity below.

Activity

Read these two extracts and then answer the questions which follow each

1. Some common public interest factors in the favour of prosecution

Para 6.4 The more serious the offence, the more likely it is that a prosecution will be needed in the public interest. A prosecution is likely to be needed if:

- *a* a conviction is likely to result in a significant sentence;
- *b* a weapon was used or violence was threatened during the commission of the offence;

c   the offence was committed against a person serving the public (for example, a police or prison officer, or a nurse);

d   the defendant was in a position of authority or trust;

e   the evidence shows that the defendant was a ringleader or an organiser of the offence;

f   there is evidence that the offence was premeditated;

g   there is evidence that the offence was carried out by a group;

h   the victim of the offence was vulnerable or has been put in considerable fear;

i   the offence was motivated by any form of discrimination against the victim's ethnic or national origin, sex, religious beliefs, political views or sexual orientation;

j   there is a marked difference between the actual or mental ages of the defendant and the victim, or if there is any element of corruption;

k   the defendant's previous convictions or cautions are relevant to the present offence;

l   the defendant is alleged to have committed the offence whilst under an order of the court;

m   there are grounds for believing that the offence is likely to be continued or repeated, for example, by a history of recurring conduct; or

n   the offence, although not serious in itself, is widespread in the area where it was committed.

QUESTIONS

❶ Look at the list of factors in favour of prosecution and decide if you think any of the factors should be more important than others.

❷ Are there any factors in this list which you do not think should be considered when deciding whether to prosecute a defendant?

❸ What, if any, other factors would you like to see considered?

2. Some common public interest factors against prosecution

Para 6.5 A prosecution is less likely to be needed if:

a   the court is likely to impose a very small or nominal penalty;

b   the defendant has already been made the subject of a sentence, any further conviction would be unlikely to result in the imposition of an additional sentence or order, unless the nature of the particular offence requires a prosecution;

c   the offence was committed as a result of a genuine mistake or misunderstanding (these factors must be balanced against the seriousness of the offence);

d   the loss or harm can be described as minor and was the result of a single incident, particularly if it was caused by misjudgment;

e   there has been a long delay between the offence taking place and the date of the trial, unless:
- the offence is serious;
- the delay has been caused in part by the defendant;
- the offence has only recently come to light; or
- the complexity of the offence has meant that there has been a long investigation;

f   a prosecution is likely to have a bad effect on the victim's physical or mental health, always bearing in mind the seriousness of the offence;

g   the defendant is elderly or is, or was at the time of the offence, suffering from significant mental or physical ill health, unless the offence is serious or there is a real possibility that it may be repeated . . .

h   the defendant has put right the loss or harm that was caused (but defendants must not avoid prosecution simply because they can pay compensation); or

i   details may be made public that could harm sources of information, international relations or national security.

Source: The code for Crown Prosecutors

QUESTIONS

❹ Do you think any of the factors in this list are more important than others? Give reasons for your answer.

❺ Which, if any, of the above factors do you think should not be considered when deciding whether or not to prosecute a defendant?

❻ Compare the two lists. Are they well balanced? Do they provide a good framework for deciding when it is in the public interest to prosecute?

About 12 per cent of cases are discontinued each year. In addition there are cases which continue as far as the Crown Court, but are then abandoned.

However, there are still cases in which the CPS have been heavily criticised for discontinuation; as a result of the CPS discontinuing cases, there have been instances where private prosecutions have been brought for serious crimes. For example in 1995, there was a successful prosecution in a rape case which the CPS had refused to prosecute – a press report of this case is shown on this page.

There are also criticisms that the CPS often reduces the charge against the defendant to a less serious crime than is revealed by the evidence. This makes it more likely that the defendant will plead guilty, but, as the sentence will probably be less serious as well, it can leave the victim of a crime feeling that justice has not been done.

To improve matters the 2000 code of practice stresses that victims must be told about any decision made by the CPS which makes significant difference to the case (such as reducing the charge).

Civil actions

There have also been cases in which a civil case has been taken because the Crown Prosecution Service refuse to prosecute. The standard of proof in civil cases is not as high as in criminal cases, but even so some of these cases have then spurred the Crown Prosecution Service to prosecute. In particular in 1998 the family of a murdered black woman doctor, Joan Francisco, took a

Rapist is jailed after private court case

A man was jailed for 14 years yesterday in the first successful private prosecution for rape in England and Wales.

The sentence imposed on Christopher Davies, 44, a chef, is expected to prompt a spate of actions.

The case against Davies was brought by two prostitutes, who cannot be named, after the Crown Prosecution Service decided not to proceed. Both counsel and the solicitors acted free of charge. Davies was convicted earlier this year and sentence was deferred until yesterday.

Afterwards, one of the women said: 'This case has proved all women have the right to say "no".' Yesterday Women Against Rape said: 'This is especially a victory, given that the Crown Prosecution Service dismissed the case as having insufficient evidence'.

Taken from an article by Frances Gibb in *The Times*, 20 September 1995

civil case for trespass to the person against her ex-boyfriend. The family alleged that the boyfriend had murdered her. They were successful in this civil case: The police and the Crown Prosecution Service then reviewed the evidence and discovered that there was a test for discovering very small amounts of blood which they had not used in the first investigation. When this test was used, it revealed that there were spots of the boyfriend's blood on the woman's T-shirt. The CPS then prosecuted the man for murder and in 1999, six years after the murder, he was convicted.

Activity

Use CD-ROM to find newspaper reports of the civil case and the criminal case for the murder of Joan Francisco. Read these reports and make a list of the differences between these cases, including which court heard each case and what the decision was in each case.

NB To remind yourself of the differences between civil and criminal cases look back at section 1.1.2.

9.3.4 The Glidewell Report

Because of the problems and criticism of the CPS, Sir Iain Glidewell was asked to conduct an inquiry into the service. The Glidewell Report was published in 1998. A main criticism in the Report was the number of judge-ordered acquittals, which made up over 20 per cent of all acquittals. The report stated that in one in five of these cases something appeared to have been wrong with the preparation of the case.

The report also criticised the organisation of the CPS, finding that it was too bureaucratic and over-centralised. As a result the CPS was reorganised in 1999 into 42 areas (instead of 13). New Chief Crown Prosecutors were appointed for each area and the DPP, David Calvert-Smith, stated that these Chief Crown Prosecutors would have the power to act on their own initiative. It is intended that they can place a priority on prosecution work which will benefit the local communities they serve.

The re-organisation is also intended to create better working relationships with other local agencies in the criminal justice system, including the police and the courts.

Criminal Justice Units

The Narey Report into delay in the criminal justice system suggested that CPS staff should work in police stations in order to prevent delay in cases being passed to the CPS. During 1998 and 1999 pilot schemes were run in six areas of the country. As it was impractical to have a CPS lawyer in every police station, they were assigned to Criminal Justice Units or Administrative Support Units. The evaluation of the pilot schemes found that not only did this help to prevent delay, but it also created better working practices between the police and the CPS with greater continuity in cases.

It was also found that fewer cases were discontinued by the CPS: 7 per cent in the pilot areas as against 12 per cent nationally. This was thought to be due to the fact that CPS staff were available to advise police at an early stage in a case.

By March 2001 20 Criminal Justice Units had been established with another 36 planned to come into operation by March 2002.

Chapter 10

CRIMINAL COURTS

The two courts which hear criminal trials are the Magistrates' Court and the Crown Court. As already explained in Chapter 9, the actual court for the trial is decided by the category of crime involved in the charge. Summary offences can only be tried at the Magistrates' Court, indictable offences can only be tried at the Crown Court, while triable either way offences may be tried at either court.

In both the Magistrates' Court and the Crown Court the majority of defendants plead guilty to the charge against them. In these cases the role of the court is to decide what sentence should be imposed on the defendant. Where the accused pleads not guilty, the role of the court is to try the case and decide if the accused is guilty or not guilty; the burden of proof is on the prosecution who must prove the case beyond reasonable doubt. The form of the trial is an adversarial one, with prosecution and defence presenting their cases and cross-examining each other's witnesses, while the role of the judge is effectively that of referee, overseeing the trial and making sure that legal rules are followed correctly. The judge cannot investigate the case, nor ask to see additional witnesses.

10.1 Magistrates' Courts

There are about 430 Magistrates' Courts in England and Wales. They are local courts so there will be a Magistrates' Court in almost every town, while big cities will have several courts. Each court deals with cases that have a connection with its geographical area and they have jurisdiction over a variety of matters involving criminal cases. Cases are heard by magistrates, who may be either qualified District judges or unqualified lay justices (see Chapter 14 for further details on magistrates). There is also a legally qualified clerk attached to each court to assist the magistrates.

10.1.1 Jurisdiction of the Magistrates' Courts

So far as criminal cases are concerned the courts have jurisdiction in a variety of matters. They have a very large workload and they do the following:

1. Try all summary cases.
2. Try any triable either way offences which it is decided should be dealt with in the Magistrates' Court (see section 10.1.3).
   These first two categories account for about 97 per cent of all criminal cases.
3. Act as examining magistrates in committal proceedings for any triable either way offences which are going to the Crown Court. This means the magistrates take a preliminary look at the evidence, and if there is a *prima facie* case, send the case for trial to the Crown Court.
4. Deal with the first hearing of all indictable offences. These cases are then sent to the Crown Court.
5. Deal with all the side matters connected to criminal cases, such as issuing warrants for arrest and deciding bail applications.
6. Try cases in the Youth Court where the defendants are aged 10–17 inclusive.

Civil jurisdiction

The Magistrates' Courts also have some civil jurisdiction. Strictly speaking, this side of their work belongs in Chapter 6 – however, for completeness, and to illustrate the wide variety of work carried out by Magistrates' Court, this side of their work is listed below. It includes:

- Licensing pubs and restaurants to sell alcoholic drinks
- Granting licences under the betting and gaming laws
- Enforcing council tax demands and issuing warrants of entry and investigation to gas and electricity authorities
- Family cases including orders for protection against violence and maintenance orders (NB Magistrates' Courts cannot grant divorces)
- Proceedings concerning the welfare of children under the Children Act 1989

10.1.2 Summary trials

These are the least serious criminal offences and are sub-divided into offences of different 'levels' – level one being the lowest level and level five the highest. The use of levels allows a maximum fine to be set for each level which is increased in line with inflation from time to time. The current maximum fines date from the Criminal Justice Act 1991 and are level one: maximum £200, level two: £500, level three: £1,000, level four: £2,500 and level five: £5,000. However, for certain breaches of environmental law and health and safety legislation, business can be fined up to £20,000 by the magistrates. The maximum prison sentence that can be given on summary trial is six months.

At the start of any case, the clerk of the court will check the defendant's name and address and then ask whether he pleads guilty or not guilty. Over 90 per cent of defendants in the Magistrates' Court plead guilty and the process is then concerned with establishing an appropriate penalty for the case.

Guilty plea

The usual sequence of events in such a case is as follows.

1. The Crown Prosecutor or lay presenter from the CPS will give the court a resume of the facts of the case.
2. The defendant is asked if he agrees with those facts (if he does not the magistrates may have to hold an inquiry, called a Newton hearing, to establish the facts).
3. The defendant's past record of convictions, if any, is given to the court.
4. Other information about the defendant's background, especially his financial position, is given to the court.
5. Any relevant reports are considered by the magistrates; these may include a pre-sentence report prepared by a probation officer and/or a medical report on the defendant's mental health.
6. The defendant or his lawyer can then explain any matter which might persuade the magistrates to give a lenient sentence. This is called making a speech in mitigation.
7. The magistrates decide the sentence.

This is shown in a flow chart form in Figure 10.1.

Not guilty plea

When a defendant pleads not guilty the procedure is longer and more complicated, as both sides produce evidence to the court. Since the burden of proof is on the prosecution, they will begin the case – usually by making a short speech outlining what the case is about and what they hope to prove. The prosecution witnesses will then be called one at a time to give evidence, and the prosecutor will question each to establish what he or she saw and heard. This is called the examination in chief. After the prosecution finishes the examination in chief of a witness, the defence will then cross-examine that witness to test their evidence

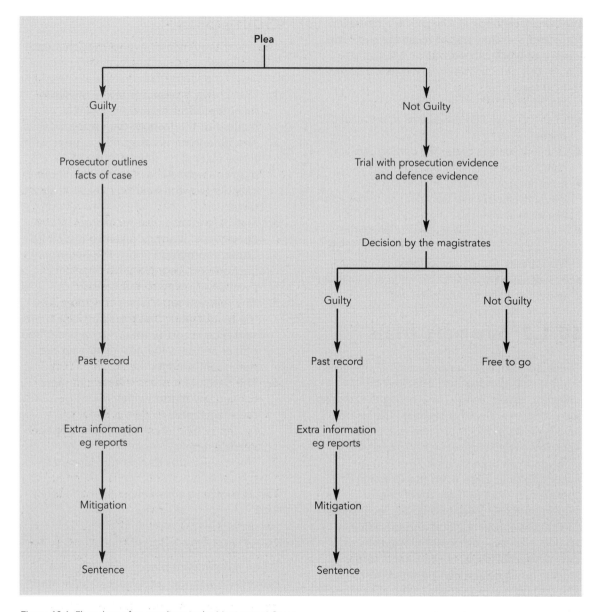

Figure 10.1 *Flow chart of proceedings in the Magistrates' Court*

and try to show that it is not reliable. The prosecution may also produce relevant exhibits, such as property found in the possession of the defendant or documents which help establish the case.

At the end of the prosecution case the defence can submit to the magistrates that there is no case to answer and that the case should be dismissed at this point. This is

because the prosecution has to prove the case and if their evidence does not establish a case, then it must be dismissed.

Only a very small number of cases will be dismissed at this stage. In the vast majority the case will continue and the defence will have to give their evidence to the court. The defendant himself will usually give evidence, though he does not have to. However, since the Criminal Justice and Public Order Act 1994, the magistrates can draw their own conclusions from the fact that the accused stays silent and does not explain his side of the matter. If the defendant does give evidence, he can be cross-examined by the prosecutor, as can any defence witnesses. The defence can call any witnesses and produce any evidence that they believe will help to disprove the prosecution's case.

Once all the evidence has been given, the defence have the right to make a speech pointing out the weaknesses of the case to the magistrates and try to persuade them to acquit the defendant. Further speeches are not usually allowed unless there is a point of law to be argued. The magistrates then decide if the defendant is guilty or not guilty. If they convict, they will then hear about his past record and may also look at reports and hear a speech in mitigation from the defence. They will then pass sentence.

If the magistrates dismiss the case, the defendant is free to go and cannot usually be tried for that offence again. There is, however, one exception when the defendant can be retried. This is where the prosecution successfully appeals against the acquittal in a 'case stated' appeal (see section 10.3.2 for the rules on these).

10.1.3 Triable either way offences

Plea before venue

Under the plea before venue procedure set out in the Criminal Procedure and Investigations Act 1996 the defendant is first asked whether he pleads guilty or not guilty. If he pleads guilty, then he has no right to ask to go to the Crown Court although the magistrates may still decide to send him there for sentence.

Mode of trial

If the defendant pleads not guilty then the magistrates must carry out 'mode of trial' proceedings to establish where the case will be tried. In this the magistrates first decide if they think the case is suitable for trial in the Magistrates' Court and whether they are prepared to accept jurisdiction.

Under section 19 of the Magistrates' Court Act 1980 they must consider the nature and seriousness of the case, their own powers of punishment and any representations of the prosecution and defence.

Cases involving complex questions of fact or law should be sent to the Crown Court. Other relevant factors which may make a case more suitable for trial at the Crown Court include:

- where there was breach of trust by a person
- where the crime was committed by an organised gang
- where the amount involved was more than twice the amount the magistrates can fine the defendant.

In rare cases where the Attorney-General, Solicitor-General or the Director of Public Prosecutions is the prosecutor, the magistrates, under section 19(4) of the Magistrates' Court Act 1980, must send the case to the Crown Court if that is what the prosecution wants. In other cases the prosecution's wishes are just part of the matters to be considered by the magistrates before they decide whether they are prepared to hear the case or whether it should be tried at the Crown Court.

Defendant's election

If the magistrates are prepared to accept jurisdiction, the defendant is then told he has the right to choose trial by jury, but may be tried by the magistrates if he agrees to this course. However, he is also warned that if the case is tried by the magistrates and at the end of the case he is found guilty, the magistrates can send him to the Crown Court for sentence if they feel their powers of punishment are insufficient.

10.1.4 Choosing trial by jury

Since 1997 defendants pleading guilty to a triable either way offence at the Magistrates' Court in the plea before venue procedure have not been able to choose to go to the Crown Court. This is sensible since there will be no trial of the case, so the defendants are not losing a right to trial by jury. Defendants who are pleading not guilty have had the right to choose where they want the case to be dealt with. This has been seen as an important part of civil liberties, as trial by jury is viewed as a protection of individual rights.

However not many defendants elect to go to the Crown Court. It was noticeable that when all defendants could choose to go to the Crown Court less than one out of 20 elected to do so.

Implications of choosing jury trial

There are several factors involved in a defendant's choice of the Crown Court as the venue for his trial. The main reason for choosing the Crown Court is that the decision on guilt or innocence is made by a jury and this gives a better chance of an acquittal. Only 20 per cent of defendants who plead not guilty at the Magistrates' Court will be found not guilty by the magistrates, whereas 60 per cent of those who plead not guilty at the Crown Court are acquitted. This does not mean the jury acquit a large number as this figure includes cases where the case is discharged by the judge without a trial. This is when the prosecution at the Crown Court does not offer evidence against the defendant. This

may be because by the time the case reaches the Crown Court, the prosecution accept that the defendant is not guilty, or it may be because witnesses have failed or refused to come to court and the prosecution are left with insufficient evidence for the case to proceed.

Other points to be considered are that:

- There will be a longer wait before the trial and there will also be committal proceedings in the Magistrates' Court before the case goes to the Crown Court
- Cases at the Crown Court are more expensive, but the defendant is also more likely to get legal representation through the Criminal Defence Service
- If the defendant is represented this must be by a barrister or solicitor with a certificate of advocacy giving rights of audience at the Crown Court
- There is a risk of a higher sentence if the defendant is found guilty in the Crown Court.

A study by Hedderman and Moxon showed that most defendants who chose the Crown Court did so on the advice of their lawyers and the main factor was the higher chance of an acquittal. There were many factors, however, which influenced the choice, including (where defendants were in custody) a wish to serve part of the sentence in a remand prison!

Should the right to choose trial by jury be kept?

It is very much more expensive to hold trials at the Crown Court than at the Magistrates' Court. In addition, statistics show that many of the defendants who choose jury trial then go on to plead guilty at the Crown Court. This has led to the questioning of whether defendants should have the right to elect trial by jury in cases where they are charged with a triable either way offence. In fact this right to jury trial has already been eroded by the fact that many offences which used to be triable either way have been reclassified as summary offences. These include the offences of assaulting a police officer in the execution of his duty, and driving whilst disqualified and drink driving.

The Runciman Commission in 1993 recommended that in all triable either way offences the right to choose trial by jury should be removed from the defendant.

In 1995 the Home Secretary under the Conservative Government issued a consultation paper on whether defendants should keep the right to choose trial by jury. There were many arguments against abolishing the right. Those against included the then shadow Home Secretary, Jack Straw, who said that it was 'unfair, short-sighted and likely to prove ineffective'. However, in 1997 when Jack Straw became Home Secretary in the Labour Government, he changed his mind. In 1998 he issued a consultation paper, *Determining Mode of Trial in Either-way Cases*, and in 1999 announced that he would be introducing law to abolish the right of defendants to elect trial by jury.

Two Bills were introduced into Parliament but on both occasions (once in 1999 and once in 2000) the House of Lords voted against the change.

The Auld Review

In 2001 Sir Robin Auld in a review of the criminal justice system recommended that decisions as to where trials should be held should be made by the magistrates (see 10.6 for other recommendations).

All these suggestions that the defendant's right to choose jury trial for triable either way offences should be abolished have been opposed by civil liberties groups. They point out that jury trial is a major part of democratic rights and that it promotes confidence in the legal system.

Activity

The following extract is from an editorial article in the *New Law Journal* which comments on a debate over the right to elect trial by jury. Read the extract and then answer the questions which follow.

'*Charles Clarke of the Home Office reiterated the official line that the right to jury trial must be curtailed, not only on the grounds of expense but also on the grounds that for justice to succeed it must be efficient. At present no one suggests that it is efficient. What Mr Clarke believes is that the present system of allowing defendants the right of a trial by jury costs more than a case in a Magistrates' Court, wastes police time and causes inconvenience and worry to witnesses and victims. What apparently has been happening is that defendants opt for trial by jury and throw their hands in [that is, plead guilty]. He believes this is an effort to manipulate the system, with defendants hoping that witnesses will not turn up or that their recollection of events will have dimmed as time goes on. In a minority of cases witnesses may well have been nobbled.*

He is probably quite correct. A number of defendants prefer to sit out much of their time on remand with no intention of actually defending a case; a number do hope that witnesses will go away or will forget but that is not a good argument for taking away the right of trial by jury from the many. In fact research, which may be out of date anyway shows that only one in 25 exercise the right to trial by jury. At least we should have up to the minute research.

Those who elect trial by jury and contest the case are statistically far more likely to be acquitted. As we have said, time and again, the truth is that defendants, particularly from ethnic minorities, do not trust justice in the Magistrates' Court. Nor for the matter are we altogether confident of it. Defenders of the magistracy will say there have been reforms and that critics such as we are out of date, but there have been far too many empirical examples of magistrates favouring "our police" or "our prosecutor" to have overall confidence in the system.'

New Law Journal, 29 October 1999

QUESTIONS

❶ The Home Office official put forward reasons for abolishing the right to choose trial by jury. What are those reasons?
❷ Why does the editorial not agree with the proposal to abolish the right to trial by jury?
❸ Explain with reasons which side of the argument you prefer.

10.1.5 Sending cases to the Crown Court

Where the trial is going to be held at the Crown Court, the magistrates must officially send the case to the Crown Court. For triable either way offences committal proceedings are used, while indictable offences are now transferred without these proceedings.

Committal proceedings

Committal proceedings originally involved all the witnesses in the case coming to the Magistrates' Court and giving their evidence. If there was sufficient evidence, the magistrates could commit the case to be tried at the Crown Court.

Since 1967 witness statements have been used at committal proceedings rather than calling the witnesses to give evidence in court although the defence could ask for some witnesses to attend court.

Present position

Under section 47 of and Schedule 1 to the Criminal Procedure and Investigations Act 1996 no witnesses are called at committal proceedings. All prosecution evidence must be handed to the court in a written form. If the defence want to challenge whether there is sufficient evidence for the case to be sent to the Crown Court, all this written evidence is read out. The defence and prosecution

then have the right to make oral statements on whether the case should be sent to the Crown Court or whether the defendant should be discharged.

Where there is no dispute that there is enough evidence for the case to be sent to the Crown Court, and provided that the defendant has legal representation, then the written statements are not read by the magistrates. The committal proceedings are just a formality.

Remember that committal proceedings only take place for triable either way offences which are to be tried at the Crown Court.

Transfer proceedings

For indictable offences the case is transferred to the Crown Court immediately from the first hearing at the Magistrates' Court. This is under section 51 of the Crime and Disorder Act 1998. The idea is to speed up the way cases are dealt with.

10.1.6 Committals for sentence

Magistrates can commit a defendant charged with a triable either way offence for sentence to the Crown Court if, at the end of a case, having heard the defendant's past record, they feel that their powers of punishment are insufficient.

The magistrates must be of the opinion that the offence, or the combination of offences, is so serious that a greater punishment than they have power to inflict should be imposed. In cases of violent or sexual offences, the magistrates may commit for sentence if they think that a long sentence of imprisonment is necessary to protect the public from serious harm.

After the introduction of plea before venue (see section 10.1.3) the number of committals for sentence more than doubled.

About 28,000 defendants each year are sent by the magistrates to the Crown Court for sentencing. There are criticisms that magistrates commit too many defendants for sentence, since a significant percentage of those committed for sentence do not receive more than the magistrate could have imposed on them.

10.1.7 The role of the clerk

Every bench of magistrates is assisted by a clerk. The senior clerk in each court has to be a barrister or solicitor of at least five years' standing. The role of the clerk is to guide the magistrates on questions of law, practice and procedure. The clerk makes sure that the correct procedure is followed in court. For example at the start of a case it is the clerk who will ask the defendant if he pleads guilty or not guilty. The clerk is not meant to take part in the decision-making process; that is the magistrates' role. This means that the clerk should not retire with the justices when they leave the court at the end of a case to consider their verdict.

The senior clerk has been granted greater powers to deal with routine matters which previously had to be done by magistrates. For example clerks can now issue warrants for arrest, extend police bail, adjourn criminal proceedings (where the defendant is on bail and the terms on the bail are not being changed), and conduct early administrative hearings.

10.2 Youth courts

Young offenders aged from 10 to 17 are dealt with in the Youth court which is a branch of the Magistrates' Court. Children under the age of 10 cannot be charged with a criminal offence. Those aged 17 used to be tried in the ordinary courts, but since the Criminal Justice Act 1991, they are now also dealt with in the Youth court.

There are some exceptional cases in which young offenders can be tried in the Crown Court. These are cases where the defendant is charged with murder or manslaughter, rape, and causing death by dangerous driving. In addition it is possible for those aged 14 and over, to be sent to the Crown Court for trial in any case where they are charged with a serious offence (usually one which for an adult carries a maximum prison sentence of at least 14 years). Apart from these provisions, a young offender who is jointly charged with an adult may be tried with that adult in the ordinary courts. However, if the young offender is found guilty it is usual in such cases for him to be sent back to the Youth court for sentencing.

The court sits in private with only those who are involved in the case allowed into the court room. Members of the press may be present, but they cannot publish the name of any young offender or other information which could identify him, such as address or school.

The magistrates who sit on the bench in these courts must be under 65 and have had special training to deal with young offenders. There must be at least one female magistrate and one male magistrate on the bench. The procedure in the court is less formal than in the adult courts and the parents or guardian any child under 16 are required to be present for the proceedings. The court can also ask parents of those aged 16 or 17 to attend.

10.3 Appeals from the Magistrates' Court

There is a system of appeal routes available from a decision by the Magistrates' Court. The route used will depend on whether the appeal is only on a point of law, or whether it is for other reasons. The two appeal routes are to the Crown Court, or to the Queen's Bench Divisional Court.

10.3.1 Appeals to the Crown Court

This is the normal route of appeal and is only available to the defence. If the defendant pleaded guilty at the Magistrates' Court, then he can only appeal against sentence. If the defendant pleaded not guilty and was convicted, then the appeal can be against conviction and/or sentence. In both cases the defendant has an automatic right to appeal and does not need to get leave (permission) to appeal.

At the Crown Court the case is completely re-heard by a judge and two magistrates. They can come to the same decision as the magistrates and confirm the conviction, or they can decide that the case is not proved and reverse the decision. In some cases it is possible for them to vary the decision and find the defendant guilty of a lesser offence.

Where the appeal is against sentence, the Crown Court can confirm the sentence or they can increase or decrease it. However, any increase can only be up to the magistrates' maximum powers for the case.

Over the last few years there have been about 15,000 appeals to the Crown Court each year, and judicial statistics published by the Lord Chancellor Department show that the appeal is allowed in approximately one quarter of cases, while the magistrates' order is varied in about another quarter. This means that about half of those who appeal have some success.

If it becomes apparent that there is a point of law to be decided, then the Crown Court can decide that point of law, but there is the possibility of a further appeal by way of a case stated appeal being made to the Queen's Bench Divisional Court (see section 10.3.2). A diagram setting out the appeal routes from the Magistrates' Court is shown in Figure 10.2.

10.3.2 Case stated appeals

These are appeals on a point of law which go to the Queen's Bench Divisional Court. Both the prosecution and the defence can use this appeal route and it can be direct from the Magistrates' Court, or following an appeal to the Crown Court. The magistrates (or the Crown Court) are asked to state the case by setting out their findings of fact and their decision. The appeal is then argued on the basis of what the law is on those facts; no witnesses are called. The appeal is heard by a panel of two or three High Court judges from the Queen's Bench Division, though in some cases a judge from the Court of Appeal may form part of the panel.

This route is only used by the defendant against a conviction, or by the prosecution against an acquittal. It cannot be used to challenge the sentence. The appeal is because they claim the magistrates came to the wrong decision because they made a mistake about the law. The Divisional Court may confirm, vary or reverse the decision or remit (send back) the case to the Magistrates' Court for the magistrates to implement the decision on the law.

There are only a small number of appeals by way of case stated made each year. In 2000 there were 125 appeals to the Queen's Bench Divisional Court.

Further appeal to the House of Lords

From the decision of the Queen's Bench Divisional Court there is a possibility of a further appeal to the House of Lords. Such an appeal can only be made if:

1. The Divisional Court certifies that a point of law of general public importance is involved.
2. The Divisional Court or the House of Lords gives leave to appeal because the point is one which ought to be considered by the House of Lords.

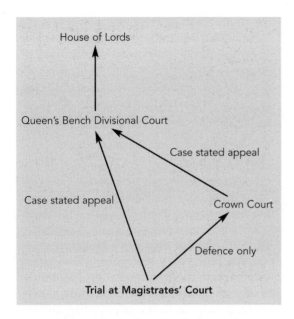

Figure 10.2 Appeal routes from the Magistrates' Court

An example of a case which followed this appeal route was *C v DPP* (1994). This case concerned the legal point about the presumption of criminal responsibility of children from the age of 10 up to their fourteenth birthday. Until this case, it had been accepted that a child of this age could only be convicted if the prosecution proved that the child knew he was doing wrong. The Divisional Court held that times had changed and that children were more mature and the rule was not needed. They decided that children of this age were presumed to know the difference between right and wrong, and that the prosecution, did not need to prove 'mischievous discretion'.

The case was then appealed to the House of Lords who overruled the Divisional Court, holding that the law was still that a child of this age was presumed not to know he or she was doing wrong, and therefore not to have the necessary intention for any criminal offence. A child of this age could only be convicted if the prosecution disproved this presumption by bringing evidence to show

that the child was aware that what he or she was doing was seriously wrong. The House of Lords ruling was on the basis that it was for Parliament to make such a major change to the law, not the courts. The courts were bound by precedent.

10.4 The Crown Court

Until 1971 very serious criminal cases were dealt with by High Court judges when they toured the country holding Assize Courts. Other indictable offences were heard at Quarter Sessions, which were intended to sit four times a year. This system was out of date and unable to cope with the growing number of criminal cases – following the Beeching Commission Report 1969, both Assizes and Quarter Sessions were abolished. In their place, the Courts Act 1971 set up the Crown Court to deal with all cases which were not tried at the Magistrates' Court.

The Crown Court currently sits in 90 different centres throughout England and Wales. There are three kinds of centre:

1. **First tier**
   These exist in main centres throughout the country, for example there are first tier Crown Courts in Bristol, Birmingham, Leeds and Manchester. At each court there is a High Court and a Crown Court with separate judges for civil and criminal work. The Crown Court is permanently staffed by High Court judges as well as Circuit judges and Recorders, and the court can deal with all categories of crime triable on indictment.
2. **Second tier**
   This is a Crown Court only, but High Court judges sit there on a regular basis to hear criminal cases, as well as Circuit judges and Recorders. All categories of crime triable on indictment can be tried here.

3. **Third tier**

This is staffed only by Circuit judges and Recorders. The most serious cases, such as murder, manslaughter and rape are not usually tried here as there is no High Court judge to deal with them.

10.4.1 Preliminary matters

The indictment

This is a document which formally sets out the charges against the defendant. Although the defendant will have been sent for trial charged with specific crimes, the indictment can be drawn up for any offence that the witness statements reveal. In more complicated cases the indictment may be for several counts. Figure 10.3 shows a sample indictment.

Disclosure by prosecution and defence

The Criminal Procedure and Investigations Act 1996 places a duty on both sides to make certain points known to the other. The prosecution, who have already given the defence statements of all the evidence they propose to use at the trial, must also disclose previously undisclosed material 'which in the prosecutor's opinion might undermine the case for the prosecution against the accused'. This is designed to prevent the sort of miscarriage of justice which occurred in Stefan Kiszko's case (see Chapter 8) through the prosecution 'hiding' something which could help prove the innocence of the defendant. However, defence lawyers have pointed out that since 1981 when the Attorney-General first issued guidelines on prosecution disclosure, the courts have laid down wideranging rules which have meant that the defence was entitled to know about almost all unused material. The 1996 Act is a backward step as it leaves exactly what is to be disclosed to the judgment of the prosecution.

DONBRIDGE CROWN COURT

The Queen v John Wilkie
charged as follows:

STATEMENT OF OFFENCE
Murder contrary to the common law

PARTICULARS OF OFFENCE
John Wilkie on the 4th day of April 1997 murdered Abraham Lincoln

---

Figure 10.3 Sample indictment

The 1996 Act also imposes a new duty on the defence in cases which are to be tried on indictment. In these, after the prosecution's primary disclosure, the defence must give a written statement to the prosecution setting out in general terms the nature of the accused's defence, indicating the matters on which he takes issue with the prosecution and why he takes issue over these matters. This forces the defence to disclose their case before the trial, and appears to run contrary to the concept that the burden of proof is on the prosecution.

Following the defence disclosure, the prosecution have a duty to disclose any previously undisclosed material which might 'reasonably be expected to assist the accused's defence'.

The Auld Review (2001) recommended that the disclosure system should be simplified with automatic disclosure of certain documents. It also recommended that the prosecutor rather than the police should be responsible for identifying all potentially disclosable material.

Plea and directions hearing (PDH)

Since 1995 a preliminary hearing called a 'plea and directions' hearing has been held in cases sent to the Crown Court for trial. It is held as soon as possible after the case has been sent to the Crown Court, normally within four weeks if the defendant is being held in custody, and six weeks if the defendant is on bail. The first purpose of a PDH is to find out whether the defendant is pleading guilty or not guilty. All the charges on the indictment are read out to the defendant in open court, and he is asked how he pleads to each charge. This process is called the 'arraignment'.

If the defendant pleads guilty, the judge will, if possible, sentence the defendant immediately. This means that defendants who plead guilty will not have an unnecessarily long wait for their case to come to court.

Where a defendant pleads not guilty the judge will require the prosecution and defence to identify the key issues, both of fact and law, that are involved in the case. He will then give any directions that are necessary to organise the actual trial, for instance the prosecution and defence may agree that certain witnesses need not attend court as their evidence is not in dispute. Other points such as whether it will be necessary to use a video link for any witnesses are also agreed on. The aim of the PDH is to speed up the actual trial process and to ensure that time will not be wasted on unnecessary points. It also allows the court to plan its lists. However, the combined effect of this and the duty of defence disclosure under the Criminal Procedure and Investigations Act, means that the defence are prevented from asking questions, 'fishing' for information or looking for a loophole in the prosecution evidence. This can be viewed as tilting the balance in the prosecution's favour.

Preparatory hearings

These have been introduced by the Criminal Procedure and Investigations Act 1996 for complex cases. The judge assigned to the case decides if a preparatory hearing is necessary – as with PDHs the main aim is to

identify the issues and speed up the trial. The judge can deal with the same points that would occur in a PDH, but he can also hear legal arguments on points of law and admissibility of evidence and decide these points.

Plea bargaining

This is the name for pre-trial informal discussions between defence and prosecution on whether it might be possible for the defendant to plead guilty to a lesser offence. In addition, in some cases the judge might be unofficially approached as to what sentence the accused could expect to receive if he pleaded guilty. This was not supposed to happen, but in practice it occurred, and still occurs, quite widely.

The Auld Review recommends that there should be a formal system of indicating in advance the sentence a defendant is likely to receive if he pleads guilty.

10.4.2 The trial

It is normal for a defendant appearing at the Crown Court to be represented, usually by a barrister, although solicitors who have a certificate of advocacy can also appear at the Crown Court. Defendants can represent themselves, but there was concern over the effect this could have on witnesses who were cross-examined at length by a defendant in person. As a result the Youth Justice and Criminal Evidence Act 1999 forbids cross-examination in person by defendants who are charged with sexual offences, or where there is a child witness.

At the trial where the defendant pleads not guilty, the order of events will normally be:

1. The jury is sworn in to try the case (for further information on juries see Chapter 14).
2. The prosecution will make an opening speech to the jury explaining what the

case is about and what they intend to prove.

3. The prosecution witnesses give evidence and can be cross-examined by the defence; the prosecution will also produce any other evidence such as documents or video recordings.

4. At the end of the prosecution case the defence may submit that there is no case to go to the jury; if the judge decides there is no case he will direct the jury to acquit the defendant.

5. The defence may make an opening speech provided they intend calling evidence other than the defendant.

6. The defence witnesses give evidence and are cross-examined by the prosecution; the defendant does not have to give evidence personally but the judge may comment on the failure to do in his summing up to the jury.

7. The prosecutor makes a closing speech to the jury pointing out the strengths of the prosecution case.

8. The defence makes a closing speech to the jury pointing out the weaknesses of the prosecution.

9. The judge sums up the case to the jury and directs them on any relevant law.

10. The jury retire to consider their verdict in private.

11. The jury's verdict is given in open court.

12. If the verdict is guilty the judge then sentences the accused; if the verdict is not guilty the accused is discharged and, under the doctrine of *autrefois acquit*, can never be tried for that offence again.

10.5 Appeals from the Crown Court

It is important that there should be adequate routes of appeal, and the functions of an appeal process serve not only to protect the defendant from a miscarriage of justice, but also to allow uniform development of the law.

10.5.1 Appeals by the defendant

The defendant has the possibility of appealing against conviction and/or sentence to the Court of Appeal (Criminal Division). So, at the end of any trial in which a defendant has been found guilty, his lawyer should advise him on the possibility of an appeal. This can be done verbally at the court, or in writing within 14 days of the trial, and is intended to make sure that each defendant has advice within the time limits for making an appeal. In order to appeal, a notice of appeal must be filed at the Court of Appeal (Criminal Division) within 28 days of conviction.

Leave to appeal

The rules on appeals are set out in the Criminal Appeal Act 1995 and in all cases the defendant must get leave to appeal from the Court of Appeal, or a certificate that the case is fit for appeal from the trial judge. The idea of having to get leave is that cases which are without merit are filtered out and the court's time saved.

The application for leave to appeal is considered by a single judge of the Court of Appeal in private, although if he refuses it is possible to apply to a full Court of Appeal for leave. It is difficult to get leave to appeal – in 2000, 7,348 applications were considered by a single judge, but leave to appeal was granted in only 2,105 cases (about 28 per cent). Even when a defendent gets leave to appeal that does not mean that the actual appeal will be successful.

The Criminal Appeal Act 1995

The Criminal Appeal Act 1995 simplified the grounds under which the court can allow an appeal. The Act states that the Court of Appeal:

'(a) shall allow an appeal against conviction if they think that the conviction is unsafe; and
(b) shall dismiss such an appeal in any other case.'

Since the European Convention on Human Rights has been incorporated into our law by the Human Rights Act 1998, the Court of Appeal has taken a broad approach to the meaning of 'unsafe'. In particular, a conviction has been held to be 'unsafe' where the defendant has been denied a fair trial.

New evidence

The Criminal Appeal Act also changes the criteria under which new evidence can be produced at an appeal. The new evidence must appear to be capable of belief and would afford a ground for an appeal. This has to be considered together with whether it would have been admissible at the trial and why it was not produced at that trial.

Court of Appeal's powers

The Court of Appeal can allow a defendant's appeal and quash the conviction. Alternatively it can vary the conviction to that of a lesser offence of which the jury could have convicted the defendant. So far sentence is concerned the court can decrease, but not increase it on the defendant's appeal. Where the appeal is not successful, the court can decide to dismiss the appeal.

The Court of Appeal also has the power to order that there should be a re-trial of the case in front of a new jury. The power was given to it in 1988, but initially was not often used, for example in 1989 only one re-trial was ordered. However, its use has increased with over 70 re-trials being ordered in each of the years 1998, 1999 and 2000.

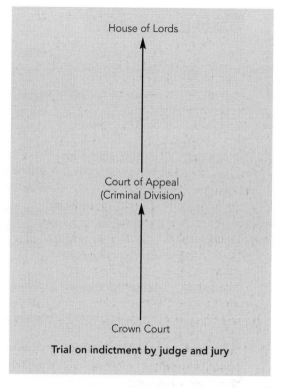

Figure 10.4 Appeal routes from the Crown Court

10.5.2 Appeals by the prosecution

Originally the prosecution had no right to appeal against either the verdict or sentence passed in the Crown Court. Gradually, however, some limited rights of appeal have been given to them by Parliament.

Against an acquittal

With one small exception, the prosecution cannot appeal against a finding of not guilty by a jury. The exception is for cases where the acquittal was the result of the jury or witnesses being 'nobbled', i.e. where some jurors are bribed or threatened by associates of the defendant. In these circumstances, provided there has been an actual conviction for jury nobbling, the Criminal Procedure and Investigations Act 1996 allows an application to be made to the High Court for an order quashing the acquittal. Once

KEY FACTS

Party	Court which hears appeal	Reason for appealing	Relevant Act of Parliament
Defence	Court of Appeal	against sentence and/or conviction need leave to appeal	Criminal Appeal Act 1995 conviction 'unsafe'
Defence	further appeal to House of Lords	on point of law of general public importance need leave to appeal	
Prosecution	High Court	asking for order to quash acquittal because of interference with witness or jury	Criminal Procedure and Investigations Act 1996
Prosecution	Court of Appeal	Attorney-General's reference on a point of law: does not affect acquittal	Criminal Justice Act 1972
Prosecution	Court of Appeal	Attorney-General against lenient sentence	Criminal Justice Act 1988
Prosecution	Further appeal to House of Lords	on point of law of general public importance need leave to appeal	

Figure 10.5 Key fact chart on appeal rights from the Crown Court

the acquittal is quashed, the prosecution could then start new proceedings for the same offence. As yet this power has never been used.

Referring a point of law

However, the prosecution have a special referral right in cases where the defendant is acquitted. This is under s 36 of the Criminal Justice Act 1972 which allows the Attorney-General to refer a point of law to the Court of Appeal, in order to get a ruling on the law. The decision by the Court of Appeal on that point of law does not affect the acquittal but it creates a precedent for any future case involving the same point of law.

Against sentence

Under s 36 of the Criminal Justice Act 1988 the Attorney-General can apply for leave to refer an unduly lenient sentence to the Court of Appeal for re-sentencing. This power was initially available for indictable cases only, but was extended in 1994 to many triable either way offences, provided that the trial of the case took place at a Crown Court. This power has been used successfully in a number of cases, including one where a boy of 15 had been given a supervision order for three years for raping a girl (and his parents ordered to pay £500 compensation to her). His sentence was increased to a two years' custodial sentence in a Young Offenders

Institution. It has also been used in other cases, such as that of Orlando Baker, who in May 1996 had his nine-year sentence for rape increased to life imprisonment.

The main difficulty is: how does the Attorney-General learn of cases which ought to be referred to the Court of Appeal? In fact, about 160 cases are brought to the Attorney-General's attention each year, with most of these being sent to him by the Crown Prosecution Service. However, it is possible for the public to write to the Attorney-General's office and about 12 cases a year are reported in this way, usually by distressed relatives of the victim of the crime, who feel that the original sentence was inadequate. Members of Parliament will also sometimes refer cases to the Attorney-General on behalf of aggrieved constituents.

Whenever a case is sent to the Attorney-General he will look through the papers on the trial and decide whether to refer the case to the Court of Appeal.

10.5.3 Appeals to the House of Lords

Both the prosecution and the defence may appeal from the Court of Appeal to the House of Lords, but it is necessary to have the case certified as involving a point of law of general public importance, and to get leave to appeal, either from the House of Lords or from the Court of Appeal. There are very few criminal appeals heard by the House of Lords. In 2000 there were 18 petitions for leave to appeal considered, but leave was granted in only four of these.

Comment

There have often been criticisms of the Law Lords' judgments in criminal cases. It is felt that there is a certain lack of expertise as very few of the Lords will have practised in the field of criminal law. This was emphasised in *Hyam* v *DPP* (1975) when Lord Cross in his judgment said: 'I have never before had to grapple with this obscure and highly technical branch of the law'. In the case of *R* v *Shivpuri* (1986) the judges in the House of Lords admitted that they had wrongly interpreted the law on attempts to commit a crime, in a case which they had decided only the year before. During the 1980s the law on recklessness became very complex as a result of House of Lords' rulings. Some of these decisions have been subsequently overruled by later House of Lords' decisions in the 1990s. This type of haphazard development of the law does little to instil confidence in the House of Lords as the final appeal court for criminal cases.

References to the European Court of Justice

Where a point of European law is involved in a case it is possible for any court to make a reference to the European Court of Justice under Article 177 of the Treaty of Rome (see Chapter 4). However, this is a fairly rare occurrence in criminal cases, as most of the criminal law is purely 'domestic' and not affected by European Union law.

10.6 The Auld Review

In 2001 Sir Robin Auld published his review of the criminal justice system. He made 328 recommendations. Some of these were very wide-ranging. For example, he recommended the codification of the criminal law and also that there should be codes for procedure, evidence and sentencing.

A new court structure

The main recommendation was for a unified criminal court with three divisions:

- a Crown Division for all indictable offences and the more serious triable either way offences;
- a District Division of a District Judge and at least two lay magistrates to exercise jurisdiction over a mid range of either-way offences meriting up to two years' custody and in which the District judge would be the sole arbiter of law;
- a Magistrates Division with a District Judge or lay magistrates (as at present).

He thought that the allocation of either-way cases to the divisions should be by the Magistrates' Division. They would decide this according to seriousness of the alleged offence and possible outcome. Where there was a dispute over venue, this would be decided by a District Judge after hearing representations from prosecution and defence. The defendant's right to elect jury trial would be lost.

Appeals

There should be new appeal routes for the Divisions with a single line of appeal from the Magistrates' Division to the Crown Division (judge sitting alone). The case stated appeal to the Queens Bench Divisional Court would be abolished and replaced, if necessary, with appeal to the Court of Appeal.

There were a large number of recommendations about juries and these are set out in the chapter on juries at section 14.2.7.

Other recommendations

To ease the workload on the Magistrates' Division, offences such as failing to pay the TV licence fee or Council Tax should be decriminalised and become subject to fixed penalties.

The report also recommended that courts in some areas should sit in the evening or at weekends. This idea is already being tried with a pilot scheme of late sitting Magistrates' Courts which started in September 2001.

The review supported the Law Commission's recommendations that the double jeopardy rule should be abolished in murder cases where there is 'compelling' evidence. However, the Auld Review goes beyond this and suggests extending the prosecutor's right of appeal to other grave offences punishable with life or long terms of imprisonment.

The Government will be issuing a White Paper some time in 2002 setting out the Government's conclusions with a view to introducing legislation 'when Parliamentary time allows'.

However, it seems unlikely that the idea of a new District Division for mid-range crimes will be brought in.

10.7 The Criminal Cases Review Commission

The large number of miscarriages of justice (see section 8.1.2) which had not been corrected through the normal appeal system led to demands for a review body. It was true that the Home Secretary had power to review cases and refer them to the Court of Appeal, but cases such as the Birmingham Six and Judith Ward left people feeling that the Home Secretary was not sufficiently independent of the Government. The Runciman Commission, when considering the question, recommended that an independent review body should be set up to consider possible miscarriages of justice. This recommendation was implemented by the Criminal Appeal Act 1995 which set up the Criminal Cases Review Commission.

The Commission has the power to investigate possible miscarriages of justice (including summary offences) and to refer cases back to the courts. In addition the Court of Appeal may direct the Commission to investigate and report to the court on any matter which comes before it in an appeal if it feels an investigation is likely to help the court resolve the appeal.

The members of the Commission are appointed by the Queen – at least one third are legally qualified and at least two thirds have relevant experience of the criminal justice system. They have about 60 support staff, treble the number previously used in the Home Office for such work. However, most of the re-investigation work is done by the police. This is felt to be unsatisfactory as it does not really make such a re-investigation independent, although it is true to say that many of the past miscarriages of justice have come to light as the result of investigation by other police forces.

Work

The Criminal Cases Review Commission took over the investigation of miscarriages of justice at the beginning of April 1997.

The main bulk of cases it investigates are brought to its attention by defendants themselves or by defendants' families, though some cases have been referred by the Court of Appeal and others have been identified by the Commission itself. Some of the first cases it investigated were alleged miscarriages of justice from over 40 years ago, such as the case of Derek Bentley. Bentley was hanged for murder in 1953, while his co-defendant, Craig, who actually fired the fatal shot, was not hanged due to his youth. Over the years there have been

many attempts to have the case re-opened but it was not until the Criminal Cases Review Commission took over the investigation that the case was referred back to the Court of Appeal. In July 1998 the Court of Appeal held that the summing-up of the judge at the trial had not been fair and it quashed the conviction.

Other cases are more recent, such as the case of Ryan James who was convicted in 1995 of murdering his wife. A year after his trial an apparent suicide note written by his wife was found. This was investigated by the Commission and the decision made to refer the case back to the Court of Appeal. Mr James' conviction was then quashed by the Court of Appeal in 1998.

Referrals to the Court of Appeal

In the first four and a half years of work the Criminal Cases Review Commission received almost 4,500 applications and had dealt with about 3,500 of these. The Commission had referred 145 cases to the Court of Appeal. 73 of these had been heard and the convictions quashed in 55 cases.

Activity

Check the website for the Criminal Cases Review Commission (*www.ccrc.gov.uk*) and find out:

1. How many cases has the Commission now dealt with?
2. How many cases has it referred to the Court of Appeal?
3. In how many cases has the defendant had his or her conviction quashed?

Chapter 11

SENTENCING

Whenever a person pleads guilty, or is found guilty of an offence, the role of the court is to decide what sentence should be imposed on the offender. Judges and magistrates have a fairly wide discretion as to the sentence they select in each case, although they are subject to certain restrictions. Magistrates can only impose a maximum of six months' imprisonment for one offence (12 months' for two) and a maximum fine of £5,000. Judges in the Crown Court have no such limits; they can impose up to life imprisonment for some crimes and there is no maximum figure for fines. Figure 11.1 shows the percentages of different sentences imposed for triable either way and indictable offences at the Magistrates' Court and the Crown Court in 2000. The differing percentages of offenders given an immediate custodial sentence stresses that the Crown Court is dealing with more serious offences.

However, there are other restrictions, both in the Magistrates' Court and the Crown Court. Each crime has a maximum penalty for that type of offence set by Parliament – for example the crime of theft has a fixed maximum of seven years' imprisonment, so that no matter how much has been stolen, the judge can never send an offender to prison for longer that this. Some offences have a maximum sentence of life imprisonment: these include manslaughter and rape. In such cases the judge has complete discretion when sentencing; the offender may be sent to prison for life or given a shorter prison sentence, or a non-custodial sentence may even be thought appropriate. Murder is the exception as it carries a mandatory life sentence; in other words, the judge has to pass life imprisonment: there is no other sentence available.

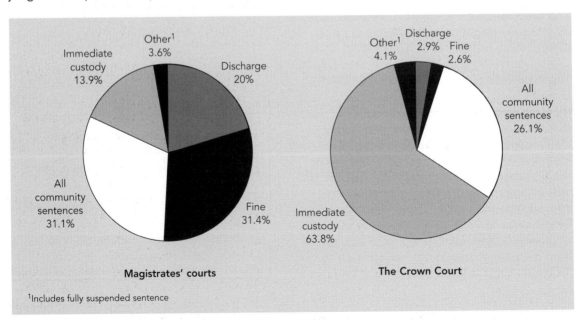

[1]Includes fully suspended sentence

Figure 11.1 Offenders sentenced at Magistrates' Court and Crown Court by types of sentence

Source: Home Office Statistical Bulletin 20/01

Minimum sentences

Although Parliament has set down various maximum sentences for offences, there are no minimum sentences for first time offenders. However, Parliament in the Crime (Sentences) Act 1997 set down minimum sentences for some persistent offenders. This idea followed American laws which impose minimum sentences for those who offend repeatedly. As well as minimum sentences for drug dealers and burglars, the Crime (Sentences) Act 1997 brought in an automatic life sentence for those who commit a second serious or violent offence. These provisions are very controversial and are considered further in section 11.6.

11.1 Aims of sentencing

When judges or magistrates have to pass a sentence they will not only look at the sentences available, they will also have to decide what they are trying to achieve by the punishment they give. There are six main different, and sometimes conflicting, aims of sentencing. These are: retribution, denunciation, incapacitation, deterrence, rehabilitation and reparation. Each of these will now be examined in turn.

11.1.1 Retribution

This is based on the idea of punishment because the offender deserves punishment for his or her acts. It does not seek to reduce crime or alter the offender's future behaviour. This idea was expressed in the nineteenth century by Kant in *The Metaphysical Elements of Justice* when he wrote:

> 'Judicial punishment can never be used merely as a means to promote some other good for the criminal himself or for civil society, but instead it must in all cases be imposed on him only on the ground that he has committed a crime.'

Retribution is therefore concerned only with the offence that was committed and making sure that the punishment inflicted is in proportion to that offence.

The crudest form of retribution can be seen in the old saying 'an eye for an eye and a tooth for a tooth and a life for a life'. This was one of the factors used to justify the death penalty for the offence of murder. In America, at least one judge has been known to put this theory into practice in other offences, by giving victims of burglary the right to go, with a law officer, to the home of the burglar and take items up to the approximate value of those stolen from them. In other crimes it is not so easy to see how this principle can operate to produce an exact match between crime and punishment.

Court of Appeal guidelines

Retribution, today, is based more on the idea that each offence should have a set tariff. This can be seen in the guidelines laid down by the Court of Appeal, particularly during the 1980s, as to the 'correct' punishment for certain offences. In *R v Aramah* (1983) the different tariffs for drug offences were spelled out according to the type, value and amount of drug involved. In *R v Billam* (1986) the Court of Appeal set out tariffs for rape.

The Crime and Disorder Act 1998 now requires the Court of Appeal to consider setting guidelines when hearing any appropriate appeal on sentence. The same Act also set up the Sentencing Advisory Panel which can put forward sentencing guidelines to the Court of Appeal. As a result many more guidelines have been issued.

Tariff sentences

Some states in America operate a very rigid system in which each crime has a set tariff with the judge being allowed only to impose a penalty within the tariff range. This removes almost all the element of discretion in sentencing from the judges and ensures that sentences for offences are uniform. The objections to this are that it does not allow sufficient consideration of mitigating factors, and may produce a sentence which is unjust in the particular circumstances. The concept of retribution and giving the offender his 'just deserts' should not be so rigid as to ignore special needs of the offender.

There is also a problem in applying this principle to fines. A tariff system of fines involves having a fixed sum as the correct fine for particular offences, however, this takes no account of the financial situation of the offender. So a fine of £500 might be a very severe penalty for an offender who is unemployed, while the same amount would be negligible to a millionaire.

Revenge

Retribution contains an element of revenge: society (and the victim) is being avenged for the wrong done. It is on the basis of revenge that long prison sentences for causing death by dangerous or drink driving can be justified. In 1993 the Government, in response to public opinion, increased the maximum penalties available these offences from five years' to 10 years' imprisonment.

11.1.2 Denunciation

This is society expressing its disapproval of criminal activity. A sentence should indicate both to the offender and to other people that society condemns certain types of behaviour. It shows people that justice is being done. Lord Denning when giving written evidence to the Royal Commission on Capital Punishment put it in this way:

> 'Punishment is the way in which society expresses its denunciation of wrong doing: and in order to maintain respect for the law it is essential that the punishment inflicted for grave crimes should adequately reflect the revulsion felt by the great majority of citizens for them.'

Denunciation also reinforces the moral boundaries of acceptable conduct and can mould society's views on the criminality of particular conduct – for example, drink driving is now viewed by the majority of people as unacceptable behaviour. This is largely because of the changes in the law and the increasingly severe sentences that are imposed. By sending offenders to prison, banning them from driving and imposing heavy fines, society's opinion of drink driving has been changed.

The ideas of retribution and denunciation were foremost in the concepts behind the Criminal Justice Act 1991. That Act was based on the Government White Paper on Crime and Punishment (1990) which stated that: 'The first objective for all sentences is the denunciation of and retribution for crime.'

However, other sentencing aims were not ruled out as the White Paper went on to say:

> 'Depending on the offence and the offender, the sentence may also aim to achieve public protection, reparation and reform the offender, preferably in the community.'

This stresses that though one aim may predominate, it is also sometimes possible to combine aims within the same case.

11.1.3 Incapacitation or protection of the public

The concept behind this and the next three principles of sentencing is that the punishment must serve a useful purpose. Useful in this context can mean that it serves a purpose for society as a whole, or that it will help the offender in some way. Incapacitation means that in some way the offender is made incapable of re-offending. Of course, the ultimate method of incapacitation is the death penalty, and in some countries the hands of thieves are cut off to prevent them re-offending. Another controversial method of incapacitation is the use in some American states of medical means to incapacitate sex offenders, and thus ensure that they cannot re-offend.

Incapacitation is also thought of as protecting society from the criminal activities of the offender. This is achieved today in Britain by removing dangerous offenders from society through the use of long prison sentences. This is shown by the Powers of Criminal Courts (Sentencing) Act 2000 in which section 79 states that a prison sentence should only be imposed where the offence is so serious that imprisonment is justified, or where the offence is a violent or sexual offence and only such a sentence would be adequate to protect the public.

The use of minimum sentences for persistent offenders is aimed at protecting the public from their repeated criminal activities. Electronic tagging of offenders is a method of protecting the public from the offender without having to send the offender to prison.

There are other penalties that can be viewed as incapacitating the offender – for example in driving offences, the offender can be banned from driving. There is also a move to using community-based sentences that will incapacitate the offender in the short term and protect the public. These include exclusion orders under which an offender is banned from going to the place where he offends (usually a pub or a football ground), and curfew orders which order an offender to remain at a given address for certain times of the day or night. There is also the provision of electronic tagging to help supervise curfew orders.

11.1.4 Deterrence

This can be individual deterrence or general deterrence. Individual deterrence is intended to ensure that the offender does not re-offend, through fear of future punishment. General deterrence is aimed at preventing other potential offenders from committing crimes. Both are aimed at reducing future levels of crime.

Individual deterrence

There are several penalties that can be imposed with the aim of deterring the individual offender from committing similar crimes in the future. These include a prison sentence, a suspended sentence or a heavy fine. However, prison does not appear to deter as about 55 per cent of adult prisoners re-offend within two years of release. With young offenders, custodial sentences have even less of a deterrent effect.

Critics of the theory of deterrence point out that it makes an assumption about criminal behaviour that is not borne out in practice. It assumes that an offender will stop to consider what the consequences of his action will be. In fact most crimes are committed on the spur of the moment, and many are committed by offenders who are under the influence of drugs or alcohol. These offenders are unlikely to stop and consider the possible consequences of their actions.

It is also pointed out that fear of being caught is more of a deterrent and that while crime detection rates are low, the threat of an unpleasant penalty, if caught, seems too remote. Fear of detection has been shown to be a powerful deterrent by the success rate of closed circuit televisions used for surveying areas. In one scheme on London's District line of the underground system there was an 83 per cent reduction in crime in the first full year that surveillance cameras were used.

General deterrence

The value of this is even more doubtful as potential offenders are rarely deterred by severe sentences passed on others. However, the courts do occasionally resort to making an example of an offender in order to warn other potential offenders of the type of punishment they face. This will usually be where there is a large increase in a particular type of crime. An example of this occurred in the case of *R v Whitton* (1985) in which the trial judge passed a sentence of life imprisonment on a football hooligan as a warning to other football hooligans, although the Court of Appeal subsequently reduced this to three years'.

General deterrence also relies on publicity so that potential offenders are aware of the level of punishment they can expect. Unless the sentence is exceptionally severe, as in the case of *Whitton*, the story may not be sufficiently newsworthy for the media to publish it. Deterrent sentences will, therefore, be even less effective in cases of drug smuggling by foreign nationals, yet this is one of the crimes in which the courts seem tempted to resort to the hope that a severe sentence passed on one (or more) offender, will somehow deter other potential offenders. In 2002 crime statistics showed that in the previous year there had been about one million offences of street robbery involving taking a mobile phone. In an effort to deter offenders, the Lord Chief Justice said that stiffer sentences were needed and increased a sentence of six months to three and a half years. He also stated that offenders should be given a custodial sentence unless there were very exceptional circumstances.

General deterrence is in direct conflict with the principle of retribution, since it involves sentencing an offender to a longer term than is deserved for the specific offence. It is probably the least effective and least fair principle of sentencing.

11.1.5 Rehabilitation

Under this the main aim of the penalty is to reform the offender and rehabilitate him or her into society. It is a forward-looking aim, with the hope that the offender's behaviour will be altered by the penalty imposed, so that he or she will not offend in the future (it aims to reduce crime in this way). This principle of sentence has come to the fore in the second half of the twentieth century with the development of sentences such as probation (now called community rehabilitation orders) and community service orders (now called community punishment orders).

As the abuse of drugs is the cause of many offences, there have also been two new community sentences – drug testing and treatment orders and drug abstention orders – aimed at trying to rehabilitate drug abusers.

Reformation is a very important element in the sentencing philosophy for young offenders, but it is also used for some adult offenders. The court will be given information about the defendant's background, usually through a pre-sentence report prepared by the probation service. Where relevant, the court will consider other factors, such as school reports, job prospects, or medical problems.

Individualised sentences

Where the court considers rehabilitation, the sentence used is an individualised one aimed at the needs of the offender. This is in direct contrast to the concept of tariff-sentences seen in the aim of retribution. One of the criticisms of this approach is, therefore, that it leads to inconsistency in sentencing. Offenders who have committed exactly the same type of offence may be given different sentences because the emphasis is on the individual offender. Another criticism is that is tends to discriminate against the underprivileged. Offenders from poor home backgrounds are less likely to be seen as possible candidates for reform.

Persistent offenders are usually thought less likely to respond to a reformative sentence.

KEY FACTS

Theory	Aim of theory	Suitable punishment
Retribution	Punishment imposed only on ground that an offence has been committed	• Tariff sentences • Sentence must be proportionate to the crime
Denunciation	Society expressing its disapproval Re-inforces moral boundaries	• Reflects blameworthiness of the offence
Incapacitation	Offender is made incapable of committing further crime Society is protected from crime	• Death penalty for murder • Long prison sentences • Tagging
Deterrence	Individual – the offender is deterred through fear of further punishment General – potential offenders warned as to likely punishment	• Prison sentence • Heavy fine • Long sentence as an example to others
Rehabilitation	Reform offender's behaviour	• Individualised sentence • Community Rehabilitation Order • Community Punishment Order
Reparation	Repayment/reparation to victim or to community	• Compensation Order • Community Punishment Order

Figure 11.2 *Key fact chart on aims of sentencing*

The Powers of Criminal Courts (Sentencing) Act 2000 states that, in considering the seriousness of an offence, the court may take into consideration any previous failures to respond to previous sentences.

11.1.6 Reparation

This is aimed at compensating the victim of the crime usually by ordering the offender to pay a sum of money to the victim or to make restitution, for example by returning stolen property to its rightful owner. The idea that criminals should pay compensation to the victims of their crimes is one that goes back to before the Norman Conquest to the Anglo-Saxon courts. In England today, the courts are required to consider ordering compensation to the victim of a crime, in addition to any other penalty they may think appropriate. Under section 130 of the Powers of Criminal Courts (Sentencing) Act 2000 courts are under a duty to give reasons if they do not make a compensation order. There have also been some experimental projects to bring offenders and victims together, so that the offenders may make direct reparation.

The concept of restitution also includes making reparation to society as a whole. This can be seen mainly in the use of Community Punishment Orders where offenders are required to do so many hours work on a community project under the supervision of the probation service.

Activity

Read the following article and answer the questions below

Unlocking the door to prison reform

The statutory purpose set out in the Prison Rules, first made under the Prisons Act 1898, is the rehabilitation of offenders. For years it has been accepted by those working in the prison service that this is an unattainable objective. But if rehabilitation is impracticable, what should be the object, or objects, of a prison sentence? So far there has been no answer. Is the purpose deterrence? Those with experience of the courts know that offenders with previous convictions are likely to reappear in the courts, whereas, for about 80 per cent of first offenders, appearing in court and being convicted – not the sentence imposed – is what deters.

No-one knows whether prison sentences stop others from committing crime. Perhaps they do, but probably not among that section of society which seems to produce so many of the criminals.

By the Prisons Act 1865, Parliament approved a rigorous prison regime. Courts were empowered to impose sentences of imprisonment with hard labour. Some were put to work breaking stones in quarries, others excavating sites for new docks. The object was to make prisons terrifying places, but they did not stop recidivists.

The public conscience was disturbed by the brutality of the regime. In 1895, the Gladstone Committee was set up to report. It advised that the regime should be abandoned and that the object of prison administration should be rehabilitation. The Prisons Act 1898 was passed to implement the recommendations.

There is some value in imposing custodial sentences for the purpose of preventing crime. Persistent burglars cannot break into houses while in prison. Judges know that when they send a burglar with previous convictions to prison the probabilities are that he will take to crime again within weeks of being released. But if the prison sentences for this kind of offender are for the purpose of preventing crime, they should be longer, rather than shorter.

Twice this century, in 1908 and 1948, Parliament tackled this problem. In 1908 the offence of being a habitual offender was created. Juries did not like returning verdicts of guilty and the Act fell into disuse. The Criminal Justice Act 1948 gave judges power to pass extra long sentences on habitual offenders. Judges were reluctant to do so. By the 1960s few such sentences were being passed. The inference is that the public rejects the concept of a penal policy based on the prevention of crime by long sentences.

If rehabilitation is impractical, deterrence useless and sentencing for the prevention of crime unacceptable, what should be the purpose of a prison sentence? Of the four classical reasons for imposing prison sentences only retribution remains; but not in the sense of causing pain because of antecedent offences, but because society has to take action to show its disapproval of anti-social conduct. Since the 1820s, when most corporal punishments were abolished and the number of capital offences reduced from about 160 to four, the deprivation of liberty has become the only way of showing society's disapproval.

Taken from an article by Sir Frederick Lawton in *The Times*, 27 August 1991

QUESTIONS

❶ The article identifies four 'classical' reasons for imposing prison sentences; what are they?

❷ Which one does the author give as the only valid reason for imposing a prison sentence?

❸ Why does he reject the other three?

❹ Do you agree with his arguments in rejecting these other three? Give reasons for your answer.

11.2 Sentencing practice in the courts

The court will usually consider both the offence and the background of the offender, as well as the aims of sentencing. In order to do this, the court must know details of the offence, so where the defendant pleads guilty the prosecution will outline the facts of the case. As seen in Chapter 10, the defendant is asked if he agrees with those facts and, if not, a Newton hearing will be held for the facts to be established. This is important as the details of the offence can affect the sentence. Where the defendant has pleaded not guilty and been convicted after a trial, the court will have heard full information about the case during the trial.

11.2.1 Factors surrounding the offence

In looking at the offence, the most important point to establish is how serious was it, of its type? For example, in a case of theft how much was stolen, and was the defendant in a position of trust? In a case of assault the court will need to know what injuries were inflicted and whether the assault was premeditated; was the victim particularly vulnerable (perhaps elderly) or was there a racial motive behind the attack? A premeditated crime is usually considered to be more serious than one committed on the spur of the moment. Where the offender in a position of trust and abused that trust, then again, the offence will be considered as being more serious and meriting a longer than usual sentence.

Where several defendants are convicted of committing a crime jointly, the court will want to know if any of them played a greater part than the others, and who was involved in planning it. The sentences that each receive will reflect the part they played in the offence.

Another increasingly important factor is whether the offender showed any remorse and, in particular, at what stage did he indicate that he would be pleading guilty. An early plea of guilty can be rewarded by up to one third off the sentence.

Finally in 2001, the Lord Chief Justice issued a statement that the effects of the offence on the victim should be taken into consideration when sentencing.

11.2.2 The offender's background

Previous convictions

So far as the offender is concerned, the court will want to know whether he has any previous convictions. The court may also take into account the failure of an offender to respond to previous sentences, in deciding the seriousness of the current offence. The past record of the offender will also determine whether he has to receive a minimum sentence or an automatic life sentence for certain offences.

Another important factor is whether the offender was on bail when he committed the offence. The Powers of Criminal Courts (Sentencing) Act 2000 states that if this is the case, the court shall treat that fact as an aggravating factor.

Pre-sentence reports

These are prepared by the probation service. The court does not have to (but usually will) consider such a report before deciding to impose a custodial sentence, though for very serious offences such a report may not be relevant. Where the court is considering a community sentence, they are likely to have a report before they decide on the sentence. The report will give information about the defendant's background and suitability, or otherwise, for a community-based sentence. The defendant's background may be important in showing both why the offender committed a crime, and indicate if he is likely to respond to a community-based penalty.

Medical reports

Where the offender has medical or psychiatric problems, the court will usually ask for a report to be prepared by an appropriate doctor. Medical conditions may be important factors in deciding the appropriate way of dealing with the offender; the courts have special powers where the defendant is suffering from mental illness. The treatment of mentally ill defendants is considered further in section 11.5.

The financial situation of the offender

Where the court considers that a fine is a suitable penalty, it must inquire into the financial circumstances of the offender, and take this into account when setting the level of the fine.

11.2.3 Sentencing guidelines

Section 80 of the Crime and Disorder Act 1998 places the Court of Appeal's making of sentencing guidelines on a statutory basis. Whenever the Court of Appeal hears an appeal against sentence or an Attorney-General's reference against an unduly lenient sentence, the court shall consider whether to frame guidelines or, where guidelines exist, whether to review them.

If the court decides to make guidelines, it must have regard to:

- The need for consistency in sentencing
- The sentences imposed by courts for offences of the relevant category
- The cost of different sentences and their relative effectiveness in preventing re-offending
- The views of the Sentencing Advisory Panel.

Sentencing Advisory Panel

Also under the Crime and Disorder Act 1998 a Sentencing Advisory Panel has been set up by the Lord Chancellor. When the Court of Appeal decides to make or revise guidelines, the Court must notify the Panel. In addition, the panel will have the power to propose that sentencing guidelines be made or revised for a particular category of offence.

11.3 Types of sentences

As already indicated, the courts have several different types of sentences available to them. There are four main categories: custodial sentences, community sentences, fines and discharges. The courts also have the power to make additional orders such as compensation orders, and, in motoring offences have other powers such as disqualification from driving.

11.3.1 Custodial sentences

The age of the offender is important here, as there are different custodial sentences available for different age groups. Young offenders can only be given custodial sentences in exceptional circumstances and are always held in separate units from adults.

The Powers of Criminal Courts (Sentencing) Act 2000 states that a custodial sentence should not be passed, unless the court considers that the crime was so serious that only a prison sentence is justified, or the case involves a violent or sexual offence, and only a prison sentence would be adequate to protect the public. When considering the seriousness of the offence, the court may take into account any previous convictions, or any failure of the offender to respond to previous sentences. In addition, the fact that an offence was committed while on bail for another offence is an aggravating factor and makes the offence more serious.

The court must state its reason for imposing a custodial sentence, and in the case of the Magistrates' Court, that reason must be written on the warrant of commitment and entered in the court register.

In the guidelines of suggested 'entry points' published by the Magistrates' Association, a custodial sentence is advised for offences such as assaulting a police officer in the execution of his duty, and burglary of a residential property.

Prison sentences

A sentence of imprisonment is only available for offenders aged 21 and over. For the crime of murder the only sentence the court can impose is life imprisonment. Where this happens the judge may recommend a minimum number of years the offender should serve, before he can be considered for parole and the Home Secretary will then set the tariff. In some cases, for example the Moors murderers, Ian Brady and Myra Hindley, the Home Secretary has indicated that they are very unlikely to be considered for release. For other crimes, the length of the sentence will depend on several factors, including the maximum sentence available for the particular crime, the seriousness of the crime and the defendant's previous record. Imprisonment for a set number of months or years is called a 'fixed term' sentence.

Prisoners do not serve the whole of the sentence passed by the court. Anyone sent to prison for less than four years is automatically released after they have served half of the sentence. Long-term prisoners serving a sentence of four years or more will be automatically released after two-thirds of the time, but may be released on licence after they have served half their sentence. The exact length of the time they spend in jail will be determined by their behaviour in prison. Except for those serving less than a one year sentence, all prisoners are supervised after release.

Home Detention Curfew

The Crime and Disorder Act 1998 allows early release from prison on condition that a curfew condition is included. The period of curfew is increased with the length of sentence. There is no automatic right to be released on curfew; each prisoner is assessed to see if he or she is suitable. If a Home Detention Curfew order is not made, then the prisoner must serve half the sentence before release on licence.

The reason for introducing such Home Detention Curfews is to encourage recently released prisoners to structure their lives more effectively as well as prevent re-offending. Also by releasing prisoners early in this way the prison population is reduced.

Extended sentences

Section 85 of the Powers of Criminal Courts (Sentencing) Act 2000 gives the sentencing court power to pass an extended sentence for a sexual or violent offence. This means that the offender is given a custodial sentence plus a further period (the 'extension period') during which the offender is at liberty on licence. The extension period cannot exceeds 10 years for a sexual offence or five years for a violent offence.

The idea behind this sentence is to have greater control over sexual offenders when they leave prison. Such offenders are also required to register with the police so that it is known where they are living.

Suspended prison sentences

An adult offender may be given a suspended prison sentence of up to two years (six months maximum in the Magistrates' Court). This means that the sentence does not take effect immediately. The court will fix a time during which the sentence is suspended; this can be for any period up to two years. If, during this time, the offender does not commit any further offences, the prison sentence will not be served. However, if the offender does commit another offence within the period of suspension, then the prison sentence is 'activated' and the offender will serve that sentence together with any sentence for the new offence.

A suspended sentence should only be given where the offence is so serious that an immediate custodial sentence would have been appropriate, but there are exceptional circumstances in the case that justify suspending the sentence.

Suspended sentences can be combined with a fine or compensation order, but even so they are viewed as a 'soft' option by many offenders. Prior to the Criminal Justice Act 1991, they were used frequently by the courts, but many defendants then re-offended and ended up serving the suspended sentence.

Suspended sentences are passed by magistrates in only 0.2 per cent of cases, and by the Crown Court in 2.5 per cent of cases.

11.3.2 Custodial sentences for young offenders

There has been a lot of debate as to whether young offenders, particularly those under the age of 15, should be given custodial sentences. Government policy on this point has changed frequently during the past few years. It is argued that many young offenders need help rather than punishment and that this is best provided by sentencing orders which keep the offender in the community. Custodial units for young offenders have often been called 'universities of crime'. However, there are at the moment several different types of custodial sentence which can be given, depending on the type of offence, the age of the offender and whether he or she has offended before.

Young Offenders' Institutions

Offenders aged 18 to 20 can be sent to a Young Offenders' Institution as a custodial sentence. The minimum sentence is 21 days and the maximum is the maximum allowed for the particular offence. If the offender becomes 21 years old while serving the sentence, he will be transferred to an adult prison.

Detention and training orders

The Crime and Disorder Act 1998 created a new custodial sentence, called a detention and training order, for young offenders. The sentence must be for a specified period with a minimum of four months and a maximum of 24 months. In between these, the order can be for six months, eight months, 10 months, 12 months or 18 months. No other length of time can be given.

A detention and training order can be passed on offenders from the age of 12 to the age of 21, but for those under the age of 15 this order can only be made if they are persistent offenders.

There is also power for the Home Secretary to extend the use of detention and training orders to offenders aged 10 and 11. If this is introduced it can only apply where the court is of the opinion that only a custodial sentence is adequate to protect the public from further offending.

Detention for serious crimes

For very serious offences, the courts have additional power to order that the offender be detained for longer periods. For 10 to 13-year-olds this power is only available where the crime committed carries a maximum sentence of at least 14 years' imprisonment for adults, or is an offence of indecent assault on a woman under section

14 of the Sexual Offences Act 1956. For 14 to 17-year-olds, it is also available for causing death by dangerous driving, or for causing death by careless driving while under the influence of drink or drugs. The length of detention imposed on the young offender cannot be more than the maximum sentence available for an adult.

Originally 10 to 13-year-olds were not included in these provisions, but the law was amended in 1994 to include them, after a court had been unable to give a custodial sentence to a 13-year-old boy who had been found guilty of raping a 12-year-old girl.

Detention at Her Majesty's Pleasure

Any offender aged 10 to 17 who is convicted of murder must be ordered to be detained during Her Majesty's Pleasure. This is an indeterminate sentence which allows the offender to be released when suitable. The judge in the case can recommend a minimum number of years that should be served before release is considered, and the Lord Chief Justice will then set the tariff.

If an offender reaches 21 while still serving a sentence he or she will be transferred to an adult prison.

Comment

Critics of the use of custodial sentences for young offenders point out that such penalties do not appear to have any reformative effective. Home Office research in 1994 revealed that for male prisoners, 82 per cent of those aged 17–20 re-offended within two years of being released, while the figure for those aged 15–16 was even higher at 92 per cent. However, there are also statistics to show that persistent offenders are likely to re-offend regardless of whether they are given a custodial sentence or a community-based one.

Since 1997 one of the aims of the Labour Government has been to try to prevent young offenders becoming persistent offenders. They have introduced a range of new non-custodial measures for dealing with young offenders. These include referrals to Youth Offending Teams and action plan orders which can create an intensive programme aimed at rehabilitation.

Activity

The following extract explains some of the changes in custodial sentences for young offenders and also gives some of the problems involved. Read the extract and answer the questions which follow.

'In September 1990 David Waddington, the then Home Secretary, announced that the Government's forthcoming Criminal Justice Bill would remove 14-year-old boys from the scope of custodial sentences. (Parliament had acted to remove girls of this age some years earlier.) At the time it seemed likely that all young people of school age would, in due course, be barred from the prison system. Within two years, however, it had become clear that it was good-bye to all that and more. The announcement to Kenneth Clarke of five "secure training centres" to hold children as young as twelve was an early indication that an unprecedented U-turn on criminal policy was underway.

The prominent place given to this new sanction in the Criminal Justice and Public Order Act 1994 was reinforced by the Labour Party's studied abstention. Penal reformers were disappointed but hardly surprised when the Labour Government quickly made it clear that it would not only honour the first contract for the Medway Secure Training Centre near

> *Rochester in Kent but would proceed with other proposed centres. Under the Crime and Disorder Act 1998 the secure training centre order will be replaced by the new detention and training order which will be available for 12–14-year-old "persistent" offenders and 15–17-year-olds. Powers are provided by the legislation for the minimum age to be reduced to ten.'*
>
> Taken from *Locking up children* by Andrew Rutherford, *New Law Journal*, 12 February 1999

QUESTIONS

❶ What changes in the sentencing of young offenders does this extract highlight?

❷ At what age can young offenders be given a detention and training order?

❸ To what age group does legislation allow the order to be extended?

❹ Do you think that all or any these age groups should be given a custodial sentence? Give reasons for your answer?

11.3.3 Community sentences

The Powers of the Criminal Courts (Sentencing) Act 2000 sets out five community orders which can be used in sentencing offenders over the age of 16.

These are:

- Community Rehabilitation Orders
- Community Punishment Orders
- Community Punishment and Rehabilitation Orders
- Curfew Orders
- Drug Treatment and Testing Orders

In addition the Criminal Justice and Courts Services Act 2000 has created two extra community sentences. These are:

- Exclusion Orders
- Drug Abstinence Orders

There are also additional community sentences which can only be used for young offenders. These are set out in section 11.4.

Community Rehabilitation Order

This places the offender under the supervision of a probation officer for a period of between six months and three years. During this time the offender must keep in regular contact with the probation officer and must lead an 'industrious and honest' life. Other conditions may be included by the court such as:

- A residence order, requiring the offender to live at a certain address
- An order that the defendant take part in specified activities for up to 60 days
- A condition that the defendant attends a probation centre.
- A treatment order requiring the offender to attend for medical or psychiatric treatment or undergo treatment for drug or alcohol abuse

From these conditions it can be seen that the main aim of the order is to rehabilitate the offender. However, Home Office figures published in 1999 suggest that a Community Rehabilitation Order does not prevent re-offending, with about 60 per cent being reconvicted within two years.

Community Punishment Order

This requires the offender to work for between 40 and 240 hours on a suitable project organised by the probation service. The exact number of hours will be fixed by the court, and those hours are then usually worked in eight-hour sessions, often at weekends. The type of work involved will vary, depending on what schemes the local probation service have running. The offender may be required to paint school buildings, help build a play centre or work on conservation projects. When Eric Cantona, the French footballer, was found guilty of assaulting a football fan, the court ordered that he help at coaching sessions for young footballers.

One criticism is that the number of hours is not enough – other countries which run similar schemes can impose much longer hours. However, re-offending rates are lower than for other community sentences.

Community Punishment and Rehabilitation Order

This is a combination of up to 100 hours of work on a Community Punishment and a Community Rehabilitation Order. The offender will have to complete the required number of hours of community work, and keep the terms of the rehabilitation order. The aim behind combining these orders was to strengthen community penalties and give the courts more flexibility in what they could impose.

Curfew Orders

Under these, an offender can be ordered to remain at a fixed address for between 2 and 12 hours in any 24 hour period. This order can last for up to six months and may be enforced by electronic tagging (where suitable). Courts can only make such an order if there is an arrangement for monitoring curfews in their area. Such monitoring can be done by spot-checks, with security firms sending someone to make sure that the offender is at home or offenders may be electronically tagged.

The cost of tagging is quite expensive, being estimated at £675 per offender per month. However, this does compare favourably with the cost of keeping an offender in prison as the estimated cost of this is £1,555 per month per offender.

This is the government's latest idea for a community sentence.

Statistics show that in the first two years of using electronic tagging, a very high percentage (80+) of offenders completed the tagging period successfully.

Drug Treatment and Testing Orders

Sections 61 to 64 of the Crime and Disorder Act 1998 created a new community penalty of drug treatment and testing for offenders aged 16 and over. This is now set out in sections 52 to 58 of the Powers of Criminal Courts (Sentencing) Act 2000. Such an order can last for between six months and three years. An order can only be made if the offender is willing to comply with it. The court must also be satisfied that arrangements have been made or can be made for the treatment. The treatment can be residential or non-residential and the court must set the minimum number of tests required from the offender each month. The court must hold reviews of the order in which the offender must attend at court and a written report of progress, including results of drug testing, must be provide before each review.

Pilot schemes, which started in October 1998 for a period of 18 months, showed that the amount of drug abuse by those placed on this scheme fell considerably. However, there were only a small number of offenders given such an order.

Exclusion Orders

Offenders are ordered not to go to certain places. The order can specify different places for different periods or days. This is intended to keep offenders away from areas where they are most likely to commit crime. For example, a persistent shoplifter could be banned from certain shopping areas. The order can be for up to two years for offenders 16 and over, and a maximum of three months for those under 16.

Drug Abstinence Orders

These can only be made where the offender is dependent on drugs or has a propensity to misuse them *and* the offence is a 'trigger offence' or was caused or contributed to by the misuse of drugs. It orders the offender to abstain from misusing specified Class A drugs. It is enforced by drug-testing. An order can only be made for offenders aged 18 or over and it can last for a period of between six months and three years.

11.3.4 Fines

This is the most common way of disposing of a case in the Magistrates' Court where the maximum fine is £5,000 for an individual offender. The magistrate can impose a fine of up to £20,000 on businesses who have committed offences under various regulatory legislation, such as health and safety at work. In the Crown Court only a small percentage of offenders are dealt with by way of a fine.

Unpaid fines

A major problem of using fines as a sentencing power is the high level of non-payment. This has two effects: it makes the punishment ineffective; and it leads to a large number of defendants being imprisoned for non-payment. This high number of defaulters who end up in prison is an expensive waste of prison resources.

11.3.5 Discharges

These may be either a conditional discharge or an absolute discharge. A conditional discharge means that the court discharges an offender on the condition that no further offence is committed during a set period of up to three years. It is intended to be used where it is thought that punishment is not necessary. If an offender re-offends within the time limit, the court can then impose another sentence in place of the conditional discharge, as well as imposing a penalty for the new offence. Conditional discharges are widely used by Magistrates' Courts for first-time minor offenders.

An absolute discharge means that, effectively, no penalty is imposed. Such a penalty is likely to be used where an offender is technically guilty but morally blameless. An example could be where the tax disc on a vehicle has fallen to the floor – it is technically not being displayed and an offence has been committed. So, in the unlikely situation of someone being prosecuted for this, the magistrates, who would have to impose some penalty, would most probably decide that an absolute discharge was appropriate.

11.3.6 Disqualification from driving

Where a defendant is charged with a driving offence, the courts may also have the power to disqualify that person from driving for a certain period of time. The length of the disqualification will depend on the seriousness of the driving offence. Usually the courts will impose a fine as well as disqualification. For a first-time drink-driving offence the courts have to disqualify the defendant for a minimum of 12 months, unless there are very exceptional reasons not to disqualify. If an offender has a previous drink-drive conviction, then the minimum is usually three years' disqualification.

The courts can use this power to disqualify in any other crime where the offender has used a vehicle to commit an offence. For example a defendant who drives a car in order to do a burglary could be disqualified from driving, but this power is not often used.

11.3.7 Other powers available to the courts

The courts have other powers which are aimed at compensating victims and/or making sure that the defendant does not benefit from his or her crimes.

Compensation orders and restitution orders

Courts can make an order that the defendant pay a sum of money to his victim in compensation. They are encouraged to use this order by the fact that they must give reasons if they do not make a compensation order in any case in which they have the power to do so. In the Magistrates' Court the maximum amount of compensation is £5,000.

If the defendant still has the property he obtained from the victim, then the courts can make an order that the property is returned. This is called a restitution order.

Deprivation and forfeiture orders

A court can order an offender to be deprived of property he has used to commit an offence. For example a person convicted of drink-driving could be ordered to lose his car. There is special power to order forfeiture in drug-related cases. The Proceeds of Crime Act 1995 also gives the courts powers to take from criminals all profits from crime for up to six years before conviction.

Deferred sentences

Where the judge has a good reason to believe that the offender's circumstances are about to change, the sentence may deferred for up to six months. This is to see if the change makes a difference to the defendant's behaviour. A sentence should only be deferred where the change in circumstances is such that punishment will not be necessary, or a lesser penalty be more suitable as a result of the change. The offender has to consent to sentence being deferred.

11.4 Young offenders

This term includes all offenders under the age of 21. However there are considerable variations in the different sentences available for those under 18, under 16, under 14 and under 12. The main aim in sentencing young offenders is reformation and rehabilitation. As already seen in Chapter 10, offenders under 18-years-old are normally dealt with in the Youth Court.

11.4.1 Available sentences

As with adult offenders, the courts have, in general, powers to order custodial sentences, community sentences, fines and discharges, but different sentences are available, and also restrictions on what the courts can order (especially for the youngest offenders). The custodial sentences available have already been explained in section 11.3.1. So far as community sentences are concerned, young offenders aged 16 and over can be given the same sentences as adults. These are Community Rehabilitation and Community Punishment Orders and Drug Testing and Treatment Orders. These sentences cannot be used for offenders under the age of 16. However, Curfew Orders can be used for offenders from the age of ten upwards.

There are a number of other orders which are aimed at young offenders. These are explained next.

Attendance Centre Orders

This type of order is only for those under 21, and is available for all young offenders from the age of 10 upwards. It involves attendance at a special centre for two or three hours a week – up to a maximum of 36 hours for 16 to 20-year-olds, and 24 hours for 10 to 15-year-olds. The minimum number of hours is usually 12, but can be less for offenders under the age of 14. The centres used to be run by the police but are now under the supervision of the probation service; they are usually held on Saturday afternoons and will include organised leisure activities and training. An attendance centre order cannot be made if the offender has served a period of detention previously.

Supervision Orders

Those under 18 can be placed under the supervision of one of the following:

- the local social services
- a probation officer
- a member of a Youth Offending Team

This can be for a period of up to three years.

Action Plan Orders

Section 69 of the Crime and Disorder Act 1998 creates a new community order called an Action Plan Order which the courts can impose on offenders under the age of 18. In the White Paper *No More Excuses*, the Government said it was intended to be 'a short intensive programme of community intervention combining punishment, rehabilitation and reparation to change offending behaviour and prevent further crime'.

The order places the offender under supervision and also sets out requirements the offender has to comply with in respect to his actions and whereabouts during a period of three months.

These requirements can be any of the following:

- To participate in set activities
- To present himself to a specified person at set times and places

KEY FACTS

Types of sentence	Age limitations
Custodial sentences	• Prison only for 21 + • Young Offenders' Institution 18–20-year-olds • Detention and training order for 12–17-year-olds • Powers of detention for 10–17-year-olds in serious cases
Community sentences	• Community Rehabilitation and Community Punishment and Drug Treatment and Testing Orders for 16 + • Curfews and Exclusion Orders 10 + • Attendance centres for 10–20-year-olds • Supervision Orders for 10–17-year-olds • Action Plan Orders for 10–17-year-olds
Fines	• Over 18s – Magistrates' Court maximum £5,000 (Crown Court no limit) • 14–17 Maximum £1,000 • 10–13 Maximum £250
Discharges	• Conditional discharge – 10 + • Absolute discharge – 10 +
Other powers	• Disqualification from driving – 10 + • Compensation orders – 10 +

Figure 11.3 *Key fact chart on sentencing powers of the courts*

- To attend at an attendance centre
- To stay away from certain places
- To comply with arrangements for his education
- To make reparation.

Fines

The maximum amount of a fine varies with the age of the offender: 10 to 13-year-olds can only be fined a maximum of £250, while for 14 to 17-year-olds the maximum is £1,000. Those aged 18 and over are subject to the normal maximum of the Magistrates' Court of £5,000.

Reparation Orders

A Reparation Order may be imposed on offenders under the age of 18. This order cannot be made in combination with a custodial sentence, Community Service Order, a combination order, a Supervision Order or an Action Plan Order.

An order will require the offender to make reparation as specified in the order:

- To a person or persons who were victims of the offence or were otherwise affected by it; or
- To the community at large.

The order is for a maximum of 24 hours' work and the reparation order must be completed under supervision within three months of its imposition. An order for direct reparation to a victim can only be made with that person's consent.

Discharges

These may be used for an offender of any age, and are commonly used for first-time young offenders who have committed minor crimes.

However, the courts cannot conditionally discharge an offender in the following circumstances:

- Where a child or young offender who is convicted of an offence has been warned within the previous two years; unless there are exceptional circumstances which must be explained in open court
- Where the offender is in breach of an anti-social behaviour order
- Where the offender is in breach of a sex offender order.

Reprimands and warnings

These are not sentences passed by a court, but methods by which the police can deal with offenders without bringing the case to court. For either a reprimand or warning to be given there must be evidence that a child or young person has committed an offence and admits it. In addition, the police must be satisfied that it would not be in the public interest for the offender to be prosecuted. A reprimand or warning can only be given if the offender has never been convicted of any offence.

There is a limit to the number of times and the occasions on which an offender can be 'cautioned'. The first step is the reprimand. This can only be given if the child or young person has not been previously reprimanded or warned. Even then it should not be used where the constable considers the offence to be so serious as to require a warning.

An offender may be warned only if he has not been warned before or if an earlier warning was more than two years before. When warned the child or young offender must be referred to a Youth Offending Team. This team assesses the case and, unless it considers it inappropriate to do so, arranges for the offender to participate in a rehabilitation scheme.

11.4.2 Parental responsibility

If the parents agree, they can be bound over to keep their child under control for a set period of up to one year. If the child commits an offence during this period the parents will forfeit a sum of money up to a maximum of £1,000. If a parent unreasonably refuses to be bound over, the court has the power to fine that parent instead. Parents can also be bound over to ensure that a young offender complies with a community sentence.

Where an offender under 16 years old is fined or ordered to pay compensation, the court must require the offender's parents to pay, and the financial situation of the parent is taken into account in deciding the amount of the order.

Parenting orders

This is intended to offer training and support to parents to help change their children's offending behaviour. In this way it is more practical than the existing provisions which merely make a parent responsible for their child's offending behaviour. Under such an order a parent can be required to attend counselling or guidance sessions for up to three months on a maximum basis of once a week.

In addition, the parent may be required to comply with conditions imposed by the courts; for example, escort the child to school or ensure that a responsible adult is present in the home in the evening to supervise the child. A court may make a parenting order where:

- The court makes a child safety order
- The court makes an anti-social behaviour order (or sex offender order) in respect of a child
- A child or young person is convicted of an offence
- A parent is convicted of an offence relating to truancy under the Education Act 1996.

An order should only be made if it is desirable in the interests of preventing the conduct which gave rise to the order. Where a person under the age of 16 is convicted of an offence, the court should make a parenting order unless it is satisfied that it is not desirable in the interests of preventing the conduct which gave rise to the order. In this case the court must state in open court that it is not satisfied and explain why not.

11.4.3 Youth Offending Teams

The Crime and Disorder Act makes it the duty of each local authority to establish one or more Youth Offending Teams (YOTs) in their area. The main idea in establishing these teams is to build on co-operation between agencies involved, especially social services and the probation service. These teams are to co-ordinate the provision of youth justice services in the area.

A YOT must include a probation officer, a local authority social worker, a police officer, a representative of the local health authority and a person nominated by the chief education officer. Any other appropriate person may also be invited to join the team.

The role of YOTs is highlighted by the fact that, under section 66 of the Crime and Disorder Act 1998, any offender who is warned must be referred to the local YOT. Youth courts may also refer offenders to the YOT.

Activity

Suggest a suitable sentence for the following offenders and explain what the aim of the sentence would be.

QUESTIONS

❶ Kevin, aged 22, has been found guilty by the magistrates of two charges of criminal damage. The amount of damage involved is estimated at £600. He is single, unemployed and has no previous convictions.

❷ Melanie, aged 15, appeared before the local youth court and admitted shoplifting on five occasions. She also admitted two offences of taking and driving a car without the owner's consent. She has appeared before the youth court on two previous occasions for similar offences.

❸ Andrew, aged 26, has been found guilty at the Crown Court of an assault causing grievous bodily harm. He committed this offence while on bail charged with another offence of violence.

11.5 Mentally ill offenders

The law recognises that, so far as possible, mentally ill offenders should not be punished but should receive treatment. Where an offence has been committed by an offender who is mentally ill, the courts have a wider range of powers available to them. In addition to the ordinary sentences which can be given, there are special provisions aimed at treating such offenders in a suitable way.

The main additional powers available to the courts are to: place the offender on probation, with an order that he or she attends for treatment; make a hospital order or to make a restriction order under section 41 of the Mental Health Act 1983.

A probation order combined with a treatment order will be made where the court is satisfied that the mental condition is treatable, and that there is no need to make a hospital order. A hospital order will be made if the condition makes it appropriate that the offender should stay in hospital for treatment.

However, there are some cases in which the protection of the public is a key element. Under section 41 of the Mental Health Act 1983 offenders with severe mental problems, who are considered to be a danger to the community, can be sent to a secure hospital such as Broadmoor. Magistrates' Courts cannot make such an order; it can only be made by a Crown Court. The order can be that the offender be detained for a set period or, where necessary, for an indefinite period. If an offender is ordered to be detained for an indefinite period, the hospital can only discharge him with the permission of the Home Secretary or the Mental Health Review Tribunal.

11.6 Penal policies and their effects

Sentencing policies have an effect on the number of offenders who are sent to prison. The United Kingdom sends a higher percentage of its population to prison than any other European Union country. The changes in sentencing policy over the last few years are reflected in the changing size of prison population as the Government has first attempted to reduce the number of defendants sent to prison for relatively minor offences, and then (to some extent) reversed their policies in an effort as being seen as the party of 'law and order'.

Minimum sentences

The Crime (Sentences) Act 1997 introduced automatic life sentences for anyone aged 18 or over, who is convicted for a second time of a serious sexual or violent offence. This does not remove all discretion from the judge, however, as the trial judge can recommend the minimum period to be served, before the offender could be considered for release. Also the judge has a discretion not to impose an automatic life sentence in 'exceptional circumstances'.

There is a minimum sentence of seven years for anyone aged 18 or over, who is convicted on three separate occasions of dealing in class A drugs. There is also a minimum sentence of three years for those convicted of burglary of a residential building for a third time. Judges can impose a lesser sentence if there are exceptional circumstances.

It is accepted that the measures regarding burglars are likely to increase the prison population. This shown by the fact that the provision for persistent burglars was not implemented until December 1999 when new prison places were available.

Home detention curfews

Since 1998 it has been possible for some prisoners to be released early by being electronically tagged on a home curfew order. It is available for those serving sentences of between three months and four years, but it is not an automatic right. It will only be used where it is thought that the prisoner does not pose a risk to society. For example, it was used with the ex-MP Jonathan Aitken when he was released early from his prison sentence for perjury.

The introduction of early release on home detention curfew reduced the prison population slightly in 1999 and 2000. However, by the end of 2001 the prison population had risen to over 68,000.

Because of the rising prison population the Lord Chief Justice, Lord Woolf, in October

2001 called on judges and magistrates not to send people to prison unless it was really necessary. He also asked them when they were going to impose a short-term sentence to pause and ask whether half the sentence would do. He pointed out that short-term sentences were often ineffective.

11.6.1 Prison population

Statistics show that there has been a considerable increase in the prison population in England and Wales during the second half of the twentieth century. In 1957 there were on average 21,700 male prisoners and 900 female prisoners in prison on any given day, but by 1987 this had more than doubled to 47,200 male prisoners and 1,800 female prisoners. Concern over this rising number of offenders was one of the factors which led to a complete re-appraisal of sentencing policies, and the passing of the Criminal Justice Act 1991, with its emphasis on community-based penalties. This had an marked effect in reducing the number of prisoners. However, by 1995 the average prison population was 49,000 males and nearly 2,000 females. This figure included those on remand. The numbers have continued to increase at a rapid rate with the prison population in 1998 reaching over 67,000, of whom over 3,000 were women.

In 1999 and 2000 there was a slight decrease in the prison population due to the system of early release and home detention curfews. However, in 2001 the numbers in prison reached an all time high at over 68,000, of whom 4,000 were women.

A report, *Alternatives to Prison Sentences*, by the Home Affairs Committee (September 1998), came to the conclusion that:

> *'many people currently being sentenced to imprisonment could be dealt with effectively – and at far less expense – by a non-custodial sentence.'*

The Chief Inspector of Prisons, Sir David Ramsbotham, told the committee that perhaps 70 per cent of women prisoners and 30–40 per cent of young offenders did not need to be in prison.

11.6.2 Prison riots

Prisons are seen as a way of containing violent offenders but there can be problems within them. There have been serious disturbances within prisons, with one of the worst incidents occurring in 1990 at Strangeways Prison. An independent public inquiry, under the chairmanship of Lord Justice Woolf, was set up to look at the causes of these riots and to make recommendations. The Report revealed that there were several factors which were possible causes of the disturbances. These were: poor physical conditions, especially poor sanitation and overcrowding; the fact that prisoners were locked up in their cells for long periods of time; complaints about food; the attitude of the staff towards the inmates and a certain amount of 'copycat' response by prisoners.

There are criticisms that there are insufficient constructive activities to give prisoners skills, and so help them on their return to the community. The fact that the re-offending rate for released prisoners is very high, also shows that more needs to be done. The former Chief Inspector of Prisons, Judge Tumim, has said:

> *'Most prisoners . . . are male and under 30. Their offences are connected with stealing cars, burglary and occasionally drugs, but they are not given to violence. They were failures at school and they know too little to lead useful lives outside . . . They need to be taught working skills and they need social training to cope with the problems of drink, drugs, Aids, and above all their own offending behaviour.'*

11.6.3 Racism in sentencing

Statistics reveal that ethnic minorities are very much over-represented in the prison population. Since 1997, they have accounted for about 18 per cent of male prisoners and 25 per cent of female prisoners. This is compared with 6 per cent of the male and female populations of England and Wales. However, part of this imbalance is because of the sizeable proportions of foreign nationals who are in British prisons for drug-smuggling offences, or are being held under the Immigration Act 1971.

However, even when these are discounted, the percentage of ethnic minority prisoners (in particular, black prisoners) is still above the proportions found in the population as a whole.

It is difficult to discover whether there is a racist element in sentencing, or whether there are other factors. There were studies in the 1980s that suggested that black defendants were more likely to be sent to prison than their white counter-parts.

A study by Hood (Race and Sentencing 1992) came to the conclusion that about 80 per cent of the difference between the proportion of black males in the general population, and their proportion among those serving prison sentences, was due to the fact that proportionately more black males appeared at the Crown Court, and that the offences they were convicted of were more serious. The remaining 20 per cent was due to different treatment by the courts, but some of this was in itself due to the fact that more black defendants pleaded not guilty, and would therefore be liable to receive a longer term. Only in about 7 per cent of cases did there appear to be a 'race-effect' and Hood argues that some of this was due to bias on the part of individual judges.

In the 1990s there has been an effort to improve training for judges and to include racial awareness as part of that training.

In 1999 information was collected from five pilot areas of details on racial background and the type of sentence imposed. This showed that there was no evidence of substantial differences in the use of custody at Magistrates' Courts. The only difference was that black defendants were more likely to be sentenced to a community sentence.

11.6.4 Women and sentencing

The number of women serving prison sentences is still considerably lower than the number of males serving sentences in prison, and they make up only a few per cent of the prison population. However, women commit considerably fewer offences than men. Despite this, the number of women prisoners does (to some extent) support the findings of certain surveys which show that women are treated more harshly than men when being sentenced by the courts.

A study in 1990 by the National Association for the Care and Resettlement of Offenders found that only 11 per cent of males serving a prison sentence had never been to prison before. This was in contrast to the fact that 33 per cent of women prisoners had not previously served a jail sentence. The study also found that most women prisoners were in prison for minor, non-violent offences.

In contrast, a Home Office study by Hedderman and Hough in 1994 (Does the Criminal Justice System treat men and women differently?) found that women were, if anything, treated more favourably than men. They reported that women were far less likely than men to receive a custodial sentence for virtually all indictable offences except for drug offences; that women who received a prison sentence tend to be given shorter sentences than men, and that women were less likely to receive prison sentences, irrespective of the number of previous convictions. However, these figures did not look at the individual particulars of the offences committed by male and female offenders. This point is important as women commit less serious offences than men, and so a direct comparison is difficult.

Regardless of whether women offenders as a whole receive harsher treatment, there is support for the view that women who are single or divorced, or who have children in care are more likely to receive a custodial sentence than women who have a stable family life. This suggests a 'hidden' element of discrimination against women who are thought to be failing in their traditional role.

One worrying problem is that many of the women in prison are mothers. 55 per cent have at least one child under 16 and over a third of these have a child under the age of five.

Activity

Read the following extract from a newspaper article and then answer the questions below.

Rape claim student jailed for wasting police time

'A university student who bound her wrists and ankles with tape and rolled down a muddy bank in an elaborate attempt to claim that she had been raped was jailed for two months yesterday.

Rowena Jones, 21, gave detectives a detailed, 27 page statement claiming that she had been raped by a stranger on the campus of Exeter University.

More than 60 policemen were diverted from murder, manslaughter and genuine rape cases to the investigation.

But six weeks later, after an inquiry involving more than 900 man hours and costing more than £11,000, Jones, of Newport, Shropshire, admitted that her allegation was false.

Exeter magistrates were told that Jones made up the claim because she had been raped previously by a boyfriend but had not reported the attack because she thought that no one would believe her.

Jones, who obtained a 2.2 in Greek and Roman Studies in her exams this year, admitted wasting police time.'

Taken from an article by Sean O'Neill, *The Daily Telegraph*, 30 October, 1999

QUESTIONS

❶ What sentence did the woman in this article receive?

❷ What aim of sentencing do you think the magistrates had in mind when this sentence was given?

❸ What other sentences could the woman have been given?

❹ Discuss whether the sentenced passed by the magistrates was justified.

Chapter 12

THE LEGAL PROFESSION

In England and Wales there are two types of lawyers (barristers and solicitors) jointly referred to as the legal profession. Most countries do not have this clear-cut division amongst lawyers: a person will qualify simply as a lawyer, although, after qualifying, it will be possible for them to specialise as an advocate, or in a particular area of law. This type of system is seen in this country in the medical profession, where all those wishing to become doctors take the same general qualifications. After they have qualified, some doctors will go on to specialise in different fields, perhaps as surgeons, and will take further qualifications in their chosen field.

In England, not only are the professions separate, but there is no common training for lawyers, although there have been increasing calls for this. As far back as 1971 the Ormrod Committee was in favour of a common education for all prospective lawyers. In 1994 the Lord Chancellor's advisory committee on legal education, under Lord Steyn, recommended that, instead of having separate training for barristers and solicitors, 'the two branches of the profession should have joint training. All those qualifying would then work for six months or a year at a solicitors', with those who wished to become barristers going on to do extra training at the Bar. Yet despite these recommendations, the training of the two professions remains separate.

12.1 Solicitors

There are about 80,000 solicitors practising in England and Wales and they are controlled by their own professional body, the Law Society.

12.1.1 Training

To become a solicitor it is usual to have a law degree, although those with a degree in a subject other than law can do an extra year's training in core legal subjects, and take the Common Professional Examination. The next stage is the one-year Legal Practice Course. This is much more practically based than the previous Law Society Finals course and includes training in skills such as client-interviewing, negotiation, advocacy, drafting documents and legal research. There is also an emphasis on business management, for example keeping accounts. Even when this course has been passed, the student is still not a qualified solicitor. He or she must next obtain a training contract under which they work in a solicitors' firm for two years, getting practical experience. This training period can also be undertaken in certain other legal organisations such as the Crown Prosecution Service, or the legal department of a local authority. During this two-year training contract the trainee will be paid, though not at the same rate as a fully qualified solicitor, and will do his own work, supervised by a solicitor. He will also have to complete a 20 day Professional Skills Course which builds on the skills learnt on the LPC. At the end of the time, the trainee will be admitted as a solicitor by the Law Society and his name will be added to the roll (or list) of solicitors. Even after qualifying, solicitors have to attend continuing education courses to keep their knowledge up to date.

There is also a route under which non-graduates can qualify as solicitors by first becoming legal executives. This route is only open to mature candidates and takes longer

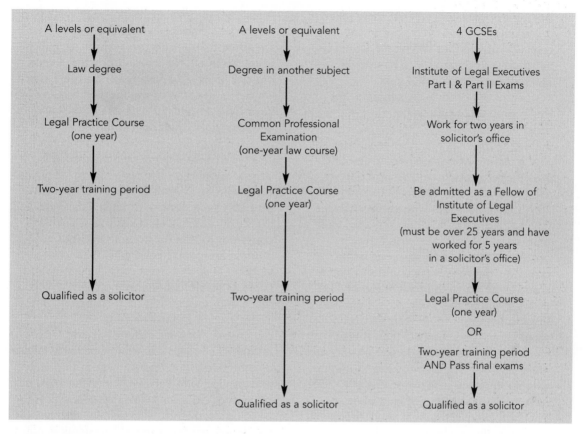

Figure 12.1 Training routes to become a solicitor

than the graduate route. The three routes to becoming a solicitor are shown in Figure 12.1.

Criticisms of the training process

There are several criticisms of the training process.

1. The first of these is a financial problem, in that students will usually have to pay the fees of the Legal Practice Course (about £6,000) and support themselves during this year. This problem has arisen because, as the LPC is a post-graduate course, students must pay all the cost. The result of this policy is that students from poor families cannot afford to take the course and are therefore prevented from becoming solicitors, even though they may have obtained a good law degree. Other students may take out bank loans, so that although they qualify, they start the training period with a large debt. In order to overcome this problem a few universities have started offering four year degree courses, combining a law qualification and a practical course, so students pay only £1,000 per year for fees. This financial problem is also one faced by prospective barristers.

2. A point common to barristers, is that non-law graduates do only one year of formal law for the Common Professional Course. The Ormrod Committee which reported on legal education in 1971 thought that the main entry route should be via a law degree, but in practice 25

per cent of solicitors will not have taken a law degree. One critic posed the question of whether the public would be satisfied with doctors who have only studied medicine for one year, concentrating on only six subjects. Yet this is precisely what is occurring in the legal profession.

3. A third problem is one of over-supply, so that students who have passed the LPC are unable to obtain a training contract. When the LPC was set up in the early 1990s to replace the Law Society's Finals Course, a greater number of places were made available. This stopped the previous criticism that students with good law degrees were unable to find a place to go on to the next stage of training, but at the same time it created the problem that there were far more students passing the LPC than there were training contracts. In some years, as many as three out of every five students who successfully completed the LPC have been unable to obtain a training contract. Even in the best years there will be one in three who pass all the solicitor's examinations and cannot qualify as a solicitor because of the shortage of training places in law firms. Clearly there is something wrong with a system which allows students to get as far as this, often incurring large debts on the way, only to prevent qualification at such a late stage.

12.1.2 Solicitors' work

The majority of those who succeed in qualifying as a solicitor will then work in private practice in a solicitors' firm. However, there are other careers available, and some newly-qualified solicitors may go on to work in the Crown Prosecution Service or for a Local Authority or Government Department. Others will become legal advisors in commercial or industrial businesses.

A solicitor in private practice may work as a sole practitioner or in a partnership. There are some 8,700 firms of solicitors, ranging from the small 'high street' practice to the big city firms. The number of partners is not limited, and some of the biggest firms will have over a hundred partners as well as employing assistant solicitors.

The type of work done by a solicitor will largely depend on the type of firm he or she is working in. A small high street firm will probably be a general practice advising clients on a whole range of topics such as consumer problems, housing and business matters and family problems. A solicitor working in such a practice is likely to spend some of his time interviewing clients in his office and negotiating on their behalf, and a large amount of time dealing with paperwork. This will include: writing letters on behalf of clients, drafting contracts, leases or other legal documents, drawing up wills and dealing with conveyancing (the legal side of buying and selling flats, houses, office buildings and land). The solicitor may also, if he wishes, act for some of his clients in court. Standing up in court and putting the client's case, and questioning witnesses is known as advocacy. Some solicitors will specialise in this and spend much of their time in court.

Although some solicitors may be general practitioners handling a variety of work it is not unusual even in small firms, for a solicitor to specialise in one particular field. The firm itself may only handle certain types of cases (perhaps only civil actions) and not do any criminal cases, or a firm may specialise in matrimonial cases. Even within the firm the solicitors are likely to have their own field of expertise. In large firms there will be an even greater degree of specialisation with departments dealing with one aspect of the law. The large city firms usually concentrate on business and commercial law. Amounts earned by solicitors are as varied as the types of firm, with the top earners in big firms on £500,000 or more, while at the bottom end of the scale some sole practitioners will earn less than £25,000.

Conveyancing

Prior to 1985 solicitors had a monopoly on conveyancing: this meant that only solicitors could deal with the legal side of transferring houses and other buildings and land. This was changed by the Administration of Justice Act 1985 which allowed people other than solicitors to become licensed conveyancers. The Courts and Legal Service Act 1990 then extended this right of doing conveyancing to banks and building societies. As a result of the increased competition in this area, solicitors had to reduce their fees, but even so they lost a large proportion of the work. This led to a demand for wider rights of advocacy.

Rights of advocacy

All solicitors have always been able to act as advocates in the Magistrates' Courts and the County Courts, but their rights of audience in the higher courts used to be very limited. Normally a solicitor could only act as advocate in the Crown Court on a committal for sentence, or on an appeal from the Magistrates' Court, and then only if he or another solicitor in the firm had been the advocate in the original case in the Magistrates' Court.

Until 1986 solicitors had no rights of audience in open court in the High Court, though they could deal with preliminary matters in preparation for a case. This lack of rights of audience was emphasised in *Abse* v *Smith* (1986) in which two Members of Parliament were contesting a libel action. They came to an agreed settlement, but the solicitor for one of them was refused permission by the judge to read out the terms of that settlement in open court. Following this decision the Lord Chancellor and the senior judges in each division of the High Court issued a Practice Direction, allowing solicitors to appear in the High Court to make a statement in a case that has been settled.

Certificate of advocacy

The first major alteration to solicitors' rights of audience came in the Courts and Legal Services Act 1990. Under this Act, a solicitor in private practice had the right to apply for a certificate of advocacy which enabled him to appear in the higher courts. Such a certificate was granted if the solicitor already had experience of advocacy in the Magistrates' Court and the County Court, took a short training course and passed examinations on the rules of evidence. The first certificates were granted in 1994 and by the end of 2001 about 1,100 solicitors had qualified to be an advocate in the higher courts. Figure 12.2 sets out the changes to the rights of audience of solicitors.

Solicitors with an advocacy qualification are also eligible to be appointed as Queen's Counsel (see section 12.2.2) and also to be appointed to higher judicial posts (see section 13.1.1).

The Access to Justice Act (s 36) provides that all solicitors will automatically be given full rights of audience. New training requirements will be brought in to allow solicitors to obtain these rights.

Multi-discipline partnerships

Section 66 of the Courts and Legal Services Act 1990 allows solicitors to form partnerships with other professions, for example accountants. This would give clients a wider range of expertise and advice in a 'one-stop shop'. However, the Law Society and the Bar Council have rules which prohibit the creation of multi-discipline partnerships. Section 66 allows the Law Society and the Bar Council to continue to operate such rules, so that, as yet, 'one-stop' shops are not allowed by the professional bodies that govern solicitors and barristers.

KEY FACTS

Original rights	To present cases in County Court and Magistrates' Court also at Crown Court on committal for sentence or appeal from Magistrates' Court
Practice Direction 1986	Following *Abse* v *Smith* allowed to make statement in High Court in cases in which terms had been agreed
Courts and Legal Services Act 1990	Solicitors allowed to apply for certificate of advocacy to conduct cases in the higher courts. Must have experience of advocacy, take course and pass examinations
Access to Justice Act 1999	Solicitors to have full rights of audience

Figure 12.2 Key fact chart on solicitors' rights of audience

12.1.3 Complaints against solicitors

A solicitor deals directly with clients and enters into a contract with them. This means that if the client does not pay, the solicitor has the right to sue for his fees. It also means that the client can sue his solicitor for breach of contract if the solicitor fails to do the work.

A client can also sue the solicitor for negligence in and out of court work. This happened in *Griffiths* v *Dawson* (1993) where solicitors for the plaintiff had failed to make the correct application in divorce proceedings against her husband. As a result the plaintiff lost financially and the solicitors were ordered to pay her £21,000 in compensation.

Other people affected by the solicitor's negligence may also have the right to sue in certain circumstances. An example of this was the case of *White* v *Jones* (1995) where a father wanted to make a will leaving each of his daughters £9,000. He wrote to his solicitors instructing them to draw up a will to include this. The solicitors received this letter on 17 July 1986 but had done nothing about it by the time the father died on 14 September 1986. As a result the daughters did not inherit any money and they successfully sued the solicitor for the £9,000 they had each lost.

Negligent advocacy

It used to be held that a solicitor presenting a case in court could not be sued for negligence. However, in *Hall* v *Simons* (2000), the House of Lords decided that advocates can be liable for negligence. This case is discussed more fully in section 19.2.3.

Office for the Supervision of Solicitors

There have been problems with the complaints procedures operated by the Law Society. One of the main concerns has been that the Law Society is in the position of acting as a regulatory body to protect the interests of clients, while at the same time representing solicitors. This is seen as a conflict of interests and was highlighted in 1986 with a High Court decision that Glanville Davies, a solicitor and member of the Law Society's Council, had over-charged a client by £131,000. The Law Society had previously investigated the complaint and held that Glanville Davies had acted properly. However, following the court decision the Law Society struck off Glanville Davies, and realised that it needed a more independent complaints procedure. This led to the setting up of the Solicitors' Complaints Bureau.

However, the Solicitors' Complaints Bureau itself came under attack for its own delays and inefficiency in dealing with complaints. A survey by the Law Society in 1995 found that in a sample of 2,246 complainants, two out of every three were dissatisfied with the outcome of their complaint.

As a result of these findings, and also in response to criticism by the Legal Services Ombudsman, in 1996 the Law Society abolished the Solicitors' Complaints Bureau and in its place set up the Office for the Supervision of Solicitors. However, this new 'watchdog' is still funded by the Law Society, so that the criticism of lack of an independent complaints body is still valid. In addition, the Office for the Supervision of Solicitors has been criticised for delays.

Access to Justice Act 1999

Schedule 7 to this Act gives greater powers to the Law Society to inspect solicitors' files and accounts. Also section 35 sets up a Legal Services Consultative Panel. This panel will report to the Lord Chancellor on the effectiveness of the Law Society's regulation of its members.

The Legal Services Ombudsman

Under the Courts and Legal Services Act 1990, the post of Legal Services Ombudsman was created to examine complaints against solicitors, and also barristers and licensed conveyancers, where the professions' own regulatory bodies did not provide a satisfactory answer. Under the Access to Justice Act 1999 the Ombudsman has power to order that the solicitor

concerned should pay compensation or that the Law Society itself should compensate the client.

12.2 Barristers

There are about 10,000 barristers in independent practice in England and Wales. Collectively barristers are referred to as 'the Bar' and they are controlled by their own professional body – the General Council of the Bar. All barristers must also be a member of one of the four Inns of Court: Lincoln's Inn, Inner Temple, Middle Temple and Gray's Inn, all of which are situated near the Royal Courts of Justice in London.

12.2.1 Training

Entry to the Bar is normally degree-based, though there is a non-degree route for mature entrants, under which a small number of students qualify. As with solicitors, graduate students without a law degree can take the one year course for the Common Professional Examination in the core subjects, in order to go on to qualify as a barrister. All student barristers have to pass the Bar Vocational Course which emphasises the practical skills of drafting pleadings for use in court, negotiation and advocacy.

Until 1997 only the Inns of Court School of Law (Bar School) could run this course, but from September 1997 six other bodies have been validated to offer the course. These are: the BPP Law School and the College of Law in London, and Law Schools in Nottingham, Northumbria, Bristol and Cardiff. This will allow more students to obtain a place on the Bar Vocational Course, but will bring the same problems that solicitors are facing, with more people qualifying than there are work placements available for.

All student barristers must join one of the four Inns of Court and used to have to dine there 12 times before being called to the Bar. Since October 1997 students may attend in a different way, for example, a weekend residential course. This will help students on the courses outside London as travelling costs will be lower. The idea behind the rule requiring all trainee barristers to dine was that they met senior barristers and judges and absorbed the traditions of the profession. In practice, few barristers dine at their Inns and students are unlikely to meet anyone except other students.

Once a student has passed the Bar Vocational Course, he or she is then 'called to the Bar'. This means that they are officially qualified as a barrister. However, there is still a practical stage to their training which must be completed. This is called pupillage.

Pupillage

After the student has passed the Bar Vocational Course there is 'on the job' training where the trainee barrister becomes a pupil to a qualified barrister. This effectively involves 'work shadowing' that barrister, and can be with the same barrister for 12 months or with two different pupil masters for six months each. There is also a requirement that they take part in a programme of continuing education organised by the Bar Council. After the first six months of pupillage, barristers are eligible to appear in court and may conduct their own cases. During pupillage trainee barristers are paid a small salary, usually about half the amount paid to trainee solicitors.

The various training routes are shown in Figure 12.3.

12.2.2 Barristers' work

Barristers practising at the Bar are self-employed, but usually work from a set of chambers where they can share administrative expenses with other barristers. Most sets of chambers are fairly small comprising of about 15 to 20 barristers. They will employ a clerk as a practice administrator – booking in cases and negotiating fees – and they will have other support staff. One of the problems facing newly qualified barristers is the difficulty of finding a tenancy in chambers. Many will do a third six-month pupillage and then 'squat' as an unofficial tenant before obtaining a place. The rule on having to practise from chambers has been relaxed, so that it is technically possible for barristers to practise from home. However, despite the fact that a tenancy in chambers is not essential, it is still viewed as the way to allow a barrister to build a successful practice.

The majority of barristers will concentrate on advocacy, although there are some who specialise in areas such as tax and company law, and who rarely appear in court. Barristers have rights of audience in all courts in England and Wales. Even those who specialise in advocacy will do a certain amount of paperwork, writing opinions on cases, giving advice and drafting documents for use in court. Clients cannot, as a general rule, go direct to a barrister but must use a solicitor who will then brief a barrister if it becomes necessary. Certain professions, including accountants and surveyors, can brief a barrister directly without the need for a solicitor as an intermediary. Also, clients from abroad can contact a barrister directly without having to go through a solicitor. There is pressure to allow direct access to the Bar for all prospective clients.

Employed barristers

The employed Bar, which includes those barristers working for the Crown Prosecution Service, can appear in the Magistrates' Court, but used not to be able to conduct cases in the Crown Court, High Court or appellate courts. As these barristers will have

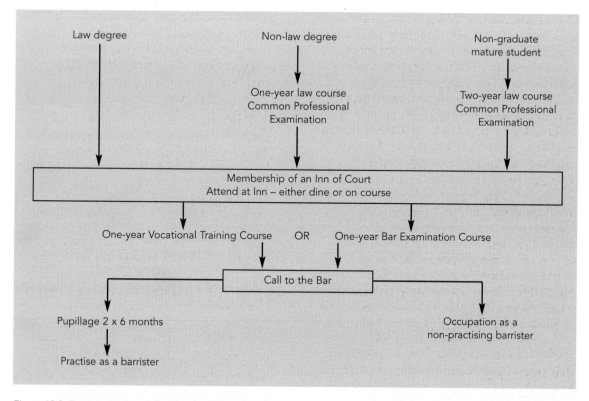

Figure 12.3 *Training routes to become a barrister*

done exactly the same training as the independent Bar this was seen as being unnecessarily restrictive. The Access to Justice Act 1999 now allows barristers working for the CPS or other employers to keep their rights of audience. The Act also allows barristers who work in solicitors' firms to keep the right to present cases in court.

Queen's Counsel

After at least 10 years as a barrister or as a solicitor with an advocacy qualification, it is possible to apply to the Lord Chancellor to become a Queen's Counsel (QC). About 10 per cent of the Bar are Queen's Counsel and it is known as 'taking silk'. QCs usually take on more complicated and high profile cases than junior barristers (all barristers who are not Queen's Counsel are known as 'juniors'), and they can command higher fees for their recognised expertise. Often a QC will have a junior barrister to assist with the case.

The Lord Chancellor's criteria for selecting QCs has been criticised as being too secretive. Barristers have to apply and, if they were not appointed, they were not told why they were not considered. Since 1999 those applying to become a QC must pay a fee, but if they are not appointed the reasons are given to them. There is also the fact that less than 10 per cent of QCs are women and only a very few are from ethnic minorities. In turn, this has an effect on the composition of the judiciary since senior judges are usually chosen from the ranks of Queen's Counsel. The position of women and ethnic minorities in the legal profession is considered in more detail in section 12.4.

12.2.3 Complaints against barristers

A barrister does not enter into a contract with his client and so cannot sue if his fees are not paid. Similarly, the client cannot sue for breach of contract. However, they can be sued for negligence. In *Saif Ali* v *Sydney Mitchell and Co* (1980) it was held that a barrister could be sued for negligence in respect of written advice and opinions. In that case a barrister had given the wrong advice about who to sue, with the result that the claimant was too late to start proceedings against the right person.

In *Hall (a firm)* v *Simons* (2000) the House of Lords held that lawyers could also be liable for negligence in the conduct of advocacy in court. This decision overruled the earlier case of *Rondel* v *Worsley* (1969) in which barristers were held not to be liable because their first duty was to the courts and they must be 'free to do their duty fearlessly and independently'.

The Law Lords in *Hall (a firm)* v *Simons* felt that in light of modern conditions it was no longer in the public interest that advocates should have immunity from being sued for negligence. They pointed out that doctors could be sued and they had a duty to an ethical code of practice and might have difficult decisions to make when treating patients. There was no reason why advocates should not be liable in the same way.

They also pointed out that allowing advocates to be sued for negligence would not be likely to lead to the whole case being re-argued. If an action against an advocate was merely an excuse to get the whole issue litigated again, the matter would almost certainly be struck out as an abuse of process.

Barristers can be disciplined by the Senate of the Inns of Court if they fail to maintain the standards set out in their Code of Conduct. In extreme cases the Senate can disbar a barrister from practising. There is also a Lay Complaints Commissioner who can investigate complaints. The Bar Council

has the power to pay compensation for poor service.

Legal Services Ombudsman

As set out earlier in section 12.1.3, there has been a Legal Services Ombudsman since 1991, whose work involves investigating complaints about all the legal professions. There are comparatively few complaints against barristers and the Ombudsman has found that the Bar Council handles 90 per cent of complaints satisfactorily.

12.3 The future

12.3.1 The OFT report 2001

In March 2001 The Office of Fair Trading issued a very critical report on the legal profession. It identified restrictions which have the effect of 'preventing, restricting or distorting competition in professional services to a significant extent'. Amongst other matters it recommended that:

- people should be allowed direct access to the bar; this means that members of the public would be able to brief a barrister without going to a solicitor;
- mixed professional partnerships should be allowed, the so-called 'one-stop shop';
- advertising of comparative fees and comparative success rates should be allowed.

The report also criticised the silk system saying it is 'questionable what the value of the system is to consumers'.

12.3.2 The professions' response

In reply the Bar Council pointed out that 'the rules under challenge go to the heart of the distinction between the profession of barrister and that of solicitor'. They rejected the idea that barristers should be allowed to

KEY FACTS

	Solicitors	Barristers
Professional body	Law Society	Bar Council
Basic qualifications	Law degree OR degree in another subject PLUS Common Professional Exam	Law degree OR degree in another subject PLUS Common Professional Exam
Vocational training	Legal Practice Course	Bar Vocational Course
Practical training	Training contract	Pupillage
Number in profession	80,000	10,000 (including 600 QCs)
Method of working	Firm of partners OR as sole practitioner	Self-employed, practising in chambers
Rights of audience	Normally only County Court and Magistrates' Court After Access to Justice Act 1999 will be able to have full advocacy rights	All courts
Relationship with client	Contractual	Normally through solicitor BUT accountants and surveyors can brief barristers directly
Liability	Liable in contract and tort to clients May also be liable to others affected by negligence (*White* v *Jones*)	No contractual liability BUT liable for negligence (*Hall* v *Simons*)

Figure 12.4 Key fact chart comparing solicitors and barristers

form partnerships as the present system maximises competition and choice; and minimises cost. It also preserves the cab-rank rule.

The Law Society is in favour of limited multi-disciplinary practices. They recommend that non-solicitors should be able to join a law firm as partners provided the partnership operates to offer legal services and any other business, such as financial advice is ancillary to it. In addition, the solicitor-partners must remain in control of the partnership.

Direct access

The Bar has already given wider rights of direct access under the BARDIRECT scheme which started in 2000. This allows direct access to a wide variety of groups who are in a position to have the skills and resources to do the work normally done by a solicitor. These groups include police, fire services, insurers, banks, employment consultants, advice agencies, racial equality councils, trading standards officers and trades unions. This is in addition to professionals such as accountants and surveyors who already had direct access.

The advantages of retaining direct access are that it enables smaller firms of solicitors to compete with larger firms; it also enables barristers to concentrate on their role as advocates.

12.3.3 Advocacy rights

Although the Access to Justice allows for all new solicitors to become advocates automatically, the new training procedures to allow this to happen have not yet been agreed.

The Bar sees the two main competitors for the work currently undertaken by independent barristers as being 'in-house' solicitors who will be able to represent their employer and employed barristers who are likely to be given full rights of audience.

In addition, the work available at the Crown Court for barristers is diminishing. By the beginning of 2001, nearly 300 Crown Prosecutors had obtained higher court advocacy rights so that they can conduct prosecutions in the Crown Court. The CPS is carrying out a training programme so that there will be an increasing number of advocate-prosecutors. At the same time the amount of work in the Crown Court is decreasing and, if the Auld Review recommendations are accepted, will decrease further.

12.3.4 Fusion

A major debate used to be whether the two professions should be merged into one profession. The advantages of fusion were thought to be:

- reduced costs as only one lawyer would be needed instead of a solicitor and a barrister;
- less duplication of work because only one person would be doing the work, instead of a solicitor preparing the case and then passing it on to a barrister;
- more continuity as the same person could deal with the case from start to finish.

The disadvantages of fusion were seen as:

- a decrease in the specialist skills of advocacy;
- loss of the independent bar and the lack of availability of advice from independent specialists at the bar;
- less objectivity in consideration of a case; at the moment the barrister provides a second opinion;
- loss of a cab-rank principle under which barristers have to accept any case offered to them (except when they are already booked on another case for the same day). This principle allows anyone to get representation, even if their case is unpopular or unlikely to win.

The argument for fusion is no longer so important since the changes made by the Courts and Legal Services Act 1990 and the Access to Justice Act 1999 mean that barristers and solicitors can take a case from start to finish. Under the Access to Justice Act barristers have the right to do litigation (i.e. the preliminary work in starting a case) which has in the past always been done by solicitors. At the same time solicitors have wider rights of advocacy and may represent clients in all courts.

12.4 Women and ethnic minorities in the legal profession

The legal profession has an image of being white male-dominated. Both women and ethnic minorities are under-represented in the higher levels of the legal professions.

Women

Women are forming an increasing number of the entrants to the professions. They now make up just over half of new solicitors and just under half of new entrants to the Bar. Despite this there are very few women at the higher levels in either profession. For example at the bar only about 7 per cent of QCs are women. Women solicitors tend to be in junior positions as assistant solicitors or junior partners, even though a third of practising solicitors are women.

One of the reasons put forward to explain this is that the increase in entrants is a fairly recent phenomena. Twenty years ago there were comparatively few women going into the legal professions, and so it is not so surprising that there are correspondingly fewer women in senior positions. This is shown by the much smaller number of women who apply to become QCs. About 50 women apply each year compared to 450 men. However, women applicants have a higher success rate.

In the solicitors' profession about 19 per cent of partners are women. This figure is increasing, but a survey in 2001 found that many women solicitors did not want to become partners.

Women also tend to earn less than their male counterparts, even when they do achieve higher status, especially in the solicitors' ranks. Women solicitors do not earn the same level of salary as male solicitors. Even the starting salaries of women are lower. The gap becomes bigger the higher up the profession, with men earning on average £15,000 more per year than women.

Activity

Read the following article and answer the questions below.

No room at the bar

The Lord Chancellor, Lord Mackay, is urging more women lawyers to apply to become QCs and judges. And of the women who applied for silk this year, 19 per cent were successful this month, compared with only 14 per cent of men.

At first sight it looks as though traditional barriers to women's advancement in the male-dominated legal profession are toppling. Yet a closer look at the new QCs list shows that even the most successful senior women barristers remain concentrated in the lower-paid, less prestigious fields of family law and crime. Cherie Booth, wife of the Labour leader Tony Blair, one of eight women out of 71 new silks, is exceptional in specialising in the 'male' fields of employment and public law and few women have managed to break into the most lucrative commercial work.

'Women feel they're not being given the opportunities,' says Susan Ward, chairwoman of the Association of Women Barristers. 'By and large, they're channelled into stereotyped women's work. The clerks negotiate lower fees for women than for men. And when it comes to appointments, the rules of the game are still made by men for men to play.'

Women are joining both branches of the legal profession in unprecedented numbers: nearly half of the new barristers, and more than half the new solicitors, are female. Yet both anecdotal

> **evidence and hard research show that most are set for less glittering careers than the men they qualify with.**
>
> **Without Prejudice, an independent study in 1992, commissioned by the Bar Council and the Lord Chancellor's Department, painted a picture of institutional discrimination at all stages of barristers' careers. Women had a harder time finding pupillages and permanent places in chambers, continued to be asked questions about marriage and children at interviews, earned less than men and were less likely to find work in the field of their choice.**
>
> Taken from an article by Clare Dyer in *The Guardian*, 25 April 1995

QUESTIONS

❶ What evidence is there to show that women in the legal profession suffer from discrimination?

❷ Is there any evidence to show that there has been an improvement in women's position in the legal profession?

❸ Is the imbalance between men and women likely to have an adverse effect on the profession as a whole?

Ethnic minorities

Proportionate to the composition of the general population, ethnic minorities are quite well represented at the Bar. In 2000 minority lawyers made up 8 per cent of barristers in private practice. However, they experience even more difficulty in achieving higher positions than women do. There are still only a few Queen's Counsel of ethnic minority origin. This may reflect the fact that many of the ethnic minority at the Bar are fairly newly qualified, so that in time the number of QCs should improve.

In the solicitors' profession ethnic minorities are slightly under-represented, making up about 5 per cent of the profession. However, in the last few years the number of ethnic minority entrants has risen substantially. In 2000, 19 per cent of those admitted as solicitors were from ethnic minority backgrounds.

12.5　Legal executives

Legal executives work in solicitors' firms as assistants. To become a legal executive it is necessary to pass the Part I and Part II examinations of the Institute of Legal Executives, and to have worked in a solicitors' firm (or an organisation such as the Crown Prosecution Service) for at least five years. Legal executives will often deal with the more straightforward cases themselves, for example preparing simple wills or leases. They also have limited rights of audience in court, mainly making applications in the County Court where the case is not defended. The Institute of Legal Executives is seeking the right for its members to have further rights of audience, in relation to matters which will be dealt with by a District judge in the County Court and applications to the Magistrates' Courts in cases which are started by a complaint or application; this would include family proceedings and applications under the licensing and gaming legislation. They also want to be able to conduct cases in front of tribunals.

The partners in the firm of solicitors for whom the legal executive works are responsible for his or her work.

Chapter 13

THE JUDICIARY

When speaking of judges as a group, they are referred to as the judiciary. There are many different levels of judges, but the basic function is the same at all levels: judges are there to adjudicate on disputes in a fair, unbiased way, applying the legal rules of this country. There is no clear-cut division between civil and criminal judges, as many judges at the various levels are required to sit for both types of case. This in itself causes problems as, before their appointment, most judges will have specialised in one area of law. The head of the judiciary is the Lord Chancellor. This position is a political appointment and is considered in detail in section 13.6.

When considering judges the first point is that there is a marked difference between what are called superior judges and inferior judges. This affects the method of appointment, the training, the work and the terms on which they hold office, so it is as well to start by understanding which judges are involved at each level.

Types of judges

Superior judges are those in the High Court and above. Starting from the top and working down these are:

- The Lords of Appeal in Ordinary (the Law Lords) in the House of Lords
- The Lords Justices of Appeal in the Court of Appeal
- High Court judges (known as puisne judges) who sit in the three divisions of the High Court and, note that in addition, judges from the Queen's Bench Division also sit in the Crown Court

The head of the House of Lords is the Lord Chancellor. Specific judicial posts heading the different divisions of the Court of Appeal and the High Court are as follows:

- **The Lord Chief Justice** is second only to the Lord Chancellor in the judicial hierarchy. He is the President of the Criminal Division of the Court of Appeal and technically the senior judge in the Queen's Bench Division of the High Court.
- **The Master of the Rolls**, President of the Civil Division of the Court of Appeal.

- **The President of the Family Division of the High Court**, the senior judge in that division. In 1999 the first woman President was appointed
- **The Vice-Chancellor of the Chancery Division of the High Court**, the day-to-day head of that division. The Lord Chancellor is nominally the head of the division but rarely, if ever, actually sits as a judge there

The inferior judges are:

- Circuit judges who sit in both the Crown Court and the County Court
- Recorders who are part-time judges sitting usually in the Crown Court, though some may be assigned to the County Court
- District judges who hear small claims and other matters in the County Court
- Stipendiary magistrates who sit in Magistrates' Courts in London and other major towns and cities
- Chairmen of tribunals

13.1 Appointment

The Lord Chancellor is the key post in the appointment of judges. He either nominates

The Lord Chief Justice, Lord Woolf and Master of the Rolls, Lord Phillips of Worth Matravers

or appoints all the lower ranks of the judiciary, and although the higher ranks are appointed by the Queen (on the advice of the Prime Minister), the Lord Chancellor will still be very influential.

The relevant qualifications for the different judicial posts are now contained in the Courts and Legal Services Act 1990. This Act broke the previous monopoly that the Bar held on all superior judgeships, by basing qualifications on the relevant advocacy qualifications, and providing for promotion from one level to the next. To become a judge at any level it is necessary to have qualified as a barrister or solicitor. It is no longer essential to have practised, as the Courts and Legal Services Act provided for academic lawyers to be appointed. In 1994, the Lord Chancellor lifted the ban which prevented lawyers in the civil service and Crown Prosecution Service from becoming judges. These changes have all helped to widen the pool of potential candidates for judgeships, and may eventually help to make the composition of the bench a wider cross-section of society.

13.1.1 Superior judges

The appointment of judges to the House of Lords and the Court of Appeal is by way of invitation; i.e. it is not possible to apply for such a position. Judges for the High Court may apply, although many are still invited.

Before 1986 little was known about how such invitations were decided, but in 1986, the then Lord Chancellor, Lord Hailsham, published a document called 'Judicial Appointments' which gave some explanation of the selection process. This involves the Lord Chancellor's Department keeping files on all possible candidates and collecting confidential information and opinions about those candidates from judges. These files are secret so that the subjects do not know what is in them – this could lead to errors remaining uncorrected. Not surprisingly, this system of selection is seen as secretive and tending to perpetuate the white-male dominance of these positions, as it relies heavily on word of mouth and the confidential opinion of existing judges.

There is now a Judicial Appointments Commissioner to act as a 'watchdog'. The Commissioner monitors how judges are selected but does not have any say in their appointment. Those not appointed can make complaints to him.

The Law Lords

These are appointed from those who hold high judicial office (for example as a judge in the Court of Appeal), or from those who have been qualified to appear in the Supreme Court for at least 15 years. As the House of Lords is the final appellate court for Scotland and Northern Ireland as well, judges can also be appointed from those who have practised as an advocate in Scotland for at least 15 years, or as a member of the Bar in Northern Ireland for at least 15 years, or held high judicial office in their own legal system. There are 12 Lords of Appeal in Ordinary and, in addition, the Lord Chancellor is entitled to sit as one of the Appellate Committee of the House of Lords (this is the correct title for the House of Lords in its judicial capacity).

Law Lords are made life peers and are entitled to sit in the House of Lords in its legislative capacity and take part in debates. The appointments are made by the Queen after being nominated by the Prime Minister; in fact, the normal procedure is understood to be that the Lord Chancellor draws up a short list in order of preference and the Prime Minister selects from this list. In nearly all cases the first choice candidate of the Lord Chancellor will be the one who is appointed, but it is known that Mrs Thatcher on at least

one occasion vetoed the first choice and nominated the second choice. No woman has yet been appointed as a Law Lord.

Judges in the House of Lords hear civil and criminal appeals where a point of law is involved. The work, however, is mostly civil with about 50 cases each year, many of which involve narrow fields of law such as planning and taxation; only about five criminal cases are dealt with each year.

Lords Justices of Appeal

These must have a 10-year High Court qualification or be an existing High Court judge. In practice nearly all Lords Justices of Appeal have been appointed from existing High Court judges. As with the Law Lords, they are appointed by the Queen after being nominated by the Prime Minister, but clearly, as with the House of Lords, the Lord Chancellor will play a major part in the recommendations. As solicitors can be appointed High Court judges, it means that it is possible for a solicitor to become a judge in the Court of Appeal, but at the moment (2002) all the judges in the Court of Appeal have been barristers.

The first woman Lord Justice of Appeal, Elizabeth Butler-Sloss, was appointed in 1988. Until 1994, she had to be addressed in court as Lord Butler-Sloss, since the Supreme Court Act 1981 which governs the appointments sets out that the judges 'shall be styled Lords Justices of Appeal'. However in 1994, the then Master of the Rolls, Sir Thomas Bingham, announced that in future she should be addressed as My Lady, Lady Justice Butler-Sloss. In making the announcement he said that 'Procedure in the Court of Appeal can now recognise the happy fact that the holders of the highest judicial office include women'. It was not until 1999 that the second woman was appointed to the Court of Appeal, Lady Justice Hale, and a third in 2000. In February 2001 an all-female Court of Appeal panel sat for the first time.

The Lords Justices of Appeal sit in both divisions of the Court of Appeal and thus can hear both civil and criminal cases. Their workload is much heavier than the House of Lords. High Court judges are often used to form part of the panel to help with the workload of the Court of Appeal (Criminal Division), so that there may be one Lord Justice of Appeal sitting with two High Court judges.

High Court judges

In order to be eligible to be appointed as a High Court judge it is necessary either to have had the right to practice in the High Court for at least 10 years, or to have been a Circuit judge for at least two years. Prior to the Courts and Legal Services Act only those who had practised as a barrister for at least 10 years were eligible. The new qualification routes give solicitors the chance to become High Court judges, either by promotion from a circuit judgeship (as happened in 1993 to the first solicitor to be appointed, Sir Michael Sachs), or by holding a certificate of advocacy for the required time. A second solicitor was appointed as a High Court judge in 2000.

The Act also allows academic lawyers to be appointed as it is no longer necessary to have actually practised. One of the first academics to be appointed as a High Court judge was Brenda Hale QC who is now a judge in the Court of Appeal.

High Court judgeships have been advertised since 1998, but the Lord Chancellor can also invite people to become a High Court judge.

Judges in the High Court are appointed by the Queen on the advice of the Lord Chancellor. On appointment they are assigned to one of the three divisions, although they are technically able to sit in all three divisions. This is designed to allow the Lord Chancellor to ensure that the judges in each division have expertise in that area of law.

One recent problem on the appointment of High Court judges is that the present rates of salary are not attractive to top barristers and some have declined appointment as a judge. The gap in potential earnings is probably getting wider, as a top QC could now expect to earn well over £500,000 a year, whilst the pay of a High Court judge is only in the region of £125,000. In the past the financial security of a pension at the end of 15 years' service as a judge was an added incentive, but judges are now required to serve 20 years before being eligible for a full pension.

There has been an increasing use of Deputy High Court judges trying cases in the High Court. This reflects the increasing workload and the fact, that despite some extra judges being appointed, it is generally thought that the number of High Court judges needs to be increased.

Activity

Look at law reports in the papers, especially *The Times* and *The Independent*, and find reports from the High Court, the Court of Appeal and the House of Lords. You can do this on CD-ROM or the Internet.

TRY TO FIND

❶ A law report in which there was a female judge.

❷ A report of the Court of Appeal in which at least one of the judges is only of High Court level. The title they are given should tell you this. (If you need help, turn to Appendix 1 which explains how judges' titles are written.)

❸ A report from the High Court in which the judge sitting is only a Deputy High Court judge.

13.1.2 Inferior judges

The Lord Chancellor is responsible for appointing all lower levels of the judiciary, and at this level potential candidates apply for such a position. In the past this was always by a general application, without knowing whether there was a vacancy at the required level. This still occurs for what is regarded as the first post on the judicial ladder – recorder. However, for the positions of Circuit judge and District judge, advertisements are now placed in the legal press.

Circuit judges

There are different routes to becoming a Circuit judge. The candidate can either have had rights of audience for at least 10 years (in either the Crown Court or the County Court) or have been a recorder. This route via being a recorder has existed since 1971 and allows solicitors who have not got the required certificate of advocacy, a route into the judiciary. About 10 per cent of Circuit judges are solicitors. The Courts and Legal Services Act 1990 also allows for promotion after being a District judge, stipendiary magistrate or chairman of an employment tribunal for at least three years. These proposals widen the pool of potential judges and should lead to a better cross-section amongst the judges.

The usual route, however is to be appointed first as a recorder before becoming a Circuit judge. Since 1995, posts of Circuit judges (and District judges) have been advertised. The first advert that appeared stated that applicants should normally be aged between 45 and 60, and have served as a recorder for two years. Applicants are shortlisted and interviewed by a panel which includes a serving judge, an official from the Lord Chancellor's Department and a lay person. The interview panel put their view to the Lord Chancellor and the appointment is then made by the Queen on the advice of the Lord Chancellor.

Recorders

This is a part-time post. The applicant must have practised as a barrister or solicitor for at least 10 years, though in practice it is rare

to be appointed with less than 15 years' experience. Recorders sit as a judge for 20 days in the year; the rest of the time they continue in their private practice as a solicitor or barrister. The appointment is for five years and most recorders work in the Crown Court, though it is also possible for them to sit in the County Court.

District judges

These need a seven-year general qualification. This means they can be appointed from either barristers or solicitors, but in practice the vast majority of District judges are solicitors. They work in the County Court and are concerned only with civil cases.

District judges (Magistrates' Courts)

These used to be called stipendiary magistrates. Most sit in London, although the number who can be appointed to posts outside London was increased from 40 to 50 in 1996. They need a seven-year general qualification, so, as with District Judges, any barrister or solicitor with this length of experience is eligible.

Activity

Read the following article and answer the questions below

A system of ill-judged appointments

A QC was being sounded out by the Lord Chancellor about a High Court judgeship. They knew each other well, had been colleagues at the Bar. But the

QC, a top earner, could not afford the move. He had family commitments. The incident illustrates the personal aspect of the patronage at the Lord Chancellor's disposal. Lord Irvine of Lairg knows as friends many people he can now promote; those he does not know – the wider pool of solicitors for instance – can feel disadvantaged. But what if the Lord Chancellor records no judicial appointments? The verdict is positive: they include the top promotions of Lord Bingham of Cornhill to senior law lord, of Lord Woolf to Lord Chief Justice, of Dame Butler-Sloss to President of the Family Division – the first woman to reach such a rank. Yet the face of the judiciary remains similar to that of four years ago [when Lord Irvine took over as Lord Chancellor], despite efforts to promote more women and ethnic minorities. Merit remains the acid test. Of 125 circuit judges appointed, only one is known to be black, 20 were solicitors and 20 were women.

Taken from an article by Frances Gibbs in *The Times*, 27 February 2001

QUESTIONS

❶ Why might some lawyers refuse to be appointed as a judge?
❷ Why could some groups feel at a disadvantage when the appointment of new judges is being considered?
❸ Give one good point about recent judicial appointments.
❹ Give one bad point about recent judicial appointments.

Research

The article names three judges. Look up these judges on the Lord Chancellor's Department's website (www.lcd.gov.uk and use menus to find pages on judges) and list any information you can find about them and their judicial careers.

13.1.3 Composition of the bench

One of the main criticisms of the bench is that it is dominated by elderly, white, upper-class males. There are very few women judges, and even fewer judges from ethnic minorities. With the introduction of a younger retirement age, the average age of judges will be slightly reduced, but it is unusual for any judge to be appointed under the age of 40, with superior judges usually being well above this age.

Women in the judiciary

The number of women in judicial posts is very small, although there has been an improvement in recent years. During the 1990s there was an increase in the number of women appointed to the High Court. The first woman judge in the Queen's Bench Division was appointed in 1992, and the first in the Chancery Division in 1993. By the beginning of the year 2002 the total number of women judges in the High Court was still only nine out of nearly 100 judges, with only two women out of 35 judges in the Court of Appeal and no women judges in the House of Lords.

Lower down the judicial ladder, there are slightly more women being appointed than in the past. At the beginning of 2002, 9 per cent of Circuit judges and 12 per cent of recorders were female. The highest percentages of women were for District judges (16 per cent and 20 per cent for deputies).

In 1994 the then Lord Chancellor announced a nine-point package designed to encourage more women and people from ethnic minority backgrounds to apply for judicial posts. This ranged from persuading senior members of the judiciary and the legal profession to encourage suitably qualified candidates to apply, to publicising the fact that the Lord Chancellor is prepared to be flexible over upper age limits so as not to rule out women who have taken a career break to have children.

Ethnic minorities

There are no judges from ethnic minorities in the higher courts and even at the lower levels ethnic minorities are still poorly represented. At the beginning of 2002 only 1 per cent of Circuit judges and 3 per cent of recorders were from an ethnic minority. However, there have been improvements at lower levels with 5.5 per cent of deputy district judges being from an ethnic minority.

Educational and social background

At the higher levels judges tend to come from the upper levels of society, with many having been educated at public school and nearly all attending Oxford or Cambridge University. A survey by the magazine, *Labour Research*, found that of the 85 judges appointed from 1997 to mid 1999, 73 per cent had been to public school and 79 per cent to Oxbridge. Judges (especially superior judges) will have spent at least 20 years working as barristers and mixing with a small group of like-minded people. As a result, judges are seen as out of touch with society. Occasionally the media report actions or comments which appear to support this view, for example where a judge said of an eight-year-old rape victim that she 'was no angel'. Since 1995 training in human awareness has been given to prevent such offensive remarks. Lord Taylor, the former Lord Chief Justice, who was one of the few senior judges who had attended a state school, pointed out that judges live in the real world and do ordinary things like shopping in supermarkets.

13.2 Training

The training of judges is carried out by the Judicial Studies Board, which was set up in 1979. Most of the training is, however, focused at the lower end of the judicial scale, being aimed at recorders. Once a lawyer has been appointed as a recorder in training, they go on a one-week course run by the Judicial Studies Board, and then shadow an experienced judge for a week. After this they will sit to hear cases, though there will be one-day courses available from time to time, especially on the effect of new legislation.

Critics point out that the training is very short, and that even if all the people involved are experienced lawyers this does not mean that they have any experience of doing such tasks as summing up to the jury or sentencing. There is also the fact that some recorders will not have practised in the criminal courts as lawyers, so their expertise is limited and a one-week course a very short training period.

There is no compulsory training given to new High Court judges, although they are invited to attend the courses run by the Judicial Studies Board. The attitude of the judiciary to training has changed considerably over the last 20 years. Training used to be seen as insulting to lawyers who had spent all their working lives in the courts building up expertise in their field. It was also seen as a threat to judicial independence. However, the need for training is now fully accepted.

Human awareness training

In 1993 the Judicial Studies Board recommended that training should include racial awareness courses. This was accepted by the Lord Chancellor and all Circuit judges and recorders now have to attend a course designed to make them aware of what might be unintentionally discriminatory or offensive, such as asking a non-Christian for their Christian name. The Board has also introduced training in human awareness, covering gender awareness, and disability issues. The training explores the perceptions of unrepresented parties, witnesses, jurors, victims and their families, and tries to make judges more aware of other people's viewpoints.

Legal research

Another problem that exists is the lack of research facilities for judges at all levels – this is especially true of the appellate courts, where the cases are likely to involve complex legal points. The judges in the Court of Appeal have only four days a month for legal reading, and, unlike many foreign courts, there are no lawyers attached to the court to research the law. In the European Court of Justice there are Advocates-General who are independent lawyers working for the court, whose task is to research legal points and present their findings.

13.2.1 Should there be a 'career' judiciary?

In many continental countries becoming a judge is a career choice made by students once they have their basic legal qualifications. They will usually not practise as a lawyer first, but instead are trained as judges. Once they have qualified as a judge they will sit in junior posts and then hope to be promoted up the judicial ladder. This has two distinct advantages over the system in use in this country:

- The average age of judges is much lower, especially in the bottom ranks. In this country an assistant recorder will normally be in their late thirties or early forties when appointed, and the average age for appointment to the High Court bench tends to be late forties/early fifties
- Judges have had far more training in the specific skills they need as judges

The disadvantage of the continental system is that judges may be seen as too closely linked to the government as they are civil servants. In this country judges are generally considered as independent from the government. This point of judicial independence is explored more fully in section 13.5.

Elected judges

In the United States of America judges at state and local level are elected to their posts. This may cause pressure groups to canvass voters actively for or against judges, according to the views the judges hold. Judges in the federal courts are appointed by the President but the appointment has to be confirmed by the Senate. Before voting on a new appointee the Senate can question him or her about their background and past life and this is usually televised. This makes the appointment system very public, but can lead to political overtones in the appointment system, with one political party voting for a candidate and the opposing party voting against that candidate.

13.3 Retirement and dismissal

It is important that judges should be impartial in their decisions and, in particular, that the Government cannot force a judge to resign if that judge makes a decision with which the Government of the day disagrees. In this country judges are reasonably secure from political interference. The only exception to this rule is the Lord Chancellor. His is a political appointment and the Prime Minister can dismiss the Lord Chancellor at any time, just as the Prime Minister has the right to dismiss any other Cabinet member. The Lord Chancellor will also change with a change of Government.

13.3.1 Security of tenure of superior judges

Superior judges have security of tenure in that they cannot be dismissed by the Lord Chancellor or the Government. This right originated in the Act of Settlement 1701 which allowed them to hold office while of good behaviour (previously the Monarch could dismiss judges at will). The same provision is now contained in the Supreme Court Act 1981 for High Court judges and Lords Justices of Appeal, and in the Appellate Jurisdiction Act 1876 for the Law Lords. As a result they can only be removed by the Monarch following a petition presented to him or her by both Houses of Parliament. This gives superior judges protection from political whims and allows them to be independent in their judgments.

This power to remove a superior judge has never been used for an English judge, though it was used in 1830 to remove an Irish judge, Jonah Barrington, who had misappropriated £700 from court funds.

The Lord Chancellor can, however, after consulting with senior judges, declare vacant the office of any judge who (through ill-health) is incapable of carrying out his work and of taking the decision to resign. This power was first introduced in the Administration of Justice Act 1973 and is now contained in the Supreme Court Act 1981.

In fact what has happened on two occasions in the past is that pressure has been put on unsatisfactory High Court judges to resign. The first of these was in 1959 when the Lord Chancellor asked Mr Justice Hallett to resign; the second in 1998 when Mr Justice Harman resigned after criticisms by the Court of Appeal.

13.3.2 Tenure of inferior judges

These do not have the same security of tenure of office as superior judges since the Lord Chancellor has the power to dismiss inferior judges for incapacity or misbehaviour. A criminal conviction for dishonesty would obviously be regarded as misbehaviour and would lead to the dismissal of the judge concerned. This has happened only once, in the case of Bruce Campbell, a Circuit judge, who was convicted of evading Customs duty on cigarettes and whisky. The Lord Chancellor has also indicated that drunken driving would probably be seen as misbehaviour, as would racial or sexual harassment.

So far as recorders are concerned, their appointment is for a period of five years. As a result the Lord Chancellor can refuse to re-appoint at the end of that period without having to give an explanation. This can be viewed as an unreasonable power and has led to allegations of political interference in the judiciary on the part of the Lord Chancellor.

13.3.3 Retirement

Since the Judicial Pensions and Retirement Act 1993 all judges now have to retire at the age of 70, though there are some situations in which authorisation can be given for a judge to continue beyond that age. Prior to this Act judges in the High Court and above could remain sitting as judges until they were 75. All inferior judges now also retire at 70.

13.4 Doctrine of the separation of powers

The theory of separation of powers was first put forward by Montesquieu, a French political theorist, in the eighteenth century.

The theory states that there are three primary functions of the state and that the only way to safeguard the liberty of citizens is by keeping these three functions separate. As the power of each is exercised by independent and separate bodies, each can keep a check on the others and thus limit the amount of power wielded by any one group. Ideally this theory requires that individuals should not be members of more than one 'arm of the state'.

Some countries, for example the United States of America, have a written constitution which embodies this theory. In the United Kingdom we have no such written constitution, but even so the three organs of State are roughly separated. However, there is some overlap, especially in the fact that the Lord Chancellor is involved in all three functions of the state.

The three arms of the State identified by Montesquieu are:

1. **The legislature.** This is the law-making arm of the State and in our system this is Parliament.
2. **The executive or the body administering the law.** Under the British political system this is the Government of the day which forms the Cabinet.
3. **The judiciary who apply the law.** In other words, the judges.

There is an overlap between the executive and the legislature, in that the ministers forming the Government also sit in Parliament and are active in the law-making process. With the exception of the Lord Chancellor, there is very little overlap between the judiciary and the other two arms of the state. This is important because it allows the judiciary to act as a check and ensure that the executive does not overstep its constitutional powers. This is in accordance with Montesquieu's theory. However, it is open to debate whether the judiciary is truly independent from the other organs of government.

13.5 Independence of the judiciary

As already stated, an independent judiciary is seen as important in protecting the liberty of the individual from abuse of power by the executive. Judges in the English system can be thought of as being independent in a number of ways.

13.5.1 Independence from the legislature

Judges are generally not involved in the law-making functions of Parliament. Full-time judges are not allowed to be members of the House of Commons, although the rule is not as strict for part-time judges so that recorders and assistant recorders can be Members of Parliament. However, judges can be members of the House of Lords in its legislative function, as the Law Lords are life peers and can take part in debates on new laws. In addition any judge who is also a peer may sit in the House of Lords.

There is a convention that the Law Lords will not take part in very political debates, but over recent years there have been instances where they have entered into controversial areas of law making. One area has been the Government's policies on sentencing, where Lord Taylor, in particular, was highly critical of the 1996 White Paper proposals to bring in minimum sentences.

As well as the fact that judges are increasingly willing to enter into areas that in the past would have been the sole domain of politicians, judges play a role in law-making through the doctrine of judicial precedent. In this way there is an overlap of roles, although in some instances the judges will refuse to change past precedent saying that it is for Parliament to make changes in the law. This was seen in *C v DPP* (1994) regarding the criminal responsibility for children (see section 10.3.2).

KEY FACTS

Judges	Court/s	Qualifications	Tenure
Lords of Appeal in Ordinary (Law Lords)	House of Lords	15-year Supreme Court qualification OR hold high judicial office for two years	'whilst of good behaviour' (Appellate Jurisdiction Act 1876 s 6)
Lords Justices of Appeal	Court of Appeal	10-year High Court qualification OR be a High Court judge	'whilst of good behaviour' (Supreme Court Act 1981 s 11(3))
High Court judges (puisne judges)	High Court Crown Court for serious cases	10-year High Court qualification OR be a Circuit judge for two years	'whilst of good behaviour' (Supreme Court Act 1981 s 11(3))
Circuit judges	Crown Court County Court	10-year Crown Court or County Court qualification OR be a recorder OR hold other judicial post (Stipendiary magistrate, District judge, tribunal chairman) for three years	Can be dismissed by Lord Chancellor for incapacity or misbehaviour (Courts Act 1971 s 17(4))
District judges	County Court Magistrates' Court	seven-year general qualification	Can be dismissed by the Lord Chancellor
Recorders	Crown Court Some may sit in County Court	10-year Crown Court or County Court qualification	Appointed for period of five years; Lord Chancellor can decide not to re-appoint

Figure 13.2 Key fact chart on judges

13.5.2 Independence from the executive

Superior judges cannot be dismissed by the Government and in this way they can truly be said to be independent of the Government. They can make decisions which may displease the Government, without the threat of dismissal. The extent to which judges are prepared to challenge or support the Government is considered in section 13.5.4 and also in the section on judicial review in Chapter 16. However the appointment of judges is not independent from the executive as the Lord Chancellor, who is a member of the Government, is involved in the appointment of judges at all levels and the Prime Minister is responsible for the nomination of the most senior judges.

Since 1998 the Lord Chancellor has also monitored complaints about judges. Further action has been taken by the Lord Chancellor in 23 cases. This has been either writing to the judge or arranging for the judge to be seen by officials. This could be viewed as pressure from the executive.

13.5.3 Freedom from pressure

There are several ways in which judges are protected from outside pressure when exercising their judicial functions.

1. They are given a certain degree of financial independence, as judicial salaries are paid out of the consolidated fund so that payment is made without the need for Parliament's authorisation. This does not completely protect them from Parliamentary interference with the terms on which they hold office. As already seen, changes can be made to retirement ages and qualifying periods for pensions.

2. Judges have immunity from being sued for actions taken or decisions made in the course of their judicial duties. This was confirmed in *Sirros* v *Moore* (1975) and is a key factor in ensuring judicial independence in decision-making.

3. As already noted, the security of tenure of the superior judges protects them from the threat of removal.

However, it is still possible for pressure to be placed on them by the Lord Chancellor. This happened in 1993 in the case of Mr Justice Wood, the High Court judge who chaired the Employment Appeals Tribunal. The Lord Chancellor was concerned that Mr Justice Wood was not using his powers to full effect under the Employment Appeal Tribunal Rules. After some correspondence on this point the Lord Chancellor wrote to Mr Justice Wood to: 'ask you again for your immediate assurance that Rule 3 is henceforth to be applied in full'. The letter went on to say 'if you do not feel that you can give me that assurance, I must ask you to consider your position.' This implied that the Lord Chancellor would ask him to resign if he did not conform to the Lord Chancellor's wishes, although the Lord Chancellor denied that he had meant this.

The controversy led to a debate in the House of Lords in which one of the Law Lords, Lord Ackner, pointed out that 'However unwitting the Lord Chancellor may have been in the expression which he used, this clearly was, in the circumstance, an unconstitutional way of applying pressure.'

David Pannick QC, writing in an article in *The Times*, says that this type of dispute is a 'reminder of the unique constitutional relationship between the Lord Chancellor and the judiciary'. Pannick feels that true independence for the judiciary requires that 'judges be given responsibility for administering their courts out of funds provided by Parliament'.

13.5.4 Independence from political bias

This is the area in which there is most dispute over how independent the judiciary are. Writers, such as Professor Griffith, point out that judges are too pro-establishment and conservative with a small 'c'.

This view is partly supported by the admission of Lord Justice Scrutton in the 1920s that it was difficult to be impartial, saying: 'I am not speaking of conscious partiality, but the habits you are trained in, the people with whom you mix, lead to your having a certain class of ideas of such a nature that when you deal with other ideas you do not give as sound and accurate judgments as you would wish.'

Pro-Government decisions

Griffith cites cases such as the 'GCHQ case' in showing that judges tend to support the establishment. This case, *Council of Civil Service Unions* v *Minister for the Civil Service* (1984), concerned the minister for the Conservative Government withdrawing the right to trade union membership from civil servants working at the intelligence headquarters in Cheltenham. The House of Lords upheld the minister's right, and the decision was seen as anti-trade union. In *Attorney-General* v *Guardian Newspapers Ltd* (1987) (the 'Spycatcher' case) the House of Lords granted an interlocutory injunction to the Government banning the sale of a book about the security services, on the grounds that it was in the national interest of security to do so. This injunction was granted even though the book had already been published in America and Australia.

Anti-Government decisions

There is, however, evidence that judges are not as pro-establishment as sometimes thought. Lord Taylor, when giving the Dimbleby Lecture in 1992, pointed out that this could be seen in the case of the Greenham Common women who had camped by an RAF base in protest against nuclear missiles. In *DPP* v *Hutchinson* (1990) some of the women were prosecuted under a bylaw for being on Ministry of Defence property unlawfully. The case went, all the way to the House of Lords, where the Law Lords ruled in the women's favour, holding that the Minister had exceeded his powers in framing the bylaw so as to prevent access to common land.

Judicial review

More recently there have been several challenges, by way of judicial review, to ministerial actions. In a sizeable number of cases the judges have ruled against the minister concerned. This has occurred in *R* v *Home Secretary, ex parte Fire Brigades Union* (1995) in which it was held that the changes to the Criminal Injuries Compensation Scheme made by the Home Secretary were unlawful. Also in *R* v *Secretary of State for Foreign Affairs, ex parte World Development Movement* (1995) the courts decided that the Foreign Secretary, Douglas Hurd, had acted unlawfully over the development of the Pergau Dam. In *R* v *Lord Chancellor, ex parte Witham* (1997) the judges ruled that the

Lord Chancellor had gone beyond his powers when he changed the rules on payment of court fees.

The development of European Union law has also led to judges being more progressive in their application of the law. An example of this was in *R* v *Secretary of State, ex parte Equal Opportunities Commission* (1994) in which the House of Lords held that the British employment law which gave a lower level of protection to part-time workers than to full-time workers discriminated against women, and was incompatible with Article 141 of the Treaty of Rome. This decision prompted the Government to change the regulations for part-time workers and bring them into line with those for full-time workers. In cases such as this the judiciary has played an important role in protecting individual rights.

Human rights

With the Human Rights Act 1998 incorporating the European Convention on Human Rights, judges can declare that an Act is incompatible with the Convention. This puts pressure on the Government to change the law. The first case in which this happened was *H* v *Mental Health Review Tribunal* (2001).

The courts also have a duty to interpret laws in a way which is compatible with the Convention. In two cases this has led judges to interpret an Act so that the effect is not what the Government intended. This happened in *R* v *Offen* (2001) in which the courts have widened the circumstances when the mandatory life sentence for a second serious offence need not be imposed. The other case is *R* v *A* (2001) where the House of Lords ruled that a defendant should have been allowed to cross-examine a victim in a rape case about her past sexual history, despite the restrictions placed on this by the Youth Justice and Criminal Evidence Act 1999.

So, while it is true that judges are still predominantly white, male, middle-class and elderly, it is possible to argue that they are no longer so out of touch with the 'real world', and that they are increasingly prepared to challenge the establishment.

13.5.5 The Pinochet case

In December 1998, the judges in the House of Lords heard an appeal by the former head of state of Chile, Ugarte Pinochet, and decided that he did not have immunity from arrest and extradition. The allegations against Pinochet were about torture and deaths which occurred in Chile during the period he was head of state. Amnesty, the human rights movement, had been granted permission to intervene in the appeal and had made written submissions to the House of Lords. One of the judges who heard the case, Lord Hoffmann, was an unpaid director of Amnesty International Charitable Trust.

When the lawyers acting for Pinochet discovered that Lord Hoffmann had this connection, they asked the House of Lords to set aside the decision and have the case re-heard by a completely independent panel of judges. The Law Lords decided that the original decision could not be allowed to stand. Judges had to be seen to be completely unbiased. The fact that Lord Hoffmann was connected with Amnesty meant that he could be said to have an interest in the outcome of the case.

This decision upheld the idea that judges must be impartial.

Human rights

The test for bias has been influenced by the European Convention on Human Rights. In the case of *Re Medicaments (no 2), Director General of Fair Trading v Proprietary Association of Great Britain* (2001) the Court of Appeal followed decisions of the European Court of Human Rights. It said that

the test was an objective one of whether the circumstances were such as to lead a fair-minded and informed observer to conclude that there was a real possibility of bias.

13.6 The Lord Chancellor

The Lord Chancellor's position is in direct contradiction to the doctrine of the separation of powers. The position is a political appointment in that he is appointed (and can be dismissed) by the Prime Minister. He also holds office only while Government of the day is in power: if there is a change of Government there will be a new Lord Chancellor. Looking more closely, it can be seen that he plays a role in all three arms of the state as he is:

- The Speaker of the House of Lords when it is sitting in its legislative capacity, and takes part in debates there; he can also introduce new Bills for consideration
- A member of the Cabinet
- One of the judges in the House of Lords, head of the Chancery division in the High Court and entitled to act as judge in both courts; he is also one of the judges of the Judicial Committee of the Privy Council

His role also runs contrary to the doctrine, in regard to the powers that he has in respect of the appointment of the judiciary.

Many past Lord Chancellors have been highly involved in politics before their appointment as Lord Chancellor. In some cases the appointment could be seen as a reward for their political support. Lord Hailsham, who was Lord Chancellor from 1979 to 1987, had sat as a member of the House of Commons for many years. He had even been regarded as a possible candidate for the position of Prime Minister in 1964. The last Lord Chancellor, Lord Mackay, was rare in that he was not a politician, but had come from the Scottish Bar and had been Lord Advocate in

KEY FACTS

Role in legislature	Role in executive	Role in the judiciary
Speaker in the House of Lords	Member of the Cabinet	Head of the judiciary Sits as judge in House of Lords Head of Chancery Division
Takes part in debates on new laws; introduces new Bills on matters connected with justice into the House of Lords	Part of the Government of the day; is appointed to this office by the Prime Minister	Plays major role in appointment of judges; also has power to dismiss inferior judges

Figure 13.3 *Key fact chart on the Lord Chancellor*

Scotland. Most Lord Chancellors in recent times have also been barristers at the English Bar, so again the appointment of Lord Mackay broke with tradition.

The present Lord Chancellor (in 2002) is Lord Irvine. There have been criticisms that, as he is a close friend of the Prime Minister, Tony Blair, he is not sufficiently independent.

Activity

Read the following extract and answer the questions below.

Appointments made recently have sparked fresh debate over the Lord Chancellor, Lord Irvine's record in appointing to silk and the judiciary – and over the appointments system as a whole. The gibe of cronyism has been a current theme of this Government. Top-heavy with lawyers, the Government has unrivalled links with the legal profession.

There was the promotion to the Court of Appeal of Sir David Keene (Tony Blair stays in his chateau) and Sir Andrew Longmore (married to the sister of Lord Irvine's wife). But why, asked one Tory lawyer, should such people not be debarred? But Lord Irvine would argue that just because someone comes from his chambers, or is known to him, should they not be promoted?

The recent rumpus has fuelled the case for a full-blown judicial appointments commission. Whether it would do a better job is not known. It would still need to be accountable to a government minister; but that minister would not have such a personal hand in appointments.

Adapted from an article by Frances Gibbs in *The Times*, 27 February 2001

QUESTIONS

❶ Briefly explain the Lord Chancellor's role in the appointment of judges.
❷ In the article, why has the Lord Chancellor been criticised over judicial appointments?
❸ Are there any advantages in the Lord Chancellor having close links with the legal profession?
❹ Explain the reasons for having an independent judicial appointment commission.

As well as his functions listed above, the Lord Chancellor has important administrative functions, as by virtue of the Courts Act 1971 he has the responsibility of appointing court staff and providing, equipping and managing the buildings used for court business. In addition the Lord Chancellor oversees the Community Legal Service. He is also responsible for overseeing the work of the Law Commission and the Council on Tribunals, and other bodies including the Official Solicitor's Department, the Land Registry and the Public Trustee Office. He is head of the Lord Chancellor's Department which is part of the civil service and has a staff of over 10,000.

One of the more controversial areas in recent years has been the extent of the Lord Chancellor's power over Government funding of cases. The Access to Justice Act 1999 gives the Lord Chancellor very wide powers in this area.

An earlier Lord Chancellor, Lord Elwyn-Jones, admitted that the Lord Chancellor's office infringed the doctrine of the separation of powers, but described his position as being the 'universal joint in the machinery' allowing the maintenance of the separation of powers to flourish.

13.7 Law Officers

There is also a Law Officers' department within the Government for advising on legal matters that affect the Government. There are two Law Officers: the Attorney-General and the Solicitor-General. Both are members of the Government of the day and are appointed by the Prime Minister. Both will usually be members of the House of Commons. The Attorney-General appoints the Director of Public Prosecutions, who heads the Crown Prosecution Service.

13.7.1 The Attorney-General

The Attorney-General is the Government's chief legal adviser. He is not a member of the main Cabinet, though he may sit on the Legislation and Home Affairs Committees of the Cabinet. He advises the Government on legislative proposals and on criminal proceedings which have a political or public element. He is also responsible for major litigation which involves the Government.

The Attorney-General is always appointed from those members of Parliament who are barristers and he can represent the Government in court proceedings. He is head of the English Bar although while he holds the post of Attorney-General he cannot practise privately as a barrister. He will sometimes act as the prosecuting barrister in high-profile criminal cases, for example in cases of treason. He can also represent the Government or Government departments in civil cases. This occurred in the case of *Pepper v Hart* (1993) (see section 3.3.9) in which the Attorney-General appeared for the Inspector of Taxes at the hearing in the House of Lords.

His consent is required before a prosecution can be started in certain cases such as corruption, possessing explosive substances and hijacking. He can grant immunity from prosecution and he can stop proceedings for any indictable offence by entering a *nolle prosequi* (do not prosecute). This power was used in 1982 when Mary Whitehouse prosecuted the director of the play, *Romans in Britain*, under the Sexual Offences Act 1956 because the play contained a simulated homosexual rape. The Attorney-General prevented the prosecution from continuing. He can also instruct the Director of Public Prosecutions to take over any private prosecution.

The Attorney-General also has the right to refer criminal cases to the Court of Appeal

(Criminal Division) for a point of law to be considered, following an acquittal in the Crown Court, and he can appeal against a sentence which is considered to be too lenient.

13.7.2 The Solicitor-General

The Solicitor-General acts as deputy to the Attorney-General and carries out such functions as are delegated by the Attorney-General. In 2001 Harriet Harman was the first woman to be appointed as Solicitor-General.

13.7.3 The Director of Public Prosecutions (DPP)

The office of DPP was established as long ago as 1879, but the duties have changed with the establishment of the Crown Prosecution Service. The DPP's duties are set out in the Prosecution of Offences Act 1985, which created the Crown Prosecution Service. The DPP must be a barrister or solicitor of not less than 10 years' standing. The appointment is made by the Attorney-General to whom the DPP is accountable – the DPP has to make a yearly report to him or her which is then put before Parliament.

The main function of the DPP is to head the Crown Prosecution Service. The other functions are set out in section three of the Prosecution of Offences Act 1985. These are:

- To take over the conduct of all criminal proceedings instituted by the police
- To institute and have the conduct of criminal proceedings where the importance or difficulty of the proceedings makes this appropriate
- To take over the conduct of binding over proceedings brought by the police
- To give advice to police forces on all matters relating to criminal offences

- To appear for the prosecution in certain appeals

The position of DPP has become much more high profile with the publicity that has been generated by the problems of the Crown Prosecution Service. The Director has had to defend the large number of cases which are discontinued by the Service and has issued the Code of Crown Prosecutors (see Chapter 9).

13.8 Should there be a Ministry of Justice?

Under the present system the administration of justice is split between different Government departments: the Lord Chancellor's Department, the Home Office and the Law Officers. However, the Lord Chancellor's Department has the major share of responsibility covering, as we have seen, the appointment of judges, administration of the courts, civil and criminal procedure and legal aid. The Home Office, under the Home Secretary, is responsible for reform of the criminal law and procedure, sentencing policy, prisons and the probation service. The Home Office is also responsible for the police and the maintenance of law and order. Until 1992 the Magistrates' Courts also came under the jurisdiction of the Home Office, but they have now been transferred to the Lord Chancellor's Department. The Home Office is also responsible for matters connected with immigration and civil rights.

In addition to the above, the Attorney-General has responsibility for acting as legal adviser to the Government as well as being responsible for prosecutions, with the Director of Public Prosecutions being answerable to him or her. The Treasury Solicitor is responsible for Government litigation and reports to the Chancellor of the Exchequer, while the Parliamentary counsel, who draft Bills for proposed new statutory law put forward by the Government, are technically attached to the Prime Minister's office. Finally, other ministers have responsibility for putting forward law reforms for matters connected to their own departments.

13.8.1 Criticisms of the present system

This muddled and overlapping system is subject to a number of criticisms, in particular the rather arbitrary and illogical division of work between the Lord Chancellor's Department and the Home Office. Is there really a need for two departments? Could one comprehensive Ministry of Justice carry out all the functions more efficiently?

A major problem is that the Home Office has roles which are potentially in conflict with each other. The responsibility for law and order (in particular, overseeing the police forces and being in charge of immigration policies) is not always compatible with the enforcement of civil rights of the individual. During the last few years there have been an increasing number of successful applications for judicial review of the Home Secretary's decisions, both in immigration cases and in other areas. In such cases the courts ruled that the Home Secretary had acted unlawfully in making decisions to deport certain immigrants. This highlights the difficulties facing the Home Office in trying to balance its conflicting roles.

Another problem is the Lord Chancellor's position in Parliament. He is not a member of the House of Commons and is not, therefore, available for questioning in the House of Commons. This calls into question the principle of ministerial accountability, under which ministers can be questioned by members of Parliament in the House of Commons about their department's work. This problem was partially solved by the creation of a new appointment in 1992 of parliamentary secretary in the Lord Chancellor's Department. The holder of this position is a Government member of the House of Commons, and has a regular session in which he may be questioned about the workings of the Lord Chancellor's Department. It could be said that the Lord Chancellor himself can be made accountable in the House of Lords, but, even here, the fact that the Lord Chancellor holds the position of Speaker makes full accountability difficult.

Another point is that the Lord Chancellor is a member of the Cabinet, but the Attorney-General, who is the main law officer in the House of Commons, is not.

This division of duties means that there is no particular department with responsibility for law reform. This has led to gaps in the law which have gone unchanged and has proved a particular problem for 'pure' law areas such as the proposed draft criminal code (see Chapter 5). A major problem is that low priority is given to the quality of the statute book, so that there are obsolete laws, contradictory laws and, in some cases, very badly drafted laws in force, which need to be changed. Some attention has been paid to these problems in that since 1993, reforms proposed by the Law Commission have been given more Parliamentary time. The Lord Chancellor's Department is also intending to review the whole statute book to establish exactly which laws are in force. However, these initiatives do not fully solve the problem.

13.8.2 Proposals for a Ministry of Justice

There have been suggestions that the whole system should be rationalised and as long ago as 1918 the Haldane Committee recommended the creation of a Ministry of Justice. It was felt that this would lead to greater political accountability, increased efficiency and more momentum for reform. More recently, some political parties have indicated that they would reform the present system.

However, there are points to be considered: should a new department retain the specialist legal knowledge of the Lord Chancellor and other law officers who are all qualified lawyers? In other government departments, the Minister is a politician and does not necessarily have any personal expertise in the subject matter of the department. For example the Minister of Health will have no medical qualifications, but relies on experts in the department for advice. Is it important that a Minister of Justice should have legal qualifications?

The other main issue is: would it be feasible for the same minister to be responsible for all aspects of justice and law? If the Home Office has a conflict of interests at present, then it would seem that one department would increase this problem – the way to resolve it would be to have two government departments, and divide the work between them in a more rational way than is at present done.

The other main criticism is that a ministry of justice could erode the independence of the judiciary, by leading to a continental system in which judges are civil servants. This could be avoided if other reforms, especially in the method of appointing judges, were made at the same time (for example an independent Judicial Appointments Commission would remove this aspect from the political arena).

Chapter 14

LAY PEOPLE IN THE LEGAL SYSTEM

There is a tradition of using lay people, i.e. people who are not legally qualified, in the decision-making process in our courts. Today this applies particularly to the Magistrates' Courts and the Crown Court. However, in the past lay people were also frequently used to decide civil cases in the High Court and the County Court, and there are still some cases in which a jury can be used in the civil courts. There are also lay people with expertise in a particular field who sit as part of a panel as lay assessors. This occurs in the Patents Court and the Admiralty Court in the High Court as well as in tribunals (especially employment tribunals and social security appeals tribunals).

14.1 Lay magistrates

There are about 29,000 lay magistrates sitting as part-time judges in the Magistrates' Courts; another name for lay magistrates is Justices of the Peace. They sit to hear cases as a bench of two or three magistrates. The size of panel has been limited to a maximum of three, whereas before 1996 there could be up to seven magistrates sitting together to hear a case. A single lay magistrate sitting on his or her own has very limited powers. They can, however, issue search warrants and warrants for arrest and conduct Early Administrative Hearings.

There are also District judges (Magistrates' Courts) who work in Magistrates' Courts. These are not lay people but are qualified lawyers who can sit on their own to hear any of the cases that come before the court. Under section 16(3) of the Justices of the Peace Act 1979 they have the same powers as a bench of lay magistrates. Since the duties of these District judges are the same as those of lay magistrates and since the history of the two is linked, details of District judges (formerly known as stipendiary magistrates) are also included in this chapter.

14.1.1 History of the magistracy

The office of Justice of the Peace is very old, dating back to the twelfth century at least – in 1195 Richard I appointed 'keepers of the peace'. By the mid-thirteenth century the judicial side of their position had developed and by 1361 the title Justice of the Peace was being used. Over the years they were also given many administrative duties, for example, being responsible for the poor law, highways and bridges, and weights and measures. In the nineteenth century elected local authorities took over most of these duties, though some remnants remain, especially in the licensing powers of the Magistrates' Courts.

The poor quality of the local Justices of the Peace in London and the absence of an adequate police force became a matter of concern towards the end of the eighteenth century. This led to seven public offices with paid magistrates being set up in 1792 and until 1839 they were in charge of the police as well as hearing cases in court. Outside London the first appointment of a paid magistrate was in Manchester in 1813. In 1835 the Municipal Corporations Act gave a general power for boroughs to request the appointment of a paid magistrate. At the beginning a paid magistrate did not have to have any particular qualifications, but from 1839 they could only be appointed from barristers. Solicitors did not become eligible to be appointed until 1949.

14.1.2 Qualifications

Lay magistrates

As already stated, lay magistrates do not have to have any qualifications in law. There are, however, some requirements as to their character, in that they must be suitable in character, integrity and understanding for the work they have to perform. In 1998, the Lord Chancellor set out six key qualities which candidates should have. These are:

- Good character
- Understanding and communication
- Social awareness
- Maturity and sound temperament
- Sound judgment
- Commitment and reliability.

They must have certain 'judicial' qualities – it is particularly important that they are able to assimilate factual information and make a reasoned decision upon it. They must also be able to take account of the reasoning of others and work as a team.

Apart from this, there are formal requirements as to age and residence: lay magistrates must be aged between 21 and 65 on appointment. It is unlikely that a person under 27 will be considered as it is felt they will not have enough experience.

Before 1906 there was a property qualification which meant that magistrates had to be home owners or tenants of property above a certain value. Also before 1919 the bench was an all-male affair with women becoming eligible for appointment only in that year.

Lay magistrates must live within the commission area of the court or within 15

miles of the boundary of that area. Since the commission area is likely to cover an entire county, it is preferred if magistrates live or work in the area covered by the actual court they sit in. They have to give a commitment that they will sit in court a minimum of 26 times per year and that they will to do the necessary training.

Some people are not eligible to be appointed. These include people with serious criminal convictions, though a conviction for a minor motoring offence will not automatically disqualify a candidate. Others who are disqualified include undischarged bankrupts, members of the forces and those whose work is incompatible with sitting as a magistrate, such as police officers and traffic wardens. Relatives of those working in the local criminal justice system are not likely to be appointed as it would not appear 'just' if, for example, the wife of a local police officer were to sit to decide cases. In addition people whose hearing is impaired, or who by reason of infirmity cannot carry out all the duties of a justice of the peace cannot be appointed. Close relatives will not be appointed to the same bench.

Activity

1. Put the list of six key qualities into order with the one that you think is most important first and the least important last.
2. Compare your list with those of two other people.
3. Explain what other qualities you think magistrates need.

District judges (Magistrates' Courts)

These were previously known as stipendiary magistrates. They must have a seven-year general qualification, that is a right of audience as an advocate, and are usually chosen from practising barristers or solicitors, or from others with relevant experience such as court clerks. They are only appointed to courts in London or other big cities such as Birmingham, Liverpool and Manchester. Before becoming a District judge they will usually be an acting judge sitting part-time for two years to gain experience of sitting judicially, and to establish their suitability for full-time appointment.

14.1.3 Appointment

Lay magistrates

About 1,500 new lay magistrates are appointed each year, to one commission area only. Outside London, a commission area means a county (metropolitan or non-metropolitan) and in London there are six commission areas, though there are plans to reduce the number of commission areas in the country and streamline the administration. The appointments are made by the Lord Chancellor, or in Lancashire by the Chancellor for the Duchy of Lancaster, on behalf of the Queen. In order to decide who to appoint the Lord Chancellor relies on recommendations made to him by the local advisory committees and this method of appointment is much criticised.

Local Advisory Committees

The membership of the committees used to be secret but since 1993 all names must be published. The members tend to be current or ex-Justices of the Peace and often the Lord Lieutenant of the county is the chairman of the committee. About half the members have to retire in rotation every three years. The committees should have a maximum of 12 members and that these should include a mixture of magistrates and non-magistrates.

Names of potential magistrates can be put forward by anyone. It is even possible for an interested person to ask that they

themselves should be considered. Normally names are put forward by groups such as the local political parties, trade unions and chambers of commerce. To try and encourage as wide a range of potential candidates as possible committees have advertised for individuals to put themselves forward with advertisements being placed in local papers, or newspapers aimed at particular ethnic groups, and even on buses! For example, in Leeds, radio adverts have been used and people encouraged to come to open evenings at their local Magistrates' Court in order to get as wide a spectrum of potential candidates as possible.

The intention is to create a panel that is representative of all aspects of society. In 1966 the then Lord Chancellor, Lord Gardiner, issued a directive to advisory committees telling them to bear in mind people's political allegiances in order to get a balance. At the time this caused a stir, but the reason behind it was to try to get better balanced panels of magistrates. That directive said:

> 'The Lord Chancellor cannot disregard political affiliations in making appointments, not because the politics of an individual are a qualification or a disqualification for appointment, but because it is important that justices should be drawn from all sections of the community and should represent all shades of opinion.
>
> This object would not be attained if appointments were made in too large a degree from supporters of any one political party. It is the aim of the Lord Chancellor to preserve a proper balance by the appointment of suitable parties from the main political parties, and, if they can be found, from persons who are independent of any political party.
>
> For these reasons the Lord Chancellor wishes advisory committees to have regard for the political affiliations of the persons whom they recommend for appointment.'

This is still the case today – Lord Irvine, the Lord Chancellor, wants to find an alternative way of getting a good social balance on Magistrates' panels. However, he announced in 1999 that he had reluctantly concluded that, for the moment, political balance remained the most practicable method.

A balance of occupations is also aimed at. The Lord Chancellor has set down 11 broad categories of occupations, and advisory committees are recommended that they should not have more than 15 per cent of the bench coming from any one category.

The advisory committees will interview candidates and then submit names of those they think are suitable to the Lord Chancellor. He will then appoint new magistrates from this list. Once appointed, magistrates may continue to sit until the age of 70.

14.1.4 Composition of the bench today

The traditional image of lay justices is that they are 'middle-class, middle-aged and middle-minded'. This image is to a certain extent true. Most magistrates are in the 45 to 65 age bracket. Magistrates under the age of 40 are still rare. The majority are supporters of the Conservative party; this is so even in areas where there is a high Labour vote. For example, figures issued by the Lord Chancellor's Department in 1992 showed that in St Helens, Lancashire only 26 per cent of the magistrates supported Labour even though the Labour party had taken 60 per cent of the votes in the general election. Ethnic minorities are under-represented with only about 2 per cent of the bench coming from ethnic minority backgrounds – this is so despite an effort to persuade more people to put themselves forward for appointment and an increase in the numbers that are appointed each year.

Activity

Read the following article and answer the questions below.

Calling all those who would be magistrates

The public perceives a JP as a middle-aged, middle-class person who 'knows the right people'. Up to a point, this is true; it may well be the 'right people' who suggest you apply to be a JP. But after that, you're on your own. Your application and references will be thoroughly vetted, and you will undergo a searching interview. However, if you are appointed, you will probably be nearer 40 than 30 – possibly older.

Why don't we see younger JPs? 'Lack of maturity/experience' is usually given as the reason for not appointing many applicants in the 25 to 30 age group, but this begs the question of why comparatively few JPs are in their thirties or forties.

Since most defendants are under 40, why aren't there more JPs of a similar age? It is unlikely that the selection procedure is at fault – age is not a qualification *per se*. A more probable reason is that people from this age group submit fewer applications, which may well be through lack of awareness. For example, did you know that you do not have to be nominated by someone else – you can nominate yourself? Why don't we see more 'recruitment' advertising that emphasises this point? Perhaps the Lord Chancellor's Department thinks it would not be able to cope.

More probably, it is outside factors that inhibit younger applicants. JPs have to sit at least 26 times a year, plus 'training days'. How many people can take this kind of time off work? Will their employer pay them? Will they be passed over for promotion because they are 'hardly ever there'? Employers do not take kindly to someone who wants to take off more than two days a month. Civic responsibility does not contribute to company profits. Nevertheless, employers should take the wider view and encourage service as a JP. Spin-off from this policy would be employees who have received training in analysing situations in a structured manner – a rarity in many firms.

If we grant that there is a preponderance of 40 to 60-year-olds on the bench, it is not surprising that many an 18-year-old driver considers the bench that fined him £100 for speeding were a bunch of old fogeys and that he has not had a hearing by his peers.

If you think that *he* has a point, how do you think a young *black* person feels? Only about 6 per cent of newly appointed magistrates come from ethnic minorities, creating an enormous imbalance from the point of view of race.

In practice, the standard complement of three JPs in court ensures that an extremist view held by one member cannot decide the verdict. And, if such views *were* expressed by a JP, he or she could well be asked to resign. The lay magistracy is certainly not a breeding ground for any kind of racial bias.

But, as the old adage that is repeated *ad nauseam* has it, 'Justice must be seen to be done'. And many a convicted defendant from an ethnic minority may feel that he or she did not have a fair hearing purely and simply because all the JPs were white. It won't be true but that doesn't stop him or her from thinking it.

There is no easy answer as to why ethnic minorities are under-represented. It may be that many are in blue-collar jobs, and therefore cannot take the time off work. Perhaps they feel they will be out of place in an institution that is dominated by white people? Or do they fear rejection by their own people?

Nobody is suggesting that positive discrimination be practised in order to boost the number of JPs from ethnic minorities. But with constant criticism of the fact that there is a disproportionate number of such people in prison, surely it would be a positive step to encourage applications actively from ethnic minorities?

Taken from an article by Derek Edmunds in *The Times*, 21 February 1995

QUESTIONS

❶ What reasons does the article put forward for the lack of young JPs?
❷ Why is it suggested that there should be more young JPs?
❸ Why does the article suggest that more magistrates from ethnic minorities should be appointed?
❹ Do you think that it is necessary for the lay bench to be a wide cross-section of society? Give reasons for your answer.

The Home Affairs Committee of the House of Commons reported in 1996 that a balance had not yet been achieved in the magistracy.

The one area in which there is now near parity is in the number of male and female lay justices. There has been a steady increase of the number of women over the last few years so that from making up 37 per-cent of the magistracy in 1978, women now account for 49 per cent of lay magistrates.

Lord Irvine, the Lord Chancellor, has encouraged disabled people to apply to become magistrates. In 1998 the first blind lay magistrates were appointed.

14.1.5 Magistrates' duties

They have a very wide workload which is mainly connected to criminal cases, although they also deal with some civil matters, especially family cases. They try 97 per cent of all criminal cases and deal with preliminary hearings in the remaining 3 per cent of criminal cases. This will involve Early Administrative Hearings, remand hearings, bail applications and committal proceedings. They also deal with civil matters which include the enforcing of debts owed to the utilities (gas, electric and water), non-payment of the council tax and non payment of television licenses. In addition they have powers to grant licences for the sale of alcohol and licences for betting and gaming establishments.

Specially nominated and trained justices form the Youth Court panel to hear criminal charges against young offenders aged 10 to 17-years-old. These magistrates must be under 65 and a panel must usually include at least one man and one woman. There is also a special panel for the Family Court to hear family cases including orders for protection against violence, affiliation cases, adoption orders and proceedings under the Children Act 1989.

Lay magistrates also sit at the Crown Court to hear appeals from the Magistrates' Court. In these cases the lay justices form a panel with a qualified judge.

14.1.6 Training of lay magistrates

The training of lay magistrates is supervised by the Magistrates' Committee of the Judicial Studies Board. This Committee has drawn up a syllabus of the topics which lay magistrates should cover in their training. However, because of the large numbers of lay magistrates, the actual training is carried out in local areas, sometimes through the clerk of the court, sometimes through weekend courses organised by universities with magistrates from the region attending.

Training

In 1998 the Lay Magistrates New Training Initiative started. Under this scheme newly-appointed magistrates have to achieve four basic competencies. These are:

- an applied understanding of the framework within which magistrates operate;
- an ability to follow basic law and procedure;
- an ability to think and act judicially;
- an ability to work as an effective member of a team.

Mentors

Each new magistrate keeps a Personal Development Log of their progress and has a mentor (an experience magistrate) to assist them. The first competence (understanding the framework within which magistrates operate) is usually covered before the new magistrate starts sitting in court. This is done through observing cases in court and by attending training sessions.

Appraisal

During the first two years of the new magistrate sitting in court, between eight and eleven of the sessions will be mentored. In the same period the magistrate is also expected to attend about seven training sessions. After two years, or whenever it is felt that the magistrate is ready, there will be an appraisal of the magistrate to check if they have acquired the competencies.

Any magistrate who cannot show that they have achieved the competencies will be given extra training. If they still cannot achieve the competencies, then the matter is referred to the local Advisory Committee, who may recommend to the Lord Chancellor that the magistrate is removed from sitting.

This new scheme involves practical training 'on the job'. It also answers the criticisms of the old system where there was no check made on whether the magistrate had actually benefited from the training session they attended.

Those magistrates who chair the bench are also appraised for this role, so that the quality of the chairing in court should also improve.

14.1.7 Retirement and removal

The retirement age is 70, but when magistrates become 70 they do not officially retire – instead their names are placed on the Supplemental List. This means that they can no longer sit in the Magistrates' Court. However, they can continue to carry out some administrative functions mainly connected with signing documents. Lay magistrates who move from the commission area to which they were appointed cannot continue as magistrates in that area. If they wish to continue as magistrates their names will be placed on the Supplemental List until there is a vacancy in their new area. Lay magistrates may, of course, resign from office at any time and many will resign before reaching 70.

The Lord Chancellor can also remove a magistrate for good cause, and usually about 10 a year are removed. The main reason for removal is a criminal conviction but in the past, magistrates have been dismissed for other reasons such as transvestite behaviour or taking part in a CND march. Removal from the bench for such reasons has been criticised.

14.1.8 The magistrates' clerk

Every bench is assisted by a clerk. The senior clerk in each court has to be qualified as a

barrister or solicitor for at least five years. The clerk's duty is to guide the magistrates on questions of law, practice and procedure. This is set out in section 28(3) of the Justices of the Peace Act 1979 which says:

> 'It is hereby declared that the functions of a justices' clerk include the giving to the justices . . . of advice about law, practice or procedure on questions arising in connection with the discharge of their functions.'

The clerk is not meant to assist in the decision-making and should not normally retire with the magistrates when they go to make their decision. In *R v Eccles Justices, ex parte Farrelly* (1992) the Queen's Bench Divisional Court quashed convictions because the clerk had apparently participated in the decision-making process.

Clerks deal with routine administrative matters and in May 1993 were given increased powers so that they can now issue warrants for arrest, extend police bail, adjourn criminal proceedings. The Crime and Disorder Act 1998 also gives clerks the powers to deal with Early Administrative Hearings.

14.1.9 Advantages and disadvantages of lay magistrates

Providing a cross-section of society

The system involves members of the community and provides a wider cross-section on the bench than would be possible with the use of professional judges. This is particularly true of women, with 49 per cent of magistrates being women against 7 per cent of professional judges. Also, even though there is a shortage of ethnic minority magistrates, there is still considerably more involvement of ethnic minorities than in the

KEY FACTS

Qualifications	Live within 15 miles of commission area
	Need common sense, integrity
	Disqualified for serious criminal record, bankruptcy or work that is incompatible
Appointment	By Lord Chancellor on the recommendation of local advisory committees
Training	Four basic competencies:
	Personal Development Log of progress
	Mentors and mentored sessions
	Attend about seven training sessions
	Appraisal
Composition of bench	29,000 lay magistrates, 51 per cent men 49 per cent women
	Over-representation of Conservative supporters
	Under-representation of young working class and ethnic minorities
Work	Summary trials
	Committal proceedings
	Ancillary matters e.g. issuing warrants, bail applications
	Youth court
	Family court

Figure 14.1 Key fact chart on lay magistrates

main judiciary. However, as lay magistrates tend to be 'middle-class, middle-aged and middle-minded' they are not a true cross-section of the local community, and will have little in common with the young working-class defendants who make up the majority of defendants.

Local knowledge

Since lay magistrates have to live within 15 miles of the area covered by the commission it is intended that they should have local knowledge of particular problems in the area. However, as most magistrates come from the professional and managerial classes, it is unlikely that they live in, or have any real knowledge of, the problems in the poorer areas. Their main value is that they

will have more awareness of local events, local patterns of crime and local opinions than a professional judge from another area.

Cost

The use of unpaid lay magistrates is cheap. The cost of replacing them with paid stipendiary magistrates has been estimated at £100 million a year (there would also be the problem of recruiting sufficient qualified lawyers). The cost of a trial in the Magistrates' Court is also much cheaper than in the Crown Court – the Home Office Research and Planning Unit has estimated the average cost of a contested trial in the Magistrates' Court at £1,500 and a guilty plea at £500. The comparative figures for the Crown Court are £13,500 and £2,500.

Part of this difference is due to the fact that cases in the Crown Court are more complex and therefore likely to take longer, but even so, it is clear that the cost both to the Government and to defendants who pay for their own lawyer is much higher.

Training

Improved training means that lay magistrates are not complete 'amateurs'. The majority of decisions require common sense rather than professional training. However, there are the criticisms that the training is variable in quality and inadequate for the workload. This poor training may be the cause of marked variations in sentencing and granting of bail between different benches.

Inconsistency in sentencing

Several studies in recent years have revealed worrying differences in the number of defendants sent to prison.

In 1995 Home Office figures revealed that there were major differences in sentencing practice for the same type of offence. For example, while 70 per cent of those driving whilst disqualified were jailed in West Derbyshire, nobody went to prison for such an offence in Cirencester, Gloucester or Beverley in Humberside. Other crimes were also treated very differently by different benches. Common assault (which it is true can vary in seriousness) showed a big variation, with some London Magistrates' Courts sending about one out of every three offenders to prison, while in Northampton no offenders were jailed and half of them received only a discharge. These variations were also pointed out in 1996 by the National Association of Probation Officers. Sentencing is claimed to be a 'geographical lottery' with, for example, a person convicted of theft being three times more likely to be jailed in Folkestone than in Brighton.

Even in Youth courts there are variations in sentencing. Home Office figures for 1999 show that courts in the north of England were generally tougher in sentencing than those in the south. But there were also variations between courts within the same area. For example, in Chester-le-Street in County Durham only 8.1 per cent of young offenders were given an immediate custodial sentence, while in the city of Durham 17.2 per cent were given an immediate custodial sentence.

However, it is also interesting to note that a study by Professor Diamond in 1991 found that lay magistrates were more lenient in the sentences they passed than stipendiary magistrates.

Advice of the clerk

The lack of legal knowledge of the lay justices should be offset by the fact that a legally qualified clerk is available to give advice. However, this will not prevent inconsistencies in sentencing since the clerk is not allowed to help the magistrates decide on a sentence. In some courts it is felt that the magistrates rely too heavily on their clerk.

Prosecution bias

It is often said that lay magistrates tend to be prosecution-biased, believing the police too readily. However, part of the training is aimed at eliminating this type of bias. It is also true that at courts outside London they will see the same Crown Prosecution Service prosecutor frequently and this could affect their judgment. There is a low acquittal rate in Magistrates' Courts with only 20 per cent of defendants being acquitted. By comparison 60 per cent of defendants pleading not guilty at the Crown Court were acquitted, though many of these acquittals were because the prosecution offered no evidence (see section 14.2.7).

Against this, there is the fact that comparatively few defendants appeal against the magistrates' decision, and many of the appeals are against sentence and not against the finding of guilt. In fact, the number of appeals to the Crown Court has fallen in recent years from 25,000 in 1995 to less than 15,000 in 2000. There are also very few appeals by way of case stated to the Queen's Bench Divisional Court. Of the appeals to the Crown Court, rather less than half of the appeals are usually successful. This is out of a total workload of over 1.5 million criminal cases dealt with in the Magistrates' Courts.

From this it can be argued that despite the amateur status of lay magistrates, and despite all the problems, they do a remarkably good job.

14.1.10 The Auld Review

This review, which was completed in 2001, was supportive of the use of lay magistrates in Magistrates' Courts. It recommended an extended role for them in a new 'middle' level court, the District Division. The review suggested that these courts should be staffed by a panel of one District judge sitting with two lay magistrates. They should deal with middle-range offences and have the power to sentence offenders to up to two years' imprisonment.

14.2 Juries

14.2.1 History of the jury system

Juries have been used in the legal system for over 1,000 years. There is evidence that they were used even before the Norman conquest. However, in 1215 when trial by ordeal was condemned by the Church and (in the same year) the Magna Carta included the recognition of a person's right to trial by 'the lawful judgment of his peers', juries became the usual method of trying criminal

cases. Originally they were used for providing local knowledge and information, and acted more as witnesses than decision-makers. By the middle of the fifteenth century juries had become independent assessors and assumed their modern role as deciders of fact.

The independence of the jury

The independence of the jury became even more firmly established following *Bushell's Case* (1670). In that case several jurors refused to convict Quaker activists of unlawful assembly. The trial judge would not accept the not guilty verdict, and ordered the jurors to resume their deliberations without food or drink. When the jurors persisted in their refusal to convict, the court fined them and committed them to prison until the fines were paid. On appeal, the Court of Common Pleas ordered the release of the jurors, holding that jurors could not be punished for their verdict. This established that the jury were the sole arbiters of fact and the judge could not challenge their decision. A more modern-day example demonstrating that judges must respect the independence of the jury is *R v McKenna* (1960). In that case the judge at the trial had threatened the jury that if they did not return a verdict within another 10 minutes they would be locked up all night. The jury then returned a verdict of guilty, but the defendant's conviction was quashed on appeal because of the judge's interference.

14.2.2 Modern-day use of the jury

Only a small percentage of cases is tried by jury today. However, juries are used in the following courts:

- Crown Court for criminal trials on indictment
- High Court, Queen's Bench Division (but only for certain types of cases)

KEY FACTS

Court	Type of case	Role	Number on jury
Crown Court	Serious criminal cases: e.g. murder, manslaughter, rape	Decide verdict Guilty or Not guilty	12
High Court	Defamation False imprisonment Malicious prosecution Any case alleging fraud	Decide liability If find for the claimant also decide amount of damages	12
County Court	Defamation False imprisonment Malicious prosecution Any case alleging fraud	Decide liability If find for the claimant also decide amount of damages	8
Coroners' Court	Deaths: • In prison • In policy custody • Through an industrial accident • Where health and safety of public is involved	Decide cause of death	7–11

Figure 14.2 Key fact chart on the use of juries

- County Court (for similar cases to the Queen's Bench Division)
- Coroners' Courts (in some cases)

Juries in criminal cases

The most important use of juries today is in the Crown Court where they decide whether the defendant is guilty or not guilty. Jury trials, however, account for less than 1 per cent of all criminal trials. This is because 97 per cent of cases are dealt with in the Magistrates' Court and of the cases that go to the Crown Court, about two out of every three defendants will plead guilty. Also some of the cases at the Crown Court, in which the defendant has entered a not guilty plea, will not go before a jury as the case will be discharged by judge without any trial. This occurs where the Crown Prosecution Service withdraw the charges, possibly because a witness refuses to give evidence. A jury in

the Crown Court has 12 members.

Juries in civil cases

Juries in civil cases are now only used in very limited circumstances, but where they are used they have a dual role. They decide whether the claimant has proved his case or not, then, if they decide that the claimant has won the case, the jury also go on to decide the amount of damages that the defendant should pay to the claimant.

Up to 1854 all common law actions were tried by jury, but from 1854 the parties could agree not to use a jury and gradually their use declined. Then in 1933 the Administration of Justice Act limited the right to use a jury, so that juries could not be used in disputes over breach of contract. The present rules for when juries may be used in civil cases are set out in section 69 of the Supreme Court Act 1981 for High Court cases, and section 66 of the County Courts Act 1984 for cases in that court. These Acts state that parties have the right to jury trial only in the following types of case:

- Defamation, i.e. cases of libel and slander (this is the most frequent use of juries)
- False imprisonment
- Malicious prosecution
- Fraud

All these cases involve character or reputation and it is for this reason that jury trial has been retained. Even for these cases a jury trial can be refused by the judge if the case involves complicated documents or accounts or scientific evidence and is therefore thought to be unsuitable for jury trial.

Use of juries in personal injury cases

In other civil cases in the Queen's Bench Division of the High Court the parties can apply to a judge for trial by jury, but it is very rare for such a request to be granted. This follows the case of *Ward* v *James* (1966) where the plaintiff was claiming for injuries caused in a road crash. In this case the Court of Appeal laid down guidelines for personal injury cases. These were:

- Personal injury cases should normally be tried by a judge sitting alone, because such cases involve assessing compensatory damages which have to have regard to the conventional scales of damages
- There have to be exceptional circumstances before the court will allow a jury to be used in such a case

The decision in *Ward* v *James* effectively stopped the use of juries for personal injury cases. The following cases show how the courts have proved very reluctant to let juries be used. In *Singh* v *London Underground* (1990) a request for a jury to

try a personal injury case arising from the King's Cross underground fire was refused. It was held that the case was unsuitable for jury trial because it involved such wide issues and technical points.

The case of *H* v *Ministry of Defence* (1991) further reinforced the rule in *Ward* v *James*; the defendant was a soldier who had received negligent medical treatment necessitating the amputation of part of his penis. He applied for jury trial, but it was held that jury trial for a personal injury claim would only be allowed in very exceptional circumstances and this case was not such a one. The court said that an example of when jury trial might be appropriate was where the injuries resulted from someone deliberately abusing their authority and there might well be a claim for exemplary damages.

Trial by jury in the County Court had become very rare, but since 1991 with the changes in the jurisdiction (defamation actions can be transferred for trial to the County Court) there are occasionally cases in which a jury is used. Where a jury is used in the High Court there will be 12 members; in the County Court a jury consists of eight.

Coroners' courts

In these courts a jury of between seven and 11 members may be used to enquire into deaths. A jury has to be used in four types of case; these are where there has been a death in:

- Prison
- An industrial accident
- Circumstances where the health and safety of the public is involved; for example the Herald of Free Enterprise disaster or the Marchioness tragedy on the Thames
- Police custody or resulting from an injury caused by a police officer in the execution of his duty

Rules about jury service

Some people cannot be jurors by law. These people are **not qualified** for jury service.

Other people may, by law, **have the right to be excused** from jury service.

Are you qualified for jury service?

> **Warning**
> You may have to pay a fine if you serve on a jury knowing that you are not qualified for jury service.

You are qualified for jury service if

> you will be at least 18 years old
> and under 70 years old
> on the day you start your jury service

and your name is on the Register of Electors for Parliamentary or Local Government elections

and you have lived in

> the United Kingdom
> **or** the Channel Islands
> **or** the Isle of Man
> for a period of at least 5 years
> since you were 13 years old.

But you are not qualified for jury service if

> you are someone listed in
> Box A
> **or** Box B
> **or** Box C (on page 3)
> **or** Box D (on page 3).

Do you have the right to be excused from jury service?

The law gives some people the right to be excused from jury service if they want to be excused.

You may ask the jury summoning officer to excuse you from jury service if

> you are more than 65 years old

or you have been on jury service during the past 2 years. **This does not apply if you were a juror at a coroner's court.**

or you have been a juror and the court excused you for a period that has not yet ended.

or you are someone listed in Box E (on page 3).

Please turn to page 4>

Box A Convictions

You are not qualified for jury service

■ if you have **ever been** sentenced
> to imprisonment for life
>
> **or** to imprisonment, or youth custody for 5 years or more
>
> **or** to be detained during Her Majesty's Pleasure or during the pleasure of the Secretary of State for Northern Ireland

■ if you have in the **last 10 years**
> served any part of a sentence of imprisonment, youth custody or detention
>
> **or** received a suspended sentence of imprisonment or an order for detention
>
> **or** been subject to a community service order

■ if you have in the **past 5 years** been placed on probation

■ if you are currently on bail in criminal proceedings

This list relates to sentences passed in the United Kingdom, the Channel Islands or the Isle of Man.

Box B Mental disorders

You are not qualified for jury service

■ if you suffer, or have suffered, from a mental disorder and, because of that condition,
> you are resident in a hospital or other similar institution
>
> **or** you regularly attend for treatment by a medical practitioner

■ if you are in guardianship under section 37 of the Mental Health Act 1983

■ if a judge has decided that you are not capable of managing and administering your property or affairs because of mental disorder.

If you are in any doubt whether this list applies to you, please talk to your doctor or ask someone to explain it to you.

Figure 14.3 Extract from a jury summons

Box C   The Judiciary and other people concerned with the Administration of Justice

The Judiciary

You are not qualified for jury service if you are, or ever have been

- a judge
- a stipendiary magistrate
- a justice of the peace
- the Chairman or President; the Vice-Chairman or Vice-President; the registrar or assistant registrar of any tribunal.

Others concerned with the Administration of Justice

You are not qualified for jury service if you have been, **at any time within the last 10 years**

- an authorised advocate, or authorised litigator
- a barrister, a barrister's clerk or assistant
- a solicitor or articled clerk
- a legal executive employed by solicitors
- a Public Notary
- a member of the staff of the Director of Public Prosecutions
- an officer employed under the Lord Chancellor and concerned with the day to day administration of the legal system
- an officer, or member of the staff, of any court whose work is concerned with the day to day administration of the court
- a coroner, deputy coroner or assistant coroner
- a justices' clerk, deputy clerk or assistant clerk
- one of the Active Elder Brethren of the Corporation of Trinity House of Deptford Strond
- a shorthand writer in any court
- a court security officer
- a governor, chaplain, medical officer or other officer of a penal establishment
- a member of the board of visitors of a penal establishment
- a prisoner custody officer
- the warden, or a member of the staff, of a probation home, probation hostel or bail hostel
- a probation officer or someone appointed to help them
- a member of a Parole Board, or of a local review committee
- a member of any police force (this includes a person on central service, a special constable, or anyone with the powers and privileges of a constable)
- a member of a police authority or of any body with responsibility for appointing members of a constabulary
- an Inspector or Assistant Inspector of Constabulary
- a civilian employed for police purposes or a member of the metropolitan civil staffs
- someone employed in a forensic science laboratory

Box D   The Clergy

You are not qualified for jury service if you are

- in holy orders
- a regular minister of any religious denomination
- a vowed member of any religious order living in a monastery, convent or other religious community.

Box E   People who have the right to be excused

You have the right to be excused if you are one of the following people

Parliament
- a Peer or Peeress who is entitled to receive a writ of summons to attend the House of Lords
- a Member of the House of Commons
- an Officer of the House of Lords
- an Officer of the House of Commons

European Assembly

A representative to the assembly of the European Communities.

Medical and other Professions
- a dentist
- a nurse
- a medical practitioner
- a Veterinary surgeon or a Veterinary practitioner
- a midwife
- a pharmaceutical chemist

if you are practising the profession and you are registered, enrolled or certificated under the law which relates to your profession

The Forces

You may be excused if you are a full-time member of

- the army, navy or air force
- the Queen Alexandra's Royal Naval Nursing Service
- any Voluntary Aid Detachment serving with the Royal Navy

and your commanding officer certifies to the jury summoning officer that your absence would be 'prejudicial to the efficiency of the service'.

others concerned
- A practising member of a religious society or order whose tenets or beliefs are incompatible with jury service.

Figure 14.3 Continued

Since 1977 a coroner is no longer obliged to summon a jury to decide cases involving road accidents or suspected homicide. He has a discretion as to whether a jury should be used in such cases.

14.2.3 Jury qualifications

Basic qualifications

The qualifications for jury service were revised in 1972 following the Morris Committee Report on jury service. Before this date there was a property qualification – in order to be a juror it was necessary to be the owner or tenant of a dwelling. This restriction meant that women and young people who were less likely to own or rent property were prevented from serving on a jury. The Morris Committee thought that being a juror should be the counterpart of being a citizen. As a result, the qualifications for jury service were widened in the Criminal Justice Act 1972 and based on the right to vote. The present qualifications are set out in the Juries Act 1974 (as amended) so that to qualify for jury service a person must be:

- Aged between 18 and 70
- Registered as a parliamentary or local government elector
- Ordinarily resident in the United Kingdom, the Channel Islands or the Isle of Man for at least five years since their thirteenth birthday

However, certain people are not permitted to sit on a jury even though they are within these basic qualifications; these are people who are disqualified or ineligible for various reasons.

Disqualification

Some criminal convictions will disqualify a person from jury service. The type of sentence and the length of a prison sentence decide whether the person is disqualified and the period for which that disqualification lasts. A custodial sentence, including a suspended sentence always results in disqualification, as do a community service order and probation. In addition the Criminal Justice and Public Order Act 1994 disqualified anyone who is currently on bail in criminal proceedings. The full list of those who are disqualified is shown in box A of the jury summons on page 242.

If a disqualified person fails to disclose that fact and turns up for jury service, they may be fined up to £5,000.

Ineligibility

Those who are considered ineligible for jury service are in three broad categories. These are:

1. Those suffering from certain mental disorders (see box B of the jury summons)
2. The judiciary who cannot sit on a jury; others who are in occupations concerned with the administration of justice, or who have been so within the last 10 years; this is a very wide category as can be seen from the list in box C (page 243)
3. Those with a religious vocation (see box D); it should be noted, though, that the Runciman Commission on criminal justice suggested that these people should be allowed to do jury service

Excusals as of right

There are also some groups of people who are eligible to serve on a jury but who have the right to be excused from jury service. It is said that they are excusable 'as of right'. This type of excusal must not be confused with the discretionary excusal which is explained below. Those who are entitled to be excused as of right include:

- Anyone between 65 and 70 years old
- Anyone who has served on a jury within the past two years
- Members of Parliament
- Those in the armed forces

- People in essential professions such as doctors, nurses, dentists and chemists
- Practising members of a religious group whose beliefs are not compatible with jury service

The complete list is shown in box E of the jury summons.

Discretionary excusals

Anyone who has problems which make it very difficult for them to do their jury service, may ask to be excused, or for their period of service to be put back to a later date. The court has a discretion to grant such an excusal but will only do so if there is a sufficiently good reason. Such reasons include being too ill to attend court, suffering from a disability that makes it impossible to sit as a juror, or being a mother with a small baby. Other reasons could include business appointments that cannot be undertaken by anyone else, examinations or holidays that have been booked. In these situations the court is most likely to defer jury service to a more convenient date, rather than excuse the person completely. If a person is not excused from jury service they must attend on the date set, or they may be fined up to £1,000 for non-attendance.

Lack of capacity

A judge at the court may discharge a person from being a juror for lack of capacity to cope with the trial. This could be because the person does not understand English adequately or because of some disability which makes them unsuitable as a juror. This includes the blind, who would be unable to see plans and photographs produced in evidence. Section 9B(2) of the Juries Act 1974 (which was added into the Act by the Criminal Justice and Public Order Act 1994 s 41) makes it clear that the mere fact of a disability does not prevent someone from acting as a juror. The judge can only discharge the juror if he is satisfied that the disability means that that juror is not capable

of acting effectively as a juror.

In June 1995 a deaf man was prevented from sitting on a jury at the Old Bailey despite wishing to serve and bringing with him a sign language interpreter. The judge pointed out that that would mean an extra person in the jury room and this was not allowed by law. He also said that the way in which witnesses gave evidence and the tone of their voice was important: 'a deaf juror may not be able to pick up these nuances and to properly judge their credibility.'

In November 1999 another deaf man challenged the ban on him sitting as a juror. The judge in this case felt that there was no practical reason why he should not sit, but the law only allowed the 12 jury members to be present in the jury room. It did not allow a 13th person – a sign-language interpreter – to be present. This made it impossible for the deaf man to be a juror.

Activity

State with reasons whether the following people could serve on a jury

- A 65-year-old retired company director
- A 17-year-old car mechanic
- A 19-year-old mother who has a six month old baby
- A 22-year-old woman who was placed on one year's probation four years ago
- A midwife
- A legal executive
- A 23-year-old man who was fined last week for shoplifting
- A prison chaplain
- A 52-year-old man with five previous convictions for burglary and who served a three year prison sentence for his last offence 12 years ago
- A court shorthand writer

14.2.4 Selecting a jury

At each Crown Court there is an official who is responsible for summonsing enough jurors to try the cases that will be heard in each two week period. This official will arrange for names to be selected at random from the electoral registers, for the area which the court covers. This is done through a computer selection at a central office. It is necessary to summons more than 12 jurors as most courts have more than one court-room and it will not be known how many of those summonsed are disqualified, ineligible or entitled to an excusal. In fact, at the bigger courts up to 150 summons may be sent out each fortnight.

Those summonsed must notify the court if there is any reason why they should not or cannot attend. All others are expected to attend for two weeks' jury service, though, of course, if the case they are trying goes on for more than two weeks they will have to stay until the trial is completed. Where it is known that a trial may be exceptionally long, such as a complicated fraud trial, potential jurors are asked if they will be able to serve for such a long period.

Vetting

Once the list of potential jurors is known, both the prosecution and the defence have the right to see that list. In some cases it may be decided that this pool of potential jurors should be 'vetted', i.e. checked for suitability. There are two types of vetting.

1. Routine police checks are made on prospective jurors to eliminate those disqualified. In *R v Crown Court at Sheffield, ex parte Brownlow* (1980) the defendant was a police officer and the defence sought permission to vet the jury panel for convictions. The judge gave permission but the Court of Appeal, while holding that they had no power to interfere, said that vetting was 'unconstitutional' and a 'serious invasion of privacy' and not sanctioned by the Juries Act 1974. However, in *R v Mason* (1980) where it was revealed that the Chief Constable for Northamptonshire had been allowing widespread use of unauthorised vetting of criminal records, the Court of Appeal approved of this type of vetting. Lawton LJ pointed out that, since it is a criminal offence to serve on a jury whilst disqualified, the police were only doing their normal duty of preventing crime by checking for criminal records. Furthermore, the court said that, if in the course of looking at criminal records convictions were revealed which did not disqualify, there was no reason why these should not be passed on to prosecuting counsel, so that this information could be used in deciding to stand by individual jurors (see page 248 for information on the right of stand by).

2. A wider check is made on a juror's background and political affiliations. This practice was brought to light by the 'ABC' trial in 1978 where two journalists and a soldier were charged with collecting secret information. It was discovered that the jury had been vetted for their loyalty. The trial was stopped and a new trial ordered before a fresh jury. Following these cases, the Attorney-General published guidelines in 1980 on when political vetting of jurors should take place. These guidelines were revised in 1988 in a Practice Note (Jury: Stand By: Jury Checks) (1988) and state that:

a) vetting should only be used in exceptional cases involving:
   - national security where part of the evidence is likely to be given *in camera*
   - terrorist cases
b) vetting can only be carried out with the Attorney-General's express permission.

At court

The jurors are usually divided into groups of 15 and allocated to a court. At the start of a trial the court clerk will select 12 out of these 15 at random. If there are not enough jurors to hear all the cases scheduled for that day at the court, there is a special power to select anyone who is qualified to be a juror from people passing by in the streets or from local offices or businesses. This is called 'praying a talesman'. It is very unusual to use this power but it was used at Middlesex Crown Court in January 1992 when about half the jury panel failed to turn up after the New Year's holiday and there were not sufficient jurors to try the cases.

KEY FACTS

Court	Crown Court
Qualifications	18–70 age Registered to vote Resident in UK for at least five years since age 13
Disqualified	Sentenced to five years' or more imprisonment – disqualified for life Served a prison sentence OR suspended sentence OR a community service order – disqualified for 10 years Placed on probation – disqualified for five years On bail – disqualified while on bail
Ineligible	Mentally ill Those working in the administration of justice Minister of religion or member of religious order
Excusals	As of right – MPs, medical professions, armed forces, over 65 Discretionary – ill, business commitments, or other 'good reason'
Selection	A central office selects names from the lists of electors Summons sent to these people Must attend unless disqualified, ineligible or excused
Vetting	May be checked for criminal record – R v Mason (1980) In cases of national security may be subject to a wider check on background subject to Attorney-General's guidelines
Challenges	Individual juror may be challenged for cause, e.g. knows defendant Whole panel may be challenged for biased selection – but no right to a multi-racial jury (R v Ford (1989)) Prosecution may 'stand by' any juror
Function	Decide verdict – Guilty or Not guilty Sole arbiters of fact but judge directs them on law
Verdict	Must try for a unanimous verdict BUT if cannot reach a unanimous verdict then a majority verdict can be accepted of 10–2 or 11–1

Figure 14.4 Key fact chart on the use of juries in criminal cases

Challenging

Once the court clerk has selected the panel of 12 jurors, these jurors come into the jury box to be sworn in as jurors. At this point, before the jury is sworn in, both the prosecution and defence have certain rights to challenge one or more of the jurors. There are two challenges which can be made and, in addition, the prosecution have a special right of 'stand by'. These are:

1. **To the array**
    This right to challenge is given by section 5 of the Juries Act 1974 and it is a challenge to the whole jury on the basis that it has been chosen in an unrepresentative or biased way. This challenge was used successfully against the 'Romford' jury at the Old Bailey in 1993 when, out of a panel of 12 jurors, nine came from Romford, with two of them living within 20 doors of each other in the same street. In *R v Fraser* (1987) this method of challenging a jury was also used, as the defendant was of an ethnic minority background but all the jurors were white. The judge in that case agreed to empanel another jury. However, in *R v Ford* (1989) it was held that if the jury was chosen in a random manner then it could not be challenged simply because it was not multiracial.

2. **For cause**
    This involves challenging the right of an individual juror to sit on the jury. To be successful the challenge must point out a valid reason why that juror should not serve on the jury. An obvious reason is that the juror is disqualified, but a challenge for cause can also be made if the juror knows or is related to a witness or defendant. If such people are not removed from the jury there is a risk that any subsequent conviction could be quashed. This occurred in *R v Wilson* and

R v Sprason (1995) where the wife of a prison officer was summoned for jury service. She had asked to be excused attendance on that ground, but this request had not been granted. She served on the jury which convicted the two defendants of robbery. Both defendants had been on remand at Exeter prison where her husband worked. The Court of Appeal said that justice must not only be done, it must be seen to be done and the presence of Mrs Roberts on the jury prevented that, so that the convictions had to be quashed.

3. **Prosecution right to stand by jurors**
    This is a right that only the prosecution can exercise. It allows the juror who has been stood by to be put to the end of the list of potential jurors, so that they will not be used on the jury unless there are not enough other jurors. The prosecution does not have to give a reason for 'standing by', but the Attorney-General's guidelines issued in 1988 make it clear that this power should be used sparingly.

Peremptory challenge

Before 1989 the defence used to have the right to challenge jurors without giving any reason. Initially the right allowed seven jurors to be removed in this way, but this number was reduced to three before the right was abolished altogether because of abuse of the system. The problem arose mainly in trials where there were several defendants each with a right of peremptory challenge. This meant that an unbalanced jury could result. For example it was used in the Cyprus Secrets case in 1986 to get a young jury, in the Greenham Common case in 1985 to get an all-female jury and in 1982 in the Bristol riots case to provide an all-black jury.

14.2.5 Criticisms of the selection of juries

Use of electoral register

The method of selecting jurors from the list of registered voters is open to criticism as it does not always give a representative sample of the population. It excludes some groups such as the homeless who cannot register to vote, and not every one who is eligible registers to vote. This is especially true of the young and ethnic minorities. While the poll tax was operating in the early 1990s the number of people registered to vote went down by well over a million. All these facts cast doubt on the representative nature of the electoral register.

Where the jury is selected by manual methods, as opposed to a randomised computer selection, there is a possibility that too many of the jury will come from the same small area. As seen above, this happened with the 'Romford' jury.

Multi-racial juries

One of the problems is whether it is desirable for the jury to be racially mixed, where the defendant or victim is from an ethnic minority. Research in 1979 by Baldwin and McConville found that ethnic minorities were severely under-represented on juries. They looked at a sample of 3,912 jurors and found there were only 28 jurors from ethnic minorities, while census figures indicated that the figure should have been 10 times higher. However, more recent research by Zander and Henderson in 1993 found that non-white jurors made up 5 per cent of jury panels. This was only just below the proportion in the population, as a whole, of 5.9 per cent. Despite this, there is no guarantee that there will be any ethnic minority jurors on a particular case and, as decided in R v Ford (1989), there is no power for the judge to empanel a multi-racial jury.

Surprisingly, up until 1870 there was statutory power where a non-English person was on trial, for a jury to be specially selected so that it contained equal numbers of English people and foreigners. The Runciman Commission (1993) has recommended that in exceptional cases it should be possible for either the prosecution or the defence to apply for the selection of the jury to contain up to three jurors from ethnic minorities. Furthermore, that it should be open to the defence or prosecution to argue the need for one or more of the three jurors to come from the same ethnic minority as the victim or defendant. These proposals have not been implemented.

Disqualified jurors

Although some checks are carried out, many disqualified people fail to disclose this fact and sit on juries. One survey of Inner London juries estimated that one in every 24 jurors was disqualified. In one instance at Snaresbrook Crown Court a man with 15 previous convictions sat as a juror in three cases and was the jury foreman in two of them. He later admitted that as far as he was concerned all defendants were not guilty unless they 'had been molesting kids'.

Excusals

If there are too many discretionary excusals it may lead to an unrepresentative jury. In 1979 Baldwin and McConville found that young mothers were often excused so that women were under-represented on juries. However, the research in 1993 by Zander and Henderson found that women were proportionately represented, so this problem may no longer exist. Home Office research in 1999 found that over one in every three jurors was excused from serving. The main reasons for excusal were medical conditions, looking after children or elderly relatives and business commitments. This wide spread use of the discretionary excusal can again prevent juries from being a true cross-section of the local population. The

Runciman Commission recommended that wherever possible, alternative dates should be offered to people who cannot sit on the date first suggested.

Prosecution's right of 'stand by'

The prosecution's right of stand by was kept even when the defence's peremptory challenge was withdrawn. This might be seen as giving the prosecution an advantage in 'rigging' the jury, particularly when combined with vetting. However, even when a jury has been vetted, it does not always give the prosecution an advantage. This was seen in *Ponting's case*, where the defendant was charged with an offence against the Official Secrets Acts and the jury was vetted. Despite the vetting the jury returned a not guilty verdict (see page 251 for further comment on this case).

14.2.6 The jury's role in criminal cases

The jury is used only at the Crown Court for cases where the defendant pleads not guilty. This means that a jury is used in about 20,000 cases each year.

Split function

The trial is presided over by a judge and the functions split between the judge and jury. The judge decides points of law and the jury decides the facts. At the end of the prosecution case, the judge has the power to direct the jury to acquit the defendant if he decides that, in law, the prosecution's evidence has not made out a case against the defendant. This is called a directed acquittal and occurs in about 10 per cent of cases.

Where the trial continues, the judge will sum up the case at the end, to the jury and direct them on any law involved. The jury retire to a private room and make the decision on the guilt or innocence of the accused in secret.

Initially the jury must try to come to a unanimous verdict, i.e. one on which they are all agreed. The judge must accept the jury verdict, even if he or she does not agree with it. This long established principle goes back to *Bushell's case* (1670). The jury do not give any reasons for their decision.

Majority verdicts

If, after at least two hours (longer where there are several defendants), the jury have not reached a verdict, the judge can call them back into the courtroom and direct them that he can now accept a majority verdict. Majority verdicts have been allowed since 1967. Where there is a full jury of 12, the verdict can be 10–2 or 11–1 either for guilty or for no guilty. If the jury has fallen below 12 for any reason (such as the death or illness of a juror during the trial) then only one can disagree with the verdict. That is, if there are 11 jurors, the verdict can be 10–1; if there are 10 jurors it can be 9–1. If there are only nine jurors the verdict must be unanimous. A jury cannot go below nine.

Majority verdicts were introduced because of the fear of jury 'nobbling', that is jurors being bribed or intimidated by associates of the defendant into voting for a not guilty verdict. When a jury had to be unanimous, only one member need be bribed to cause a 'stalemate' in which the jury were unable to reach a decision. It was also thought that the acquittal rates in jury trials were too high and majority decisions would result in more convictions.

Where the jury convict a defendant on a majority verdict, the foreman of the jury must announce the numbers both agreeing and disagreeing with the verdict in open court. This provision is contained in section 17(3) of the Juries Act 1974 and is aimed at making sure the jury have come to a legal majority, and not one, for example of eight to four, which is not allowed. However, in *R v Pigg* (1983), the Court of Appeal held that, provided the foreman announced the number who had agreed with the verdict, and that number was within the number allowed for a majority verdict, then the conviction was legal. It did not matter that the foreman had not also been asked how many disagreed with the verdict. About 20 per cent of convictions by juries each year are by majority verdict.

Secrecy

The jury discussion takes place in secret and there can be no inquiry into how the jury reached its verdict. This is because section eight of the Contempt of Court Act 1981 makes disclosure of anything that happened in the jury room a contempt of court which is a criminal offence. It is a contempt 'to obtain, disclose or solicit any particulars of statements made, opinions expressed, arguments advanced or votes cast by members of a jury in the course of their deliberations in any legal proceedings'. The section was brought in because newspapers were paying jurors large sums of money for 'their story'. This is obviously not desirable, but the total ban on finding out what happens in the jury room means that it is difficult to discover whether jurors have understood the evidence in complex cases.

The Runciman Commission suggested that this section should be amended to allow research into the workings of juries. It was thought that in particular there should be research into the influence that jurors with criminal convictions may have on jury verdicts. The Lord Chief Justice Lord Bingham also announced in 1996 that he was in favour of allowing research into jury verdicts.

14.2.7 Advantages and disadvantages of jury trial

Public confidence

On the face of it, asking 12 strangers who have no legal knowledge and without any training to decide what may be complex and technical points is an absurd one. Yet the jury is considered as one of the fundamentals of a democratic society. The right to be tried by one's peers is a bastion of liberty against the state and has been supported by eminent judges. For example, Lord Devlin said juries are 'the lamp that shows that freedom lives'. The tradition of trial by jury is very old and people seem to have confidence in the impartiality and fairness of a jury trial. This can be seen in the objection to withdrawing the right to jury trial from cases of 'minor' theft.

Jury equity

Since juries are not legal experts, are not bound to follow the precedent of past cases or even Acts of Parliament, and do not have to give reasons for their verdict, it is possible for them to decide cases on their idea of 'fairness'. This is sometimes referred to as jury equity. Several cases have shown the importance of this, in particular *Ponting's case* (1984) in which a civil servant was charged under the old wide-ranging section 2 of the Official Secrets Act 1911. He had leaked information on the sinking of the ship, The General Belgrano, in the Falklands war to a member of Parliament. At his trial he pleaded not guilty, claiming that his actions had been in the public interest. The jury refused to convict him even though the judge ruled there was no defence. The case also prompted the Government to reconsider the law and to amend section 2.

However this type of decision can be seen as a perverse decision and one which was not justified. Juries have refused to convict in other clear cut cases such as *R v Randle and Pottle* (1991) where the defendants were charged with helping the spy George Blake to escape from prison. Their prosecution did not occur until 25 years after the escape, when they wrote about what they had done and the jury acquitted them, possibly as a protest over the time lapse between the offence and the prosecution.

Activity

Read the following article and use it as a basis for a discussion on 'jury equity'.

Jet case verdict is hard to understand, says minister

Talks with the Home Office and the Attorney-General are being sought by the Treasury Minister Michael Jack into the acquittal of a group of women who caused £1.5 million of damage to a British Aerospace Hawk destined for Indonesia.

Mr Jack, MP for Fylde, said yesterday: 'I, and I am sure many others, find this jury's decision difficult to understand. It would appear there is little question about who did this damage. For whatever reason that damage was done, it was just plain wrong. The ramifications of the case are, however, very important in terms of future security, jobs and the question of being able to do damage and getting off with it.'

On Tuesday, the jury at Liverpool Crown Court cleared Lotta Kronlid, 28, Andrea Needham, 30, and Joan Wilson, 33, of causing criminal damage to the jet at a BAe factory at Warton, near Preston, in January. They and a fourth defendant, Angela Zelter, 45, were cleared of conspiring to damage the jet.

The women admitted breaking into a hangar and using hammers to damage the £10 million aircraft. However, they denied the charges claiming that their actions were justified. The jury accepted their claim that they had a lawful excuse to damage the aircraft because they were using reasonable force to prevent a greater crime. They said that disarming the jet, one of a consignment of 24 bought by Indonesia, would prevent it being used against the civilian population in East Timor.

Taken from an article by Kate Alderson in *The Times*, 2 August 1996

Open system of justice

The use of a jury is viewed as making the legal system more open. Justice is seen to be done as members of the public are involved in a key role and the whole process is public. It also helps to keep the law clearer as points have to be explained to the jury, enabling the defendant to understand the case more easily. Against this is the fact that the jury deliberate in private and that no-one can inquire into what happened in the jury room. In addition, the jury do not have to give any reason for their verdict. When a judge gives a judgment he explains his reasoning and, if he has made an error, it is known and can be appealed against.

Secrecy of the jury room

This can be seen as an advantage, since the jury are free from pressure in their discussion. Jurors are protected from outside influences when deciding on the verdict. This allows juries to bring in verdicts that may be unpopular with the public as well as allowing jurors the freedom to ignore the strict letter of the law. It has been suggested that people would be less willing to serve on a jury if they knew that their discussions could be made public.

There is also the disadvantage that, as no reasons have to be given for the verdict, there is no way of knowing if the jury did understand the case and came to the decision for the right reasons. One of the most unusual cases was *R v Young* (1991) in which the defendant was charged with the murder of two people. The jury had to stay overnight in a hotel as they had not reach a verdict by the end of the first day of discussion. During this stay at the hotel some members of the jury held a seance using a ouija board to try to contact the dead victims and ask who had killed them. The next day the jury returned a verdict of guilty. When the fact that the ouija board had been used became known, the defendant appealed and the Court of

Appeal quashed the verdict and ordered a retrial of the case. The court felt able to inquire into what had happened as it was in a hotel and not part of the jury discussions in the jury room.

Impartiality

A jury should be impartial as they are not connected to anyone in the case. The process of random selection should result in a cross-section of society and this should also lead to an impartial jury, as they will have different prejudices and so should cancel out each others' biases. No one individual person is responsible for the decision. A jury is also not case hardened since they sit for only two weeks and are unlikely to try more than three or four cases in that time. After the end of the case the jury dissolves and, as Sir Sebag Shaw said, it is 'anonymous and amorphous'.

Racial bias

However, although jurors have no direct interest in a case, and despite the fact that there are 12 of them, they may still have prejudices which can affect the verdict. Some jurors may be biased against the police – this is one of the reasons that those with certain criminal convictions are disqualified from sitting on a jury. In particular there is the worry that some jurors are racially prejudiced. This is why the fact that the selection process can produce an all white jury to try a defendant from an ethnic minority is viewed with suspicion. In *Sander* v *United Kingdom* (2000) the European Court of Human Rights ruled that there had been a breach of the right to a fair trial under Article 6 of the European Convention on Human Rights. In the case one juror had written a note to the judge raising concern over the fact that other jurors had been making openly racist remarks and jokes. The judge asked the jury to 'search their consciences'. The next day the judge received two letters, one signed by all the jurors in which they denied any racist

attitudes and a second from one juror who admitted that he may have been the one making the jokes. Despite the discrepancies between these two letters the judge allowed the case to continue with the same jury. The European Court of Human Rights held that in these circumstances the judge should have discharged the jury as there was an obvious risk of racial bias.

The possibility of racial bias was shown by the research into juries by Baldwin and McConville in 1979 in which the legal professionals in the cases had serious doubts about the correctness of convictions in one out of every 20 convictions. It was apparent that black defendants were more likely to fall into this 'doubtful' conviction category than white defendants. This risk of racial prejudice is the reason that the Runciman Commission recommended that up to three jurors should be drawn from ethnic minority cases in suitable cases.

Another way of preventing bias and allowing 'justice to be seen to be done' is to reinstate the defence's right of peremptory challenge. This would allow defendants a limited choice over who sits on a jury and might create a racially mixed jury.

Media influence

Media coverage may influence jurors. This is especially true in high-profile cases, where there has been a lot of publicity about police investigations into a case. This occurred in the case *R* v *West* (1996) in which Rosemary West was convicted for the murders of 10 young girls and women, including her own daughter. From the time the bodies were first discovered, the media coverage was intense. In addition, some newspapers had paid large sums of money to some of the witnesses in order to secure their story after the trial was completed. One of the grounds on which Rosemary West appealed against her conviction was that the media coverage had made it impossible for her to receive a fair trial. The Court of Appeal rejected the appeal, pointing out that otherwise it would mean that if 'allegations of murder were sufficiently horrendous so as to inevitably shock the nation, the accused could not be tried'. They also said that the trial judge had given adequate warning to the jury to consider only the evidence they heard in court.

Another case which highlighted media influence on the jury's decision was *R* v *Taylor and Taylor* (1993) in which two sisters were charged with murder. Some newspapers published a still from a video sequence which gave a false impression of what was happening. After the jury convicted the two defendants, the trial judge gave leave to appeal because of the possible influence this picture could have had on the jury's verdict and the Court of Appeal quashed the convictions.

Lack of understanding

There are worries that jurors may not understand the case which they are trying. This fear was only partly borne out by a survey carried out in 1992 for the Runciman Commission, in which jurors were asked whether they thought they had been able to understand the evidence. Over half (56 per cent) of the jurors questioned thought that the jury as a whole had understood the evidence with another two-fifths (41 per cent) believing that most of the jury had understood the case. However just under 10 per cent of jurors admitted that they had had difficulty. When the foremen of juries were questioned on the same point, they thought that a small number of jurors (0.2 per cent) could not understand English sufficiently well to follow a case. The foremen also thought that about 1 per cent of jurors could not understand the details of a case, while another 1 per cent could not understand any case. These may be small numbers, but it is still worrying that in some cases a defendant's future is being decided by some members of the public who do not understand the case. For example, in one case at Snaresbrook Crown Court, the jury after they had retired to consider their verdict sent a note to the judge asking what they had to do! The judge discharged that jury from the case.

Fraud trials

Fraud trials with complex accounts being given in evidence can create special problems for jurors. Even jurors who can easily cope with other evidence may have difficulty understanding a fraud case. These cases are also often very long, so that the jurors have to be able to be away from their own work for months. A long fraud trial can place a great strain on jurors. Such cases also become very expensive, both for the prosecution and for the defendants.

The Roskill Committee in 1986 suggested that juries should not be used for complex fraud cases. However, this reform has not been implemented. One of the difficulties is in deciding which fraud cases are sufficiently complex to withdraw them from the right to jury trial. A possible solution is the system used in New Zealand, where the defendants can choose not to be tried by a jury, but instead to be tried by a judge sitting on his own. Another solution would be for all fraud cases to be tried by a judge and two lay assessors who have expertise in accounts and business management.

High acquittal rates

Juries are often criticised on the grounds that they acquit too many defendants. The figures usually quoted in support of this are that about 60 per cent of those who plead not guilty at the Crown Court are acquitted. However, this figure does not give a true picture of the workings of juries as it includes cases discharged by the judge and those in which the judge directed an acquittal.

The judicial statistics for 2000 show that more than half of the acquittals were ordered by the judge without a jury even being sworn in to try the case. This happens where the prosecution drop the case at the last minute and offer no evidence against the defendant. Another 15 per cent of acquittals were by a jury but on the direction of a judge. This occurs where the judge rules that there is no case against the defendant; it might be because of a legal point or because the prosecution evidence is not sufficient in law to prove the case. When these decisions are excluded from the statistics it is found that juries actually acquit in less than 40 per cent of cases.

Other disadvantages

The compulsory nature of jury service is unpopular, so that some jurors may be against the whole system, while others may rush their verdict in order to leave as quickly as possible. Jury service can be a strain, especially where jurors have to listen to horrific evidence. Jurors in the Rosemary West case were offered counselling after the trial to help them cope with the evidence they had had to see and hear.

Jury 'nobbling' does occur and in some cases jurors have had to be provided with police protection. In order to try to combat this, the Criminal Procedure and Investigations Act 1996 allows for a retrial to be ordered if someone is subsequently proved to have interfered with the jury.

The use of juries makes trials slow and expensive. This is because each point has to be explained carefully to the jury and the whole procedure of the case takes longer.

14.2.8 The Auld Review

This review recommended a number of changes to the jury system in criminal courts. The way in which a jury is selected was criticised and it suggested that:

1. Juries should be more representative with the entitlement to be on the electoral roll as the criteria rather than actually having name on roll. A wider method than just using the electoral roll should be used to include more of those eligible.
2. Ineligibility and excusable as of right to be abolished. This would mean that judges, lawyers, doctors and nurses would have to sit on juries. This idea can be criticised as a lawyer on the jury could have a major influence on the decision. A judge or lawyer might even explain the law to the jury if they had not understood the judge's summing up in the court room. The problem with making doctors and nurses sit on jury is that there is a shortage of medical staff in the health service and they cannot afford the time to sit on a jury. They are too badly needed in the health service.
3. Provision should be made for ethnic minority representation on juries where race is likely to be an issue. This is the same recommendation as made by the Runciman commission in 1993 but never been brought in to effect. The Government has indicated that they are unlikely to follow this recommendation.

In some situations the review recommended that juries should not be used. For example, fraud cases in the Crown Court should be heard by a judge and two lay people taken from a special panel. It also recommended that defendants at the Crown Court could opt for trial by judge alone. The right to elect jury trial should be taken away from defendants charged with triable either way offences. Instead the magistrates should decided where these cases should be tried. This last point is particularly controversial as supporters of the present system say the right to elect jury trial gives people confidence in the legal system.

Jury verdicts

There were also recommendations about how jury verdicts were reached. The most important of these were:

1. Juries should be given a more structured summing up by the judge and, where the judge thinks it appropriate, they should be required to answer questions and declare a verdict in accordance with those answers.
2. Juries should not have the right to acquit defendants in defiance of the law or in disregard of the evidence. The prosecution should have the right to appeal against a 'perverse' verdict. This is a particularly worrying recommendation as it removes the jury's independence.
3. The law should not be amended to allow jury research, but the Court of Appeal should be entitled to examine alleged improprieties in the jury room.

The Government is likely to bring in legislation on some of these points in 2003 or 2004.

14.2.9 Special problems of using juries in civil cases

Amount of damages

Juries in civil cases decide both the liability of the parties in the case and also the amount of damages that will be awarded. The awards vary greatly as each jury has its own ideas and does not follow past cases. The amount is, therefore, totally unpredictable which makes it difficult for lawyers to advise on settlements. Judges look back to past awards when deciding awards of damages in personal injury cases, and then apply an inflation factor so that there is consistency between similar cases. Juries in defamation cases cause particular problems with very large awards; one judge

called it Mickey Mouse money. In 1989 Lord Aldington was awarded one-and-a-half million pounds; this is the highest award to date. If the amounts in personal injury cases are compared to this, it can be seen that this size of award would only be given to a very severely injured person who had been permanently disabled.

Until 1990 the Court of Appeal had no power to correct awards which were thought to be far too high. They could only strike out the award and order a re-trial. This was both time-consuming and expensive and rarely happened. As a result of cases in which there were overgenerous awards, Parliament enacted section eight of the Courts and Legal Services Act 1990 which gives the Court of Appeal special powers in such cases. This allows the Court of Appeal to order a new trial or substitute such sum as appears proper to the court, if they feel the damages were excessive or inadequate. This power was first used in a case brought by the MP Teresa Gorman where the Court of Appeal reduced the damages awarded to her by the jury from £150,000 to £50,000. It was also used in *Rantzen* v *Mirror Group Newspapers* (1993) when the award to Esther Rantzen, the founder of 'Childline' (a charity set up to help abused children) over allegations that she had deliberately kept quiet about the activities of a suspected child abuser, was reduced from £250,000 to £110,000.

Unreasoned decision

The jury does not have to give a reason either for its decision or for the amount it awards. A judge always gives a judgment, this makes it easier to see if there are good grounds for an appeal.

Bias

The problems of bias in civil cases is different to that encountered in criminal cases. In some defamation cases the claimants and/or the defendants may be public figures so that jurors will know and possibly hold views about them.

Alternatively there is the fact that the defendant in a defamation case is often a newspaper and jurors may be biased against the press or may feel that 'they can afford to pay'.

Cost

Civil cases are expensive and the use of a jury adds to this as the case is likely to last longer. At the end of the case the losing party will have to pay all the costs of the case which may amount to hundreds of thousands of pounds. As a result of this, the Lord Chancellor has introduced some reforms so that defamation actions will be less costly. Firstly, with the increase in County Court jurisdiction, parties can now agree that their case should be transferred to the County Court. Here a jury of eight may be used and the trial is likely to be less expensive than one in the High Court. Secondly, the parties may also agree to the case being tried by a judge alone without a jury. The Defamation Act 1996 allows the claimant to seek a limited sum (up to £10,000) in a quick procedure dealt with by a judge. This allows those who want to clear their name and get immediate compensation at a lower cost to do so.

14.2.10 Alternatives to jury trial

Despite all the problems of using juries in criminal cases, there is still a strong feeling that they are the best method available. However, if juries are not thought suitable to try serious criminal cases, what alternative form of trial could be used?

Trial by a single judge

This is the method of trial in the majority of civil cases which is generally regarded as producing a fairer and more predictable result. Trial by a single judge is also used for

some criminal trials in Northern Ireland. These are called the Diplock courts and were brought in on the recommendation of Lord Diplock to replace jury trial because of the special problems of threats and jury nobbling that existed between the different sectarian parties.

However, there appears to be less public confidence in the use of judges to decide all serious criminal cases. The arguments against this form of trial are that judges become case-hardened and prosecution-minded. They are also from a very elite group and would have little understanding of the background and problems of defendants. Individual prejudices are more likely than in a jury where the different personalities should go some way to eliminating bias. But, on the other hand, judges are trained to evaluate cases and they are now being given training in racial awareness. This may make them better arbiters of fact than an untrained jury.

A panel of judges

In some continental countries cases are heard by a panel of three or five judges sitting together. This allows for a balance of views, instead of the verdict of a single person. However, it still leaves the problems of judges becoming case-hardened and prosecutionminded and coming from an elite background. The other difficulty is that there are not sufficient judges and our system of legal training and appointment would need a radical overhaul to implement this proposal. It would also be expensive.

A judge plus lay assessors

Under this system the judge and two lay people would make the decision together. This method is used in the Scandinavian countries. It provides the legal expertise of the judge, together with lay participation in the legal system by ordinary members of the public. The lay people could either be drawn from the general public, using the same method as is used for selecting juries at present or a special panel of assessors could be drawn up as in tribunal cases. This latter suggestion would be particularly suitable for fraud cases.

A mini-jury

Finally, if the jury is to remain, then it might be possible to have a smaller number of jurors. In many continental countries when a jury is used there are nine members. For example in Spain, which reintroduced the use of juries in certain criminal case in 1996, there is a jury of nine. Alternatively a jury of six could be used for less serious criminal cases that at the moment can have a full jury trial, as occurs in some American states.

Chapter 15

LEGAL FUNDING

When faced with a legal problem, the average person will usually need expert help from a lawyer, or from someone else with expertise in the particular type of legal difficulty. Most often the need is just for advice, but some people may need help in starting court proceedings and/or presenting their case in court. For the ordinary person seeking legal assistance there are three main difficulties:

1. **Lack of knowledge.** Many people do not know where their nearest solicitor is located or, if they do know this, they do not know which solicitor specialises in the law involved in their particular case.
2. **People often have a fear of dealing with lawyers**; they feel intimidated.
3. **The final difficulty is one of cost.** Solicitors charge from about £80 an hour for routine advice from a small local firm, to over £300 an hour for work done by a top city firm of solicitors in a specialist field.

Access to justice

Where a person cannot get the help they need, it is said they are being denied access to justice. Access to justice involves both an open system of justice and also being able to fund the costs of a case. There have been various schemes aimed at making the law more accessible to everyone – for example, the national network of Citizens' Advice Bureaux was started in 1938 and now operates in most towns. More recently the Law Society has relaxed the rules so that solicitors are allowed to advertise and inform the public of the areas of law they specialise in.

However, the problem of cost still remains a major hurdle. A judge, Mr Justice Darling, once said 'The law courts of England are open to all men like the doors of the Ritz hotel'. In other words, the courts are there for anyone to use but cost may prevent many people from seeking justice. The cost of civil cases in the High Court will run into thousands of pounds. Even in the cheaper County Court the cost will possibly be more than the amount of money recovered in damages. There is the additional risk in all civil cases that the loser has to pay the winner's costs. In criminal cases a person's liberty may be at risk and it is essential that they should be able to defend themselves properly.

15.1 History of legal aid and advice schemes

A system of Government-funded legal aid and advice began after the report by the Rushcliffe Committee in 1945. This was the era of the development of the Welfare State and access to legal services was viewed as being as important as access to medical services.

The Government accepted the proposals in principle and this led to the Legal Aid and Advice Act 1949. The initial scheme only covered civil cases. It was not until 1964 that the scheme was extended to criminal cases. Other parts of the scheme were gradually set up. The main areas of advice came from the Green Form scheme of advice which was set up in 1972. Then, following the Police and Criminal Evidence Act 1984, duty solicitor schemes in police stations and Magistrates' Courts were established. The entire system was consolidated in the Legal Aid Act 1988, when the handling of civil legal aid was taken from the Law Society and given to a specially created Legal Aid Board.

Eligibility

When the scheme started in 1949, about 80 per cent of the population were eligible. This was in line with the idea of the Rushcliffe Committee that the scheme should be available not only to the poor but also to those of moderate means. Because the financial limits for qualifying did not keep pace with inflation, the number qualifying gradually went down to about 48 per cent by 1978. In 1979 the limits were revised upward and once more nearly 80 per cent of the population qualified. This did not last long and in 1993 there were severe cuts to the limits so that only 40 per cent qualified and many of these had to pay large contributions towards their funding.

15.2 The Access to Justice Act 1999

The cost of funding cases under the legal aid scheme was very expensive. There were also criticisms that advice was not available to those who really needed it. In their White Paper, *Modernising Justice*, which preceded the Access to Justice Act, the Government stated that it needed to tackle the following problems:

- Inadequate access to good quality information and advice
- The inability to control legal aid
- The need to target legal aid on real legal needs, within a budget the taxpayer can afford.

The advice sector was described as 'fragmented and unplanned' with the result that providers of legal services could not work together to achieve the maximum value and effect.

Under the Access to Justice Act the old legal aid scheme was replaced by two new schemes. These are the Community Legal Service for civil matters and the Criminal Defence Service for criminal cases. The Community Legal Service came into effect on 1 April 2000. The Criminal Defence Service started in April 2001. To oversee the public funding of legal services there is a Legal Services Commission.

15.2.1 The Legal Services Commission

Section 1 of the Access to Justice Act 1999 set up the Legal Services Commission. The members of the Commission are appointed by the Lord Chancellor. When appointing members he should try to make sure that, between them, they have a wide range of expertise and experience. This expertise should cover the advice sector and other legal services, the work of the courts, consumer affairs, social conditions and management.

The Legal Services Commission took over funding of civil cases from the Legal Aid Board. It is responsible for managing the Community Legal Service Fund and it is able to make contracts with providers of all types of legal service. The Commission is also responsible for developing local, regional and national plans to match the delivery of legal services to needs and priorities which have been identified. It also has a role in respect of criminal legal aid and the new Criminal Defence Service (see section 15.6).

15.2.2 The Community Legal Service

The Access to Justice Act 1999 establishes a Community Legal Service which provides the following services for matters involving civil law:

- General information about the law and legal system and the availability of legal services
- Legal advice
- Help in preventing or settling or otherwise resolving disputes about legal rights and duties
- Help in enforcing decisions by which such disputes are resolved
- Help in relation to legal proceedings not relating to disputes.

The explanatory notes to the Act state that the scheme includes advice, assistance and representation by lawyers and, as well, the services of non-lawyers. It also covers services such as mediation. The money to pay for this service is met by the Community Legal Service Fund.

15.2.3 The Community Legal Service Fund

This fund is maintained by the Legal Services Commission from money paid to the Commission by the Lord Chancellor. The Lord Chancellor is responsible for determining how much is appropriate each year though, obviously, he has to work within the Government's total budget. This means that there is a set limit for the fund and it is a main difference from the old legal aid system which was demand led. In other words, under the old system, Government funding was provided for any case which qualified; while under the new system there is a limit or cap on the amount of money available and it is possible that some people will be refused funding because the money has run out.

For 2001–2002 the Lord Chancellor set the budget at £732 million but indicated that he intended decreasing it in the following years.

Within the set budget for the Community Legal Service Fund, there are two sub-budgets – civil and family. The Legal Services Commission will have limited flexibility to switch money between the two. Money will be allocated to regional offices of the Commission according to the amount identified as necessary for that area. However, this could result in one area not having enough to fund all the cases it needs to, while in another area there is enough funding. To help this problem very expensive cases will be funded on a case-by-case basis through individually negotiated contracts from a central fund.

15.2.4 Excluded matters

Certain types of legal matters **cannot** be funded by the Community Legal Service Fund. These are:

- Allegations of negligently caused injury, death or damage to property, apart from allegations of clinical negligence
- Conveyancing
- Boundary disputes
- The making of wills
- Matters of trust law
- Defamation or malicious falsehood
- Matters of company or partnership law, or
- Other matters arising out of the carrying on of a business.

Most of these were excluded from receiving legal aid under the previous system, but some of the categories used to be able to get help. In particular, people who suffer injury or damage through someone else's negligence used to be able to get legal aid, but are now excluded from Government funding. This type of case can be funded by conditional fees (see section 15.4).

Court cases

Funding is available for cases in the County Court, High Court and appeal courts. However, cases for amounts of under £5,000 cannot get funding. There is also another 'gap' in the system as funding is not available for most tribunal hearings. The exceptions are cases before the Mental Health Tribunal, which are funded because they involve the liberty of the individual, as the Mental Health Tribunal decides whether detention of people under the Mental Heath Acts is justified. It is also hoped that there will be funding for cases before immigration tribunals.

Even where funding is allowed, individuals must show that they meet the other criteria before funding will be given. These criteria are discussed in section 15.2.6.

15.2.5 Priority for funding

Section 6 of the Access to Justice Act 1999 states that priorities shall be set in accordance with any directions given by the Lord Chancellor. In February 2000 the Lord Chancellor directed the Legal Services commission to give priority to child protection cases and cases where a person is at risk of loss of life or liberty. The available resources should be managed so that all cases in these categories that meet the merits criteria can be funded.

After that the Commission should give high priority to:

- other cases concerning the welfare of children;
- domestic violence cases;
- cases alleging serious wrong-doing or breaches of human rights by public bodies; and
- 'social welfare' cases, including housing proceedings, and advice about employment rights, social security entitlements and debt.

This direction only covers advice about most 'social welfare' matters. Funding is not available for representation in employment tribunals or social security tribunals.

15.2.6 Funding criteria

Under section 7 of the Access to Justice Act 1999, regulations are issued on financial eligibility for funding. This is known as means testing and there are two matters taken into consideration. These are the person's disposable income and their disposable capital:

Disposable income and capital

Disposable income is the amount of income available to a person after taking into account essential living expenses. Disposable capital is the assets owned by the person such as money in the bank or building society, valuables such as jewellery, stocks and shares or other investments. It also includes the value of the house which the person owns, but only if that value is more than £100,000 after deducting the amount of mortgage up to £100,000 which is still owing.

For December 2001 the levels of income and capital allowed to qualify for legal help or representation in civil cases have been simplified. For all types of service the person's gross income must not be more than £2,000 per month.

Where the client qualifies on gross income, then their disposable income and capital must be calculated. For most cases the maximum level is £601 per month disposable income and £3,000 disposable capital. The levels for family cases and mediation are slightly higher. People receiving Income Support or Income Based Job Seekers' Allowance automatically qualify.

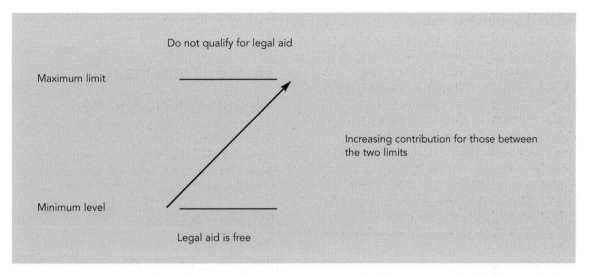

Figure 15.1 Minimum and maximum limits for legal aid

Those below a certain amount of disposable income will not have to pay any contribution. Those above this minimum level will have to pay a contribution which increases the higher their income is. This idea of minimum and maximum levels is best explained by a diagram and is shown in Figure 15.1.

Since December 2001 those with a monthly disposable income below £259 do not have to pay any contributions. For income levels above this the contributions are graded into bands. Those bands are:

Monthly disposable income	Monthly contribution
A £260 to £380	¼ of income in excess of £2,555
B £381 to £505	£31.25 + ⅓ of income in excess of £380
C £506 to £683	£72.91 + ½ of income in excess of £505

This idea of minimum and maximum levels is best explained by a diagram and is shown in Figure 15.1.

Criteria for funding

There is a code about provision of funded services. This code sets out criteria on which it is decided whether to fund services.

The factors which are considered are:

- The likely cost of funding and the benefit which may be obtained
- The availability of sums in the Community Legal Fund
- The importance of the matters for the individual
- The availability of other services
- The prospects of success
- The conduct of the individual
- The public interest and
- Such other factors as the Lord Chancellor may require the Commission to consider.

So even if a person is financially poor enough to qualify for help, other factors will also be considered. For example, if another type of service such as mediation is thought to be a better way of dealing with the case, then the case will not qualify. Also if it is thought that the applicant could fund the case in another way such as by a conditional fee agreement, funding is not available.

Merits of the case

Another factor which is taken into consideration is whether the case is likely to be successful. There must be a realistic chance of the case succeeding before public money is made available for it. But even if there is a realistic chance of success this is not a guarantee that funding will be given. The test is now wider. Do the merits of the case, in the context of the Government's priorities and available resources, justify public spending? It cannot be assumed that any case necessarily has an automatic right to public funding because of its intrinsic merits.

The funding code specifically states that full representation will be refused unless:

a) where the prospects of success are very good (80 per cent +) the likely damages will exceed costs; or

b) where the prospects of success are good (60 per cent – 80 per cent) the likely damages will exceed costs by a ratio of 2 to 1; or

c) where the prospects of success are moderate (50 per cent – 60 per cent) the likely damages will exceed costs by a ratio of 4 to 1.

From all of this it can be seen that even if a person is poor enough to qualify for help with funding a legal case, it does not mean that they will automatically get help.

15.3 Providers of legal services

Legal services are provided by a wide range of people and organisations. Local solicitors are a main source of legal services, but there are also advice agencies, welfare associations and consumer protection groups who can offer help and advice. The Government wants to extend the range of bodies that provide legal services and to make sure that services are more evenly distributed through the country.

15.3.1 Franchises

The Legal Service Commission grants contracts to services providers. About 5,000 firms of solicitors have contracts. This is considerably lower than the number who were allowed to do legal aid work under the previous scheme.

Quality Marks

All providers must reach certain minimum standards. There are three different Quality Marks. These are for:

- Information
- General help
- Specialist help.

An information provider must be able to provide leaflets and other reference material, access to the CLS directory and/or website. This may, for example, be at a community centre or a library. To be a general help provider they must be able to advise on what action to take and give basic assistance. Many CABx are general help providers. A specialist help provider must be able to advise and help with complex points of law. These are likely to be solicitors' firms or law centres.

Advice agencies such as Citizens' Advice Bureaux and Law Centres can also be given contracts to provide Government-funded legal advice. The intention is that the Legal Services Commission should identify areas which lack adequate services and make sure that, so far as finances will allow, each area has provision for legal services.

15.3.2 Community Legal Service website

To help people get legal advice there is a Community Legal Service website (www.justask.org.uk). The Government hopes that by the year 2002 every public library will be online, so that everyone can have access to the website. The website provides a wide range of advice, including how to deal with different types of legal problem. It makes help more accessible for everyone, but especially people living in remote locations, or confined to home by disability.

▶ Comment

Although it is accepted that the previous legal aid scheme was not working properly, there are several worrying features about the new schemes. First, the Community Legal Services Fund is capped with each region having a set budget.

The fact that cases which have a reasonable chance of success do not automatically receive funding is another problem with the new scheme. People who are poor enough to receive help with funding are no longer guaranteed that they can have access to justice. Also the reduction in the numbers of firms of solicitors who have contracts to do publicly funded work means that people may not have services available locally. Fewer outlets may create a problem of access to justice with people unable to have the solicitor of their choice and having to travel a distance to their nearest franchised firm.

Although there will be a website available, many people do not understand the nature of their legal problem so that they do not know what to look up in such a site. The most disadvantaged people in society often have literacy problems and will find trying to

'do-it-yourself' on a website beyond them.

Another problem is that Government funding has been withdrawn from personal injury cases. Someone who has been seriously injured in a car crash or at work needs to be able to get advice and support. Conditional fees do not give enough assistance, even though the new legislation allows claimants to recover insurance premiums. The problems arise because there are heavy costs in preparing such a case. Claimants cannot afford to pay these out. These are items which are not part of the solicitors' fees, but items which have to be paid to other people; matters such as insurance premiums to protect against paying costs if the case is lost and payment of experts (such as doctors) for reports.

15.4 Conditional fees

A major problem in taking a civil case to court is that it is not possible to know in advance exactly how much that case will cost. This is because it is not known how serious the other party is about defending the case. It may be that, once a court case is started, the other side will admit liability and the case will not actually go to court; it will be settled quickly and comparatively cheaply. However, if a case is defended then costs start to rise. Apart from lawyers' fees, there will be expenses of getting evidence, perhaps the cost of an expert's report on the matter, as well as the court fees to pay. In big cases in the High Court, the costs of a case can run to hundreds of thousands of pounds.

If the claimant wins then they should be able to get most of the costs, if not all, back from the defendant. But there is the risk that if the claimant loses the case, then they will have to pay the defendant's costs as well as their own. This uncertainty about the actual

Normal fee	£2,000		
Success fee	£1,000		
Cap on success fee	25%		

Result of case	**Client pays**	
Case is lost	Nothing	
Case is won: Client gets £20,000 damages	£3,000	£2,000 + £1,000
Case is won: Client gets £2,000 damages	£2,500	£2,000 + £500*

*This £500 is because the success fee cannot be more than 25 per cent of the damages.

Figure 15.2 *Illustration of conditional fees*

cost of a case means that for most people taking a court action is too risky, even though they may be advised that they have a very strong case.

Conditional fees agreements were developed in order to help people in this situation. They were first allowed by section 58 of the Courts and Legal Services Act 1990 in personal injury, insolvency and human rights cases. By 1998 the use of conditional fees was extended to all civil cases except family cases. Under the Access to Justice Act 1999 conditional fees form an important part of the Government strategy for funding civil cases.

15.4.1 How conditional fees work

The solicitor and client agree on the fee which would normally be charged for such a case. The agreement also states what the solicitor's 'success fee' will be. This can be an 'uplift' of up to 100 per cent of the agreed normal fee. If the solicitor does not win the case, then the client pays nothing. If the solicitor is successful then the client pays the normal fee plus the success fee. Most solicitors will also include a 'cap' on the success fee, which means that it cannot be more than 25 per cent of the damages which are awarded to the successful claimant. This

is easier to understand by looking at an example.

As the success fee is an extra fee, it used not to be possible for the successful party to claim this from the other side as part of the normal costs of the case. However, the Access to Justice Act 1999 now allows courts to order that the losing party pays the amount of the success fee to the winning party.

In *Callery* v *Gray* the Court of Appeal decided that an after-the-event insurance premium was recoverable by the claimant from the defendant as part of the costs of the case under s 29 Access to Justice Act 1999 even though the policy was taken out in contemplation of proceedings rather than after the issue of proceedings. This extended to Rule 44.12A which enabled pre-action costs to be recovered where an action had been settled before substantive proceedings had been commenced. However, the cost of the premium had to be reasonable.

15.4.2 Insurance premiums

There is still the problem that a person who loses the case will normally be ordered to pay the costs of the other side. To help protect against this it is possible to insure against losing a case. The insurance premium will have to be paid in advance of the case even if the case is eventually won. This can cause problems to people who cannot afford the cost of the premium. There was also the fact that this premium could not be claimed as part of the costs of the case from the other side. This second point has been amended by s 29 of the Access to Justice Act 1999 which allows the court to order that the winning party recovers the cost of insurance premiums from the losing party.

In *Callery* v *Gray* (2001) the court also ruled that a success fee could be recovered where an action had been settled before substantive proceedings had been commenced. But in normal cases the recoverable success fee would be limited to 20 per cent.

The court drew attention to the possible use of a two-stage success fee in cases with a higher success fee where the case did not settle. In such cases an uplift of 100 per cent could be included as the second stage of the success fee.

15.4.3 Are conditional fees working?

Since conditional fee agreements (CFAs) were allowed they have been used in over 50,000 cases for claims for personal injury. This shows that CFAs have allowed a number of people to get access to justice and bring a case which they would probably not have been able to do otherwise.

However, there are still problems. Research in 1998 by Sheffield University found that:

- The poorest clients were not able to afford insurance premiums or disbursements
- Those with risky cases were likely to have to shop around for a solicitor prepared to take on the case
- The amount of work needed to be done on some types of personal injury case, especially from an accident at work, meant that that it

was difficult to estimate the cost, and such cases had cost solicitors more than the 100 per cent uplift fee.

A survey of solicitors in 2001, by accountancy firm BDO Stoy Hayward, suggested that solicitors were becoming more choosy about accepting CFA cases. They usually only accepted them where there was a strong case and a clear opportunity for profit.

Where there is a less certain outcome solicitors preferred such cases to be covered by an insurance policy which would pay both sides' costs.

15.4.4 Claims firms

There are a number of claims firms who negotiate for compensation on behalf of people. These are widely advertised on television. These firms operate the same sort of conditional fee agreement as solicitors. However, some claims firms have been accused of charging very high rates for insurance cover in such claims.

The levels of settlement agreed by claims firms are thought to be lower than if the person had been represented by a solicitor. However, these firms do provide a service to people who would probably not go directly to a lawyer. Also, where the case cannot be settled, the claim firm arranges for legal representation.

15.5 Advice agencies

A number of different advice schemes are available. The main ones are Citizens' Advice Bureaux and law centres. They can apply for contracts to do Government-funded work. However, there are other agencies which offer specialist advice on certain topics, for example the RAC and the AA offer members some help in traffic matters, while Trade

Unions will help members with legal problems, particularly in work-related matters. There are also charities, such as Shelter which offers advice to people with housing problems. About 300 not-for-profit agencies have contracts to do Community Legal Service work.

The legal profession offers assistance with schemes run by solicitors which provide cheap or free advice. In addition solicitors are now allowed to offer a 'conditional fee' service under which they will agree a set fee for a court case, but are entitled to an increased the fee if they win.

Another way of funding a court case is by legal insurance. Most motor insurance policies offer cover (for an additional small amount) for help with legal fees in cases arising from road accidents, and there are policies purely for insurance against legal costs.

15.5.1 Citizens' Advice Bureaux

These were first set up in 1938 and today there are about a thousand throughout the country, with a bureau existing in most towns. They give general advice free to anyone on a variety of issues mostly connected to social welfare problems and debt, but they also advise on some legal matters. They can provide information on which local solicitors do legal aid work or give cheap or free initial interviews. Many have arrangements under which solicitors may attend at the bureau once a week or fortnight to give more qualified advice on legal matters.

The Benson Commission in 1979 emphasised the importance of CABx as a first tier legal advice service and recommended that they should be staffed by 'para-legals' (people who have had some legal training but who are not qualified lawyers) and given more Government funding. This has not happened

so far – funding is still patchy and CABx rely heavily on volunteers. However, there is a training system for these volunteers and many become quite expert in certain fields. The Legal Services Commission has awarded contracts for some CABx to provide Government-funded advice.

15.5.2 Law centres

These offer a free, non-means tested legal service to people in their area. The first law centre opened in North Kensington in 1970. This stated its aims as providing 'a first class solicitor's service to the people . . . a service which is easily accessible, not intimidating, to which they can turn for guidance as they would to their family doctor, or as someone who can afford it would turn to his family solicitor'. Their aim is to provide free legal advice (and sometimes representation) in areas where there are few solicitors.

Funding

Funding is a major problem for law centres. Although the Home Office provides some funding, and some have managed to get financial support from local businesses, law centres are largely reliant on Local Authority funding which is patchy. As a result some have been forced to close.

However, in 2001 there was the largest expansion of law centres for 20 years. This was mainly as a result of funding from the Community Legal Service. Local authorities are still reluctant to fund centres.

Role

Law centres have played a pioneering role in identifying previously unrecognised areas of need and are oriented to the needs of the particular community they serve. The most common areas of work include housing, planning and environment, welfare, problems connected with employment, discrimination, immigration and children's rights. Some centres have set up duty solicitor schemes in the local County Court to deal with housing cases and try to help prevent evictions.

15.5.3 Schemes run by lawyers

Cheap/free interviews

Some solicitors offer an initial interview of about half an hour either free or up to a maximum of £25 on a non-means tested basis. Many solicitors run such a scheme and advertise the fact, both at their offices and in the press and even on the radio. Above there is a photograph of a solicitors' firm showing a such an advert. The local CABx will have a list of solicitors who offer this service and can refer people to these solicitors.

ALAS

This is the Law Society's free Accident Legal Advice Service which is aimed at helping accident victims claim compensation. Solicitors in the scheme will give a free initial interview to advise whether a person has a case worth pursuing. In addition the Law Society has an Accident Line – a freephone telephone service to put accident victims in contact with solicitors who do legal aid personal injury work.

Free Representation Unit

Since 1992 the Bar has set up schemes in different areas, aimed at helping those who are ineligible for legal aid present their case in court. Barristers will represent clients in court at no cost. More than 2,000 cases per year are handled in this way.

15.6 The Criminal Defence Service

Under s 12 of the Access to Justice Act 1999, the Legal Services Commission was required to establish a Criminal Defence Service. This service is aimed at 'securing that individuals involved in criminal investigation or proceedings have access to such advice, assistance and representation as the interests of justice require'. It came into operation in April 2001.

15.6.1 Advice and Assistance

Section 13 of the Access to Justice Act 1999 states that the Commission shall fund such advice and assistance as it considers appropriate for individuals who are arrested and held in custody at a police station or other premises.

There is no means or merits test and the service is free. Local solicitors operate a rota scheme so that, theoretically, there is a 24-hour service under which a solicitor can be contacted by almost every police station. Under the PACE Code of Practice the police must tell a detained person of the scheme. Solicitors who are on duty will either give advice to the detainee by telephone or come to the police station to be present when the police interview the detainee. Suspects do not have to use it, they may choose to pay for their own solicitor.

◀ Comment

In 1989 research by Sanders and others showed that only about 20 per cent of those held in the 10 police stations surveyed received legal advice and that the actual percentage varied very widely between police stations. Later research in 1993 by Sanders found that police officers were likely to try to avoid suspects receiving legal advice by failing to inform them of the duty solicitor scheme, or by not telling them it was free or, where they did inform the suspect of his rights, warning them that it would mean delay or would not be very helpful.

The revised Code of Practice under PACE (see Chapter 8) tackled this problem in two ways. Firstly, posters must be prominently displayed in custody areas of police stations and, secondly, detained persons must be told orally of the availability of the duty solicitor scheme and given a written notice about it. There are also some London police stations which are piloting a scheme of having a solicitor in the station at 'peak' times, so that there is no delay.

In 1997, it was found that the number of people requesting legal advice had risen to 40 per cent.

Another problem found by the Sanders research in 1989 was that duty solicitors often gave advice over the telephone, or attended at the police station briefly giving advice and leaving before the suspect was questioned by the police. Quite often inexperienced young solicitors or unqualified clerks were sent from the solicitors' firms. By 1997 matters had improved, although telephone advice was still used in one in three cases. When a representative went to the police station, that representative was a qualified solicitor in 92 per cent of cases.

15.6.2 Duty solicitors at the Magistrates' Courts

Local solicitors work on a rota basis, attending the court to give advice to unrepresented defendants on their first appearance before the court. The solicitor may also represent a defendant in court but only in limited circumstances; this is mainly where there is a risk of the defendant being held in custody such as:

- Bail applications
- If there is a risk of prison for non-payment of a fine or breach of other order

There is no means or merits test and the defendant is not required to pay any contribution.

The basic test is whether it is in the interests of justice for the defendant to be given legal aid.

15.6.3 Representation

Courts will continue to be able to grant a defendant the right to legal representation in a case, although eventually there will be regulations giving the Legal Services Commission the power to grant rights of representation. When considering whether a defendant should have a legal representative paid by public funding, the test is whether it is in the interests of justice. The five categories to be considered are set out in the Access to Justice Act 1999 and are similar to those previously used for legal aid.

They are:

- Whether the individual would, if any matter arising in the proceedings is decided against him, be likely to lose his liberty or livelihood or suffer serious damage to his reputation
- Whether the determination of any matter arising in the proceedings may involve consideration of a substantial point of law
- Whether the individual may be unable to understand the proceedings or to state his own case
- Whether the proceedings may involve the tracing, interviewing or expert cross-examination of witnesses on behalf of the individual and
- Whether it is in the interests of another person that the individual is represented.

Means test

In 2000–2001 legal aid was granted free in criminal cases where the applicant was on job seekers' allowance, family credit or disability working allowance, or if their disposable income was not more than £52 per week. The disposable capital limit for free legal aid was capital of not more than £3,000. Above these figures a contribution is payable of a third of the excess income each week while the legal aid order is in force, and usually all the excess capital. In fact, only about 5 per cent of defendants pay contributions.

Choice of representative

It is intended that eventually there will be salaried defenders working for the Criminal Defence Service. This raises the point that a defendant will be prosecuted by one Government agency, the Crown Prosecution Service, and defended by another, the Criminal Defence Service. However, the Access to Justice Act does keep a defendant's right to choose an independent lawyer, but only from those whose firms who have a contract with the Legal Services Commission.

Research on the use of a public defender in Scotland

The Public Defence Solicitors' Office (PDSO) has been operating in Edinburgh since October 1998. In order to build up a sufficient volume of casework on which to report, accused people whose birthdays were in January or February were 'directed' to the PDSO and generally could not use 'normal' legal aid through private solicitors.

KEY FACTS

Service	Criteria	Comment
Community Legal Service Fund	• Only for those on low incomes • Case not suitable for funding in another way • In the public interest to fund case	Set budget Not available for personal injury, defamation or malicious prosecution cases Not available for most tribunals
Privately paid lawyer	Can choose any lawyer	Expensive
Conditional fees	Offered by solicitors for money claims, especially personal injury cases	Uplift fee not more than 25 per cent of damages If lose do not pay, but still liable for other side's costs
Criminal Defence Service	• Representation for those on low incomes • Must be in the interests of justice for defendant to be represented	Limited choice of lawyer Advice free to anyone detained at a police station

Figure 15.4 Key fact chart on the funding of cases

Research into the use of the PDSO showed that:

- there was resistance to using the PDSO; 60 per cent of those directed to the PDSO did not use it but used a private solicitor; of these half paid privately to do so, although the others did manage to obtain some form of legal aid;
- defendants represented by the PDSO were more likely to plead guilty at an earlier stage in the proceedings;
- there was less time wasting with the PDSO as for every 100 scheduled 'private' trials 44 did not take place (usually because of a plea or an adjournment) whilst for every 100 PDSO scheduled trials only 31 did not take place;
- 88 per cent of PDSO clients were convicted (including guilty pleas) as against 83 per cent of those represented by a private solicitor;
- client satisfaction was low for the PDSO with only 46 per cent of their defendants saying they would use them again, compared with 83 per cent of those using private firms.

Budget

The funding of criminal cases will continue to be demand led. There will not be a fixed budget. Indeed, if the cost of criminal cases becomes very heavy, then it is possible for funds from the civil budget to be transferred to the criminal budget. This ensures that criminal cases will continue to be funded, but it puts civil cases at risk of losing their funding.

Chapter 16

PROTECTION OF RIGHTS

In some circumstances there may be an infringement of a person's rights which cannot be dealt with by normal civil case procedure. This may be because the problems are caused by a decision against which there is no appeal, or the person may have tried all the normal appeal routes and yet still feel dissatisfied with the outcome. In other cases the complaint may be about delay or poor administration. In these cases there is a need for people's rights to be protected. This chapter looks at three different ways in which citizens are given protection.

16.1 Judicial review

Judicial review is where judges in the High Court are asked to 'review' the decisions (or refusals to make decisions) of inferior courts and tribunals, and also of public bodies and officials. It allows the courts to supervise the workings of a very wide range of decision-making processes.

For example judicial review has been used to challenge the magistrates' decision to dismiss a case against a defendant, when the prosecutor from the Crown Prosecution Service was late arriving at court. This occurred in *R v Hendon Justices, ex parte DPP* (1992) when the CPS had been given a list of cases by the court to be heard which, by mistake, did not include one case in which the CPS was due to prosecute. The CPS rang the court about that 'missing' case, but was told that the court due to hear the case was not sitting. As a result the CPS did not send a lawyer to court. When the case came before the magistrates and they found there was no representative from the CPS present at court, the magistrates dismissed the case against the defendants. In such circumstances there is no actual appeal against the magistrates' decision, but judicial review can be used.

Many applications for judicial review are against decisions of Government departments or ministers or local councils but, judicial review can also be used to challenge the decisions of other bodies. In *Stevenage Borough Football Club Ltd v The Football League Ltd* (1996) Stevenage Football Club used the procedure to try and challenge the refusal of the Football League to admit them to the league. Stevenage had finished top of the GM Vauxhall Football Conference, the league of semi-professional clubs, immediately below the three divisions forming the Football League. This would normally mean that they would be promoted to the third division. However, under the league's rules for promotion, any club being promoted had to show that they had a certain ground capacity and met certain financial criteria. There were set dates for these points, for example the ground capacity was taken as at the end of December of the previous year. Stevenage did not meet the criteria on the set dates, though they had made changes so that by the start date of the new football season (in August 1996) they expected to be able to comply. The league refused to admit Stevenage. The judge hearing the application held that, even though the Football League was an independent body, judicial review could be used against such a decision. The reason for this was that the league was part of the elaborate structure established for the control of professional football, in the interests of the participants and the public generally. Therefore, if the league's rules and decisions were shown to be 'arbitrary or capricious' they were open to review by the courts. However, the judge then ruled against Stevenage because the rules could have been challenged earlier. Stevenage, and all other clubs involved, had accepted them at the beginning of the 1995–96 season. The application for judicial review had been made too late. This case also illustrates that the court has a discretion in judicial review cases.

Lottery decision

In *R v National Lottery Commission, ex parte Camelot Group plc* (2001) the actions of the National Lottery Commission in deciding who should run the lottery were subject to judicial review. The Commission had invited companies to apply for the right to run the lottery. Applications were made by two firms Camelot, who had run the lottery for seven years, and the People's Lottery. The Commission then decided not to continue with the competitive process set out in its invitation to apply, but instead it announced that it would negotiate only with the People's Lottery.

Camelot challenged this decision, claiming that their exclusion was contrary to the principles of fairness and natural justice. The court decided that the Commission's decision was 'conspicuously unfair to Camelot' and ordered that it should be quashed and Camelot given the same opportunity as the People's Lottery to prove that their bid was viable.

This action of judicial review was very important since, when both bids were finally considered, the Commission awarded the right to run the lottery to Camelot.

16.1.1 Definition of 'judicial review'

In *O'Reilly v Mackman* (1982), Lord Diplock stated that:

'Judicial review . . . provides the means by which judicial control of administrative action is exercised. The subject matter of every judicial review is a decision made by some person (or body of persons) or else a refusal by him to make a decision.'

This definition can be seen in action in both the two cases described in the section above.

Judicial review is different from an appeal. An appeal is made on the merits of a case, to the correct appeal court for the particular type of case. Judicial review is concerned with the legality of the decision (or refusal to make a decision), and is always made to the Queen's Bench Division of the High Court.

In some cases it is possible that the matter could be dealt with either by an appeal or by judicial review. For example, both prosecution and defence can appeal by way of case stated, against a decision of the magistrates where it is thought an error of law has been made. However, it is also possible that either side could apply for judicial review on the basis of an error of law, or that the magistrates were acting in excess of their jurisdiction, or had violated the principles of natural justice. Generally, if there is an appeal route available, then that route should be used. Leave to apply for judicial review will only be granted when other appeal routes have been tried, and failed to overturn the decision.

In other cases there will not be any appeal route open, so that judicial review is the only possible way of challenging a decision or a refusal to make a decision. Sometimes this is because the court system does not have an appeal route for the particular situation. This was the position in *R v Hendon Justices, ex parte DPP* (1992), since the only way the prosecution can appeal from an acquittal in the Magistrates' Court is by way of case stated on a point of law. The defendants in the case had been acquitted but the case did not involve a point of law, so the only method of challenging the magistrates' actions was by judicial review.

Where cases are about decisions made by Government departments and local authorities, Lord Woolf has defined the role of judicial review as:

'Judicial review is all about the balance between the rights of the individual to be treated fairly, and the rights of government at a local and national level to do what it has been elected to do.'

16.1.2 Procedure

An applicant must first obtain leave from a single judge in the High Court to apply for judicial review. This application is made without notice to the other side. It has to be made by filing the prescribed form and an affidavit, giving supporting evidence at the court. The judge can then determine the application for leave without a hearing in court – though if the applicant requests a hearing, the judge will hear oral argument of the case. This preliminary stage is designed to filter out cases which have no merit or legal grounds. In *Commissioners of Inland Revenue v National Federation of Self-Employed & Small Business Ltd* (1983) Lord Diplock said: 'it prevents the time of the court being wasted by busybodies with misguided or trivial complaints of administrative error'.

If leave to apply for judicial review is given, then the actual application for judicial review will be heard. This will be normally be by a single judge in the Queen's Bench Division, though cases which involve criminal law will be heard by two or three judges sitting in the Queen's Bench Divisional Court. There is an appeal against decisions to the Court of Appeal, and from there to the House of Lords.

If leave to apply for judicial review is not given, then an application can be made to the Court of Appeal. If the Court of Appeal decides that the application should be granted, then it may hear the case, or it may be referred back to the Queen's Bench Division.

Time limits

The normal time limit for bringing an application for leave to apply for judicial review is three months from the decision. However, the court has a wide discretion on the matter and can allow applications to be made after the three months has expired. Equally, even if the application is made within the three months, the court may decide that the application was such that it should have been made more quickly than it actually was, and refuse leave to apply for judicial review. This was the position in the Stevenage Football club case.

Number of applications

There has been a rapid growth in the use of judicial review as a way of challenging official decisions. In 1980 there were only 525 applications for leave to apply for judicial review, whereas in 2000 there were over 4,200. About half of the applications in 2000 were on immigration matters.

16.1.3 *Locus standi*

Only people with sufficient interest in the decision can bring an application for judicial review. This is set out in s 31(3) of the Supreme Court Act 1981 which states that the court shall not grant leave to make application for judicial review unless 'it considers that the applicant has a sufficient interest in the matter to which the application relates'.

In many cases there is no difficulty about this. For example in the Stevenage Football club case, the club clearly had 'sufficient interest' as the decision affected their chances of promotion. In other cases the person bringing the case may not be so directly affected, but they may not be able to show that they have 'sufficient interest'. The leading case on this is *Commissioners of Inland Revenue v National Federation of Self-Employed & Small Businesses Ltd* (1983) (usually known as the Fleet Street Casuals case). In this case an application for judicial review was made by the National Federation of Self-Employed & Small Businesses Ltd, a taxpayers' association, who wished to challenge an agreement made by the Inland Revenue waiving the back tax of 6,000 freelance workers in the printing industry. The Inland Revenue was faced with a long-standing problem of the Fleet Street casuals who were paid without tax being deducted, and who evaded tax by supplying fictitious names and addresses (such as Mickey Mouse of Sunset Boulevard) when drawing their pay. The Inland Revenue agreed that, if the casuals registered with the tax authorities and submitted tax returns for the previous two years, then the Inland Revenue would not investigate tax evasion prior to those two years.

The National Federation of Self-Employed & Small Businesses Ltd applied for judicial review, asking for a declaration that the Inland Revenue had acted unlawfully in declaring the amnesty, and also asking that the Revenue be ordered to assess and collect all the tax due from the Fleet Street casuals. The Inland Revenue opposed the application on the ground that the federation did not have a 'sufficient interest' in the matter. The House of Lords held that the federation did not have *locus standi*, as the tax affairs of other people were confidential between the tax authorities and the taxpayer.

However, the courts have widened the scope of *locus standi* in some cases, to allow pressure groups and interest groups to make an application. For example, in *R v Secretary*

of State, ex parte Equal Opportunities Commission (1994) it was held that the Equal Opportunities Commission did have *locus standi* to bring proceedings for the purpose of determining whether the Secretary of State had acted in breach of European Community law, by deciding not to take steps to reduce, or distinguish, discrimination between men and women on the issue of part-time workers.

The Attorney-General is always entitled to bring an action for judicial review and, if a party has failed to establish *locus standi*, the Attorney-General can choose to permit the action to proceed by means of what is called a 'Realtor action'.

16.1.4 Principles on which judicial review operates

Judicial review is a review of the legality of a decision, and will only be granted if it is shown that the public body involved had gone beyond the powers given to it. This is the *ultra vires* principle. *Ultra vires* means 'beyond the powers' and the courts will consider applications on the basis that a decision had been made without the correct procedure being followed (procedural *ultra vires*), or the ground that the public body had, in law, no authority to make the decision it did (substantive *ultra vires*). This second head would be a very narrow one, but it has been widened by the courts being prepared to rule that a decision is so unreasonable that it is *ultra vires*.

In *Council of Civil Service Unions v Minister for the Civil Service* (1984) the grounds on which an administrative action is subject to control by judicial review were summarised as being:

* **Illegality** where the public authority has made an error of law
* **Irrationality** where the authority has acted so

unreasonably that no reasonable authority would have made the decision (these first two are substantive *ultra vires*)

- **Procedural irregularity** where the authority has failed in its duty to act according to standard procedure, or has breached the rules of natural justice (procedural *ultra vires*)

Substantial *ultra vires*

In some situations the courts have ruled that a decision or action has gone beyond the powers given, so that it is actually illegal. This occurred in *Bromley London Borough Council* v *Greater London Council* (1982) where it was held that the Greater London Council had acted *ultra vires* in issuing a supplemental rate precept to London boroughs, in order to finance cheap fares in London.

Unreasonable

In other cases the challenge is on the ground that the decision was unreasonable. This principle on which the courts will intervene to prevent or remedy an abuse of power by public authorities comes from *Associated Provincial Picture Houses* v *Wednesbury Corporation* (1948). In that case it was said that a decision would be held to be *ultra vires* where it was so unreasonable that no reasonable public body could have reached the same decision. In *Council of Civil Service Unions* v *Minister for the Civil Service* (1984) it was said that it had to be 'a decision which is so outrageous in its defiance of logic or of accepted moral standards that no sensible person . . . could have arrived at it'.

Proportionality

In *R* v *Secretary of State for the Home Department, ex parte Daly* (2001) the House of Lords decided that in judicial review cases of decisions by public authorities where European Convention Rights are involved, the traditional grounds of review should be replaced by a doctrine of proportionality.

Most cases would be likely to be decided in the same way, but the intensity of review is somewhat greater under the proportionality approach.

Lord Steyn pointed out first that the doctrine of proportionality may require the reviewing court to assess the balance which the decision-maker has struck, and not merely whether it is in the range of rational or reasonable decisions. Secondly, the proportionality test may go further than the traditional grounds of review, in as much as it may require attention to be directed to the relative weight accorded to interests and considerations. Thirdly, even the heightened scrutiny test developed in *Smith* (the 'gays in the military' case) is not necessarily appropriate to the protection of human rights.

In this last point Lord Steyn was acknowledging that the European Court of Human Rights ruled that there was a breach of Article 13 (right to an effective remedy) in the *Smith* case because of the limitations of the judicial review test.

The courts have gradually extended the circumstances in which this principle of unreasonableness will operate. It includes where there is an abuse of power by using those powers for an improper purpose. In *R* v *Derbyshire County Council, ex parte The Times Supplements* (1990) *The Times* challenged Derbyshire County Council's decision to stop advertising its educational posts in *Times* publications, after the *Sunday Times* had published two articles accusing the council of improper and legally dubious behaviour. The Queen's Bench Divisional Court held that the council had been motivated by bad faith and vindictiveness and this was an abuse of power.

Procedural *ultra vires*

This principle was seen in Chapter 3 (section 3.2.3) in delegated legislation in the

Aylesbury Mushroom case (1972). In that case the Minister of Labour had not carried out the correct procedure because he had not consulted the mushroom growers' association as required. As a result an order establishing a training board was invalid against mushroom growers.

However, the courts have also ruled that an order or decision can be procedurally *ultra vires* where there is a breach of natural justice. The main rules of natural justice are that no person is allowed to act as a judge in a case in which he or she has an interest, and that both sides must be given a chance to explain their side of any matter before a decision is made.

The first of these is set out in a Latin phrase, *nemo judex in causa sua*. This principle was applied in *R v Altringham Justices, ex parte Pennington* (1975) where the chairman of the lay bench of magistrates was also on local education committees as well as being a governor of two schools. A case came before the bench in which the defendants were charged with supplying short weight on vegetables to local schools. It was held that it was a breach of natural justice for the chairman of the bench to try the case, as he had an interest in the matter. The Queen's Bench Divisional Court quashed the conviction holding that there was a risk of bias and said that 'there is no better rule than the one that a man shall not be a judge in his own cause'.

The second rule of natural justice that both sides should be allowed to put their side of the case is also contained in a Latin phrase, *audi alteram partem*. It is illustrated by the case of *Ridge v Baldwin* (1964) in which Chief Constable Ridge, was dismissed from his post, following a trial for conspiracy to obstruct the course of justice in which he had been acquitted, though the trial judge had severely criticised his behaviour. The Brighton Watch Committee which had dismissed him did so without giving him a chance to defend himself. The House of Lords held that this was a breach of natural justice. Ridge should have been told what was alleged against him and allowed to put his side of the matter.

16.1.5 Remedies

The High Court has three prerogative orders that can be used where an application for judicial review is successful: *certiorari*, *mandamus* and prohibition. As well as these three remedies, the court can also issue a declaration or an injunction and awarded damages.

The prerogative orders

These come originally from the idea that the monarch had the right to control the operations of their officials. The courts have retained these rights in the name of the Crown. They are public law remedies whereas declarations, injunctions and damages are private law remedies.

1. **Certiorari** stands for *certiorari volumus* which means 'we wish to be informed' and it is an order which is used to bring a decision of an inferior body before the High Court so that its legality can be examined. If the decision is found to be *ultra vires* then the decision can be quashed. This is the order that was used in the Bromley Council case; it was also used *R v Hendon Justices, ex parte DPP* which is set out at the beginning of this chapter.
2. **Mandamus** means 'we command' and it is an order to do something. It can be an order to hear a case, for example a housing appeal that a tribunal had previously refused to hear, or it can be an order to do something such as produce accounts. It is often used with *certiorari*. The order of *certiorari* quashes the unlawful decision, and the order for *mandamus* orders that the powers be used properly.

3. **Prohibition** is an order not to do something. It is used to prevent a public body from acting unlawfully in the future. For example it was used in *R v Telford Justices, ex parte Badham* (1991) in order to prevent the magistrates from holding committal proceedings in respect of allegations of rape that had only been reported 15 years after the alleged event. The Queen's Bench Divisional Court held that the delay in the case made the committal proceedings an abuse of the process of the court.

16.1.6 Criticisms of judicial review proceedings

Need for leave to apply

In order to be able to apply for judicial review it is necessary to make an application for leave to apply. No other court action requires leave and it can be seen as a discouragement to ordinary people who wish to pursue their rights. However, it does prevent pointless applications from wasting the courts' time. The time limit of three months placed on the application for leave is also unusual and it could be argued that it is too short a time. In other cases the parties have longer time limits in which to start proceedings – often people are not aware of their rights and may not immediately realise that an application for judicial review is available to them. Against this, it is true that the courts have a discretion to allow an application for leave after the strict time limit, but the situations in which the courts will exercise their discretion are not clearly defined.

The *Wednesbury* principles of unreasonableness

In many cases it is difficult to show that a decision is so unreasonable that no reasonable public body could have come to

it. This principle also leaves a large discretion to the judge in the individual case. This was shown by a study in 1993 by the Public Law Project in which over 4,000 cases in the period 1987–89 were studied. It was shown that leave was granted by judges regarded as 'liberal' in 82 per cent of the cases they heard, whereas judges regarded as 'conservative' had only granted leave in 21 per cent of cases.

Possibly the use of the proportionality approach may improve matters.

Political role of judges

Many cases are challenges to a decision made by a Government minister or a local council and, therefore, will often have a political element involved. This means that the judiciary are required to make 'political' decisions. There is conflict even among the judges as to their powers in such situations. In *R v Home Secretary, ex parte Fire Brigades Union* (1995) Lord Keith said:

> 'The fact that the decision is of a political and administrative character means that any interference by a court of law would be a most improper intrusion into a field which lies peculiarly within the province of Parliament. The Secretary of State is unquestionably answerable to Parliament for any failure in his responsibilities.'

However, in the same case Lord Lloyd said that the duty to review executive action 'does not depend on some power granted by Parliament in a particular case. It is part of the court's ordinary function in the day-to-day administration of justice'.

There is also the accusation that judges are biased in favour of the Conservative policies and are less willing to interfere with decisions made by Conservative executives. This can be supported by cases such as *R v Boundary Commission for England, ex parte Foot* (1983) in which the former leader of the

KEY FACTS

Definition	The means by which judicial control of administrative action is exercised Also used to review and supervise decisions of inferior courts and tribunals
Procedure	Two stages: 1 Application for leave to apply for judicial review; made without informing the other side; should be made within three months of action complained about 2 If leave is granted, then an application for judicial review is made and court hears case (criminal cases are usually heard by Queen's Bench Divisional Court; all other cases usually heard by single judge in Queen's Bench Division of High Court)
Locus standi	Applicant must have 'sufficient interest in the matter to which the application relates'
Principles on which judicial review is granted	1 Procedural *ultra vires* – this is where correct procedure has not been carried out (*Aylesbury Mushroom case*) OR the rules of natural justice have been breached (*Ridge* v *Baldwin*) 2 Substantive *ultra vires* – illegality i.e. decision is beyond legal powers (*Bromley LBC* v *GLC*) OR irrationality i.e. the decision is so unreasonable that no reasonable body could have reached it (*Wednesbury principles*) OR the proportionality approach in human rights cases
Remedies	Public law – *Mandamus*; Prohibition; *Certiorari* Private law – Declaration; injunction; damages

Figure 16.1 *Key fact chart on judicial review*

Labour party, Michael Foot, tried to challenge the recommendations of the Boundary Commission for changes to the boundaries of electoral constituencies, as being unjust. His application was rejected.

However, increasingly during the 1990s, there have been cases in which the judiciary has ruled against ministers of the Conservative Government. The case of *R* v *Home Secretary, ex parte Fire Brigades Union* (1995) is an example. In that case it was ruled that the Home Secretary had acted *ultra vires* in making changes to the criminal injuries compensation scheme. In 1997 in *R* v *Lord Chancellor, ex parte*

Witham, the courts ruled that the Lord Chancellor did not have the right to withdraw the exemptions from paying court fees from people on state benefits.

16.2 Ombudsmen

In some situations a citizen may feel aggrieved by the way a matter has been handled by the administration, but there are no suitable court proceedings which can be taken. In such circumstances it may be possible to complain to an 'ombudsman'. This idea of a post to deal with complaints, originated in Scandinavian countries. The first ombudsman appointed in the United Kingdom was the Parliamentary Commissioner for Administration, who investigates complaints about Government departments. Since the creation of that position there have been other posts created to deal with complaints about: the administration of local authorities, the Health Service, the legal services and the prison service. The concept has also spread to the private sector so that other service industries such as banking and insurance now appoint their own 'ombudsmen'.

16.2.1 The Parliamentary Commissioner

The Parliamentary Commissioner Act 1967 created the post of Parliamentary Commissioner for Administration, who is known as the Ombudsman. He is appointed by the Crown on the advice of the Prime Minister. The Ombudsman's responsibility is to investigate complaints about maladministration by Government departments and agencies. This covers matters for which judicial review would not be available, such as rudeness, inefficiency or unreasonable delay in making decisions. Individuals cannot complain direct to the Ombudsman; they must instead complain to their Member of Parliament, who will then decide if the matter should be referred to the Ombudsman for him to investigate. Complaints should be made within 12 months of the incident complained of, although the Ombudsman has discretion to consider complaints made after this time limit.

The need to refer a complaint to one's MP rather than go direct to the Ombudsman has been criticised. It means that complainants have yet another hurdle to get over before their complaint is dealt with. Even the Parliamentary Commissioner himself has said that he would prefer to be able to receive complaints direct from the public. The present Commissioner, William Reid, has pointed out that of the 650 MPs there are 150 who have not referred a single complaint to him. This suggests that some complaints may not be getting through.

The Ombudsman is restricted in the type of complaint that he can investigate. In particular he will not consider any complaint where the complainant could take proceedings through a court or a tribunal, although there is some discretion for the Ombudsman to investigate if it would be unreasonable to expect the complainant to use an alternative route.

There are also restrictions in that the Parliamentary Commissioner cannot deal with complaints about the investigation of crime, or the conduct of any legal proceedings – he can investigate complaints of maladministration by administrative staff of courts and tribunals. This would cover, for example, complaints that court staff had lost files. The Ombudsman cannot deal with matters connected with national industries, or with complaints about international organisations or actions taken by Crown officials outside the United Kingdom.

Investigation of complaints

Once the Ombudsman has accepted that the complaint is suitable for him to investigate, he has power to order witnesses to attend to be questioned or to produce documents. Anyone who refuses to comply with an order of the Ombudsman and deliberately obstructs the investigation, may be treated as though in contempt of court and fined or imprisoned. Once the investigation is completed, the Ombudsman submits a report both to the Member of Parliament who raised the issue with him and to the Government office or agency which was the subject of the investigation. About 1,000 complaints are dealt with each year and about 90 per cent of these are found to be fully or partly justified.

The Ombudsman can only make recommendations, he cannot change a decision or even enforce his own recommendations. However, if his recommendations are ignored he may submit a further report to both Houses of Parliament highlighting the continuing areas of maladministration. The hope is that this further report will cause members of Parliament to place pressure on the appropriate minister to ensure that his department follows the recommendations. The Ombudsman also makes an annual report to Parliament.

The type of matter investigated by the Parliamentary Commissioner is shown by the report on the Child Support Agency published in January 1995. Complaints were referred to the Ombudsman by 95 MPs and investigations were made into 70 of those complaints. The report concentrated on just seven complaints which were representative of the majority. These complaints were about mistakes made by the Agency in wrongly identifying people as 'absent' fathers; failures to answer correspondence; delays in assessing and reviewing maintenance payments; and giving wrong and/or misleading information and advice. The Ombudsman found that the Agency was liable for maladministration, inexcusable delays and very poor service.

The report led to the chief executive of the Agency writing to the Ombudsman saying that steps were being taken to deal with the matters highlighted in the report. The junior Minister for Social Security also promised alterations to the Agency mode of working in order to improve quality, accuracy and customer service. From this it can be seen that reports by the Parliamentary Commissioner are taken seriously, even though there is no compulsion to act on the recommendations.

16.2.2 Commissioners for Local Administration

Since 1974 there have also been Ombudsmen appointed to investigate complaints of maladministration against local authorities. There are three such Ombudsmen for England, each covering a different area, and another for Wales. The posts were established by the Local Government Act 1974.

As with the Parliamentary Commissioner, these ombudsmen will not investigate any complaint where the matter can be resolved by a court or tribunal. The local authority involved must be given a chance to solve the problem, before the local ombudsman will accept a complaint as suitable for investigation. There are also restrictions on the types of complaint that can be investigated; in particular, local commissioners will not deal with a complaint about something which affects all or most of the local inhabitants, such as the level of the council tax.

Where the local ombudsmen decide that a complaint is within their jurisdiction, they then have the power to investigate it and report on it. The report is sent to the local authority involved and must also be made available to the public. However, the ombudsman can only make recommendations; like the Parliamentary Commissioner, they cannot change decisions or even enforce their own recommendations. Where recommendations are ignored, the local ombudsmen can make further reports, but their effectiveness is likely to rest on the amount of publicity and pressure group activity generated. If a local council refuses to adopt the recommendations there is nothing that can be done.

16.2.3 Other ombudsmen

There are now ombudsmen to deal with specialist areas; some of these posts have been created by statute. For example, the Courts and Legal Services Act 1990 created the Legal Services Ombudsman who investigates complaints about members of the legal profession, where the complaint has been unable to get a satisfactory response from the relevant professional body. This ombudsman is considered in more detail in section 12.1.3 (complaints against solicitors) and in section 12.2.3 (complaints against barristers).

There is also the Health Service Ombudsman who investigates complaints about the National Health Service. Any complaint must first be made locally to the hospital, clinic or surgery. Only if the complainant is not happy with the way in which the complaint has been dealt with, can the matter be referred to the Health Service Ombudsman. As with other ombudsmen, there are restrictions on the types of complaint that can be investigated. In particular, a complaint which could be taken to court or a tribunal will not be investigated. Other matters that cannot be investigated include personnel disputes over job appointments, pay or discipline. Following any investigation by the Health Service Ombudsman, a report is sent to the complaint and to the NHS body involved. Again there is no power to enforce any recommendations made by the ombudsman.

There is also a European Ombudsman, a post created by the Treaty of Rome. This Ombudsman is appointed by the European Parliament and investigates maladministration by European Union institutions. It is possible to make a complaint direct to the European Ombudsman, or to have it referred by an Member of the European Parliament, or the ombudsman may decide to investigate on his or her own initiative.

Certain businesses have also established their own ombudsmen, so that it is possible to complain about institutions such as banks, building societies and insurance companies.

However, there is the same problem, as with all ombudsmen, that their recommendations cannot be enforced. In addition some of these 'in-house' ombudsmen are felt not to be sufficiently independent from the industry they are investigating.

16.3 The European Convention on Human Rights

Up to 1998 the United Kingdom did not have a Bill of Rights which gives its citizens the right to certain basic freedoms. However as early as 1950 the United Kingdom Government signed the European Convention on Human Rights. This Convention was drawn up after the Second World War in order to try to protect people's rights from the abuses that had been seen under Hitler's rule of Germany, and followed the Universal Declaration on Human Rights made by the General Assembly of the United Nations in 1948. The Convention in its Articles sets out the rights and freedoms that the people of Europe are entitled to expect.

The Convention was adopted by the Council of Europe in 1950. The Council of Europe was formed in 1949 and is not part of the present European Union, but a separate international organisation – it has a bigger membership than the European Union, covering most European countries. During the 1990s the membership has grown rapidly, with countries from Eastern Europe joining. There are now over 40 Member States.

Although the United Kingdom signed the Convention, it was not part of our law until October 2000 when the Human Rights Act 1998 came into effect (see section 16.3.5).

In the past the Convention has been considered by our courts. In *R v Secretary of*

State for the Home Department, ex parte Brind (1990), the Court of Appeal said that an international treaty such as the European Convention 'does not directly affect the domestic law of this country'. However, the court did recognise that in some instances English law should be interpreted in line with the Convention. In *Brind* the Court of Appeal said that there was a presumption that where an Act of Parliament was ambiguous, it was to be interpreted in a 'manner which was consistent with the United Kingdom's treaty obligations'.

However, in the same case they said that this did not apply to delegated legislation or executive action taken by a minister under an enabling Act if the enabling Act was clear. They ruled that the Secretary of State had acted lawfully in banning broadcasts by members of Sinn Fein, a legitimate political party in Northern Ireland, holding that the Broadcasting Act 1981 gave him clear authority to make such directions, and his power to do this did not have to be interpreted in line with the European Convention on Human Rights.

We will now go on to consider the key Articles of the Convention and situations in which the United Kingdom has been held to be in breach of some of those Articles.

16.3.1 The right to life and liberty

Article 2 of the Convention states that everyone's right to life shall be protected by law, although it does recognise that States have the right to impose the death penalty for those convicted of certain crimes. Article 3 states that no-one shall be tortured, or suffer inhuman or degrading treatment or punishment. The United Kingdom has been found to be in breach of this Article in respect of the way that prisoners in Northern Ireland were treated during interrogation. Article 4 declares that slavery is not allowed.

Article 5 sets out that everyone has the right to liberty and that no-one shall be deprived of his liberty, except where the law allows arrest or detention. Even in these cases, the arrested person has the right to be told of the reason for the detention. Article 5(4) provides that 'everyone who is deprived of his liberty by arrest or detention shall be entitled to take proceedings by which the lawfulness of his detention shall be speedily decided by a court'. This includes those who have been given a custodial sentence, and in most cases this right is satisfied by the fact that there is the possibility of an appeal against conviction and/or sentence. However, the United Kingdom was held to be in breach of this article because the date of the release of young offenders convicted of murder used to be decided by the Home Secretary and not by a court.

16.3.2 The right to a fair hearing

Article 5 is backed up by Article 6 which states that people have the right to a fair and public hearing within a reasonable time (this is so for both civil and criminal cases). On the reasonable time element the European Court of Human Rights in *Darnell v United Kingdom* (1993) held that the United Kingdom was in breach of the Article. The case involved a question of whether a doctor had been unfairly dismissed. The dismissal had taken place in 1984 and proceedings started soon afterwards, but the final decision of the Employment Appeal Tribunal on the case had not been made until 1993.

In *Sander v United Kingdom* (2000) the European Court of Human Rights ruled that a defendant had not had a fair trial and there was a breach of Article 6. During the trial one of the jurors had written a note to the judge raising concern over the fact that other jurors had been making openly racist remarks and jokes. The judge asked the jury to 'search their consciences'. The next day the judge received two letters, one signed by all the jurors in which they denied any racist attitudes and a second letter from one juror who admitted that he may have been the one making the jokes. The judge allowed the case to continue with the same jury.

The European Court of Human Rights held that the facts should have alerted the judge to the fact that there was something fundamentally wrong and he should have discharged the jury. Allowing the trial to continue in the circumstances was an infringement of the right to a fair trial.

Article 7 states that no-one shall be found guilty of a criminal offence if his act was not a crime at the time he committed it. This means that the law is not allowed to change retrospectively; in other words, the law may be altered so as to make future acts of the type prohibited criminal offences, but it cannot look back to acts that have already been committed and declare that those are now criminal. However, in *R v R* (1991) a man was convicted of marital rape when the House of Lords overruled a previous precedent which had held that this was not a crime. R challenged this decision in the European Court of Human Rights, but that court decided that there had not been a breach of Article 7 because the law had changed in an earlier case to allow a man to be convicted of raping his wife when they were legally separated.

16.3.3 Other freedoms

Article 8 states that every person has a right to respect of his private and family life, his home and his correspondence. Although English law does give some protection to homes under the law of tort, and there is also protection of correspondence, there is no general right in English law to privacy. There have been many incidents where people with a high public profile, such as the Royal family, sports personalities, film and television stars have suffered from media intrusion into their private lives.

Privacy and respect of family life

Since the Human Rights Act has come into force, courts in the United Kingdom have taken a more positive attitude towards the right to privacy. In *Douglas and others v Hello! Ltd* (2001) the Court of Appeal had to consider whether there was a breach of Article 8 when Hello! magazine published unauthorised pictures of the wedding of Michael Douglas and Catherine Zeta-Jones. The court stated that there was a right to privacy but it had to balanced against the right to freedom of expression under Article 10. However, the court refused to make an injunction preventing *Hello!* from publishing the pictures. This refusal was mainly because Douglas and Zeta-Jones were prepared to have publicity of their wedding and had actually agreed that another magazine could publish pictures.

Article 8 can be quite wide in its application as seen in *Hatton v United Kingdom* (2001). In this case the European Court of Human Rights ruled that the increase in the level of noise caused by aircraft using Heathrow airport was a breach of the right to respect for the applicants private and family lives.

Other freedoms

Under Article 9 everyone has the right to freedom of thought, conscience and religion, while Article 10 states that everyone has the right to freedom of expression (this is the principle of freedom of speech). Article 11 also states that people have the right to freedom of peaceful assembly, and to freedom of association with others. This right includes the freedom to join trade unions.

Article 14 says that all the rights and freedoms should exist without any discrimination on any ground such as sex, race, colour, language, religion, political or other opinion, national or social origin, national minority, property, birth or status.

16.3.4 European Court of Human Rights

The European Court of Human Rights was established in 1959, in order to protect the rights set out in the European Convention on Human Rights. This court must not be confused with the European Court of Justice, which is one of the institutions of the European Union. The European Court of Human Rights sits at Strasbourg and deals only with breaches of the European Convention on Human Rights.

Member States can report another Member State to the court for apparent breaches of the Convention, though this has only happened on a handful of occasions. Individuals have the right to make an application to the court. The numbers doing so rose sharply during the 1980s and 1990s. In 1981 only 404 applications were made, but by 1997, there were 4,750 applications. Most, however, were ruled inadmissible, so that in 1997 only 119 cases were actually referred to the court.

Up to November 1998, there was a separate Commission on Human Rights which investigated the complaint and decided if the case should go to the court. With the increase in cases, this became too slow a process, so the Commission was abolished and the court became larger. The court now has 40 judges and sits full-time in a new building in Strasbourg.

Under this new system, individuals who feel that their rights have been breached by their State apply direct to the court. A Chamber of the court, consisting of a committee of three judges, decides if the complaint is admissible and, if it decides that it is, the Government of the State concerned is asked for its comments. There is then the possibility of the State and the complainant coming to a friendly negotiated settlement, but if this does not occur, then the court will hear the case in full and give a judgment on it. As well as deciding whether a state has breached the Convention, the court has the power to award compensation or other 'just satisfaction' to a successful complaint.

If the court upholds a complaint and rules against a state, that decision is final, but there is no method of forcing the member state to comply with that ruling. However, most states tend to accept the rulings. In an extreme situation it is technically possible for the Council of Europe to expel members who breach the Convention.

Complaints against the United Kingdom

Since 1966 the United Kingdom has accepted the right of an individual to petition the European Court of Human Rights. In the 30 years to 1996 the court heard 80 cases against the United Kingdom – this is more than against any other country except Italy. In 41 of the 80 cases the court found that the United Kingdom was guilty of violating human rights. The cases have involved a wide range of topics, including freedom of speech, the right to privacy, immigration rules, corporal punishment, and the rights of suspects and prisoners. Cases have led to the British Government changing the law in a variety of areas. For example, corporal punishment has been outlawed in state-run schools, terrorism suspects are now given quicker access to legal advice, and the Home Secretary can no longer set minimum jail sentences for young offenders.

The first case brought by an individual against the Government was *Golder* v *United Kingdom* (1975). Golder was a convicted prisoner who, because of the Prison Rules, had not been allowed to send confidential letters to a solicitor, nor to bring an action against a prison officer. He complained that this was in breach of Article 8 as it infringed his right to privacy of correspondence, and also a breach of Article 6 which guarantees the right to a fair hearing. The court held that the Prison Rules did breach both Articles and as a result of this ruling the British Government changed the Prison Rules.

Although some of the decisions of the court have led to the British Government changing its law, the changes have not always improved people's rights. In *Malone* v *United Kingdom* (1984) the complaint was about telephone tapping by the police and alleged that there had been a breach of Article 8 giving the right to privacy. The relevant part of the Article says:

> 'There shall be no interference by a public authority with the exercise of this right except as is in accordance with the law and is necessary in a democratic society in the interests of national security.'

The court held that there was a breach of the Article because there was no set law on telephone tapping in the United Kingdom, but the police operated under 'guidelines' on a discretionary basis. The telephone tapping had, therefore, not been 'in accordance with the law'. Following this decision Parliament passed the Interception of Communications Act 1985 under which telephone tapping can only be used where the Home Secretary has issued a warrant. This means that tapping can still take place but it is now regulated by the law.

In *Abdulaziz* v *United Kingdom* (1985) the European Court of Human Rights ruled that there was a breach of Article 14 in that the British immigration rules discriminated against women. Men who were permanently settled in the UK were allowed to bring their wives and fiancées to join them in this country, but women in the same situation were not allowed to bring their husbands or

fiancés to live here. The British Government reacted to this by changing the law so that there was no discrimination. However, this was not a change which increased human rights as the new rules prevented both men and women from bringing their partners.

On some occasions the Government has refused to change the law. This happened following the case of *Brogan* v *United Kingdom* (1988) in which the European Court ruled that the provisions of the Prevention of Terrorism (Temporary Provisions) Act 1984 were a violation of Article 5. The Act allowed suspected terrorists to be detained for up to seven days and the court held that this length of time breached the right to be brought before a judge promptly. The Government declared that the power to detain suspected terrorists for up to seven days was necessary in the interests of national security and refused to change the law.

Recent decisions of the European Court have held that the UK has been in breach of Article 10 (the right to freedom of expression) by requiring a journalist to disclose his source of information. This was decided in *Goodwin* v *United Kingdom* (1996). In December 1999 the European Court of Human Rights ruled that there had been breaches of Articles 5 and 6 in the case of Venables and Thompson (the two boys who killed two year old James Bulger). The method of trial in an adult court had violated Article 6, the right to a fair trial, as the boys could not effectively participate in the proceedings.

The court said that the formality and the ritual of the Crown Court must at times have seemed incomprehensible and intimidating for a child aged 11.

Article 5 had been breached because the tariffs for the sentences of the two boys had been fixed by the Home Secretary, who was not independent of the Government. In

addition, there had been no opportunity for the sentences to be reviewed over the years by a judicial body such as the Parole Board to decide whether the boys were still a danger to the public. This made their continuing detention unlawful.

16.3.5 The Human Rights Act 1998

This Act came into effect in October 2000. It incorporates the European Convention on Human Rights into British law and makes it unlawful for a public authority to act in a way which is incompatible with a Convention right. The Act also states that courts in England and Wales have to interpret legislation in a way that is compatible with the Convention.

This appears very wide-ranging protection as 'public authority' is defined as including courts as well as any person who has some public functions. However, there is a major limitation since 'public authority' does not include either House of Parliament or a person exercising functions in connection with proceedings in Parliament. This appears to mean that Parliament and government ministers may disregard the Convention.

Individual rights

The Act provides that a person whose rights are violated by a public authority will be able to take court action. Where an individual establishes that one of their rights has been breached, the court will be able to make any order it considers just and appropriate. However, a court can only award damages if the court is satisfied that it is necessary 'to afford just satisfaction'.

The Act in operation

Judicial review cases increased in the months immediately after the Act was brought into force. A number of cases now coming before the courts involve human rights points, although it is rarely the only issue in the case. Decisions have been made on human rights in a number of areas of law. The two main areas in which human rights points have been raised are criminal law and immigration, but there have also been issues in many other areas, for example, planning law, consumer credit and even ecclesiastical law.

Judges are required to interpret legislation, so far as possible, in a way which is compatible with the rights set out in the European convention on Human Rights. This has had an impact on statutory interpretation, with the judges in some cases interpreting Acts in a very wide manner (see section 3.3.11).

Incompatible legislation

Although courts have to read legislation and give it effect in a way which is compatible with the rights set out in the European Convention, the Act recognises that some legislation may be worded in such a way that it is impossible to give effect to the Convention. If this is so the court must apply the legislation as it stands but may make a declaration that the legislation is incompatible with the Convention. The Act then gives Government ministers the power to amend the legislation to bring it into line with the Convention. Any such amendment must be approved by Parliament. This, of course, will not help the person who is complaining that their rights have been breached, though it does mean that in the future other peoples' rights will not be breached.

The first case in which an Act was declared incompatible with Convention rights was *H v Mental Health Review Tribunal* (2001). This case concerned the fact that the burden of proof was on a patient making an application for release rather than being on the state to justify the continuing detention of the patient. As this involved the liberty of the subject it was a breach of Article 5. However, the domestic law was incompatible with the Convention and so the court could not give effect to the rights. It could only declare that the law was incompatible.

There is also the problem that the Government minister reviewing an incompatible act does not have to amend it. After the declaration of incompatibility in *H v Mental Health Review Tribunal* (2001) the Government has stated that it would change the law. However, there is no need for the Government to do so. In fact, if Parliament wishes it can deliberately pass new legislation which contravenes the Convention.

APPENDIX 1

Hints on some of the activities

This appendix gives help with the activities on pages 6, 61, and 214.

Distinguishing between civil and criminal cases (page 6)
Question 1 (Answers)
Sources A, B and D are civil cases. Sources C and E are criminal cases. This information helps with the remainder of the questions in the activity.

Statutory interpretation and the case of *Fisher* v *Bell* (page 61).
The court used the literal rule in coming to the decision in this case. The court considered the technical legal meaning of 'offer for sale' and said that this was the correct literal legal meaning. This meant that displaying knives in the window was not offering them for sale, so it was decided that the knives in the window were not 'offered for sale', neither were they actually sold or hired or lent, so the shopkeeper had not committed an offence and was found not guilty.

Judges' titles (page 214)
Judges in the House of Lords are referred to as 'Lord . . .', for example Lord Bridge.

Judges in the Court of Appeal are referred to as 'Lord Justice . . .' or the initials LJ are written after their name, for example Lord Justice Rose or Rose LJ. Sometimes in law reports where two or three Lords Justices have sat to decide a case, all their surnames will be written followed by LJJ, for example Auld, Butler-Sloss and Rose LJJ.

For the Lord Chief Justice, the full title is used or it is abbreviated to LCJ after the name. At the moment it is Lord Bingham, Lord Chief Justice or Bingham LCJ. The Master of the Rolls is referred to by that full title or the initials MR are used.

Judges in the High Court are referred to as Mr (or Mrs) Justice . . . or the initial J is written after their name, for example Mr Justice Cresswell (Cresswell J) or Mrs Justice Arden (Arden J). When there are two or more High Court judges, it is also possible to list their names and then write JJ afterwards, for example Arden and Cresswell JJ.

APPENDIX 2

Glossary of Latin terms

audi alteram partem – a rule of natural justice that each side must be given the opportunity to put their case and be heard by the court or tribunal involved.

certiorari volumus – literally 'we wish to be informed' (usually shortened to *certiorari*) – an order used by the High Court to quash a decision by an inferior court or tribunal

ejusdem generis – of the same kind – a rule used in statutory interpretation where a list of words followed by general words, will be taken to include items of the same kind

ex parte – without the other side (or party) to a case – some applications may be made to a court without informing the other party; this may be for emergency injunctions or in an application for leave to apply for judicial review. Since the Woolf reforms of civil procedure this is usually put in English – without notice. However, when looking at pre-1999 cases the Latin phrase will be used

expressio unius est exclusio alterius – the express mention of a person or thing excludes, by implication, other persons and things not mentioned; a rule used in statutory interpretation

locus standi – standing or right to take an action, especially in judicial review proceedings

mandamus – 'we command' – a command issued in the name of the Crown by the High Court ordering the performance of a public legal duty; used in judicial review proceedings

nemo judex in causa sua – no-one may act as a judge in his own case; a rule of natural justice

nolle prosequi – do not prosecute – the order used by the Attorney-General to stop a prosecution from taking place

noscitur a sociis – a word is known by the company it keeps; a rule of statutory interpretation in which words are looked at in their context

obiter dicta – 'things said by the way' – the nonbinding part of a judgment; a legal observation by a judge that is not part of his reason for the decision in the case (can be a persuasive precedent)

per incuriam – by mistake, carelessly or without taking account of a legal rule

prima facie – at first sight; on the face of it

quamdiu se bene gesserint – whilst of good behaviour – this phrase is used to explain the right of a superior judge not to be dismissed without a good reason

ratio decidendi – the legal reason for a decision – the binding part of a judgment

stare decisis – 'stand by the decision' – the fundamental principle of judicial precedent; the full version of the maxim is *stare decisis et non quieta movere* which means, stand by the decision and do nor disturb that which is settled

ultra vires – beyond or outside the powers – a concept used in deciding whether delegated legislation, or the decision of an inferior court of tribunal or administrative body are legal; if the act done was *ultra vires* it will be declared void

INDEX